The War Diary of Breckinridge Long

By the same author

NEVADA'S KEY PITTMAN (1963)

The War Diary

of

Breckinridge Long

Selections from the Years 1939–1944

Selected and Edited by

FRED L. ISRAEL

UNIVERSITY OF NEBRASKA PRESS · LINCOLN

Copyright © 1966 by the University of Nebraska Press
Library of Congress Catalog Card Number: 65–19693

MANUFACTURED IN THE UNITED STATES OF AMERICA

To Myra and Leonard

Semper Amicis Carissimis Mei

Contents

List of Illustrations

*The picture section follows page 196. All the pictures
are from the collections of the Library of Congress.*

Introduction

These are momentous days we are living in. All the things we have used as fundamentals are challenged. A revolution is on which attempts to throw over our
political, financial, social and economic structures. Potent new concepts based on
force threaten the whole framework. Some one of these days the crisis will appear.
The grand moment will arrive which will decide history for the future—and I
wonder if we will recognize it as it passes? Will we appreciate the drama and feel
the thrill of world decision? Or will the sun set inconspicuously below the horizon
and only future generations be wise enough to point back to it and say "On September 3rd, 1940. . . . How I would love to have lived that moment" and not know
that those who did were unable to distinguish that moment from any other in a
period of years? . . . Anyhow, I hope I will be in the middle of it, will be part of it
and be conscious of it. And may the decision insure that form of government for
all the world which allows free men and women a decent freedom of action in life.

Long Diary, August 31, 1940

A descendent of the distinguished Long family of North Carolina and the
Breckinridge family of Kentucky, Breckinridge Long had a deep awareness
of the past and a sense of responsibility for America's future. Throughout
his life he sought to emulate his ancestors who for generations had
been leaders in politics and public affairs and had cultivated patrician
traditions.

Long was born in St. Louis, Missouri, on May 16, 1881, the son of William
Strudwick and Margaret Miller Breckinridge Long. During his boyhood he
studied with private tutors and attended a local public high school. In the
fall of 1899, following a Breckinridge tradition, he entered Princeton University, graduating in 1904. Subsequently he studied law at Washington
University in St. Louis and was admitted to the Missouri bar in 1906.

Although Long had intended to begin his practice in the fall of that year,
a gift from his family enabled him to take a trip around the world. "In the
course of my wanderings," so he said, "I covered most of the known world."
On his return to St. Louis in June, 1907, he opened a law office. The following
year, at the age of twenty-seven, Long declared himself a candidate for state
assemblyman in a local Democratic primary. His platform consisted of the
simple declaration that he "decidedly opposed Prohibition." There were
nine candidates, and Long placed eighth. "I don't see much chance in the
political field for a young Democrat," he confided to a former classmate.

"So for the future, I am strictly practicing law and paying no attention to politics or any other diversion."[1]

Long's office records reveal that his was a small criminal and civil practice and that like many another young lawyer he had considerable difficulty in obtaining clients and collecting fees. Nevertheless a local society writer was moved to remark that "many members of his family have gained distinction as representatives of the legal profession, and the strong intellectual force and laudable ambition of Mr. Long are the basis upon which his friends rest their predictions as to a successful professional career for him."[2] In his spare time Long completed a master's thesis, "The Impossibility of India's Revolt from England," which Princeton accepted in 1909. As a hobby he compiled material for a study of American colonial governments, a subject in which he first became interested as a student in Woodrow Wilson's Constitutional Law course. In this study, published by Macmillan in 1925 under the title *The Genesis of the Constitution*, Long argued that the Constitution drew extensively from colonial precedents and was not a "result of a stroke of genius on the part of the framers."

The letters and diaries for this period show that Long continued to harbor political aspirations and that his appetite for politics was only whetted by his marriage on June 1, 1912, to Christine Graham, the wealthy and socially prominent granddaughter of Francis Preston Blair, Democratic nominee for Vice President in 1868. The young couple settled into the comfortable pattern of St. Louis society life, and with the necessity to build up his law practice no longer compelling, Long devoted more time to politics, his principal interest. Through his wife's connections he met influential Missouri Democrats and hoped for a patronage position after Wilson's 1912 victory. Senator William Stone and Representative Champ Clark, both Missourians, were enlisted to recommend the appointment of the thirty-two-year-old lawyer as Third Assistant Secretary of State. "Speaker Clark and I," reported Stone, "called on the President and talked to him about you, saying as good things as we could."[3] Long wrote to Clark that he hoped "the activity and influence of my eminent supporters will succeed in gratifying my ambition."[4] But Secretary of State William Jennings Bryan did not look with favor upon Clark's recommendation and the appointment was not forthcoming.

---

[1] B.L. to Howard Ameli, November 5, 1908, Box 16, Papers of Breckinridge Long, Library of Congress.

[2] Walter B. Stevens, *St. Louis: History of the Fourth City, 1763–1909* (Chicago: Clarke Publishing Co., 1909), II, 706.

[3] William J. Stone to B.L., March 12, 1913, Box 17. William Stone, Democrat, United States Senator from Missouri, 1903–1918.

[4] B.L. to Champ Clark, March 22, 1913, Box 17. Champ Clark, Democrat, United States Representative from Missouri, 1893–1895; 1897–1921. Clark served as House Speaker, 1911–1919.

Undaunted, Long worked zealously in Missouri politics, serving as president and financial backer of the Wilson Club, a group credited with helping the Democrats to carry the state in 1916. In addition, Long contributed more than thirty thousand dollars to the Democratic National Committee during the 1916 campaign. And when the committee met to discuss the alarming implications of their dwindling treasury, it was Long who came to the rescue. Daniel Roper, Chairman of the Organization Bureau, has recounted how Long placed a certified check for a hundred thousand dollars on the desk of Democratic National Chairman Vance McCormick. "'That's a personal loan,' Long explained. 'I guess some of us had better get busy to raise some real money.' Our spirits rose swiftly. The magnanimous act of Breckenridge [*sic*] Long put new faith and courage into all of us."[5] At the end of the hard-fought campaign Wilson managed to turn his 1912 plurality victory into a 1916 majority endorsement. "I want you to know," Wilson's secretary Joseph P. Tumulty wrote Long after the President's re-election, "that I am interested in you. . . . You were a staunch friend in the darkest days of the campaign."[6] The reward came shortly thereafter. On January 29, 1917, Long was sworn in as Third Assistant Secretary of State.

"The work was entirely new to me," recorded Long. "During my first weeks in the Department I had a perfectly terrible time. I worked from nine in the morning until midnight, or later, almost every night. . . . The supervision of the Bureau of Accounts and the entire financial end of the Department was entrusted to me. Then, I had all the ceremonial work. . . . The Far East was put under my supervision, including our relations with China and Japan, Siam, the South Sea Islands, Siberia, Australia and India. . . . I was the disbursing officer of the Department and had to sign all the warrants. I had never had much to do with finances. Bookkeeping, accounts, credits and balances were always to me unknown mysteries which I never hoped to fathom, but, here I was face to face with the necessity not only of fathoming them but of being surfeited and choked with them. The details they entailed were overwhelming. With all the things that were going on in Washington, I found myself submerged and my vision limited, temporarily almost eliminated, by the infinite details with which I found myself surrounded. . . . Each morning a large box of accounts, wrapped in little oblong bundles with rubber bands around them, was placed on my desk and awaited my approval. Each morning I would delve into them, look through allowances for salary, clerk hire, contingent expenses and all manner of other things and keep doing it until the box was empty. I gradually mastered the intricacies."

The Far East responsibilities almost overwhelmed Long. ("I am surprised

[5] Daniel C. Roper, *Fifty Years of Public Life* (Durham: Duke University Press, 1941), p. 155.
[6] Joseph Tumulty to B.L., December 11, 1916, Box 24.

how much can be done without any knowledge of it on my part.")[7] "Mr. [Edward T.] Williams who probably knows more about China than most any other man alive, was the Chief of the Far Eastern Bureau [1914–1918]. He would come down almost every day and we would talk about the Far East. . . . There were more complications internal and external than I had ever imagined and more than anybody had any right to believe. At the end of two weeks I was a trusting and confiding child at the foot of a walking encyclopedia of China. . . . Japan was easier, and Siam—poor, little Siam,— was not at all hard. With India, Siberia, and Australia I had to do only with political problems which arose there or which arose in Europe and affected those countries. . . . The details and the necessity for mastering them entirely submerged me and allowed me no opportunity for the formulation of theories or ideas."

Within three months of Long's appointment, the nation and the State Department rapidly shifted from neutrality to armed neutrality and then to belligerency against Germany. "Little Washington, the old capital, the political and social center, had ceased to exist," Long noted. "It was now an armed fortress with uniforms to be seen everywhere." New assignments were thrust upon the already burdened Assistant Secretary. One of the most time consuming but interesting of these involved preparations for the many Allied missions—military, naval, parliamentary, financial, shipping—that now streamed into Washington. Long met each with proper protocol and arranged for housing, servants, food, flags, military guards, receptions, and a thousand other details. "I went through the performance so many times I could do it in my sleep." [8]

During his service in the State Department, Long, motivated by a strong desire for higher political office, did his best to have Missourians placed on the federal payroll. He spoke, wrote to, and entertained numerous government officials, securing all sorts of varied favors for his local backers. In addition to partisan efforts within the Department, Long zealously worked for the Democratic National Committee, and his generous contributions placed him in that inner circle of politicians who mapped party strategy. Missouri was to choose a senator in 1920, and almost a full year beforehand Long's family, friends, and fortune were at work to secure him the Democratic nomination. Long resigned from the Department in June, 1920, and immersed himself in state politics. "I feel as if the situation is so favorable. . . . I hope it can continue this way," he had written earlier. [9]

The Missouri political scene, however, was far from tranquil. The League of Nations controversy became the principal issue both in the primary and

[7] Diary, March 20, 1917.
[8] Diary Notes, War Folder, Box 213.
[9] B.L. to James Baity, March 1, 1920, Box 63.

in the ensuing election. As an enthusiastic supporter of Wilson's internationalist policies, Long had participated in an intraparty fight that caused
Senator James Reed,[10] a bitter foe of the League, to be rejected as a delegate
to the 1920 Democratic national convention. Although Long soundly
defeated Reed's choice for the Senate in the August primary, the state
Democratic party was shattered. Reed refused to support either Long or the
national ticket of Governor James Cox of Ohio and Assistant Secretary of
the Navy Franklin D. Roosevelt, denouncing Wilson's foreign policy as a
treacherous betrayal of the United States. Long, nevertheless, campaigned
throughout the state on a platform that endorsed the League without any
reservations. "The one issue is whether reactionary policies shall prevail or
whether a safely progressive administration shall succeed," declared the
New York Times. "Senator Harding is a reactionary and looks backward for
inspiration. Governor Cox looks to the future."[11] But skepticism of the
League combined with the intraparty feud to sweep Missouri decisively into
the Republican column, giving Long's opponent, the incumbent Selden
P. Spencer,[12] a plurality of more than 120,000 votes.

After this defeat at the polls, Long returned to his international-law
practice which though flourishing he later described as "a very unpleasant
existence."[13] Political office still remained his goal. "The general election of
1920 should not be taken as having decided the fate of the League of Nations
for America. . . . I am committed to the League, to its philosophy, to its
objectives. I want to see it live and prosper. I want to see America a member
in it—not in a futile or ineffective organization. . . . America will join the
League as soon as political prejudices and temporary control of governmental functions find their natural level."[14] To secure his personal and political objectives, Long maintained close contact with state and national
Democratic leaders; and in 1922, when James Reed stood for re-election, he
decided to oppose the senior Senator in what became one of the bitterest
primary fights in Missouri history.

The primary campaign developed into a battle between Reed and Woodrow Wilson. The former President asserted that "Missouri cannot afford to
be represented by such a marplot and it might check the enthusiasm of
Democrats throughout the country if their comrades in Missouri should not
redeem the reputation of the party by substituting for Reed a man of the true
breed of Democratic principle."[15] Reed, who had referred to Wilson in 1920

[10] James Reed, Democrat, U.S. Senator from Missouri, 1911–1929.

[11] The *New York Times*, September 20, 1920, 14:7–8.

[12] Selden Spencer, Republican, U.S. Senator from Missouri, 1918–1925.

[13] B.L. to Desha Breckinridge, December 3, 1923, Box 71. (Desha Breckinridge was
Long's cousin.)

[14] B.L. to Arthur Balfour, June 8, 1921, Box 71.

[15] Woodrow Wilson to Lon V. Stephens, April 27, 1922, as quoted in the *New York
Times*, May 9, 1922, 1:2.

as "that long-eared animal that goes braying about the country," welcomed the challenge.[16] "The moving spirit of the Long campaign is hatred of and prejudice against Reed," observed the *New York Times*. "Democrats in talking about the campaign either praise or censure Reed. It is unusual to hear praise of Long as a candidate. . . . The Long forces are almost fanatical in opposition to Reed. The fight is not one to defeat but to annihilate the Senator. It is to drive him from the Democratic Party—to brand him as a party outlaw."[17] In spite of the former President's support, the Reed organization in cooperation with Tom Pendergast, acknowledged political boss of Kansas City, narrowly defeated Long with a majority of about 6,400 out of approximately 390,000 votes cast. Thus, both Long and the League suffered another setback.

The Missouri electorate had destroyed Long's hopes for a Senate seat, and except for occasional visits to the state he now lived at Montpelier Manor, a beautiful Georgian-style mansion near Laurel, Maryland. As he wrote, "I have felt it would be the best thing for me and the party . . . so the smoke of battle could blow away."[18] His interest in practicing law waned and most of his time was occupied by breeding and racing horses, traveling, and politics. The Teapot Dome oil scandals of the Harding administration had convinced him that "whoever is nominated [by the Democrats in 1924] will probably be elected."[19] He felt that "certain commitments I have made . . . are controlling my destiny."[20] These commitments were made to William Gibbs McAdoo, former Secretary of the Treasury in Wilson's cabinet, whom Long aided as a principal financial backer and a troubleshooter in the Californian's preconvention fight for delegates. "I have simply been living on the railroad trains . . . for the last three months," he wrote in February, 1924. "My political activity has brought me into the maelstrom and I am thickly in it."[21] "We have got to stand solidly with him [McAdoo] in order to beat Smith and the old gang," he told a fellow Missourian. "There is no one else with whom we can accomplish that object."[22] But a convention deadlock and national prosperity combined to again crush Long's political hopes.

Over the next four years, Long continued to donate considerable sums to the Democratic National Committee. By the beginning of 1928, the consensus among Democrats was that Al Smith's candidacy was growing stronger every day. McAdoo announced he would not accept the nomination, and

---

[16] *Ibid.*, June 16, 1922, 17:6.

[17] *Ibid.*, July 28, 1922, 4:2.

[18] B.L. to William Collins, June 1, 1926, Box 82.

[19] B.L. to William Collins, February 2, 1924, Box 78.

[20] B.L. to Desha Breckinridge, March 15, 1924, Box 78.

[21] B.L. to William Collins, February 2, 1924, Box 78.

[22] B.L. to C. C. Oliver, May 23, 1924, Box 173. Long's reference here is to Alfred E. Smith, Democrat, governor of New York, 1919–1921, 1923–1929, and to the Tammany Hall New York Democratic machine.

many who had opposed Smith in 1924 now considered his selection inevitable. As the convention drew closer, Long found himself "getting more or less involved in political maneuvers. . . . The mere fact that Smith's nomination seems assured does not necessarily mean that the rest of it is a ratification meeting. . . . I am going to Houston as a delegate from the District of Columbia." [23] At Houston, he fought for a strong World Court platform statement but grudgingly agreed to a compromise. [24] After the convention Long worked at New York headquarters "running the radio part of the campaign. . . . I feel proud of my job. We have put on a great show. I have neglected my family and my business, and everything except politics." [25] But on Election Day, 1928, the Democratic party suffered a most humiliating defeat. In addition to the break in the "solid South" and the loss of New York, the Far West, which had voted for Bryan and Wilson, disowned Smith. The decisive verdict—Herbert Hoover had received 444 electoral votes to Smith's 87—shocked Long: "There is no doubt now about how the American people feel." And in his diary he wrote: "Badly beaten—disgusted." [26]

The 1920's were frustrating years for the Democratic party. The loss of three successive national elections, the lack of national patronage, and the intraparty disagreement combined to splinter the Democratic oak of the Wilsonian years. Prosperity seemed to be an unbeatable issue. "My belief is that the market will continue on its upward swing for five or six years," commented Long in November, 1928. "Blue chips will advance to points during the next four or five years which seem as incredible today as would the prices of today seem two years ago." [27] Exactly one year later, however, he had had his "fingers badly burned. I could not believe that under any circumstances I. T. & T. could sell at 70 to say nothing of 50. By the grace of misfortune I am still the proud owner of all that I once possessed but I owe so much money on it that I can't kiss it goodbye and feel more or less like the Ancient Mariner. I am convinced that that venerable gentleman would have been delighted to exchange his albatross for my I. T. & T." [28]

The 1930 election returns reduced the Republican majority in the House of Representatives from 103 to 2, and in the Senate the Republican administration barely retained organizational control. The depression convinced

[23] B.L. to Desha Breckinridge, May 28; June 21, 1928, Box 88.

[24] Members of the Platform Committee sharply differed on the World Court. Opponents favored a statement of definite abstention from participation while others pleaded for American membership. The result was a compromise—the 1928 Democratic platform omitted any reference to the World Court.

[25] B.L. to H. G. Chatfield, October 30, 1928, Box 88.

[26] B.L. to Franklin Fort, November 15, 1928, Box 88; Diary, November 6, 1928.

[27] B.L. to Desha Breckinridge, November 30, 1928, Box 88.

[28] B.L. to Desha Breckinridge, November 14, 1929, Box 91.

Long that a strong leader was needed to prevent another convention split and to insure a 1932 Democratic victory. After the 1930 elections he felt sure that this strong leader had emerged in the person of Franklin D. Roosevelt. Roosevelt, who had been re-elected governor of New York by a decisive vote, seemed in the best possible position to win his party's nomination for President in 1932. In the preconvention wrangle for delegates, Long made a sizable contribution to Roosevelt's campaign chest. During the convention Long served as a floor manager, assigned to keep watch over carefully selected delegations, reporting significant developments to James Farley, Roosevelt's campaign manager. Because of this position and his monetary contributions during the previous two decades, Long hoped that a grateful party would suitably acknowledge its debt to him. This time he was not disappointed. With the 1932 Democratic sweep, Long at last was rewarded with the high political office that he had coveted for so many years. On April 20, 1933, President Roosevelt appointed him Ambassador Extraordinary and Minister Plenipotentiary to Italy.

Long's first months in Italy were a glorious and exciting adventure. Finding the embassy quarters too "dingy," he leased the magnificent Villa Taverna, "which from the exterior has all the atmosphere of Rome, while the interior has all modern conveniences." "Your Ambassador to Italy has been part of a big Show," he wrote happily to Franklin Roosevelt. "The King [Victor Emmanuel III] received me yesterday and I was taken with my whole staff. A regular procession of coaches with footmen in gorgeous uniforms attended. There were four coaches, one empty carriage, like a spare tire, and one out-rider on horseback at the head of the procession. My understanding is that there were more details of formality and of polite expressions of attention in the form of servants, soldiers, and salutes than any occasion the oldest resident at the Embassy remembers." [29]

The Ambassador's first reports and letters lauded Mussolini and Fascism. "Mussolini is an astounding character and the effects of his organized activities are apparent throughout all Italy. . . . Italy today is the most interesting experiment in government to come above the horizon since the formulation of our Constitution 150 years ago. Likewise it is the most novel since then. . . . The Head of Government [Mussolini] is one of the most remarkable persons. And he is surrounded by interesting men. And they are doing a unique work in an original manner, so I am enjoying it all." [30] "I was here twenty-odd years ago and formed the most distinct and lasting impressions. When I returned I expected reminiscences and revival of memories, but the landscape and a few donkey wagons are the only things

[29] B.L. to F.D.R., June 1, 1933, Box 105.
[30] B.L. to Joseph E. Davies, September 16, 1933; B.L. to Almy Edmunds, July 27, 1933, Box 102.

to remind one of the Italy that was. The people have changed. Their sanitary conditions have changed. The cities have changed. Rome is not to be recognized except as far as the Forum is concerned. Great avenues run through the city. The streets are clean. The people are well dressed. They move with alacrity. In the country the houses are all painted and clean. The country roads are well paved and clean. The farms are all teeming with people, just now reaping wheat by hand. The country seems as if it had been manicured every morning. The whole temper and attitude of the people have changed. They all seem happy. They all seem busy. . . . They are spending large sums on public works. The campagna is being drained, and literally small cities are being built in it. Roads have not only been built but they are all being carefully attended to and swept clean even far in the country. Construction work appears here and there in every part of Italy. Many men are in uniform. The Fascisti in their black shirts are apparent in every community. They are dapper and well dressed and stand up straight and lend an atmosphere of individuality and importance to their surroundings. . . . The trains are punctual, well-equipped, and fast. The running times have been decreased 20% to 30% and efficiency increased 100%. . . . At the end of my first four weeks I can only give you my first impressions. But I think first impressions sometimes are valuable." [31] Two years later, however, Long, sobered by time and world events, described the Fascisti as "deliberate, determined, obdurate, ruthless, and vicious." [32]

The lavish Villa Taverna provided a suitable setting for the elegant life that the Longs continued to lead. "The only parties in these days which retain any real style, any odor of oldtime opulence," wrote a *Fortune* reporter, "are those given in Rome's embassies. . . . So that it is considerably to the credit of the United States that the smooth Ambassador Breckinridge Long and his wife so very popularly hold this, the most socially exacting of our ambassadorial posts." [33] After conversations with his guests, Long, an untrained diplomat, detailed their observations in his dispatches to Washington, glowing with praise for the achievements of Fascism. Throughout 1933 his letters stressed the political novelty of the corporate state, drawing parallels to the New Deal, and especially to the National Recovery Administration. He even suggested that Attorney General Homer Cummings could benefit by making "something of a study of this new experiment in government." [34] Assistant Secretary of State Wilbur Carr was urged to read about Fascism, especially an article written by Mussolini for the Hearst press. [35] These laudatory opinions expressed in dozens of letters to American officials and

[31] B.L. to F.D.R., June 27, 1933, Box 105.
[32] B.L. to F.D.R., September 6, 1935, Box 115.
[33] *Fortune*, July 1934, p. 149.
[34] B.L. to Homer Cummings, August 11, 1933, Box 102.
[35] Memorandum, November 7, 1933, Box 163.

friends indicate that Long understood little of the operations of Fascism and still less about the subtleties of diplomacy in a rapidly changing Europe. During his first year in Italy, Long accepted the views of his immediate social circle.

The unseasoned Ambassador at first praised and supported the emerging imperialist policy of Mussolini. By 1933, Albania had come almost completely under Italian protection—Italian experts supervised an extensive internal improvement program, Italian officers organized and trained the army, Italian civilians supervised the civil servants. Annexation which occurred in 1939, was a formality. "I think that we are entirely justified in playing the game with Italy in Albania," Long advised Franklin Roosevelt in July, 1933. "I do not see the necessity of opposing Italy there. Particularly is that so when one appreciates the importance which Italy attaches to her special position in that little country. . . . If the sense of security in Italy is lacking, there is just that additional handicap to the success which can be attained by Mussolini in his efforts to maintain peace on the Continent of Europe." [36] Nineteen months later, however, he counseled the President to equip "your diplomatic and consular officers in Europe with gas masks. . . . I am satisfied [Mussolini] is looking forward to the certainty of war and is preparing. . . . I have discovered that the Italian steel mills and factories are busily engaged in the manufacture of all kinds of guns and ammunition— even large cannon. The prospect is not so good." [37]

This change in attitude, well in evidence by the beginning of 1935, ended Long's apprenticeship. His dispatches became more perceptive, his observations more acute. Instead of repeating dinner-table conversations to Washington, he now relied on the professional embassy staff assigned to him. Social engagements were curtailed as the Ambassador spent hours reading and evaluating advisory papers. The realization of the importance of his position at the center of a country bent toward war transformed the millionaire politician into a sober diplomat. Although he was a political appointee untrained in foreign affairs, Long made amazingly accurate reports—even predicting seven months in advance the week Mussolini would invade Ethiopia. His intelligence information in the early part of 1935 contained excellent analyses of the types and amounts of war materials produced throughout Italy. "We know that pith helmets and tropical equipment have been manufactured in great quantities. . . . We know that the factories in Milan have been working for months day and night making all kinds of ammunition and equipment as well as tanks, airplanes, bombs, trucks, and machine guns. . . . We know that at least 30,000 men have been sent away from Italy. . . . Six months ago I learned that horses had been bought in

[36] B.L. to F.D.R., July 7, 1933, Box 105.
[37] B.L. to F.D.R., February 3, 1935, Box 115.

Canada and mules in Oklahoma and had arrived in Italy and have been shipped to Italian East Africa. Mules are still being imported. . . . Now there is only one use for mules in an army. They are no good on the flat coastal plains, which are practically desert. They are no doubt intended for mountain work and to carry mountain artillery. If the operation involves as many as 5,000 mules, it means a rather large-scale venture into the mountains. And I am satisfied that the British Ambassador and the French Ambassador are playing the game and trying to leave the impression that the Italian Government is not doing anything extraordinary." [38] "Italy is preparing for what she thinks is a certain eventuality. While no responsible statesman in Italy will admit it, I am just as certain of it as I am that I am sitting in this chair. . . . I think we must contemplate that Europe will be at war within two years. I believe we must take into almost definite consideration that fact in making our plans for the future." [39]

As Mussolini's plans to absorb Ethiopia unfolded, Long faithfully and scrupulously reported his observations not only to the State Department, but also in confidential personal letters to the President. France, he was certain, had agreed to support Italy's African policy for fear of losing Mussolini's aid in checking Hitler. "France has undoubtedly given her consent to Italian penetration and occupation of Ethiopia," he told Roosevelt in February, 1935. "It is well understood in important circles in Milan that the French are paying the bills for the Italian military activity. It is probable that rather than give up any territory in Africa, the French have decided to make a financial contribution to permit Italy to carve it out for herself. . . . To get Italy on the side of France in direct opposition to Germany, Italy had to be bought." Long could not accurately estimate England's position in this situation, especially since "the British Ambassador is less than frank with me." [40]

Roosevelt repeatedly chided Long for his pessimistic views, to which the Ambassador responded: "You think I am a pessimist. As a matter of fact I am a realist. I see the situation in Europe as it exists. They are all prepared for war, and they have got to have it. War is the only cure for the malady with which Europe is affected. There are three and a half million men under arms here today. The Assistant Military Attaché has just returned from Milan on a tour of inspection. He was allowed to inspect very little. The factories were closed to him. However, he discovered that the airplane factories were being enlarged so that their production would be ten planes a day instead of one. The automobile manufacturing show is working day and night making military equipment and supplies. . . . I am conscious that I am walking on

[38] B.L. to F.D.R., February 15, 1935, Box 115.
[39] B.L. to F.D.R., February 21, 1935, Box 115.
[40] B.L. to F.D.R., February 15, 1935, Box 115.

delicate ground, but it is my firm belief that the success which probably awaits [Italians] in their first venture from home will only lead them on to other fields. . . . A new order is in the making, and the results of it cannot yet be foreseen." [41]

On October 3, 1935, Italy, without a declaration of war, launched the long-expected attack on Ethiopia. The League of Nations acted with unprecedented speed. On October 7, the Council declared Italy to be the aggressor, and four days later the Assembly voted to impose economic sanctions. President Roosevelt had already invoked neutrality legislation and in a proclamation he enumerated the items on which trade was restricted, mainly arms and munitions. The League list contained several additional items, but no sanctions were placed on coal or oil. "I expect I am a good deal of a cynic," Long told Roosevelt. "I am unable to see any moral element in this whole war. . . . Certainly Italy has not a leg to stand on, either moral or legal. . . . She has been condemned, and properly condemned, by the League of Nations and by practically every Government in the world. But in my opinion the League action would not have taken place without the driving force of England. While Italy has no moral justification, I doubt very much whether England has. The Italians believe, and I expect there is a good deal of truth in it, that England was preparing a commercial penetration of Abyssinia which would have enveloped the country and given her a political control which would have been peacefully consummated within a period of about three years." [42] Long believed that the only way to stop Italy would be through a united League effort—military force or strict economic sanctions.

It was soon apparent, however, that the League—largely because of the delaying tactics of the French foreign office—did not intend to impose oil sanctions against Italy. Diplomats, determined that the war would not be allowed to spread, worked to save face for Mussolini, the prestige of Great Britain, and the dignity of the League of Nations. All parties in the Ethiopian dispute wished to localize the war, especially as ominous rumblings from Germany increased. Long, who had now developed an unshakable conviction that war in Europe was inevitable, advised that an Ethiopian solution remained completely in the hands of European diplomats and that the United States should keep out of the conflict. "If you saw this thing as closely as I see it and had the veil of mysticism lifted from the picture so that you could see it in all of its naked reality, I am sure you would think so all the more." [43] Cautioning against a unilateral oil blockade, he warned that such sanctions "may be neutral from the American point of view, but it is not consonant

[41] B.L. to F.D.R., April 10; September 6, 1935, Box 115.
[42] B.L. to F.D.R., October 30, 1935, Box 115.
[43] B.L. to F.D.R., November 8, 1935, Box 115.

with the status of neutrality as fixed in the principles of international law. . . . I am motivated entirely by the desire to see the United States out of this war. I believe that an emplacement of an embargo on oil will get us involved in it. [The United States supplied about 6.3 per cent of Italian oil imports.] . . . Mussolini is wrong and has been wrong from the start. . . . Let me implore you to continue the policy of allowing Italy—and Ethiopia—to buy the same quantities they have bought in normal times." [44] Roosevelt followed Long's advice, especially after it became clear that the League would not support strong collective action against Italy.

"Europe today is like a madhouse," Long recorded in his diary, as Hitler's successive cunning triumphs threatened the peace. "Armies here and hatreds there constitute an underlying situation which sooner or later will break out again. Each time they round one corner safely you can look up the street for another corner, because they will have to round another pretty soon." [45] But Long was to be denied participation in these coming events; his health had broken and he could not continue at his post. Beginning in 1934 severe stomach ulcers caused him great pain. However, he continued to work at his post until the spring of 1936, when he had to curtail all activity and return to the United States for an operation. "I hope never to see Italy again and hope you will not ask me to go back there," he wrote Roosevelt. "I had so much physical suffering on that scene that I really hope I never set foot in the land again." [46]

"I do not need to tell you," responded the President, "how proud I am of the splendid record you made in Rome, in the midst of trying and difficult situations. . . . You are a grand fellow—and you know my devotion to you. . . . After November I shall want you again to be part of the Administration." [47] (In his forthcoming biography of Long, Professor James Watts argues that his resignation was caused by a smoldering feud between the Ambassador and the State Department—and illness was a secondary reason. Long, for example, presented his own sweeping scheme for ending the Ethiopian conflict to Mussolini without consulting Secretary of State Hull. His plan called for Germany to be given the right of qualitative equality of arms with France and England and her former African colonies to administer. In return Germany would agree to guarantee Austrian independence. Italy would receive most of Ethiopia but would have to join with Britain and France in guaranteeing the independence of the smaller Ethiopian state. And finally, the four powers would meet to resolve other outstanding issues. In addition, Long assured Fulvio Suvich, Italian Undersecretary for Foreign

[44] B.L. to F.D.R., November 29, 1935, Box 115.
[45] Diary, March 10, 1936.
[46] B.L. to F.D.R., June 15, 1936, Box 117.
[47] F.D.R. to B.L., June 18; February 22, 1936, Box 117.

Affairs, that "if Italy should become involved with another power, say with England or with France, that the Neutrality laws [of the United States] would operate against those other powers" as well as against Italy. The Department of State quickly repudiated Long when he belatedly informed them of his conversation. Watts maintains that these and similar incidents were the primary reason for Long's resignation.)

For the next three years, although he yearned to serve the Administration in almost any capacity, Long remained in semi-retirement. Periodic assurances from the White House of efforts to find him a responsible position relieved his growing anxiety and added to his burning determination to regain a prominent position, perhaps even a cabinet post. His expressions of continuing loyalty to President Roosevelt and the Democratic party finally were rewarded on the outbreak of World War II. When Germany invaded Poland on September 1, 1939, Roosevelt asked Long to serve as Special Assistant Secretary of State to handle emergency war matters. In January, 1940, he succeeded George Messersmith as Assistant Secretary of State, a position he held until December, 1944. During these years, Long had many and varied functions, but above all, he helped formulate State Department policy. The official responsibilities as Assistant Secretary were numerous—he supervised twenty-three of the forty-two divisions of the Department, including the Visa Section, Communication Defense, Legal Division, and the Foreign Service Personnel Board. When the United States entered the war, he served on several special committees to explore postwar settlements. But above all, Long now held a policy-making post.

During his State Department service, Long made extensive diary entries, recording important conversations and decisions, his observations and opinions. The bulk of Long's diary, which begins in 1906, deals with the years between 1939 and 1944; this section runs about nine hundred single-spaced closely written pages. (Most of the diary for the ambassadorial years 1933–1936 is missing.) It was Long's habit to write the entries in longhand or to dictate them to his trusted secretary at the end of each day. When time did not permit him to do so, the entry would be made the first thing the following morning. With very few exceptions the material included in the present volume was written within a day or two of the events described. The diary rarely mentions Long's personal family life; it is a record of his official work. Each evening the pages were carefully locked in his office safe.

After his retirement from the State Department, Long deposited the diaries with the Library of Congress.[48] According to his wishes they remained sealed until his death in 1958. Ever conscious of history and his family heritage, Long wrote these diaries with the idea that future generations

[48] The Breckinridge Long personal papers and diaries comprise some 65,000 items which occupy 104 linear feet of shelf space in the Library of Congress.

could better comprehend the momentous events in which he participated and understand his role in shaping them.

The Long diaries are presented here as a primary source of diplomatic history, and it has been assumed that their major importance is as a contemporaneous record of a crucial and exciting period of the American past written by an intelligent policy maker. Extensive editing, therefore, would not enhance their value. In the interests of readability and continuity I have omitted repetitious material: lengthy news dispatches; daily lists of callers; Maritime Commission meetings when the same issues were endlessly repeated (ship tonnage, crew problems, and shipping orders); and the details of the Foreign Service Personnel Board meetings. These omissions are indicated by ellipses.

FRED L. ISRAEL

City College of New York
July, 1965

The War Diary of Breckinridge Long

Called to Service

September 2, 1939

Arrived in Washington this morning and at 9:30 went to the Department and met Sumner Welles and Messersmith.[1] They asked me to take charge of a Special Division which is being created to handle emergency matters arising out of the war situation. Under the heading are relief and repatriation of Americans abroad, arrangements for steamships for that purpose, protection of American interests in war zones, both persons and property, representation of other governments, such as England and France, who have notified us that they will ask us to take charge of their Embassies in Berlin and war prisoners, if any should develop, and care and supervision on behalf of England and France in enemy (prison) camps—and any other things that may come along of an extraordinary or of an urgent nature.

After that conversation I adjourned with Messersmith to his office, and he called in Hugh Wilson, who is to be my Assistant, and Consul General George L. Brandt,[2] who is to have administrative charge of the Division. We went over policy, history, and all general matters pertaining to them. Hugh hopes to be sent on post before long, and in dictating an announcement to be made to the press he insisted it be inserted in there that he was to serve "for the time being."

I then had a talk with the Secretary.[3] He envisions the defeat of England and France and sees a very black future. He thinks that unless the war is stopped now that Hitler will divide Poland with Russia and between them they will put the screws on Roumania, Bulgaria, probably Yugoslavia, Greece, and certainly Turkey, and that they they [*sic*] will thereby establish a hegemony so that they will prevent any Europeans from trading with us except on conditions which Berlin lays down and after Russia eliminates Japan the same thing will happen in the Far East. His outlook is very black. However, his knowledge of international affairs is quite limited. He is a sweet person and a fine character, but he lacks decision and executive ability

[1] Sumner Welles, foreign service officer, Under Secretary of State, 1937–1943, and former Assistant Secretary of State, 1933–1937; George S. Messersmith, foreign service officer, Assistant Secretary of State, 1937–1940, and former minister to Austria, 1934–1937.

[2] Hugh Wilson, former ambassador to Germany, 1938–1939, and special assistant to the Secretary of State, 1939–1940; George L. Brandt, foreign service officer since 1915.

[3] Cordell Hull, Democrat, former U.S. Representative from Tennessee, 1907–1921, 1923–1931. Hull was elected to the U.S. Senate in 1930, but resigned when appointed Secretary of State on March 4, 1933, a post he held until November 27, 1944.

and he lacks a great deal of knowledge of European politics and affairs. He is too idealistic. I suggested to him that the place to pry against Hitler was with Mussolini and that Mussolini's antagonism to the Russian Pact[4] made him amenable but of course he could not be treacherous to Hitler but nevertheless could be so fortified and helped that he would be amenable to the processes which might develop later. The price of Mussolini now is a twopence as compared to the cost of a European war and particularly to the cost of a losing war. He said that he had sent over a new trade agreement with Italy recently and he thought that would help it. I said, "Why don't you accredit Phillips to the Emperor? That will do a lot to reconstitute Phillips and to help him to get more information and to place him in a better position there." He said that would raise the Japanese question and Manchukuo which was a precedent.[5] I replied that the thing to do was to deal with the question in Europe, which was most pressing, and that I thought eventually the Japanese question would take care of itself, but that we didn't have to bother about it now anyhow. Apparently my argument was without avail.

I went over to the White House to speak to General Watson[6] but he said the President wanted to see me. I found him looking very well but a little tired I thought. His mind is very active and wrapped up in the European situation. He said he sees the whole thing very involved today and somewhat mystifying. The German army has not attacked Poland in full force and it looks as if they were pulling their bluff. Deladier [sic][7] has been given full powers to act by the Chamber of Deputies, which is short of a declaration of war and postpones that eventuality. The British Parliament has done a similar thing, but nevertheless postponing the eventual hour. The eventual hour seems to be that Hitler might occupy Danzig and that part of the Corridor and Silesia which he has demanded and then say that he would make peace on terms which would confirm him in possession of those territories. The President confronted me with what should be done in those circumstances. I replied that in those circumstances Poland would probably call off England and France and try to save what was left of her country and that the chances are that Hitler's proposals would be accepted notwithstanding the English demand that he withdraw his troops before negotiating.

Mussolini has proposed a Five Power Conference with England, France,

---

[4] On August 23, 1939, Germany and Russia signed a nonaggression treaty in which each pledged to refrain from attacking the other, either individually or in alliance with other powers. Each party also agreed to remain neutral in case the other was attacked by a third country.

[5] William Phillips, ambassador to Italy, 1936–1941, remained unaccredited to King Victor Emmanuel III when the King acted as emperor of Abyssinia. The precedent here had been United States nonrecognition of the Japanese puppet state of Manchukuo.

[6] Edwin "Pa" Watson, military aide to President Roosevelt, 1933–1939, and secretary to the President, 1939–1945.

[7] Édouard Daladier, French premier, 1938–1940.

Germany, Poland, and Italy. He significantly omitted Russia. The President was at that moment waiting for a connection to be completed from Warsaw. I later learned that the Ambassador[8] there had advised that Warsaw was being bombed by "the entire German air force." My reaction was that it probably looked like the whole German air force but that the principal part of it is on the French borders awaiting developments there.

After the conversation with the President, which was general and not directed to anything particular, except the movements and news of the day, I went to Welles' office by appointment at his request.

Welles said that my going to Germany was now out of the question. The United States could not send anybody to Germany under the present conditions or in the near future. Hugh Wilson resigned yesterday as Ambassador thereby leaving it open, but Welles is of the opinion that nobody will be sent now and that they would not be sent under the present circumstances.[9] He said that Joe Davies[10] could not return to his post because of the illness of his wife (I wondered whether it was a real illness. Joe always can find lots of reasons for not doing things.) Anyhow, the President had requested him to return immediately, but he had said his wife was ill and he was afraid to leave her and couldn't take her back. Welles asked me if I would accept the post at Brussels. I replied that under the circumstances that exist at present I will do anything that he and the President want me to do; that Belgium was an active post now because it was a contiguous neutral and important but that in peace time Belgium was a nice place to take a quiet rest as far as the American Ambassador was concerned and that I had no desire to serve in that kind of a post and asked him if and when it became possible to send somebody to Germany if I could be transferred from there to Germany. He replied that he would do all he could but could make no promises and that he would like very much to see me in Germany and that that had been the plan of the President and the Secretary until the situation developed as it is. . . .

This afternoon I was back to the Department reading all the preceding dispatches and instructions concerning the work of the Division which I have just been installed in. It will be very interesting work, but I imagine it will not last very long.

I sought an interview again with Welles and told him that under the circumstances that exist in Europe, particularly vis-à-vis Mussolini and his withholding his aid from Germany, I thought it apropos and quite material to recall to his attention some of my conversations with Mussolini. I repeated

[8] Anthony J. Drexel Biddle, Jr., ambassador to Poland, 1937–1939, and former minister to Norway, 1935–1937.

[9] Earlier in the year, Welles had told Long that he might be asked by the President to serve as ambassador to Germany "in the near future."

[10] Joseph E. Davies, ambassador to Belgium, 1938–1940.

to him the circumstances of my conversations, which were definite and positive as far as Mussolini was concerned and which were uttered in such a way and under such circumstances as to leave no doubt in my mind—particularly by virtue of the repetition—that they expressed on that point his political philosophy. The conversations alluded to were that he was un-utterably opposed to a European war; that he would do everything in his power to prevent one; that he would even use force to prevent one (anomalous as that may sound, but those were his words); that the only thing he would willingly fight in Europe was Communism; that he would fight Communism every time it lifted its head, because unless you defeated it it would eventually defeat you; that a European war would be a victory for Communism and chaos would follow it and that consequently he was definitely opposed to a European war and was unendingly opposed to Communism.

I thought that could be useful today and that it should be revived in the minds of responsible officers of this Government. Apparently Mussolini would not stomach Hitler's agreement with Stalin. I can almost imagine Mussolini when he first heard the information. He must have raved in his best style, and I have no doubt he meant it. Whereas there was nothing I thought we could do in the premises, yet England and France could do a whole lot if they were convinced that this was Mussolini's attitude and philosophy.

England's Parliament and France's Chamber have met. They met yesterday; they met again today. Poland has asked them for assistance. Up to this evening neither has given that assistance. I think there is an "out" somewhere, and I still do not believe there is going to be a European war, though I do believe, as I always have, that Hitler somehow or other will get Danzig and the Corridor, or the larger part of it.

September 3, 1939

Long conference with various Department bureau heads, Maritime Commission, Army and Navy representatives. Subject, ways and means of placing additional facilities for repatriation—additional ships—for persons in Europe. Bullitt and Kennedy[11] sent long cables complaining of lack of Government efforts. They are swamped by travellers who stayed too long. Some have had accommodations cancelled by withdrawal of ships of belligerent flag. But if tourists get caught in a jam—after having had ample notice of an approaching crisis—they ought not be so critical of the Government's inability to evacuate them.

[11] William C. Bullitt, former ambassador to the Soviet Union, 1933–1936, and ambassador to France, 1936–1940; Joseph P. Kennedy, ambassador to Great Britain, 1937–1940, and former chairman of the Securities and Exchange Commission, 1934–1935.

... It is an interesting day but an awful experience again to see the world at war and on the brink of destruction.

I spent the afternoon with Messersmith and Wilson drafting cables—about repatriation and one about Diplomatic and Consular officers staying at their post in spite of threats from the air and until irresistable force or the local evacuation of civil servants—but to send wives, children and women clerks out of danger when it became imminent.

England and France declared war yesterday—England by the expiration of the ultimatum period, France by Deladier [*sic*], under authority from his Chamber. So our whole day has passed but no report has come of any fighting—which seems strange if they are going to fight. Rumors are current —that the *Bremen* has been taken by the British[12]—that four German submarines are fueling at Curacao, D.W.I.—neither confirmed. Churchill is again First Lord of the Admiralty and rumored that Eden is Minister for Dominions.[13] "Extra" editions of papers are frequently issued and called by the boys in the streets—but contain little news.

Long talk after dinner with Fumasoni-Biondi. He is Italian correspondent with very intimate relations with Italian Embassy. He said he spoke for himself only, but it was very apparent that he spoke after various and intimate conversations with the Ambassador and the Embassy staff. He talked about Italy's position. He said there was no enthusiasm for Germany. On the contrary, there was a desire not to cooperate with Germany. ... It would expose their west coast cities; that they would lose Abyssinia and Tripoli; that with Germany victor Italy and Germany would divide the Balkans all the way to the Straits, but Germany would be the principal gainer and Italy would be subordinated to her and Italy would lose. On the other hand, they feared to join the Allies because of the Brenner[14] and an invasion by Germany and an appropriation by Germany of all of Northern Italy if not more. Italy wants to save her face, and Mussolini wants a handle to grasp. ... If France would make a gesture and go to Mussolini and say that they realized they had had troubles growing out of the last war and that each of them had probably been somewhat obstinate but that they wanted Italy to feel that they

---

[12] The German merchant ship *Bremen* left New York a few days before war was declared, but successfully eluded British cruisers, and eventually reached Murmansk, U.S.S.R. In December, the *Bremen,* following Norwegian territorial waters, went to Germany.

[13] Winston Churchill was appointed First Lord of the Admiralty in Neville Chamberlain's government on September 3, 1939, and succeeded Chamberlain as Prime Minister on May 10, 1940. Anthony Eden, who had served as Secretary of State for Foreign Affairs, 1935–1938, resigning in disagreement with Chamberlain's policy at the Munich Conference, accepted the post of Secretary of State for Dominions on September 3, 1939. When Churchill became Prime Minister, he reappointed Eden as Secretary of State for Foreign Affairs.

[14] The Brenner Pass in the Alps, which connects Austria with Italy, was an important route through which many invasions of Italy had been made.

were ready to say that they would confer with them in the future and would consider generously some of the things which they thought Italy might be interested in in [*sic*] Africa and in the Mediterranean, he thought that would be sufficient. It was a long conversation of which this is only digested.

I went to bed after the President's radio speech.[15] Then the Department telephoned me about the *Athenia*'s sinking and asked for help, as it was in my Division.[16] I dressed and went to the Department and got some of the force there. Hundreds of telephones were coming in. The news of the sinking had been broadcast, and anybody who had any family aboard began telephoning to ask about the passengers on the ship, etc. I started the organization functioning and got back to bed at 12:30.

September 4, 1939

Conference this morning at 8:30 with the Secretary on hand and in his office, and Welles, Messersmith, Moore, Hugh Wilson, Truitt of the Maritime Commission, Norman Davis coming in late and going out early, Hackworth,[17] and several more and me. For hours a discussion and drafting of a message to Kennedy which was more or less expressive of American policy on repatriation and about sinking ships. Consequently it was important and somewhat delicate, as it would probably be published, and concerned belligerent ships, United States ships, etc. I tried to avoid direct reference to Germany about sinking the *Athenia* until we had more proof of her responsibility. There is a German denial of the sinking, which nobody believes because nobody else would have a reason to sink the ship, but we had nothing but an ex parte statement that the ship had been sunk by a German submarine. The Captain had not reported, and we had the statement of not a single witness. Finally that was put in the draft and submitted to the President by the Secretary, but the President wanted some reference to Germany; so we conferred again, and again I got it all agreed to talk about "belligerents" with the argument that everybody would know who we were talking about but we would have no official responsibility of charging Germany when

[15] In a special broadcast on September 3, 1939, President Roosevelt declared that every effort of his administration would be directed toward maintaining true neutrality. He warned Americans against profiteering and urged them to discriminate between fact and rumor concerning the war. (*The Public Papers and Addresses of Franklin D. Roosevelt*, compiled by Samuel I. Rosenman, 1939 volume [New York: Macmillan, 1941], pp. 460–464.)

[16] On September 3, 1939, the British liner *Athenia* with 1400 passengers en route to Canada from Glasgow was sunk about two hundred miles northwest of the Irish coast with the loss of 120 lives.

[17] R. Walton "Judge" Moore, counselor of the State Department, 1937–1941, and former Assistant Secretary of State, 1933–1937; Max Truitt, vice-chairman of the Maritime Commission, 1938–1941; Norman Davis, chairman of the American Red Cross, 1938–1944, and former Under Secretary of State, 1920–1921; Green H. Hackworth, legal adviser of the State Department, 1931–1946.

we had no proof of it. Finally I was delegated to take it up with the President over the telephone. I read it to him, and he agreed to everything except the last sentence in which the "belligerents" were mentioned. He said he wanted Germany mentioned. I argued a little, but there was no use. He had his mind made up. He was awfully mad I think that the message had arrived at the instant of his speech last night and that the contrast between the tenor of his speech and the action of Germany was so great that he could not immediately forgive it. It is quite understandable. Anyhow he listened to my arguments and agreed to the insertion of the words "reported" and "rumored" or words to that effect, so as to indicate that it was not a direct charge.

. . . Told Welles of conversation last night with Fumasoni-Biondi, withholding his name at his request, and suggested he talk with Lothian[18] today. He was to see him about noon. He is rather inclined to do so but did not say definitely he would. I urged him either to do it now or not to do it at all and that it was an emergency and was an important situation in which time was of the essence.

One thousand of the fourteen hundred people are reported safe from the *Athenia*. Perhaps others will be reported. This has shocked the country. Much planning and policy, but too much conversation and too large bodies operating in the Department. It is very slow. Can't continue that way without loss of efficiency. The war is off to a good start; belligerent ships are scurrying to neutral ports—the French attacked the Siegfried Line on the Westwall near the Swiss border and claim some gains. The British bombed German warships near the Kiel Canal and damaged two, and Germany claims bringing down several British planes. We are taking full precautionary measures to keep out, restrict travel abroad, bring citizens home, possibly convoy ships westward bound with returning passengers, etc.

Mussolini reported tried to keep war from popping but did not succeed and today announces neutrality and will start Italian ships westward. That will help evacuate our citizens there and in France.

These days have been Government holidays—Saturday, Sunday and Monday, September 2, 3, and 4, over Labor Day. . . . So it has been hard to get telegrams out, but probably was a good thing in many ways as it permitted a quiet atmosphere with only a few people around and made easier the thinking out of original problems and policy. That ought to be a slow and careful process in the beginning, ramifications of each decision projected into the future so that later action and policy will not be built on a mistaken foundation.

[18] The Marquess of Lothian, British ambassador to the United States, 1939–1940. Lord Lothian had been charged by his government to obtain supplies from the United States and support of Great Britain's war effort.

September 5, 1939

... Morgenthau[19] threw a bomb into the Cabinet session yesterday by proposing that we take over the *Normandie* and the *Queen Mary*, now in our ports, and charge it up to the war debt and operate these ships. Of course they would operate at a distinct disadvantage and a financial loss. We found that out with the *Leviathan*.[20] They are white elephants on trans-Atlantic [*sic*] runs. But the proposition was so generally considered by the Cabinet that the British and French Ambassadors were approached upon it. It even got that far, and nobody seemed to bring up the question, and very pertinent issue, that Germany would not recognize transfer of title after the declaration of war and that whatever title we did get would have a cloud on it and that the boats would be liable to be sunk by German submarines. I hope this has blown over. The respective Ambassadors received the information and said they would consult their Governments.

A large cargo of those wrecked on the *Athenia* were landed in Ireland. We consulted with the Red Cross and authorized $10,000 donated by the Red Cross and $5,000 of our own to be used on their account. The Red Cross funds are for destitute persons and our own funds are to pay railroad transportation and such expenses from the place in which they find themselves to a sailing point until a ship sails. Full details have not arrived, but we now have an official cable report that after the explosion of the torpedo the ship was shelled, one shot from a submarine at a distance of eight hundred to a thousand yards. The torpedo hit while the dining room was full of people at dinner and the floor of the dining room is reported to have collapsed. Statements from several persons have already been taken and others will follow. ...

I have been rather active all day on repatriation problems, including conferences with the Red Cross, the Maritime Commission, etc. This afternoon the President called me on the telephone and asked about the arrangements. I told him one boat was going today, another one tomorrow, and three were to follow; that they would go under blind orders and be sent to specific ports later. I also suggested that we should give priority on these or other sooner available ships for those who had been torpedoed on the *Athenia*. We still have no list of Americans injured or saved, but the reports indicate that the casualty list will be very large.

England also violated the neutrality of Holland apparently by flying airplanes over it to drop propaganda leaflets to Germany. The Dutch traced the crossing of the airplanes on a delicate recording instrument and showed

---

[19] Henry Morgenthau, Jr., Secretary of the Treasury, 1934–1945.

[20] The *Leviathan*, a German merchant ship, had been seized by the United States in 1917 and converted to a troop transport. After the war the United States Shipping Board reconverted the ship for transatlantic crossings, but without commercial success.

plainly the passage of the planes from west to east and returning from east to west. Also some of the propaganda pamphlets fell on Dutch soil. It was a cloudy night and the planes flew very high.

Little by little the new Division is fulfilling its function, and tomorrow we are to be moved into more or less permanent quarters. Miss Aderton is to be moved over and become my private secretary there, and by tomorrow night I hope to have more order and general regulation in the Division than has existed up to now.

September 6, 1939

I have had a very wearing day. Until just 5:30 this evening it looked as if some drastic change of policy would have to be made in order to repatriate American citizens. The *Orizaba* was to have sailed this morning on special trip for those desiring to return, and the *President Roosevelt* was to have sailed on its regular trip to Europe. But Labor Union troubles developed. The Unions wouldn't sign on a crew unless it was agreed that the men should have each a $200 bonus, a 40% increase in wages, and a life insurance policy paid up in the amount of $25,000 apiece and that the Unions themselves determine what was the danger zone. Of course the last was a function of the United States Government. It was very difficult to arrange, and the Maritime Commission was in almost constant negotiation during the day. Noon passed and neither ship sailed. As the afternoon wore on and it was finally proposed and I agreed for the Department of State to the text of a proposal which the operators might make to the Union representatives. In substance it was that the voyages of these two ships begin under normal conditions and that if later any arrangement was made between the Unions and the operators, with the assent of the United States Government, which would provide any of the above-mentioned benefits to the seamen for later operation, that it would be retroactive to this voyage commencing today. After various and sundry negotiations there was a final agreement that the ships sail. So the *Roosevelt* sails tonight; the *Orizaba* is now signing a crew and will sail when completed. The agreement also includes the *Manhattan,* which is due very shortly and which will turn around as quickly as possible, and also includes four other ships which we are taking over special charter for for [*sic*] repatriation purposes. So it is all cleared up for the time being, but it has been rather a hectic day in the course of which I have had to confer from time to time with the Secretary and Messersmith and Welles and even talked to Watson in order that the President might be advised if necessary. . . .

The war situation is developing rather fast in the east [*sic*]. It seems that there are eighty divisions of German troops in Poland, or a total of 1,700,000 men. There is great danger of a large part of the Polish army being trapped in Posen. However, it seems that there is in operation a major policy between

France, England, and Poland. It is believed that the Poles were to [*sic*] [will?] retire gradually after offering a stubborn resistance until they crossed the Vistula and there put up a determined stand. This would gradually lead the greater part of the German army east. It is believed that under those circumstances, and provided they can be held in the east that there may be a major attack on the West and that France will really try to break through the line and either cause the recall of thirty to forty divisions, maybe fifty divisions, or succeed in a major operation.

There have been very few bombings and very few operations on the waters or on land except in the area of Poland.

September 7, 1939

. . . Kennedy has been terribly explosive. . . . [He] seems to think that the only people needing repatriation are in the lobby of the American Embassy in London. As a matter of fact there are 2800 in Ireland; there are many thousand in France, and there are scattered and spread hundreds of them in each of Latvia, Esthonia and Finland on the wrong side of the Baltic and in Norway and Sweden, also in Denmark and Portugal and in Yugoslavia and Greece. There have been a great many in Switzerland, but the sailing of the Italian Line from Genoa and Naples has relieved that situation. George Gordon[21] in the Netherlands has done a very good job. It is not of the extent because he was not confronted with the enormous problem that London and Paris are confronted with, but he did an excellent job. He did not ask anybody's help but handled it all himself and then told us what had been done. That is the kind of a foreign representative that I like to see. Kennedy has been condemning everybody and criticizing everything and has antagonized most of the people in the Administration. Truitt and he are great friends, and Truitt has played ball with him over the long distance telephone. I talked to Truitt this afternoon and told him I thought Kennedy was hurting himself and that the impression that was created in this country and that the news stories and publicity items which went out of London with his permission if not with his origination indicated that he did not view the situation normally. Of course it is not a normal situation, but it requires a calm head and a cooperative brain rather than a vituperative tongue and a scattering of energy. . . .

Our first ship was taken by the British today because it contained some kind of rock.[22] It is the same game of a blockade of Germany and a lack of freedom of American ships. In addition there is reported an unjustified action by the British in the Caribbean. They are reported to have stopped a

[21] Foreign service officer, former envoy to Haiti, 1935–1937, and envoy to the Netherlands, 1937–1940.

[22] I have been unable to locate any mention in public records concerning this alleged incident.

Grace Line ship, demanded to see its manifest, and to have asked to have delivered to it the German citizens aboard. I heard it from the Maritime Commission and advised Welles and told him that I thought that might give Kennedy something to keep him busy there a while but first it would have to be verified. He started immediately to get proof of it if possible.

In the papers this evening there is a headline story to the effect that England has started to talk to Italy and tried to appease her. It is a great mistake things like that get into the press at this time, but it sounds like an echo of my conversation the other night. I have learned since that Halifax [23] is in entire sympathy with the ideas that I entertained but that his military and naval advisors did not agree. I learned from Welles that he probably would proceed along the lines suggested. The stories tonight seemed to be corroborative of that suggestion, though they certainly cannot be taken as authoritative.

It is still doubtful whether any fighting of any account is taking place on the western front, and it looks as if Hitler might occupy the territories he desired and then say, "Well, I will quit here if you want peace." I learned this morning that the British guarantee to Poland and their promise to support her was qualified by the understanding that Britain might not be able to be of very great assistance in the west and that the effort might be abortive. The strategy was to let the German army penetrate to the east before the French attacked, but if the British understanding with Poland is as indicated it would also carry the implication that the French army would not attack in great force—only enough to carry out the idea of support—until after the German army had occupied more than Hitler demanded. There is no doubt something like that in the bargain. I hesitate to think that there is any truth to it, but I have always felt that England would not give carte blanche to Poland to declare war for England unless there was some moderation or string attached to it.

September 13, 1939 [24]

News from abroad is pessimistic. A number of British ships are being sunk. At least one submarine was sunk near the entrance to the Mediterranean, and from London comes a report that there seems to be some

---

[23] Lord Halifax, British Secretary of State for Foreign Affairs, 1938–1940, and former leader of the House of Lords, 1935–1938.

Great Britain and France appeared willing to make substantial concessions to keep Italy neutral. On October 31, four days after conclusion of an Anglo-Italian commercial agreement, London gave *de facto* recognition to Italy's annexation of Albania. At the same time, Great Britain made formidable preparations to blockade Italy if Mussolini should join forces with Germany.

[24] From September 8–12, Long was mainly occupied in settling the complicated legal problem of sending maritime ships to bring Americans back from Europe. Long's entry for September 14 summarizes the final decisions.

pessimism in the minds of some high officials as to the eventual outcome. On the other hand in Germany Kirk[25] reports already real scarcity of foods and life under rigorous war conditions. They are having difficulty in getting food and in moving about the city. Our Consul in Warsaw is supposed to be there still, but he has been incommunicado. We have been unable to reach him, and no word has been received from him.[26] The Germans have said they would give him a wire to sending [sic] anything in plain language if they found him. The Germans have apparently not yet occupied Warsaw, and more resistance is being offered, but they have run over a very great area of land.

Russia is reported sending large reinforcements to her western border at Poland and Lithuania. No one seems to know the purpose, but it is assumed to be that they fear that a lot of Poles running from the Germans will go into Russia or that it might be that they fear that German armies might continue on.

From Italy comes the expressed opinion that the Italians are very friendly toward the French and the English in their personal contacts and the more or less expressed thought that Italy may be found on the side of England and France eventually.

The President called Congress for Special Session on the 21st. The Neutrality Bill will be the first thing up and will offer, in my opinion, a very unpleasant and difficult fight.[27] I lunched with General Watson, and he thought they had 61 votes and 9 non-committal in the Senate for passage of the Neutrality Act. He seemed to think there would be no difficulty, but my feeling is to the contrary. . . .

There is still no aerial warfare on the western front. Arthur Krock[28] tells me that the Polish Ambassador[29] calls him every day and asks him what in the world England is going to do about sending help to Poland; that Poland

[25] Alexander C. Kirk, foreign service officer, counselor of the American embassy in Berlin, 1939–1940.

As a result of the steady deterioration in relations between the United States and Germany, President Roosevelt recalled Ambassador Hugh Wilson in November 1938, leaving the counselor as the ranking American official.

[26] John K. Davis, consul general, Warsaw, 1938–1939.

[27] The Neutrality Act of 1935 had authorized the President to prohibit all arms shipments to belligerent nations. On September 5, 1939, Roosevelt proclaimed American neutrality and invoked the arms embargo. When Congress convened in special session on September 21, the President asked for repeal of the embargo. "I give to you my deep and unalterable conviction," he declared, "that by the repeal of the embargo the United States will more probably remain at peace than if the law remains as it stands today." The administration recommended the passage of a strict cash-and-carry system for all commerce with warring nations. (For a discussion of American neutrality policy 1933–1940, see Fred L. Israel, *Nevada's Key Pittman* [Lincoln: University of Nebraska Press, 1963], pp. 131–170.)

[28] Washington correspondent of the *New York Times* since 1932.

[29] Count Jerzy Potocki.

is suffering terribly. The same came today from Kennedy, relating his conversation with the Polish Ambassador there.

My own thought is that Poland should have thought of those things ahead of time. I still do not see how England or France can, or ever could have, helped Poland against Germany and in the geographical situation that exists today. Yet I do not see how they can morally accept an offer of peace which probably will be proposed to them. But if they do not accept it, the American people are very apt to take the position that England is responsible for prolonging the war and that the United States ought not to change its neutrality laws under those circumstances. Before the Congress adjourns there will be developments along this line which are apt to change public sentiment and Congressional action.

The *Bremen* is still not reported. The British were reported to have sunk her, but if so they are perfectly secret about it. If she is not sunk, she may be serving as the base for submarines somewhere at sea. It is hard to give credence to reports that one hears of submarines, but they are reported from time to time by shipping movements. One was reported just off Key West, four have been reported off Curacao, one other was reported in the Caribbean, two separate times one has been reported near Nantucket, one off George's Bank and the other off Pollack Rip Lightship. Also four strange airplanes were reported passing Haiti and were unidentified there, but none of these things have been actually identified through official sources. A lot of it is to be discounted, but there is certain to be some truth in some of it.

September 14, 1939

We have finally agreed on jurisdiction, authority and funds to move the ships. Five have been arranged for. Two have sailed; two are just about to sail; one will sail in a day or two at latest. The first is on her way to Liverpool then to Glasgow and Galway for *Athenia* survivors and return. The second goes to France—but as all Channel French ports are now closed she goes to Laver Don [Le Verdon?] near Bordeaux. The third goes to England this afternoon. The fourth goes to France, via the Azores because of some refueling or replenishing need. The fifth will sail in a day or so but destination to depend on needs of the time—either at France or England.

Every freighter has been asked to make itself available for passengers at European ports. Many have emergency capacity for 20 to 25, provided they provide life saving apparatus for that additional number and get an emergency certificate from the Consul at the port. That is being done.

. . . I figure nearly 20,000 berths will be available to sail to America out of Europe next week. So the hectic situation which existed until authority and funds could be found and until ships were actually diverted and dispatched to Europe no longer exists. Continuing is the frantic telegraphing for funds from persons abroad through the Department to their families or employers and the remission of funds and information through the Department. Also many, many inquiries from friends and families here for news of those abroad who cannot pass the censor's ban with any open messages and whose whereabouts are unknown over here. So we ask Consuls at last known address to locate them.

... In the meantime the Polish Army seems to be disintegrating. Its air force is nearly non-existent. Its resistance in the south seems to be over. Warsaw has not fallen but seems to be getting surrounded. There is our Consul still—and still unheard of or from. The Polish army in the south is threatening to flee into Roumania and Roumania undetermined whether to prevent that and Germany insisting she do and threatening if she do [sic] not. It looks black for Poland. And when that is done England and France will face a very much augmented force in the west.

Germany demanded of Hungary [that] troops be permitted to pass over Hungarian territory and into Poland. Hungary sent two divisions over night, tore up railroad tracks and mined tunnels and answered next day "no" and called [the] German Minister and told him Hungary would not only oppose any such act of Germany by firing on German Army but had massed two more divisions at Brataslava and would invade Slovakia in reprisal. Germany did not pass. A few days before this demand Ribbentrop,[30] 20 miles behind the German lines, requested the presence of the Hungarian Foreign Minister,[31] sent an Army plane for him. During conversations there Ribbentrop offered Hungary certain parts of Poland, small slices. Hungary refused, saying she wanted no single part of Polish soil. If he had said "yes" that probably would have been the price of passage of German troops through Hungary and Hungary would have been in the war on Germany's side. But it ended differently.

The situation may change drastically before our Congress meets and will certainly change so much as to confront us with the neutrality problem in a new light.

September 15, 1939

The picture abroad changes rapidly. Germany has practically annihilated Poland—air corps, army, government, morale and all. The army is in rout,

[30] Joachim von Ribbentrop, German foreign minister, 1938–1945, and former ambassador to Great Britain, 1936–1938.

After the outbreak of war in September 1939, Hungary failed to declare the customary neutrality. Although she avoided offending the Allied Powers, she continued to supply Germany liberally with agricultural products. The Hungarian policy in 1939 continued close relations with Germany in trade and external matters, yet at the same time opposed the Germanization of Hungary's internal politics.

[31] Count István Csáky, foreign minister, 1938–1941, and an advocate of close cooperation with Germany.

the populations in panic, Warsaw surrounded and threatened with bombardment unless evacuated in a few hours. Russia has made a truce with Japan in the Far East.[32] That permits Japan to increase her activity against the British in China and allows Russia an unencumbered hand to operate in Europe. Her army massing in the west, first eastern Poland is threatened and then Roumania. On the Rhine France makes slow progress against German resistance. The Westwall has not yet been reached at any point. No air attacks have been made. All in contradistinction to Germany in Poland.

Germany, Russia and Japan appear to have an understanding and to be working somewhat in common—if not in entire agreement. Italy is still out—and to all appearances wants to stay out.

But the instant picture is that the world is in an abrupt change. England's leadership is not only challenged but her existence as an empire directly threatened. Power, force, centralization, dictatorial control actually seriously threaten the ways and methods we know and live by.

September 17, 1939

Sunday morning conference in the Secretary's office. The Secretary, Davis, Wilson, Messersmith, Berle, Moffett [*sic*], Dunn[33] and Hackworth.

Two subjects were primarily discussed. One was the procedure that should be followed in dealing with British seizures of American ships and their interference with American commerce. There was some discussion of a consultation with the British Ambassador to see if we could agree upon a procedure and the drawing up of an understanding which would be quite informal and copies of which would not be exchanged. I objected seriously and rather at length to this on the basis that any agreement with the British Embassy on that subject would be wrongful, first in that it might involve a waiver of our rights or lay a predicate from which it would be difficult to insist upon our rights; and second that in case any such procedure should be adopted by agreement, it would be sure to become known sooner or later by the very manner of its operation and that when and if it did become known it would afford a substantial basis for the justification of Germany's charge that we were unneutral on the ground that we were agreeing with the British Government about ways and means that the British could operate to prevent goods being received in Germany which Germany was entitled to buy from us and needed in time of war.

[32] The Soviet-Japanese truce of September 13, 1939, ended sporadic fighting along the ill-defined frontier between the Japanese protectorate of Manchukuo and the Soviet protectorate of Outer Mongolia.

[33] Adolf A. Berle, Jr., professor of corporate law at Columbia University since 1927, and Assistant Secretary of State, 1938–1944; J. Pierrepont Moffat, foreign service officer, chief of the State Department Division of European Affairs, 1937–1940; James C. Dunn, foreign service officer, State Department Adviser on Political Relations, 1937–1943.

From objection supported at first only by Wilson I was successful in having the point of view finally adopted by the conference and limited to the fact that any arrangement which should be adopted by the Department of State should be unilateral in character and should not depend upon any agreement with the British and should not take any form in writing which could be the basis for any charge of unneutrality. . . .

September 18, 1939

First thing this morning I went to see the Secretary about the President's attitude toward neutrality, and subsequently saw General Watson at the White House. I told the Secretary that my opinion was the President should not endorse any particular plan of neutrality because if he did he was liable to endorse one that the Congress would not accept and that to have a rift between the President and the Congress at this stage of the game would be not only unfortunate from our domestic point of view but would be most harmful to our national prestige abroad. I thought he should approach the subject in general terms and leave it to Congress as to what should be done. I felt sure that something like the cash and carry plan was going to be adopted. The Secretary agreed that he thought so too, but he thought there might be some extensions of it which would be harmful. I suggested that I thought it would not be necessary for the President to mention cash and carry or any other plan but just put the baby on the lap of Congress and then to exercise his powers of control in committee and with the leaders to bring about the best modifications he could secure.

He has called the leaders of the Congress of both parties and has also asked Landon[34] and another leading Republican to meet with them. He also asked Hoover,[35] but Hoover placed some conditions upon his acceptance, and so they just dropped it. The arrogance of Hoover in placing conditions upon a conference with the President in a time like this is hard to understand.

The world moves very fast. Russia joined the fray yesterday and invaded Poland at daylight this morning with the stated intention of protecting the Russian citizens in that part of Poland and claiming it was not a violation of her neutrality. Nevertheless, her armies fought the Polish armies and routed them, and they have since announced that they shot down seven Polish planes and have captured certain Polish cities. Roumania is quaking with fear. The King[36] understands the situation he will be in if he is confronted with German or Russian forces. Some of his troops are at the border but not

[34] Alfred M. Landon, Republican, governor of Kansas, 1933–1937, and Republican presidential nominee in 1936.

[35] Herbert Hoover, former President of the United States, 1929–1933.

[36] Reference here is to Carol II, king of Rumania, 1930–1940. Throughout 1939 Rumania existed in imminent danger of invasion and dismemberment by Germany, Hungary, and Russia, but Carol managed to keep his kingdom intact.

in sufficient numbers to offer stubborn resistance. However, our Minister[37] there does not think that either Germany or Russia are ready for that movement. It looks suspicious to me as far as Russia is concerned. First, she and Germany are not in full agreement as to their respective ambitions and she realizes that Germany is on the move and that if Russia is going to occupy Roumania that Russia had better be moving quickly, else Germany might be there ahead of her. Bulgaria is prepared to permit the passage of either Russian or German troops on their way south to the Bosporus. . . . Yugoslavia is not prepared to fight anybody of any magnitude and is almost entirely lacking in equipment, airplanes, tanks and heavy guns and things of that sort. Mussolini still talks neutrality and is engaged in conversations with the French and British for commercial and industrial expansion to fill the place of German trade that is now closed. But if this war continues long and Russia and Germany insist, Mussolini may have to stop fishing and cut bait.

Our peripatetic Ambassador from Warsaw finds himself now in Bucharest and is receiving instructions tonight to accompany that Government to Paris. . . .[38]

I begin to see a few rifts in the cloud. It seems that Japan and Russia are not in accord. They have ceased fighting, but the Japanese Government has informed our Embassy that they cannot support the tenets of Communism and that their understanding goes simply to a cessation of hostilities; that they do not contemplate a non-aggression pact; that they have no sympathy with the philosophy of the Russian Government. Furthermore, it seems that Russia and Germany are not in agreement. Some of the officers of the German Government, notably one at Kaunas,[39] and several others, have intimated that their Government was perfectly surprised by the invasion of Poland by Russia. But they also intimated that there will be an agreement, or that there is the basis for an agreement, to give Lithuania back Memel[40] and to reestablish a Polish buffer state, diminutive in size, somewhere between Russia and Germany and to make a direct contact between Russia and Germany south of Lithuania but north of the prospective buffer state, such contact to take the form of a narrow corridor. This may lead to some future

[37] John F. Montgomery, minister to Hungary, 1933–1941.

[38] Ambassador Anthony Biddle, Jr. eventually went to England where he served as ambassador to the Polish government-in-exile as well as to the exile governments of Belgium, Norway, the Netherlands, Yugoslavia, Greece, Czechoslovakia, and Luxembourg.

[39] Kaunas was the provisional capital of Lithuania, 1918–1940. German troops did not formally occupy the city until 1941.

[40] The Treaty of Versailles (1919) placed the east Prussian city and port of Memel under French administration. In 1924 the city was made an autonomous region within Lithuania and had its own legislature. But, after the electoral victory of the Nazis in the city (1938), Germany served Lithuania with an ultimatum demanding the return of the area to which Lithuania complied.

trouble, like the last corridor, if it should develop into actuality.[41] It further looks as if Russia was going to occupy Latvia and Esthonia but allow Lithuania to continue, probably under the patronage of Germany.

But no one can foretell the morrow. No one yesterday saw Russia's actual entry into Poland, though we feared it. We now anticipate a proposal, either directly or through Mussolini, for an acceptance by England and France of the situation which has developed in Poland. They will refuse to accept it, and many people will hold them responsible for continuation of the war. France is prepared for a very difficult military situation in case that situation becomes a fact. They have already prepared for the evacuation of Paris, and many of the Government archives have been sent away. The American Embassy has been assigned a house in the distant country near the site the French Government will take and has been asked to be ready to leave on short notice. Other Embassies are being informed. They fear air raids and heavy destruction in Paris. . . .

September 24, 1939

Poland is completely deflated. Russia rushed into Polish Ukraine ahead of the Germans and placed themselves between Hitler and Roumania. That shuts Germany off from the Black Sea. It is not clear how much of this Russian military activity in Poland was the subject of agreement between Russia and Germany, but it seems to be understood that Russia exceeded the expectations Germany had. That may account for Germany's efforts to pass through Hungary—so they could win the race with Russia and reach Roumania first. Roumania, with Germany on the border, would be a suppliant and the Black Sea before long in Germany's back yard. But Russia wants that field to herself. At least it seems there are the seeds of discord between Stalin and Hitler which may ripen into real differences or may cause reorientation of policy on Hitler's part.

. . . There is a defeatist opinion abroad in the world as regards England. Italy, the Balkan countries, Turkey—many people here—think England is in for a bad licking. Italy is reported to be more kindly toward Germany. We have had it from Rome and from several other capitals as reports of conversations with Italian officials. Last night I had another conversation with my friend [Fumasoni-Biondi] who is intimate at the Italian Embassy here. He sought the interview and came to my apartment about nine o'clock. He betrayed the fear and the point of view that England was about to be badly beaten. The truth is that the remarkable campaign of Germany in Poland has amazed the world and has brought something akin to terror to

[41] Reference here is to the Polish Corridor, a narrow strip of territory taken from Germany and awarded to Poland under the Treaty of Versailles. This strip provided Poland with an outlet to the Baltic Sea. With the defeat of Poland in 1939, Germany annexed the Corridor.

any neighboring Government. Italy has it. He told me that Italy still wanted to stay out and had a perfectly respectable technical reason for doing so, because one of the secret clauses of the Rome-Berlin Pact provides that the obligations for military cooperation only come in effect three years from the date of signature. That could keep Italy out till 1942.

I told him we were going to keep out, improve our military forces and be ready for any eventuality on this continent—but stay out of this war. There were no "ifs" about it at this time. But that if Italy was of the opinion England was licked now she would do better not to act precipitately on that understanding. It is, I told him, too early in the race for Italy to bet on the wrong horse. We talked for an hour along those lines—and I kept the conversation open. He said he would want to see me again. I told him "any time."

This morning I told Messersmith about it. He thinks it advisable to keep it open too.

Yesterday I got off for the afternoon—later than I hoped—and missed the first nine holes of my golf game. I played the second nine with Norman Davis, Lothian and Harry Covington and dined at the Club with Elliot Wadsworth.[42]

Hull had some teeth out this morning so he did not make the conference— and there was none. I was there and went over several policies with Messersmith; then drove out to Burning Tree for lunch, by accident with Dwight Davis;[43] then drove to Montpelier, looked over the farm, horses and cows— arranged for weaning three sucklings, to ship the colt to Pons in trade for a filly—for convenience—because I can more easily handle two fillies with my Percheron filly than I could two colts under any circumstances. They would kick each other to pieces. I estimate I have 100 barrels of corn, probably more. I will sell 1/2 or 2/3 of it. My hay crop was a near failure— no Lespedeza. There are four calves now, one 5 days old, a pure bred but non-registerable heifer—2 heifers and 2 bulls. The place is all in order and ready to occupy—except for a cook. . . .

September 26, 1939

This morning we had a long session about Red Cross and all the collection and disposition of funds of that nature. It involves a great many questions and is more or less outlined in the neutrality law. There is no proposal in the new bill to change it. The Department has to register applicants, and then they go out and say they have been licensed by the Department of State and make appeals for funds. Very few of them are capable of developing

---

[42] Harry Covington, lawyer and former Democrat, U.S. Representative from Maryland, 1909-1915; Elliot Wadsworth, former Assistant Secretary of the Treasury, 1921-1925.

[43] Former Secretary of War, 1925-1929, and Governor General of the Philippine Islands, 1929-1932.

an organization abroad which would permit the proper expenditure of such funds, and many of them operate on a commission basis so that individuals soliciting funds make money out of it, so that only a part of it gets eventually to relief purposes. As long as the law places a certain responsibility on the President, and since the President has delegated that to the Department, it seems that we ought to correlate their activities. Some of them are reaching the border line of unneutrality. Bullitt, for instance, has organized ambulance units, and they are intended to be operated as parts of the French army. Of course that is a violation of our law, and we have to do something about it. Furthermore, he is sponsoring the operating of a big hospital, reserving about 40 beds for Americans and 1500 beds for French, and placing it at the disposal of the military authorities for French wounded. This is a border line activity. People are soliciting funds for the relief of Poles, but they are unable to get into Poland without cooperation of the German Government and the Russian Government, and neither of those Governments is going to let private organizations operate in territory they have occupied by their military forces. So that the funds being solicited cannot possibly be used for the purposes announced.

. . . Bullitt reports a strange interview with Daladier, saying that the British are not going to send any more into the fighting area and would not risk one plane in the danger zone, and carrying the implications of reserved but definite criticism of England, at the same time painting the picture of Communistic difficulties in France and stating that the Russian Government had spent six hundred million francs for propaganda and subversive activities in France since the beginning of hostilities in addition to their other normal expenditures.

Kennedy from London reports a laconic interview with Halifax from which the inference is drawn that the British are not very much intent on fighting at the moment. They seem to be incapable of realizing the consequences of the Russian development. They seem to be unable to see definitely where England is to fight in view of the circumstances which have brought Russia into the Danube basin and have changed the whole political attitude of the Balkan states. The implication of a Communistic Europe is foreshadowed, and British policy has not been oriented to see the new picture, and until it is oriented they will not take an active military position. These are not the words, nor is that exactly the substance, but it certainly is the sense of the interview.

September 30, 1939

This Russian affair looms very big. The implications are enormous—they are staggering. The Allies are definitely confronted now with a peace proposal. Hitler has communicated with Daladier to request a meeting at

Stockholm to settle peace. It is going to place the Allies in a difficult position, because both Stalin and Mussolini will back it up, as will probably all the neutral states. . . .

October 1, 1939

At conference this morning with the Secretary; were present Messersmith, Berle, Dunn, Hackworth, Moffat and Savage.[44] Several important matters were up for discussion. First, the Secretary read and signed my long drafted letter to the President reviewing the whole repatriation problem and recommending the discharge of the specially diverted ships when they returned from Europe. More or less in line with the letter to the President were telegrams despatched late yesterday afternoon to London and Paris.

The Secretary said the Polish Ambassador had requested to see him to notify him about the continuation of the government under different personnel in Paris. We have been advised by Bullitt that it is perfectly legal according to Polish law, and we have assured ourselves by an examination of the Polish Constitution that the Polish Government had a *de jure* existence under Polish law even though it was not now resident in Poland. The Secretary suggested that a statement be made to the press on the non-recognition of territory acquired by force and on that basis proceed to recognize the new government of Poland. I took exception to that view or to the use of that as a predicate for our position. I argued that it would lead us into trouble, as it had in the past in the case of Italy, and might have embarrassing features from the point of view of our future position and was not necessary. . . . Belgium had been referred to as a precedent. I pointed out that Belgium was not a precedent, for Whitlock[45] stayed in the capital and the King was on a fragment of Belgian soil with his army, and that in the case of Serbia later, the King of Serbia continued and did not need a delegation of his authority, and our Minister accompanied him. However, there was a precedent in Russia in 1917. The Kerensky Ambassador continued here, and our Ambassador continued on Russian soil, a part of the time in Petrograd under Lenin and Trotsky, and when forced out of there stayed in Vologda, and there continued in coordination, if not in cooperation, with local groups opposed to the Communist regime. There was also the precedent [*sic*] of Poland itself in 1918. It had been recognized when it had no country, and it could be continued now without any country. There was plenty of precedent [*sic*] in fact, and plenty of legality under Polish law, and it seemed unnecessary for us to make again a statement which had led us into embarrassment in Manchuria and in Ethiopia. . . . It was finally adopted to accept my point of view. Moffat was asked to draft a statement on those premises.

[44] Carlton Savage, assistant to the State Department counselor, 1938–1941.
[45] Brand Whitlock, ambassador to Belgium, 1913–1922.

The question of armed merchantmen came up, whether we should allow entry. It is a very delicate subject in my mind. It was the same question that led us into difficulties in 1917. The Congress is now studying a Neutrality Bill which if passed, as now drafted, will keep our ships unarmed and will prevent any of our ships from sailing for a belligerent port or into danger zones. Nevertheless, if we closed our ports to armed merchant vessels, we would be taking responsibility of placing them in the same category with battleships. Even Germany admits they are not battleships, but claims that they are entitled to be treated as armed ships to the extent to which they are armed, which means of course as far as German submarines are concerned that they will be fired on without notice. But that does not mean that we should view them as anything but what they really are, having satisfied ourselves that their armament is purely defensive. To do so would cut off our markets from European countries, because we are about to take the position that our own ships will not carry our goods to European countries. However, I suggested that it was an academic matter and that we ought to coast along as we were, having allowed the British to send merchant ships armed defensively into our ports and that it was not necessary for us to take any action until Congress should pass the Neutrality Act. It was decided to do that. . . .

October 4, 1939

I am engaged in details for the closing arrangements of repatriating Americans. Well over 50,000 have landed in 30 days, and of those remaining in Europe all who desire to come at this time will have had an opportunity by the end of the current week. There are several thousand who desire to stay longer and several small categories of persons without sufficient funds who will be investigated as to their citizenship and availability of funds and they can all be evacuated in the regular liners which will be plying for a short time longer.

The extra boats we sent were not very well patronized. Kennedy and Bullitt telegraphed their deprecatory opinions of these boats to the Department and probably made some remarks around their Embassies which were repeated. Whether it started in that way or some other way, there was certainly an "unsafe" reputation attached to these boats for the trans-Atlantic run, in spite of that fact that they had been certified by the Maritime Commission as capable and able. The result of it all was that the *Orizaba* brought back 352 passengers out of a maximum of 450, the *Shawnee* sailed with 304 estimated American citizens and about 150 Latin Americans out of a capacity of 675. The *Iroquois* left with 584 passengers with a maximum of 675. The *St. John* we do not know of yet, but the *Acadia* sailed from France with no passengers, stopped at Southampton for about 40 passengers and proceeds to Cobh, where they have probably 250. Her maximum capacity is 860. We have done our duty in making facilities available. If these people do not want to travel on safe boats and prefer the luxury of another kind of boat, and they stay in Europe for that reason, then it is certainly not the fault of the American Government that they are still in Europe.

Now we begin to turn our attention to representation of interests. Prisoners of war are just looming on the horizon as a subject matter for our handling, and we are now telegraphing to Kirk asking him what he wants in the way of organization and personnel. We have asked him once before, but apparently the rush of his work has precluded his attention to that subject.

Hugh Wilson and several of his friends want Christian Herter[46] to be sent over there to take charge of prisoners of war inspection under Kirk. I am not inclined to recommend him. He has had some experience in that matter, but he would use the appointment for the advancement of his own political fortunes in Massachusetts, where he is now Speaker of the House, and would eventually try to use any information he got through his contacts in that position in derrogation [sic] of the Administration—in my opinion—and I have known him a long time. I would like to get a man like John D. Rockerfeller [sic] III, whose name means something in its association and in whom the British and French Governments would have entire confidence. Or like Wayne Chatfield Taylor,[47] who is now on his way to Europe on a Red Cross mission and in whom our own Government and other Governments might have complete confidence. I think it is important in this position to have a person, irrespective of the person's former experience, whose reputation is above reproach, who is not a partisan in any keen sense of the word and whose character is such as to carry complete confidence. . . .

Russia has been fairly moderate in her preliminary demands upon Estonia and Latvia, though it seems probable that her foot-hold will be extended in the Baltic States. Her position vis-à-vis Germany has the appearance of being very troublesome and frightening to Germany herself. It now seems possible that Hitler may be considering withdrawing from the territories he has occupied east of the Corridor and that he is contemplating the establishment of a buffer state between him and the line of Russian occupation in that territory. Certain financial regulations promulgated in Berlin for the issuance of currency and fiscal control of these territories seem to make a distinction between them and the territories which are more properly Germanic and to carry the thought that that idea is in his head and that the origin of the idea is recent. It would seem that he feared the contiguity of Russia. But if he sets

[46] Republican, member of the Massachusetts legislature, 1931–1943, and former assistant to Secretary of Commerce Herbert Hoover, 1919–1924.

[47] European delegate of the American Red Cross, 1939–1940, and former Assistant Secretary of the Treasury, 1936–1939.

up a buffer state and withdraws his military forces, he will have Russia closer to him than the line of its present occupation. That Russia has designs upon Germany is perfectly assumable under the circumstances. Germany is dependent upon Russia for most of her supplies now and can only get oil from the Black Sea area by the courtesy of Russia through Roumania. Germany has been shut off from the Black Sea and from the Balkans and communications from Russia addressed to Communist cells in Bulgaria and passing through Roumania have been intercepted at Bucharest. Their contents indicate that Russia is planning the Bolshevization of Germany and that the present movement is only one step in the procedure.

October 5, 1939

... Kennedy telegraphed today the report of a conversation he had with Halifax. England has not yet received any peace proposal but rather expects one might come from either Turkey or Italy. Halifax's position is that if one should come, it will receive very careful consideration *and* that the neutrals will be consulted, including the United States. To my mind that means only one thing—that England is looking for a basis to end the war and will be prepared to accept a reasonable peace offer. Every neutral in Europe will advise England to accept an offer. The three Scandanavian [*sic*] countries, all the Baltic countries, Holland, Belgium, Spain, Italy, probably Switzerland, and certainly each of the Balkan States will so advise. England knows that as well as we do. There could be no reason to take into consultation governments which have that point of view unless it would be for the purpose of obtaining a basis in world opinion to justify England in abandoning the war.

Halifax is also reported to be fearful of the spread of Communism if the war continues. He might well be afraid of that. To my mind nothing is more clear than that Communism, under the aegis of Russia, will be the only winner in a prolonged war. Stalin today is trying to sell the products of Russia to each side. He is supplying Germany, and it is now reported, but not officially through our channels, that he is requesting the Scandanavian countries to rent their ships so that they can be loaded with Russian wood pulp at Murmansk, which is an open harbor, and sent to England around the danger zone of German submarines. He would like to see each side destroy the other, or so weaken themselves and each other that they could no longer resist the influences of Communism, which would spring not from without but from within from the ranks of hungry, discouraged people in each country.

In the very beginning of hostilities and during my first day of the war in Washington I discovered a little anagram which is indicative of my own thought in that matter:

> Mussolini
> Hitler
> Chamberlain
> Daladier
> Chi
> Vincera la guerra

By reading down and encircling the third letter, it reads that Stalin will win the war.

October 6, 1939

Listened to Hitler this morning at six o'clock. I could not understand his German, but I followed the interpolations in English. Having since read his speech, it appears that he has laid the basis for a move through diplomatic channels to present his peace offer to England and to France. His address was in moderate terms and more quiet than I had any idea it would be. The tone of his voice was moderate as compared to other effusions. His speech was a good presentation of his entire subject and was a very good piece of propaganda if not of statesmanship.[48]

The British Government, I have no doubt, will seriously consider the proposals if they come to them in diplomatic form. They are of course already conscious of them, but they are not in definite shape for consideration of the Government.

Bullitt once reported that Daladier had received offers from Hitler. He has since reported Daladier has not received any offer from Hitler. He now reports that the French Government is not disposed to consider the German terms. Of course the French Government will be governed entirely by what the British think. My own impression is that Chamberlain and his friends in the British Government will consider it in spite of the tone which Chamberlain took in his recent address to the Commons on that subject.[49] The counsel of Lloyd-George is apt to be the policy adopted by the British Government, Lloyd-George having been the questioner of Chamberlain on the occasion of his recent speech.[50] However, Chamberlain will have serious

[48] In his speech of October 6, Hitler proposed a conference of the leading European nations "after the most thorough preparation" to discuss restoring peace. His conditions, however, were vague. Chamberlain replied on October 12 that the "uncertain proposals contain no suggestions for righting the wrongs done to Czechoslovakia and Poland." The Prime Minister asked Hitler for "convincing proof" that he really favored peace.

[49] On October 3, Prime Minister Chamberlain affirmed to the House of Commons that he saw nothing in the Russo-German agreement partitioning Poland to cause him to modify the existing goal of mobilizing all the resources and might of the British Empire for the effective prosecution of the war.

[50] David Lloyd-George, British Prime Minister, 1916–1922, and member of Parliament, 1890–1944, was a consistent òpponent of the appeasement policy of Prime Minister Chamberlain.

opposition to any move to effect a peaceful settlement. Churchill and Eden will try to overthrow him and take charge of the Government. The probability is that the peace offer will be considered to the point where the war may dribble out. Chamberlain is no doubt fearful of the Russian development and will be glad to come to some terms largely on that account. In fact it looms large over the whole map of Europe. If peace is not arrived at within a reasonable time, it will soon develop who will probably win the war. Germany will make a terrible onslaught on England from the air, probably concentrating upon its docks and shipping and ports. If England's air force is sufficient to repel the German attacks, then England and France will probably win the war. That should develop within the next thirty days, but it will be a long war. If the British are unable to offset the German attacks and to defend themselves against the demoralization which would be caused in England by German planes, then the war ought not to last very long, and in that case Germany would be the victor.

We ought to know within thirty days if it is to be over soon, but if it is not apparent then, we will probably dig in for a long seige [sic].

October 11, 1939

The Russian menace has been moving higher and higher. There is no doubt in my mind that Hitler is scared to death. The indications are that there is considerable consternation in the high German authorities, military and otherwise. The German Minister at Kaunas admitted to our Minister that the difficulties with Russia were unexpected and serious. . . .

The thought of a Bolshevic [sic] Germany is rather staggering. It is not immediately in prospect. There were six million Communists in Germany as its boundaries existed last June. If Hitler should set up a buffer state east of the Corridor and between that line and the line of Russian occupation, as he now proposes, it would not be a stable state, because if it was not incorporated within the Reich he would not be able to fortify it and to use it for military control to the extent he would if it were part of Germany. So that if he does put up a separate buffer state, it will be easy prey for Russia to move into the east line of the Corridor. This must have a very sobering effect.

My mind reverts from time to time to Hitler's description in *Mein Kampf* of the policy of establishing an alliance with Russia. He castigated such an alliance, or the thought of one, and he now has placed himself in the position which he described with such accuracy. . . . Hitler, I have no doubt, wishes that he might clean up the western front so he could devote himself to the Russian menace or hopes that the western difficulty could be settled in order that he would have a clear hand to deal with Russia. The unfortunate part of it is that Russia will help him for the time being in his efforts to defeat

England and France, with the hope that they will all be seriously injured and that Communism will have an easy victory in all three countries.

The situation is very complicated and holds many portents of a serious nature for our future. It may be the most important moment in our modern world history, and it would be a shame if Roosevelt [by inaction] might continue a war which would mean the victory of Communism in Europe and confront us with our eventual enemy—Russia.

He should not make a move which would result in an increased power to autocratic, ruthless and dishonorable government, as represented by Hitler, a government which has repeatedly broken its word, has acted in a ruthless manner and has defied many of the rules of decent behavior and honorable conduct. In that same category is Russia, and they are militarily aligned. So that if Roosevelt was to make a move which would help them, it would militate against us and our future interests.

Delicacy enters the situation in choosing the moment and the phraseology and in finding a proper basis for any appeal or statement which might be made. We cannot base it on geographical lines. In my opinion we cannot attempt to resurrect Poland. Boundaries are now of not so great importance as the establishment of certain principles. And if when he does speak he could direct the attention of the world to the principles involved and get some agreement in general to them and have peace brought about on some proper basis, the rest of it could be settled even if Poland was not resurrected. That now seems to me a hopeless task, because it would require a military defeat of Russia to retrieve the eastern half of Poland, and the military defeat of Russia at this time seems quite improbable. . . .

I talked to Hull this afternoon. He still feels that nothing has come from Hitler which would justify the President in making any move. The British and French have given no indication that it would be agreeable to them to have the President intercede. Daladier in his address yesterday seemed to indicate that France would require assurances for security. Whom the assurances are to come from and what the nature of the security is to be desired is not specified.

It looks to me as if there was trouble brewing in Germany. In addition to our reports from Kaunas, it is unofficially reported that the head of the German Navy is very much concerned at the arrangements Ribbentrop made with Russia and which have resulted in the obtaining of naval bases on the Baltic, which will give Russia control of the Baltic.[51] The situation of responsible heads of the Army must be that they see the Russian Army at

[51] Reference here is to Admiral Erich Raeder, Commander-in-Chief of the German Navy, 1928–1943.
By the Nazi-Soviet nonaggression treaty of August 23, 1939, the Soviet Union was given a free hand in the Baltic area and the right to put naval bases along the Baltic coast.

the border of East Prussia and along their eastern front and another enemy on the west. They do not yet consider Russia their immediate enemy, but they look upon it as an essential and potential enemy. Their agreements of "friendship" are looked upon purely as expediencies and as quite temporary in nature. Yesterday there was a false rumor of an armistice in Berlin and there was reported to be great and popular rejoicing.

All of these things taken together are straws. If the responsible heads of the Government in Germany, under Hitler, are convinced that their own future safety is dependent upon making peace in the west, so that they can turn their energies against Russia in the east—if the heads of the Army, Navy and political institutions in Germany should consider that Hitler has out-lived his usefulness and that under his present activities a terrible mistake has been made—a denouement might come very rapidly. Under the program Hitler is about to attack in the west. He is waiting for the expiration of a reasonable time after his peace offer. Thereafter he is going to attack. But if his military and naval authorities are convinced that that would be bad strategy, in view of the situation vis-à-vis Russia, and if they are sufficiently strong to take a definite position, it might easily result in the retirement of Hitler and the ascendency of Goering.[52] Goering was against the Czechoslovakian movement, and until the first of August he was opposed to the Polish movement. He is a practical man and not a psychopath like Hitler. The western Powers could deal with him.

Of course this is all chimerical. . . . But it is Russia which is gaining all the time and not Germany.

October 15, 1939

. . . In conference with the Secretary this morning there was a general discussion on changes in the Neutrality Act to permit American ships to sail to belligerent territories which were not in the war zone, like Australia, Canada and other British possessions in the Pacific. The necessity is not only to ship things to them but to bring to the United States from those places wool, tin and various other products which are essentials to American industry. The question of the Mediterranean was also considered. We considered three different proposals and more or less decided in favor of one which would permit shipping south of 30° N. Lat. and west of a line which would run well off the North American, and partly off the South American, coast.

Further, there was discussed the proclamation of the President to prohibit the entrance of submarines into American waters except on the surface and to be issued under his authority under the Neutrality Law as it exists today.

---

[52] Hermann Goering, German air minister, and designated by Hitler as his successor.

October 19, 1939

. . . Day before yesterday morning Harold Dodds[53] met me at my apartment for breakfast. We then had a conversation with Norman Davis about the plans of the Woodrow Wilson Foundation vis-à-vis their donation to Princeton. Mr. Wilson's letters are going to the Congressional Library, and that removes the peg from which was suspended the proposal that the Foundation would give us all of their funds. We now propose to proceed to announce the school as the Woodrow Wilson School at Princeton. We want some occasion. The occasion might be Wilson's birthday, or the anniversary of his death. I am inclined to the latter. I suggested that the President might be obtained to make an address on the occasion and that he might tie up the present war with the last war and make some opportunity to make some expression of policy or some humanitarian appeal. Dodds returned to Princeton and will consult with some of his other advisors and then probably will ask for an appointment with the President, and he and I will go to see him.

Dodds also had in mind a suggestion that Princeton start a study for peace, to be done clandestinely but thoroughly, and just to cover all the grounds so that when this war is over some agency in this country will have explored the bases and will have collected all the data and material pertaining to America's interest in the settlement, America's interest being viewed not only from the point of view of our national necessities but from our humanitarian interest and our sympathetic desire for world peace and the basis for a lasting structure of peace. This would include disarmament and the approach of settlements in Europe on lines other than geographical, if possible, with particular reference to economic barriers. They have done more damage than almost anything else and have accentuated racial, linguistic and religious differences. . . .

It is apparent to my mind, as it has been for some time, that Germany is going to make a frantic effort, and directed principally against England and shipping interests, her control of the seas and her fleet. We ought to know before Thanksgiving whether this is going to be a long war or a short war. If she cannot destroy England in a manner similar to the way she did Poland, and if she is unable to break through the Maginot Line,[54] she will settle down to fight it out as long as she can, but will face ultimate defeat. German officials know that, certainly.

No other signs have appeared of high command opposition to the program in Germany. The success of their naval forces has obliterated that

[53] President of Princeton University, 1933–1957. Long served as a Princeton University trustee, 1937–1941.

[54] The strength of this mighty fortification system, constructed along the eastern frontier of France, was never tested, for the Germans flanked the line in their French campaign of 1940.

thought for the moment. Nevertheless the threat of Russia still continues, and she will find herself subordinated to the demands of Russia in the future. . . .

October 22, 1939

Spent last night at the farm. Up early. Went over the farm. Arranged for bringing in the harvest of corn and fodder and arranged for fall plowing.

Hours 10:00 to 1:00—Conference with Hull, Messersmith, Wilson, Hackworth and Savage; discussed: (a) Neutrality Bill situation in the House. Some doubt as to result there. Hull talked to Senator Byrnes [55] and a Member of the House on the phone. The Senate seems O.K. (b) Question of armed merchant ships. Should the President include them in a proclamation, as he did submarines? Decision in the negative. We have already advised shipping circles and instructed Collector of Customs as to inspection of armaments. We hear Bennet [*sic*] Clark[56] is preparing a resolution to deny armed ships access to our ports. (c) Proposal of Maritime Commission to run the *Washington* and *Manhattan* to Irish ports. Practical unanimity against it. I also. No need for passengers to America. All have come home who want to come home. Others there at their own risk. *St. John* bound home with only about 400 passengers out of a possible 860.

October 30, 1939

Tuesday [October 24] I saw Baruch.[57] Suggested to him that there was a movement for the Council of Foreign Relations [58] to make a study of peace bases, to do it quietly and without any publicity. I did not know how far the Department had gone. He said that he was sure that the study ought to be made and sure he ought to be active in it and that he was willing to put up expenses as far as $150,000 to $200,000.

I told him I would let him know if anything developed. Dodds has been interested in doing the same thing at Princeton but did not want to assume the responsibility alone. Dodds is a member of the Council of Foreign Relations and thought that he would approve their activity. Baruch objected to some of the personnel, and I think Dodds had some reservations on some personnel which would be in charge of it. On my return I talked to Messersmith, to whom the Council of Foreign Relations had talked. He said the

[55] James F. Byrnes, Democrat, U.S. Senator from South Carolina, 1930–1941, and former U.S. Representative, 1911–1925.

[56] Bennett Clark, Democrat, U.S. Senator from Missouri, 1936–1943.

[57] Bernard Baruch, financier, former chairman of the War Industries Board, 1918–1919, and economic adviser to President Wilson during the Paris Peace Conference, 1919.

[58] The Council on Foreign Relations, a private organization, was established in 1921 "to afford a continuous conference on international questions affecting the United States, by bringing together experts on statecraft, finance, industry, education and science."

Department could neither approve nor disapprove but was cognizant of the activity and had no objection provided it was unofficial, was thorough, worth while and in competent hands. I thought that Norman Davis and Frank Polk[59] would be active in it. Baruch had thought Davis the best equipped man to head it up. I told Messersmith that in case that did not work out as expected he could count on me to help with another effort and that I could assure him of finances in the sum indicated by Baruch, but I did not disclose the names of my contacts. . . .

At the conference yesterday morning [October 29] there were present the Secretary, Messersmith, Berle, Wilson, Norman Davis, Moffat, several others and myself. Berle was charged with getting prepared the proclamations the President will have to issue when the Neutrality Bill becomes law.[60] The Bill passed the Senate Friday night by a vote of 63 to 30. It will probably pass the House this week. The indications are there will be a majority of not less than 18 and it may be as high as 40. I still have some doubts about the action of the House. Under parliamentary procedure it will come up after a rule is passed which will be proposed by the Rules Committee. Debate will probably be limited and the only question will be consideration of the report from the Conference Committee. If the House will pass the rule to limit the debate and lay down the necessary structure, then the Bill is almost sure to pass without amendment. The test will probably come on whether the House will adopt the rules.

The other subject considered by us was the areas to be defined by the President by the authority which he will receive in the Neutrality Bill and from which will be excluded American ships. We were unanimous in excluding Holland and Belgium as ports of call for American ships. That would send them either through the North Sea or in the Channel. The question of Ireland and northern ports of Norway were considered. I was very doubtful about the advisability of granting permission to go to Bergen.[61] Bergen is entered from the North Sea and through a mined area. I said I thought it might be in contravention of the spirit of the Bill to permit American ships to go to Bergen; that they were sure to be taken by the British into Kirkwall;[62] and that to approach Bergen they would have to go north of the Faro Islands and hit the coast of Norway and then go down to Bergens fjord, but that in approaching the entrance to Bergens fjord they would be in a mined district.

[59] Washington lawyer, and former Under Secretary of State, 1919–1920.

[60] The new Neutrality Law, which Roosevelt signed on November 4, permitted belligerents to obtain war materiel from this country on a "cash and carry" basis. American citizens, vessels, and airplanes were barred from zones designated as combat areas by the President.

[61] Second largest city of Norway and its main shipping center.

[62] Located in the Orkney Islands, Scotland, and an important port on the northern trade route to Scandinavia.

As regards Ireland I thought the waters there were infested and that it would not be safe to send American ships. The British would want ships to go to Ireland, and consequently the Germans would be prepared to sink them. On the contrary, the Germans would be glad to see ships going to Bergen, and for that reason the British would be sure to seize them. No decision was made, but the Secretary was getting the gist of ideas in order to advise the President. The consensus expressed at the meeting was against Ireland, but I was one of the minority in taking a position of doubt as regards Bergen.

November 2, 1939

Today we assumed charge of British interests in that part of Poland occupied by Germany and in the Protectorate of Bohemia and Moravia. They asked us to take charge of their interests in Slovakia, but we declined. The reason for declining was not stated, but the reason was that we have no consular officers or diplomatic officers in that territory and do not care to ask for exequaturs. The government of Slovakia has requested us to recognize them, but we did not answer their communication.[63] I drafted the note to the British Embassy and the telegrams to London and Berlin and passed them on their way for signature. The French Government has asked us to do the same thing, and tomorrow I will proceed with that.

Also had a long conference today about activities under the Neutrality Act, such as efforts in this country on the part of individuals to be of assistance in various ways to belligerents, principally France. There is always a sentiment in this country to help France. People want to give hospital units, airplanes, ambulances and raise money for this or that purpose.

Some of these activities are possible under the Neutrality Act as it exists today but will not be permissible under the Neutrality Law as it is about to be revised. . . .

November 7, 1939

Today has been an interesting occupation. I had to unscramble the pattern of our representation of French interests in Germany and contiguous territories and to draft instructions to Berlin and advices to Paris. I did the same thing some days ago for England, but the telegrams did not get off till yesterday morning, the 6th, though they left my office on the second.

We assumed charge of French interests in Germany proper at the outbreak of the war. Coincidentally the French Ambassador in Warsaw asked us to assume charge of French interests in Warsaw. The French Government as

[63] On March 16, 1939, Hitler announced that Czechia thereafter belonged to the German Reich and would be known as the Protectorate of Bohemia and Moravia. On March 23 the premier of Slovakia invited Hitler to become the protector of that area, which now became a vassal state of the Reich.

such has not communicated with us further on the subject, except that on one occasion, through Bullitt, they expressed the hope that we would continue our representation in Warsaw.

After having cleared up the British situation, which in itself was a little complicated, I turned my attention to the French interests and found first, that we had been asked to take charge of French interests in Germany proper; second, that we had been asked by the French Ambassador to take charge of the French interests in Warsaw; third, that there had been no request whatsoever about taking charge of their interests in the Protectorate of Bohemia and Moravia nor in the territory of the Slovak State nor in the City of Danzig. We were advised by our Consul in Danzig that French interests there had been assumed by the Dutch.

However, since we were expected to look after the French interests, I drafted telegrams on the assumption that we were properly in charge of French interests in all of that territory, except first, the Slovak State where we are not prepared to represent either England or France, for the reason that we have no Consular representatives there, have not recognized the Slovak State and have failed to answer their communication of long standing requesting us to recognize them; and second, in Danzig, where they have committed their representation to the Dutch.

The decision had to be made on the theory that we did not recognize the right of Germany to exercise authority in the territory of former Czechoslovakia, which includes the Protectorate of Bohemia and Moravia and the Slovak State. Neither have we recognized Germany's rightful occupation of Poland or of Danzig. Naturally the British and French Governments have not done so. So a lot of assumption had to be indulged in. Our Consul in Danzig has not received an exequatur, so that there is some doubt of his authority to act. We didn't want to make a move on our own account or on the account of the British and French Governments which would be construed as recognition.

So I got the record straight, which showed that the French Ambassador had asked the Consul General in Warsaw on September 6 to assume charge of French interests in Warsaw. On September 7 we authorized the Consul so to do if the French and British left. They did leave subsequently. We were then in rightful charge of French interests in Poland. That rightful character existed at the time of the German military occupation of Warsaw. We assumed that Warsaw was assimilated into the jurisdiction of the [U.S.] Berlin Embassy after the German occupation and that Berlin inherited the function of representation in the territorial jurisdiction of the French Embassy in Warsaw as modified by the German army of occupation. So that by slow and gradual degrees I finally got the representation of French interests in Poland under the jurisdiction of the American Embassy in Berlin.

As regards the Protectorate of Bohemia, I proceeded on the assumption that the American Embassy in Berlin succeeded the British Embassy in Berlin and represented British interests in the territory which had formerly been under the territorial supervision of the British Embassy in Berlin and the same as regards the French Embassy in Berlin. As regards Danzig, it developed that the British Consul had asked the American Consul to take over thèir interests on the first of September and that he had requested permission to do so from the Senate of Danzig. The Senate, however, went out of existence before the note was accepted. He subsequently made request to the appropriate officer in the municipality, and his request was referred to the Foreign Office, but as yet he has received no word, so that he has not been granted authority to act to represent British interests there and has not received his exequatur. This was omitted from the British telegram which went a few days ago because the despatch from Danzig arrived since that telegram left my office. Consequently it had to be attended to today along with the French representation, and it developed that the French had requested the Dutch to take care of their interests there, which leaves our Embassy in Berlin in charge of French interests in all of that territory except Danzig and the Slovak State and in charge of British interests in all that territory except alone the Slovak State.

It is hoped that no repercussion is coming from the German Government in the matter and that we are not denied the right to act and placed in a position where we will have to make some formal request in order to carry out our representative duties but which might later be construed as recognition. Of course that will have to be carefully guarded against. . . .

November 9, 1939

. . . The war does not progress as a war. Few boats are being sunk. No military activity is being engaged in, and only occasional airplane manoeuvers. Yesterday nine German planes were reported shot down by nine French pursuit planes. That was the biggest manoeuver of the war so far on the Western front.

The Americans are all home from abroad. Our figures show that 75,000 have returned in North Atlantic ports up to last Friday. Several thousand additional have returned at several south Atlantic and Gulf ports from freighters.

. . . Lunched with Dean Acheson[64] and later conferred with Norman Davis. He is a little fed up with Maurice Pate[65] and the activities of the Polish Relief Committee, Incorporated. They have been unable to raise

[64] Washington lawyer, and former Under Secretary of the Treasury, May–November, 1933.

[65] President of the Committee for Polish Relief, 1939–1941, and former assistant to the American Relief Administration in Poland, 1919–1922.

money in considerable sums, and Norman says they are trying to gobble sums which different organizations have collected for the Red Cross. . . . He wants me to attend a meeting next week with the representatives of some of these organizations. He said he talked to Welles and that Welles seemed to think that the regulations might be changed so that the Secretary of State could direct that the Red Cross be the only agency for dispensing relief abroad. That seemed to me a bit drastic. Of course Herbert Hoover is behind several of these organizations, and Norman thinks that they would like to provide another spring-board for him so that he could be elected to the Presidency again on account of relief in Poland like he was on account of his Belgian relief. I remarked that I thought there would have to be a great deal of spring in the board to get Hoover elected to anything.

November 18, 1939

The war drags slowly along without much action. . . . Bullitt has just returned from a visit to the French front and reports the ground so wet and soggy that he does not see how military operations along the French-German front could be carried on until March. He is still committed to the idea that there are large concentrations of German troops on the Netherlands, Belgium and Luxembourg lines and that Germany contemplates action there. This seems doubtful from my point of view, as it would expose the German flank. It seems to me that the Germans also realize this and that the military advisors of Hitler have temporarily at least prevailed. There are reports emanating from outside Germany that there are serious differences of opinion over policy between Hitler and some of his advisors, and to my mind Hitler has certainly got his country in a terrible predicament. He is worse off today than he was three months ago with every indication that the situation will deteriorate from Germany's point of view. They are hemmed in by Russia on the north and east and are afraid to take their troops from the western front in order to operate in the southeast because that would weaken the western front. Even in the southeast they might find opposition on the part of Russia, though they would find little real opposition on the part of the local armies.

I have finally worked out the organization for Berlin, supplemental to the Embassy, to take care of prisoners of war, and we are communicating by telegram with Kirk today informing him of our decisions. The principal points are that a civilian officer must head it and not a military officer and that he be paid by the United States and that such of his entourage as will visit the camps must also be paid by the United States. They must all be civilians, with the exception of one military assistant who will not visit camps as a routine matter but will go as advisor on important cases. All these are to be charged to the United States because we do not want the idea of partiality or prejudice to appear to the Germans or to have our people subject to the suspicion of partiality or prejudice by reason of the fact that they might be paid by the Government whose interests are represented. However, all the clerical staff and expenses incidental to representation are to be paid by the Governments represented.

The telegram is going in non-confidential code, because it discusses the philosophy of the United States Government in regard to its representation of England and France in Germany, and I thought it a good thing that the Germans might read it without being officially informed.

[Joseph E.] Davies is being telegraphed today to come to the United States. He is being ordered home because no one is being given leave and it was thought advisable to make an exception in the case of Davies. So he is being ordered to return for consultation, and when he gets home he will resign. Messersmith so informed me and told me that he understood that he was to be succeeded by me. I replied that I thought that that probably had been discarded but that I only inferred that it had been discarded and had no information at all. He reiterated that it was his understanding but said that he did not know. He discussed several persons there who would be highly useful to me if I should go, but the prospect of spending a winter in a cold and wet climate is not entirely pleasing, though during the war period it would be interesting and I imagine probably effective.

The President is laying the corner stone of the building to hold his library at Hyde Park. Having been a member of the Committee, I was asked to go. I accepted the invitation formally and then talked to Steve Early and to Frank Walker[66] in New York and told them it was a pretty hard trip for me, being two nights on the train, and that I would not go unless they thought my absence would be misunderstood or unless my presence would be of value for some reason. I said that I hoped that my absence would not be interpreted as a lack of interest. They each said that it would be all right if I did not go, so I have decided not to do so. Instead I am going to the country for the week-end, leaving this afternoon and coming back Monday morning. The Secretary is away and Welles is crowded to death, being in charge in the Department and being the head of the Pan American Economic Conference now in session, and all of his own work beside.

November 24, 1939

Yesterday was Thanksgiving on the new and earlier date as proclaimed by the President. It seems to have been the occasion for several political aspersions because the new date was not adopted by all of the States. However, it was a holiday. I played golf in the morning, going out to Burning Tree with

[66] Steve Early, secretary to the President, 1937–1945; Frank Walker, former treasurer of the Democratic National Committee, 1932, and director of the President's National Emergency Council, 1935.

Stanley Reed[67] and playing in the peculiar form of tournament they have there, and in the evening dined with the Reeds at the home of Charlie Henderson[68] and had pheasant instead of turkey. The pheasant was the subject of good-natured raillery as indicating that the Hendersons were not observing Thanksgiving as proclaimed by the President.

November 27, 1939

. . . I am still wrestling with pressure from persons who want the State Department to act on behalf of non-Americans to obtain the release of their friends or relatives abroad. We refused to act except for American citizens abroad, but there is constant pressure from Congressional and organized groups in this country to have us proceed on behalf of non-Americans. So far I have been able to resist the pressure. Today Judge Moore sent down a preemptory direction to take action in one of these cases, but I sent it back to him through Messersmith, who promised to support my position.

I have only had one talk with the Secretary recently. He was off on a short vacation. When he returned I had a visit with him. He said that he was really interested in three things here; that he hoped to leave his work in those respects to be carried on when he left. The three were the cooperation of the American Republics in these two Continents; an insistence upon observing written obligations and treaties to dispense with force in international relations; and the opening up of commerce and trade in the world through the medium of trade agreements with the thought that freedom of economic and industrial activity would prevent recurrence of wars. He is very serious in these things. He is very serious anyhow. His method of oral expression is not forceful, and he resorts from time to time to invectives, but he gets an idea in the back of his head and it is pretty hard to shake him loose from it.

Davies and Kennedy somehow let it be known that they had been ordered home for consultation. The papers began to play that story up, and they finally arrived at the point where most of the Ambassadors in Europe were being ordered home for a conference, and it began to look in print as if the President were going to have an international pow-wow on his hands about Christmas time. So the President, who is now in Warm Springs, stated to the press one day that he had not ordered any of them home and that just Davies and Kennedy were coming and that they were coming at their own request.

November 28, 1939

Another long conference this morning with Norman Davis and the heads of the Polish, Jewish and other relief organizations. Discussion of various

[67] Associate Justice of the Supreme Court, 1938–1957.
[68] Charles B. Henderson, member of the board of the Reconstruction Finance Corporation, 1934–1947.

ideas and principles involved in relief. The Polish Commission wanted Davis to join in some kind of a statement which would limit the field of the Red Cross activities. This I opposed.

Lunched with Pittman.[69] He does not see how he is going to support the trade agreements plan.[70] He is opposed to the agreement with Chile because of the copper and opposed to the Argentine program because of the beef. There are seven copper producing States and nine beef states. The Senators from each of them are opposed to the inclusion of these two items in the agreements, and if it is insisted to put the items in, they may line up with the Republican and other opposition against the whole trade treaty program. Copper is the principal industry of Arizona and is responsible for the wages paid to a large proportion of its population. The same situation exists in each of the other seven States constituting the Rocky Mountain and desert section of the country.

I tried to work out some basis whereby he could reconcile his position on those two matters with the general program, and he is very willing to find a basis if it can be done but doesn't see it, nor could I convince myself that there was a basis for consistent action in two different directions. Pittman thinks that the political consequences will be very severe and that we will lose four or five, possibly as many as ten, Senators from the Middle West and West if cattle and copper are insisted upon, because the fights in the Democratic primaries will be intense and the losing opposition may vote with the Republicans.

I advised him to go and see the President and have a serious talk with him before the Chile agreement got far under way, because it would be difficult to change the administration's attitude after the Committee considering it had rendered a report, and I urged him to do it on the President's return. He was undecided whether to do so.

Played a short round of golf with Hugh Wilson.

December 6, 1939

The war has quieted down on the sea and has not started up on the land. The only exception is Finland and Russia. In spite of protestations to the contrary, Russia invaded Finland [November 30] and penetrated a few miles in the Karelian Peninsula and on the small bit of territory occupied they set up a puppet government. They have declined the request of the Swedish Govern-

---

[69] Key Pittman, Democrat, U.S. Senator from Nevada, 1912–1940, and chairman of the Foreign Relations Committee, 1933–1940.

[70] The Administration had requested a three-year extension of the Reciprocal Trade Agreement Act which was due to expire on June 12, 1940. The act, Franklin Roosevelt told Congress, "should be extended as an indispensable part of the foundation of any stable and durable peace. . . . I emphasize the leadership which this nation can take when the time comes for a renewal of world peace. Such an influence will be greatly weakened if this Government becomes a dog in the manger of trade selfishness."

ment to permit Sweden to take over Finnish interests in Moscow, stating that they could no longer deal with the regular Finnish Government but only through their puppet government, though they did not use those words.

The Finns have done very well. They are reported to have badly damaged or possibly to have sunk a Russian battleship and have brought down a number of airplanes and have apparently stopped Russian advances on their eastern border.

It does not seem possible, however, that Finland could long hold out. Russia has put her prestige at stake. She cannot be defeated by a little insignificant government of four million people. The one hundred and sixty millions of Russians must use their force to eliminate Finland. Thereafter they probably will turn their attention immediately to Roumania and try to reoccupy Bessarabia. They may even move in conjunction with Germany.

We evacuated a number of American citizens out of Finland and landed them in Sweden, where they arrived last night. . . . Norman Davis told me that the President had told him to tell me that he was going to send me abroad again very soon.

December 7, 1939

Russian troops have broken through the Finnish defenses in the Karelian Peninsula and have penetrated some distance into Finnish territory north of that. Sweden is very much concerned at the development but is afraid to help Finland and is afraid even to mobilize for fear of retaliation by Russia. If Russia should penetrate Swedish territory, it would probably be the signal for Germany to occupy Denmark and proceed up into Sweden to effect a division with Russia of the Scandinavian Peninsula. . . .

This is just part of the general picture which is very displeasing. It seems to me that the whole situation of the Allies is momentarily deteriorated and it affects the interests of all the neutral states of Europe and of the United States. . . . I have been hoping I could think of something to propose as a policy which would serve to prevent the further deterioration of the world situation and which would react to the benefit of the United States.

In contemplating possible activities my mind runs to some leadership to express the rights of neutral nations—an expression which would not lead to warfare but which would command respect. There seems no real sense in a political system which permits two or three belligerents to upset all the neutrals in the world and to prevent the neutrals from enforcing such rights as they are supposed to have. Under such a system the whole political organism of the world is based on the theory of force because as soon as force is resorted to all peaceful rights are obliterated and all peaceful hopes frustrated. It seems that some coordination of neutrals to protect their own interest *en masse,* but steps short of war, could be effected under favorable conditions and with unusual leadership. . . . With these general thoughts in mind and the political situation in the world today, it brings very serious thought to the mind of a person of responsible contact with the leaders of his Government, and I wish I could think out something clearly so that I could propose or advocate something concrete.

This evening I talked to the Secretary at some length on the subject. He sees the situation about as I do but does not see any definite step to be taken. He is afraid Europe is going to be ruined economically and financially and I think he is about of the opinion that it is already ruined morally. I told him that I was trying to find some way for us to do something which would stop the deterioration of American interests vis-à-vis the world situation but that I had been unable to find a path.

Earlier I talked to Norman Davis along the same lines. Norman agrees with the thought that the neutrals ought to take some aggressive stand, short of war, to assert their rights. Just how you can do this short of war in a world full of war I do not know.

Norman has been having some difficulty with Herbert Hoover. Hoover called him about Finnish relief and told him that he was about to take it over and then he saw the announcement that the Red Cross was doing it. Norman told him that at the time Hoover made his announcement that an airplane loaded with medical supplies was landing in Finland and that it was the natural function of the Red Cross. Hoover wanted to make some agreement with him about division of work and a joint announcement made, but Norman told him that the Red Cross could not agree to a limitation of its activity and couldn't agree with other people to divide work. Hoover is a very insistent person, and he is just itching to get into something that will help him politically, but this kind of work ought not be a political activity. However, I warned Norman that he must be very careful that there should be no evidence of partisan or personal feeling. He thoroughly sensed that. The truth is that Hoover put his men in charge of Polish relief and they have not been successful in raising funds. One of them said yesterday they had only raised $35,000. The Red Cross has already sent several hundred thousand dollars. Having failed in the Polish campaign, Hoover now wants to pick up the Finnish campaign—anything to get in the spotlight again.

December 9, 1939

Dined last night with Jesse Jones[71] and sat next to Mrs. Wilson. I broached the subject of the Woodrow Wilson Foundation and their funds and the Wilson Memorial at Princeton. She was very communicative and reviewed the whole history of her contact with the movement to have a Memorial at Princeton. She manifested a great deal of interest. It was not possible under

[71] Administrator of the Federal Loan Agency, 1939–1940, and later Secretary of Commerce, 1940–1945.

the circumstances to carry on the conversation to a conclusion, so I suggested that I have an opportunity to talk to her sometime, and she readily agreed. She said again on leaving that she hoped to see me about it again in the near future and that she would be glad to talk to me at greater length.

I told Mrs. Wilson that I thought that her decision to give Mr. Wilson's papers to the Congressional Library was the proper decision—that that is where they really belong. However, I was so devoted to Mr. Wilson and so devoted to Princeton that I hoped the effort to have a Memorial at Princeton would not be interfered with by the fact that the papers were going to the Congressional Library. She too is very much interested in a Memorial at Princeton and said she thought Mr. Wilson would have been very much pleased at the thought. She realized that the sentiment at Princeton had changed and that there was no longer any antagonism there to Mr. Wilson, only a few persons remaining on the Board who had been really opposed to him and had acted in such a bitter manner towards him. . . .

December 18, 1939

Last evening at six o'clock I listened to a broadcast by radio from Montevideo concerning the movements and destruction of the *Graf Spee*. It was the most dramatic audition I have ever experienced. This reporter stood at the water's edge with a pair of field glasses and stated into the microphone what he saw. It was thrilling. The explosion—the desertion of the ship—the fires—the gradual sinking—the additional explosions—going down by the head—then by the stern—the fires on board—the *Tacoma* standing by—the gradual disintegration of the ship with the officers and crew in small boats and launches —the final explosions and flames on the water of burning oil—told the story of morbid despair—of frustrated effort—of tragic end to the disappointing pride of the German Navy. It is assumed they destroyed her to protect Naval secrets—particularly as to her engines. . . .

The Finns are still fighting vigorously and successfully. The Baltic countries are all stirred up by the call again to Moscow of the Estonian chief—and imagine it is the prelude to either complete cooperation of Tallin[72] with Moscow or occupation and absorption by Moscow of the little country. But I suspect Russia has her hands full of prickley Finns and will try to clean that up before other things. The Balkans are still worried about Bessarabia and Sofia[73] says she will offer Russia passage over her territory if demanded and expects

[72] Tallin, capital of Estonia. Once Germany became involved in war with France and Great Britain and was no longer in a position to oppose Soviet ambitions in the Baltic, Moscow proceeded to obtain concessions, under the threat of force, from the Baltic states. By the end of 1939, Estonia's foreign and domestic policies were dictated by the Soviet Union. Formal incorporation into the U.S.S.R. took place in July 1940.

[73] Sofia, capital of Bulgaria. Toward the end of 1939 the Soviet Union made friendly overtures to Bulgaria and raised hopes that they would assist the Bulgarians in pressing their land demands with Rumania.

Roumania not to resist either losing Bessarabia or entire occupation. They get awfully jittery. And I suppose if we were so close we would be a little upset ourselves. . . .

Hull asked me to see him this afternoon. He talked the better part of an hour. He and the President had really a definite desire I be an Assistant Secretary of State. They thought me more important here now than abroad. They wanted me. He made that emphatic. Would I? Of course I would do whatever they wanted. This was no time to pursue pet ambitions. He then said Messersmith was going back in the field service—for special reasons, some personal, some official. They wanted me to take over his place, and they wanted me to assume an additional heavy work. That was to lead the fight from the Department with the opposition in the Congress which is bent on wrecking the Trade Agreements and blocking any further practice along that line. He wanted me to assume that function now—and to await, in confidence, the other change.

So it looks like I was to stay here. I would love to be in Berlin. But I will stay here and do a work which is new to me. Finance and Economics are strangers to my mind. And now I am in the midst of it. . . .

December 19, 1939

Last night when I got to bed I began to worry about the prospect of changing the line of my activity and assuming a lot of economic and financial things that I know very little about and that my mind is not adapted to. I made up my mind I wanted to have a little more time to think it over. And so this morning the first thing I went to see Hull again and told him that I spoke to him yesterday impetuously and out of a natural desire to do anything the Administration wanted me to do but that as I thought this over I would like to have a little more time—a day or so—to orient my mind to this new thought and to see whether I could really say that I would do the things that would be incumbent upon me in case I accepted his proposal. I told him that I had every desire still to be of service to the Administration but that the details of the administration of the Foreign Service and the Departmental Service and the financial things connected with Messersmith's office and the legislative activities it was necessary for him to supervise and participate in and then the additional activity in connection with the trade treaties and the economic problems involved would so occupy my mind and activity that I would be excluded from the field of policy and from actual participation in the field of foreign affairs that I had been interested in all my life and had been a participant in when I had had contacts with the Government and would do that to such an extent that I had doubts this morning.

He said that of course I could have what time I wanted to think it over and hoped that I would remember that I was the one person they had chosen above all others; that if I declined to do it they would find somebody else. However, he hoped that I would do it. He then proceeded to say that I would not be necessarily encumbered with these economic problems and that he envisioned his program as being inextricably inter-twined with the ultimate peace and as being necessarily an elemental part of an eventual settlement. He thought that the program to keep trade barriers down and to keep a free flow of trade an essential unless we were to revert to another system, which we could not contemplate. He related a lot of difficulties he had had in his administration as Secretary. He called attention to an editorial in the New York *Tribune* this morning and asked me to read it. He was friendly and in every way indicated the placing of entire confidence. He did not urge me to do it. He said do what I thought and what I wanted but he hoped I would understand they all really hoped that I would.

Last night I dined at the Italian Embassy and after dinner had a rather interesting conversation with del Drago,[74] who is in this country for about a week with his young wife. His former connections with the Embassy here and his present and former connections with the Palazzo Chigi[75] in Rome would indicate that his visit to this country had some purpose and that the shortness of the visit, considering the length of the journey, would indicate something of a confidential and important nature if it is granted that he is on an official visit.

After discussing the various phases of war in Europe and having indicated his definite repugnance of the war-like conditions in Europe and having expressed deep concern about the effect on the future of Europe of continuing the war, he asked me what I thought America would do and what would be America's real policy in the future in regard to the war. I told him that America wanted to keep out of the war but was making every preparation to be ready for any emergency but wanted to keep this country and these two continents of America outside of the conflict.

He then asked, "But would not America go into the war if it looked like England was going to be defeated?"

I was somewhat non-committal in my reply but reiterated the desire of America to keep out of war.

He asked several other questions around the fringes of that question and on several occasions during our interview reverted to the subject. He seemed trying to get a definite expression of opinion that the United States would or would not eventually go to the assistance of the Allies in case it looked that England might be defeated.

I could not but get the impression from the conversation that he had a real

[74] Prince Giovanni del Drago, Italian businessman.
[75] An old Roman palace which was the location of the Italian foreign office in downtown Rome.

purpose in mind and that it may have been the reason for his visit to the United States and that the information was wanted in Rome in order that it might be taken into consideration in determining Italy's future policy. (Of course it would be material in the determination of Italy's policy to know whether she would have to fight the Allies and the United States or whether she and Germany could fight the Allies without support from the United States.)

Del Drago said he thought the Germans were "crazy." He saw no chance for England to negotiate with Germany, because England could not negotiate with Hitler, and there was no way to displace Hitler, because he was the real head of the political organization. He expressed himself as being disgusted with the maneuvers of Ribbentrop and said that many high authorities in the military, naval and political life of Germany were very bitter against Ribbentrop; that they were real Russian haters; that they saw the advancing specter of Russia; that they now knew they could get no real help from Russia; that it would take two years for German experts, using Russian labor, to build even essential railroads in order to transport supplies; that Stalin was making progress and that Hitler was confronted with a situation he could not control and which he had himself brought on.

Del Drago also said—and I thought this very interesting—that the Italian agreement with Germany entered into at Milan [October, 1936] provided only that Italy and Germany would take military steps together when they mutually agreed to do so; that there was no compulsion of one Government to join the other in any military activity; that in the case of Poland Italy did not choose to fight Poland and under the terms of the agreement there was no obligation upon Italy to fight.

In addition, he said there was a supplemental agreement between Italy and Germany which would permit a period of peace for three years; and "within six months Hitler broke the agreement."

Reverting to the terms of the agreement for mutual assistance and speaking of the time when Germany was considering her attack upon Poland he said that Ciano[76] in his conversations at Salzburg and Berchtesgaden had told Hitler that he would have to fight England if he attacked Poland. Hitler had replied, "No. England will not fight."

Ciano had said, "You are mistaken. England will fight, and we are not going to fight."

Hitler had said that he was sure that England would not fight, and Ciano had replied, "But I warn you England will fight. We are convinced that England will fight, and you must understand that we are not bound to fight and we will not fight against Poland. We do not elect to fight against Poland and are not bound to do so under the terms of the agreement."

[76] Count Galeazzo Ciano, Italian foreign minister, 1936–1943.

Hitler replied that they were not bound to do so and that he would not rely upon Italy and that Italy was perfectly free but that Germany was forced to act.

Del Drago is in the same confidential relations with Ciano at the Palazzo Chigi he was with [Fulvio] Suvich when Suvich was Undersecretary of Foreign Affairs [1932–1936]. He was constantly in and out of the office of Suvich and was intimately concerned with the affairs that Suvich handled. He leads me to believe that he has the same relationship with Ciano. If so, his remarks are entitled to some consideration. . . .

December 20, 1939

I talked to Messersmith again, and I had this afternoon a talk with Welles. He said he had preferred the Secretary to talk to me and that he thought it was a matter of high policy that I come for a particular purpose. He said the President and Hull and he had all definitely decided that I was the one they wanted and that I would not be confined to the routine activities of that work. The Secretary had mentioned to me the Trade Agreements work. Sumner said that my contacts with the members of the Congress and my experience in political activity would be of invaluable assistance; that the Trade Agreements program was one of the most important political measures; that it just had to be successfully attended to; that he had no idea the President would be a candidate for the third term; that the President was going to back Mr. Hull; that the success of the Trade Agreements program was essential to Mr. Hull's campaign and would be a considerable factor in the election. But it was essential that it be approved and that the Congress do not upset it. He said it was for this reason they wanted me to take charge of the political end in the coming Congressional fight and that I would have plenty of technical assistance. I asked him how long this would last. He said it would last at least until the Convention. I said that to stop at the Convention right on the eve of the election would seem to leave a job unfinished and that we shouldn't consider the activity as being undertaken for such a temporary period.

Sumner was very gratified and pleased at the situation, and I suppose I am too, though I had never considered returning to the status I occupied twenty-five years ago. Nevertheless, it sounds like it would appeal to me, and I am sure that I can use the organization in Messersmith's office so that I will be freer than I expected. He is bound for Havana. However, it is all confidential. . . .

December 21, 1939

I saw Cordell again today and told him definitely that I would accept the Assistant Secretaryship. He said he was very glad. I then told him I would like to have him particularize about the Trade Agreements work; that I assumed it to be political contact and an effort to help him on the Hill and to coordinate the Department and our forces. He said that that was correct and that there were plenty of technicians here and that I would be rendered all the technical information that I needed and that various memoranda would be prepared for the use of persons there.

He then got to a reminiscent mood about his service in the Department and said that he had only two or three things in mind and as soon as they were finished he was ready to retire to private life. I told him that nobody wanted him to return to private life. He said that some of his experiences had been discouraging. There was the Moley incident,[77] which had humiliated him beyond expression in London, and there was the period when the President was thinking mostly of domestic problems and was not concentrating on any of the foreign problems, during which period he let a lot of people run around with authority, including George Peek,[78] who had worked to the detriment of Hull's ideas. He had even been furnished with several hundred thousand dollars with which to operate. Finally the President appreciated the circumstances and allowed it to be straightened out. These had been unfortunate incidents in his career, but the President had always been courteous and confiding and he felt very happy about his relationships with the President. He wanted me to feel at liberty to come in at any time and talk to him about anything and assured me of his confidence and desire to cooperate in any way and said that if any time I thought it advisable to go to the President about any of these things that he was willing I should follow my own judgment; that he was not interested in details or the manners in which things were done provided they were properly done and the main objective was achieved. He was very much afraid of the difficulties they were going to have in the fight with Congress, but the copper situation with Chile had just been arranged so as to take that out of the picture, and the difficulty with Argentina over the Trade Agreement would probably end in breaking off negotiations at the instigation of Argentina and that beef would be out of the picture. There were various political matters we touched upon, and he asked me to get down to the Trade Agreements work as quickly as I could. So I think immediately after the Christmas holidays, which begin tomorrow and last through Christmas, I shall start.

December 22, 1939

Rode down this morning with Farley. He expressed a particular fondness for Hull and said he was going to come in to see him today. He thinks Mc-

[77] Reference here is to former Assistant Secretary of State Raymond Moley and his role at the London Economic Conference of 1933. See *The Memoirs of Cordell Hull* (New York: Macmillan, 1948), pp. 256–269.

[78] Former administrator of the Agricultural Adjustment Administration, 1933.

Nutt[79] is eliminating himself from the picture. He is undignified. I told Hull that Farley was coming in and that I thought he ought to be very cordial because he could be of very great assistance in the fight coming on the Hill and that his friendly feeling toward Hull could be utilized to great advantage. He wondered with [sic] the relationship was between Farley and the President. I told him I couldn't speak for the President but that I knew pretty well about Farley. Farley had sometimes had a few misgivings as to how he was treated but he had never swerved in his devotion to the President, and I was sure there was nothing the President could ask him to do but that Farley would do it.

December 26, 1939

Talked with Hull and Welles—said I was ready now to proceed with Trade Agreements work. Hull asked me to see some of the men in the Department who had been active technicians. I did—some but not all of them. Lunched with Speaker Bankhead.[80] We are old friends and have worked together before. He is interested and will do all he can. I proposed a plan for his activity —seeing the proper members of Congress, finding out their colleagues' positions—State by State. He at first feared the Trade Agreements movement was endangered and might fail and it would be better if the Administration withheld request for renewal—else it might get beat. I argued to do so would be tantamount to defeat—just an admission on our part we were licked. Otherwise we would ask for it. In either case failure to get it would be tantamount to repudiation. He agreed eventually and undertook to help. He fears though that there are complications; that the reductions of benefits to agriculture as advocated by the President will militate against the Trade Agreements program in that the reductions will be opposed by the agricultural States and may be used by the opposition to amplify antagonism from those quarters against the Trade Agreements. Also he feels the desire of the President to increase the margin of Government debt by Congressional Act will also interfere.

I see that point and believe we should plan to push the Trade Agreements program through as quickly as possible and delay advocacy of the other two.

I told Hull part of the above hurriedly this afternoon late. He was occupied earlier with the Justice Department—which wanted to institute criminal proceedings against Amtorg, the Russian Government's fiscal and economic purchasing agency in this country. We had just cabled them [Russia] we would

[79] James A. Farley, U.S. Postmaster General 1933–1940, and chairman of the Democratic National Committee, 1932–1940; Paul V. McNutt, administrator of the Federal Security Agency, 1939–1945, and former, Democrat, governor of Indiana, 1933–1937.

[80] William Bankhead, Democrat, U.S. Representative from Alabama, 1917–1940, and Speaker of the House, 1936–1940.

not because Amtorg had obeyed our law. This was in reply to their complaint about prosecutions of another Russian Company which had acted illegally. Anyhow, I could not see him till late and hurriedly. I did suggest he ask the President to call in Bankhead and have a good talk with him—and to talk to him himself.

December 28, 1939

... Had a long talk with Bennett Clark this morning on the Trade Agreements and found him not only ready but anxious to take an aggressive part in the fight on our side. I told him that I would send him a man to help him and would put whatever material he needed for his speeches at his disposal and would be of whatever assistance we could and also suggested that he make an address on the radio.

December 29, 1939

Last night I made the address on Woodrow Wilson on his birthday at the Woman's Democratic Club. Mrs. Wilson was there—which complimented me much and embarrassed me a little. My remarks were received most enthusiastically. Mrs. Wilson was rather effusive in her commendations and men whose knowledge of him and whose own literary ability and judgment have been proven—such as Charles Warren and Sam Graham[81]—were pointedly, sincerely and profusely expressive of approval and praise. ...

Arthur Krock also, who was not present last night, said he had heard it commended so highly he was impressed. A number of people have spoken today of the favorable comment they had heard of it. The press carries shortish accounts of it and a few quotations—and the radio late last evening—around eleven o'clock—commented on it and quoted the ending—all of which pleases me. Arthur commented that I must have spent a lot of time in preparation, but I told him that was not necessary because there was nothing about the address which required delving into reference books. It was just my interpretation of his character and personality as I knew him and a relation of a few incidents in my own experience with him. ...

This day ends the working year. The next two days—Saturday and Sunday—will be holidays and the New Years Day another one. My desk is clean. The year's work is done. With me it has been a happy year. Good health, pleasant surroundings, additional honors, agreeable work.

However much personal gratification there may be in the year passing and however personally pleasing the prospect for the New Year, it is impossible to forget the unfortunate situation of the world. Millions are on relief in our own country, war raging in the Far East—another great war spreading more

[81] Charles Warren, author and constitutional lawyer; Sam Graham, former Assistant Attorney General, 1913–1919, and member of the U.S. Court of Claims, 1919–1930.

and more over Europe and the high seas, economic dislocation everywhere, nations approaching bankruptcy and the moral fibre of peoples deteriorating.

Bubonic plague is reported in Moscow. It is probably no worse than the plague which has infested that benighted country since 1917 but its development there will mean that sanitary measures will have to be taken to prevent that also from being spread to other countries. But even without the plague, fear, suspicion, hatred, insecurity, destruction and death stalk recklessly across the map of most of the world and affect the lives and happiness of hundreds of millions of people on four continents as well as the normal development and peaceful pursuits of those of us on these two American continents.

So in spite of our personal welfares the year closes in sombre atmosphere. In spite of the prospect of our own fortunes during the course of the New Year, including the pleasurable anticipation of a larger field and more important activity, the outlook for a normal world is non-existent. For even if there should come a cessation of hostilities the awful processes of readjustment would follow—social disorders, retrenchment, faltering attempts at rehabilitation, distortions of commerce and industry, discouragement and fear.

My additional work may lead me into the midst of these difficulties. If it does, I trust my health will hold out and my abilities be adequate to the circumstances. And with that expression of hope the record of this year ends.

Another European War

January 2, 1940

The press publishes today that I will be Assistant Secretary to succeed Messersmith. There is no confirmation of it. The President at his press conference this morning when asked about it said he preferred not to comment.

Had a long conversation with Pittman on Trade Agreements. I found him quite antagonistic. He is somewhat opposed to Roosevelt, but largely because of Ickes.[1] He hates Ickes with a wholesome hatred, and it does seem that Ickes goes out of his way sometimes to make things disagreeable and difficult for those Senators up there in his management of the public domain. Pittman said he was thinking of resigning as President Pro-Tem of the Senate, because it was something of an Administration preferment and he might not be in a position to support the Administration. He also said that he would be elected next fall but that he would not run again; that he would have been elected seven times to the Senate and preferred to pass the rest of his days in quiet doing some reading and writing.

I got the impression that his opposition to the Trade Agreements was largely political and that if he didn't come around for other reasons, he might be induced to support it through some political concession. The copper and cattle question with Chile and Argentina respectively have been eliminated as possibilities to disturb his State [Nevada], and I think that eventually I can be very helpful in getting him to support the program.

January 4, 1940

Attended a meeting in the Secretary's office. A large Committee is to be formed, of which I am a member, to work toward the eventual peace terms. There are three sub-committees. One is on terms of peace, of which I am a member. Another is on economics, and the third is on limitation of armaments. Welles is Chairman of the big committee, and Hugh Wilson is to be Vice-Chairman. It is all to be secret, and if anything is known about it, it is to be given the color of economic activity in support of the Trade Agreements program.

I have been very busy with the Trade Agreements program in infrequent contact with members of the Congress as yet, because my nomination was about to go up there and I did not want to be on the Hill when my name was

[1] Harold L. Ickes, Secretary of the Interior, 1933–1946.

about to appear or was pending before the Senate. Nevertheless, I have done what I could and have been studying legal phases of the situation. Some of the Senators have objections on the ground that the Trade Agreements are unconstitutional in that they are not ratified by the Senate, and others object to it because it is an improper delegation of legislative authority. These are deep questions and have to be argued with men who have studied them and have come to some opinion to support those opinions affirmatively.

My nomination went to the Senate at noon.

January 13, 1940

For a week or more I have been negligent of the record. On the 5th I went to New York to attend the meeting of the [Princeton University] Honorary Degrees Committee and stayed over Saturday to attend the Explorer's Club dinner, coming down Sunday. On Monday the papers announced the American Federation of Labor was opposing the Trade Agreements, and I got hold of Dan Tobin, who is the head of the Teamsters Union and a necessary person in the Federation. He came on from Indianapolis to attend the Jackson Day Dinner. We had an hour's conversation before the Dinner, during which I presented to him the advisability of the Federation not only taking a passive position but the possibility of its taking an affirmative position. We attended the dinner and heard the President and afterwards met again. Tuesday morning I took him to see Cordell Hull. By that time he was all prepared to adopt the entire program, to which he had originally been favorable. From the Secretary's office he called up William Green,[2] President of the Federation, and talked to him in very positive terms—in fact as positive as I ordinarily hear any man talk to another man. He told him that his organization was the biggest element in the Federation and contributed more money to the Federation than any other and that they were all for it and that they did not want to see the Federation opposed to it and they all looked to Green to do something about it. He is a blunt, outspoken fellow, and he spoke directly.

Thereafter I had a conference at luncheon with Alben Barkley, the Democratic leader of the Senate, Ed Halsey, the Secretary of the Senate, and several others to organize the Senate Democratic group in support of the Trade Treaties and come to an understanding with them. . . .

January 15, 1940

Spent the week-end quietly in the country in terrible weather. This morning had a talk with Hull. I told him I thought we ought to be very careful in extending official help to Finland; that it might be the opening wedge to an unneutral activity on our part; that if the Republicans wanted to do it and Hoover wanted to get out in front, why it seemed a very good policy for us

[2] President, American Federation of Labor, 1924–1952.

to sit by and let them do it; but that if we took any action as a Government that it might be later construed as a violation of neutrality and we might be held politically accountable for it. He agreed and said that he had taken that same position with Barkley in the Senate and with Sam Rayburn[3] in the House and that he had emphasized his point of view to the President but he did not know what Morgenthau and some others were doing in that respect.

He then reverted to the Trade Agreements. He said he thought I should be very careful in my appearances on the Hill; that he had been denouncing Lobbyists on the other side and he did not want to be caught in the position with a high official in his Department being chargeable with lobbying on his side. I assured him he might have no fears. He called attention to Joe Davies and the stories in the press of his activities in regard to the Trade Agreements. He was a little caustic on the subject. I responded that I did not get my name in the paper with the same promiscuity and avidity that other people did and that I frequently was on the Hill and had many friends there and could appear there from time to time without causing any comment but that I would be very careful. . . .

January 17, 1940

Had a session this afternoon of the Political Sub-Committee.[4] Present: Pasvolsky,[5] Wilson, Berle, Hackworth and Hornbeck,[6] under the Chairmanship of Wilson in the absence of Welles, who is on leave. I presented my idea of a plan to set before any gathering of neutrals the idea if they were to consider bringing about a peace it would be necessary to have some permanent mechanism to carry on and to secure the things which are necessary to maintain peace. I read a three or four-page paper setting out the plan. I was asked to circulate it and agreed to do so with the understanding that it was simply a suggestion but held certain ideas I thought more or less essential to any mechanism. A mechanism as rigid as the League of Nations organization with its obligations would not be acceptable to the United States and had proven a failure in Europe. It was now too soon to try to revitalize it. However, there had to be some definite undertaking. The proposal I made was with the idea that it be applicable to Europe and that it would coordinate with the Pan

---

[3] Alben Barkley, Democrat, U.S. Senator from Kentucky, 1927–1949, and Senate majority leader, 1937–1947; Sam Rayburn, Democrat, U.S. Representative from Texas, 1913–1961. A close friend of President Roosevelt, Rayburn was responsible for the successful steering of much New Deal legislation.

[4] Secretary Hull had formed a departmental committee to investigate the possibility of organizing the neutral nations behind a common peace plan. The committee in turn divided into three subcommittees—disarmament, economic, and political. The political subcommittee attempted to formulate eventual peace terms which the neutrals might suggest.

[5] Leo Pasvolsky, economist, and special assistant to the Secretary of State, 1936–1938, 1939–1946.

[6] Stanley K. Hornbeck, State Department Adviser on Political Relations, 1937–1944.

American Union. There was a long discussion, principally by Pasvolsky, on economic subjects; the impossibility of Germany and Italy to conduct their economy otherwise than by a restricted economy, the same applying to other totalitarian states; the lack of appreciation in England of the situation and the failure of England to adjust its economy to meet the needs of the states which developed into authoritarian states; and that the responsibility of neutrals and others to arrange economic conditions so that there would be a freedom of trade is an opportunity to earn. This contemplated even the possibility of transfers of gold to serve as reserves for currency and to rehabilitate currency issues. I had discussed the transfer or a loan of gold to Italy when I was in Italy some years ago, but I could never understand how there could be any security to repay the gold because gold is in itself the security in international credits and the basis for the extension of credit. Berle also had some inchoate sort of plan with the idea that the Pan American Union could be used as an international American organization to coordinate with some kind of a European organization but the thought pervading the general discussion was that it would be necessary to develop some world-wide economic cooperation as the only basis to secure a peace and that the principle underlying the Trade Agreements was possibly the most effective plan and most promising present-day possibility.

The presence of Joe Davies in the Division does not seem to grow simpler. He has ambitions, I suppose, which are undisclosed and largely personal, and he seems to have very little interest in what is going on. From some of the questions asked as to whether he could have his title of Special Assistant to the Secretary engraved on his calling cards, and whether the appointment entitled him to a special automobile number, and all that indicates that his mind is running in other directions and that probably his activity here is inspired at home and by marital influences. It grows just a little difficult—or promises to do so.

January 18, 1940

A meeting this morning on the general subject of a conference of neutrals and the agenda and plans for such a conference if possible. The meeting was in the Secretary's office. Reports were made by the Disarmament Committee, Economic Committee and Political Committee. No decisions were taken except that the thought was expressed that not later than February 15 something definite ought to be on paper as a program that could be laid before a conference if a meeting of neutrals is called. There is every indication that the conference will be called.

. . . Had a long talk with Joe Davies about the routine of the Department and the difficulties he might encounter but to which he must adjust himself. Messersmith has been delegated by the Secretary to have a very serious conversation with him and to impress him with the matters and the work in the Department and direct his attention to the affairs of this Division in particular. The Secretary has inherited him from the White House. He said to me this morning that he thought Joe was on the way out and that he wanted to be eased away from the position of Ambassador in order to return to private life. I told him I thought he was mistaken and that this was a build-up and not a let-down. Messersmith talked to the Secretary after I talked to him and the consequence is that he has been designated to have this conversation with Joe.

January 23, 1940

I took the oath of office of Assistant Secretary of State today. It was not intended that I should do it until next week, but the Secretary was sick, Welles was on leave for two weeks, Grady[7] was out of town on Departmental business, Berle was tied up with the Canadian Waterways, and Messersmith had so much to do that he was swamped, and so I was requisitioned to take the oath to comply with the requirement that an Assistant Secretary must be presiding in the Board of Examiners for entrance to the Foreign Service. I have been in attendance on the Board most of the time and will have to go through this week. It is an awful chore—from 10 A.M. to 6 P.M. with a scant hour for lunch. Today I had no time to go out for lunch and ate with Messersmith at his desk.

Borah[8] has died and is on the way to Idaho to be buried. I have never agreed with Borah. In not one single instance in twenty-five years have I been in accord with him. First I thought he was an honest and sincere man always actuated by his desire to render service and to express an honest opinion. But when in 1928 after having denounced and berated Hoover he made a glowing and impassioned speech in his behalf I had to change my mind, and again in 1936 when he withheld support from his Republican colleague and failed to support Roosevelt and concentrated purely on his own selfish efforts to be reelected I was confirmed in my 1928 opinion.

January 24, 1940

Another day on the Examining Board. They are rather emotional experiences for me for the reason that I do not like to have to deny a young man entrance to the Service after he has spent two or three years in preparation for it and his family are all expecting him to emerge victorious from the

[7] Henry F. Grady, former professor of international trade, and Assistant Secretary of State, 1939–1941.

[8] William E. Borah, Republican, U.S. Senator from Idaho, 1907–1940. Long and Borah began to disagree after World War I. Borah led the bitter-end Senate irreconcilables opposing the League of Nations, while Long ardently supported American participation in the international organization.

examinations. But it becomes a duty to resolve all doubts in favor of the Government and I have very unpleasant moments.

It is remarkable the way the Princeton boys seem to weather the storm in proportion to all other colleges. More Princeton graduates have been admitted during this examination than from any other college, and that has been the rule for the last four or five years. They stand out quite well. Of course not all of them passed. Two of them were turned down today. The School for Political and Foreign Affairs at Princeton interests the young men there in the Foreign Service and starts them seriously to studying. The result is that some very good material is made available to the Government.

After I was through with the Board this afternoon I saw young Tobin, the son of Daniel J., in regard to the release by him of an editorial which his father has written and which will be published in the International Brotherhood of Teamsters, Chauffeurs, Stablemen and Helpers official magazine. His father is an upstanding, two-fisted person, and he is supporting the Trade Agreements in every way he can. This editorial is on the Trade Agreements, and young Tobin has agreed to his father's suggestion and after my conversation to help us get publicity for it. It will offset another adverse article which was put out purporting to come from the American Federation of Labor but which does not represent the sentiments of that organization.

Dined last night with the Roumanians. Henry Wallace, Marriner Eccles[9] and various others. The Minister of Roumania was not there. He is on his way to Roumania, having been called allegedly by the serious illness of his mother. I rather have a suspicion that he went for some other reason and to talk to his Government, but I may be wrong.

January 25, 1940

Saw the President a few minutes about noon, primarily to thank him for the new expression of his confidence. He seemed tired and as having been suffering from the wear and tear of the strain he is constantly under. He is not the fresh, rosy-cheeked Franklin Roosevelt that became President seven years ago. He has grown some heavier; lines have appeared in his face; he has lost some hair and there is a great deal of gray in it. His mind is very active, however. Burt Wheeler[10] was waiting to see him as soon as I left. I had a talk with Burt before I went in and found him definitely opposed to the Trade Agreements program, but I obtained the distinct impression from him that he was opposed to it on political grounds. I mean grounds which

[9] Henry Wallace, Secretary of Agriculture, 1933–1940; Marriner Eccles, chairman of the board of governors of the Federal Reserve System, 1936–1945.
[10] Burton K. Wheeler, Democrat and Progressive, U.S. Senator from Montana, 1923–1947.

indicate to him the advisability from his own point of view of opposing the program because the passage of it would inure to the benefit of Cordell Hull and operate against his own very slim chance for the Democratic nomination, whereas the passage of it would be very helpful to Hull. I also got the idea that he was visiting the President in order to square himself a little for the publicity he got in this morning's paper as having aligned himself with John Lewis in the latter's denunciation of Roosevelt.[11]

I asked the President what he thought of John L. Lewis' activity and vouchsafed the information that he gave to me the impression of having wanted to run the entire government. The President said that that is practically what he wanted. He characterized Wheeler as an opportunist, which of course he is, but he is a pretty able citizen. He has been a radical and got his start in life as a radical, but he is now trying to hold the radical end but has become very conservative in his approaches to business and industrial personages.

The President said he is intensely interested in the Trade Agreements program and that it had to pass in the interests of our national economy. I told him it was going to be easier to get it through the House than it was through the Senate; that there were various difficulties lining up in the Senate.

Our conversation was short and, as I said, rather unsatisfactory and somewhat inconclusive.

February 9, 1940

... The efforts of the Departmental Committee seeking a basis for a plan of action between neutrals during the war and for general application subsequent to the war has not progressed very far. It has met serious obstacles in the way of lack of understanding on our own part as to what position we could take in case there were serious conversations. There are all kinds of political and economic as well as financial questions involved. Before we make a proposal it has been my thought that we should be very sure of our own ground and should be very sure of the answers we could make to the questions we would propound to the others. I think Hull has not been optimistic about it nor enthusiastic on the project of having a conference [of neutral nations]. Welles I think has been anxious. I have had various doubts and various others in the Department have had doubts, except that I think Mr. Berle has been rather progressively inclined toward the prospect of a conference. . . .

When I saw the President I mentioned my interest in the success of a movement if it could be done. We did not discuss the thing, but he expressed a

[11] President of the United Mine Workers of America, 1920–1960. Early in 1940, Lewis announced his opposition to a third term for President Roosevelt.

deep interest and said that he was going to operate in the open so that there would be no secret about it. He said that there would be no "Colonel House business."[12] Whatever he did was to be done openly, but whatever he found out he would of course treat in confidence.

Apparently following on that thought, he announced this morning that Sumner Welles would proceed to Europe and visit Rome, Berlin, Paris and London and confer with the various officials of the Governments there and would return and discuss the situation with him.

It will be a very important trip—that is, it may be. If Sumner can find any willingness on the part of the various responsible officials of any of those Governments to cease hostilities, it will be important, but if he does not find any such situation, it will probably mean that the war will continue on ad infinitum.

Of course I begin to feel that this is the same old war that started in 1914. They shoot occasionally, and they use economic methods of warfare when they are not shooting—even when they are shooting. But there has been hostility, jealousy, animosity and a nationalistic antagonism abroad in the world ever since 1914. It seems to get worse rather than better, except that the intense military warfare is not on the scale it was from '14 to '18. I have a good deal of doubt that I will ever live to see the return to the status of peace that existed prior to 1914—and I expect to live a long time.

February 17, 1940

Welles sails today for Europe. Just before he left I gave him some advice as to how to evaluate his conversations with Mussolini and with Ciano. Advice based on the personalities and characters of those two men which I know very well. He told me that the stories in the press which were so critical of him and indicated that he and the Secretary had had some dispute on the subject of his mission had all emanated from the vitriolic tongue of Bill Bullitt and that Bullitt had taken the trouble to go to the Capitol and to talk to a number of Senators and that they arranged a story of this nature to go to Chicago and to appear in the Chicago papers so that it would not have the earmarks of a Washington story.

Bullitt is here but not now in Washington. I have not seen him, particularly because he had the influenza and had to break the engagement he had with me and had to go to Philadelphia for treatment. At least that was his story.

Kennedy is also here. I saw him for several short conversations. The last conversation was about a telegram we were sending to London making

[12] Reference here is to Colonel Edward M. House, friend and confidant of President Wilson. House served as Wilson's personal representative to various European nations during World War I.

representations to the British Government because of their stoppage of Red Cross and other supplies intended for Poland. Joe did not like the telegram, but it had the approval of the Department, and the Secretary subsequently signed it. He is very much disturbed at the growth of anti-British feeling in this country. He said that a number of his contacts in the Senate had told him that they would be ready to vote for a repeal of the Neutrality Act. He also said that in his large chains of theaters throughout the country he had taken the pulse of the people and found about 80% were aggrieved at England. I told him that it would be a very good thing for him to tell the British authorities when he returned and that it could easily be explained by the British attitude to the American mails, taking American ships into the proscribed area, stoppage of our ships in transit to neutral ports and the prevention of Red Cross and other supplies reaching the stricken people of Poland; that the sooner the British realized the effect their actions were having on the American people the sooner they could expect better relations with the American Government and better support from the American people.

. . . The move to contact the neutrals was made by telegram to selected neutrals, and the responses are somewhat favorable but none has come yet from Italy or from Yugoslavia—Yugoslavia being the one selected in the Balkans and Italy selected as the one principal neutral other than the United States. I still do not know what we would say if they all agreed and said they would be glad to consider any proposal we should make. I still do not know what position we could take in any of the things we are interested in achieving. The political committee, of which I am a member, has been studying the questions, but there is a divergence of opinion as to the attitude of the United States and as to the methods of procedure. However, I suppose no harm can come of the move and some good may possibly be produced out of it, but just what the benefit can be is veiled in the mystery of the future.

The Trade Agreements program was reported out of the House Committee and is now before the House. The debate will start next week. We are now concerned as to when we shall vote and want to select a day so that all the Democrats will be in attendance. It will probably pass the House with all the Republicans voting against it and a few of the Democrats in opposition. I am having rather good luck in the Senate in having the advocates of it organized and prepared to help it on the floor. Yesterday the poll stood 45 for, 40 against and 11 doubtful. We ought to get more than an even break of the doubtful ones, so it looks as if it would pass the Senate in unamended form, but it is still pretty close.

I enlisted the support of the White House, through Steve Early, to work on a few of the individuals, and I got hold of Charlie Michaelson[13] to get a lot of

[13] Charles Michelson, Director of publicity for the Democratic National Committee, 1929–1940.

publicity started next week in rural newspapers between the Mississippi River and the coastal range. I also got Harry Woodring[14] to give out the text of a statement we prepared for him. He will be in Kansas to speak on the 22nd.

March 4, 1940

The President sent for me yesterday afternoon, and I spent an hour or more with him in his study on the second floor of the White House largely in the discussion of the policy of relief to the stricken areas of Europe. It was brought pointedly to the front by the question of Polish relief. I have discussed it on various occasions with the Secretary, and he had met the President on his arrival night before last and suggested to the President that he should talk to me.

Sol Bloom[15] had referred to his Committee in the House a number of bills, seven or eight in number, introduced to appropriate from ten to twenty million dollars for relief of the Poles in Poland. Without saying anything to the leaders in the House or to the members of his Committee, he arranged a meeting for his Committee last Thursday. When the Committee assembled they found newspaper reporters and many photographers, and there appeared Herbert Hoover to testify. He did testify, and there was much publicity. Speaker Bankhead read it in the papers next day. That was the first he knew about it. Hull had talked to Hoover at Hoover's request the day before, but Hoover had made no reference to the fact he was to testify before the Committee. Nobody knew any such matter was under consideration. Hoover had been active in Polish relief, but acted sub-rosa. He appointed his men to take charge of the movement but himself kept out of it. He was not sure at first that it would be popular. They finally got into a wrangle with the Red Cross in Berlin and were taking steps antagonistic to the Red Cross in this country. They were unable to get what they wanted in the way of supervision in Poland by representatives of their own.

The question of Finnish relief developed later. It was very popular, and Hoover jumped right in. Having been quite successful in the raising of money for the relief of Finland, he then turned his hand to Poland and the clandestine arrangement evolved into the meeting last Thursday.

Sol Bloom told me over the telephone that he thought the matter would receive the favorable action of his Committee. I got in touch with Bill Bankhead and gave him some background. He said he would take steps to ascertain the sentiment in the House and would control it and would communicate with me after he found out the situation.

I talked several times at length with the Secretary. He seemed disposed to withhold any opposition in the thought that there might be political re-

[14] Democrat, Secretary of War, 1936–1940, and former governor of Kansas, 1931–1933.
[15] Democrat, U.S. Representative from New York, 1923–1949, and chairman of the House Foreign Affairs Committee, 1940–1949.

percussions. I agreed that we should not take steps to oppose the relief but thought that if the matter could die in the Committee of the House without being killed by anybody that it would be better. He agreed to that.

I drafted a long letter for his signature to serve to advise the President of the whole situation. A copy of that letter is in my files. He did not sign the letter, but he took it to the President on his arrival from the trip to Panama. The President thought he would rather talk to me about it; so the letter was never signed or delivered, though I carried it back to the White House yesterday in case the President wanted to use it as a memorandum but did not use it and brought it back. So the letter is unsigned but still contains the history of the whole situation.

The President reacted very much in line with my own thought. He thought that if we got into Polish relief, we would have to get into other reliefs in other places; that we would have to be consistent as well as neutral. He wanted a resumé of the situation in Europe showing where the hungry and distressed people were at present, in Poland and out of Poland, and what the possibilities and probabilities would be in case the war should expand. He thought we might be committing ourselves to a program which the American people would want to consider very carefully as to its magnitude in case we would have to continue with that program in the future and extend it. . . .

The effects of the war are being felt everywhere. England has stopped buying agricultural products from us. For instance—it deranges our own trade; it causes antagonism toward England on the part of our people. There is a distinct wave of anti-British feeling in the United States. It has been caused largely by the stupidity of England. She took American help for granted—not military participation, but economic and financial and sentimental assistance. She began diverting our ships and delaying them. She then searched our mails, contrary to international convention, to which she is a party. She even stopped our airplanes at Bermuda and searched them. She stopped outward bound cargoes from Europe headed for the United States because they originated in Germany and would furnish foreign exchange for Germany. And she has stopped the purchase of tobacco in this country. And now she has stopped or limited the purchase of every agricultural product we have been in the habit of shipping her, except cotton. . . . The truth is there is a considerable anti-British feeling. There is not pro-German feeling. There is a very definite anti-Russian feeling—an antipathy that exists in 95% of the American people. Nevertheless, England's attitude has brought to the minds of the American citizens that she is not "playing fair"—as they term it—with America. The average American only sees things one at a time. He does not yet see the broad picture that the war is disturbing all trade routes, all commercial enterprises and many industrial activities. The disturbance is world-wide. . . .

At the Club the other day they got up a secret pool, each one to pay a dollar and record the persons he thought would be the Democratic and Republican nominees. Whoever comes the closest will get the pot. They put my "guess" in an envelope and sealed it so it would not be open. This was out of consideration of my contacts with the Administration. My paper contained: Democrat for President, Hull; for Vice President, Bob Jackson; Republican for President, Taft; for Vice President, Dewey.[16] Mark Sullivan, Arthur Krock, Robert L. O'Brien,[17] Charlie Warren and a lot of others recorded their views.

March 8, 1940

Cordell signed letter transmitting the Polish relief and European destitute figures and sent it over to the President. He asked me to discuss with him two other questions—one of which relates to Myron Taylor and his status and expenses.[18] Cordell does not want to pay any of his expenses. Taylor is demanding a lot of expense allowance and payment of freight to Italy for "food and personal effects." On a break-down of the bill and invoice it appears he is sending pictures, mounted big-game heads, statuary, etc., and only a small quantity of food. He wants a permanent establishment in Rome, allowances like a regular Ambassador, etc. The difficulty is two-fold—(1) There is no appropriation to pay any salary or expense, and (2) the questions he presses indicate the difference between an Ambassador and another character of representation. We do *not* want him to have an establishment in Rome. He was to occupy his villa at Florence and visit Rome only in case there should be reason for him to do so. He was to have a stenographer at the Consulate and to dictate when he would come to Rome. Tittmann[19] was to be at his disposal when necessary, coming from Geneva for these occasions. He was to serve without salary and to have his necessary expenses but to be the personal representative of the President to further the aims of peace by his official contacts with the Vatican. Phillips has cabled twice for instructions—and Cordell throws up his hands. Wants me to take it up with the Chief—keep him out. Certain members of the Congress are ready to use "Ambassador to the Vatican" as campaign material. It is political dynamite.

[16] Robert Jackson, U.S. Attorney General, 1940–1941, former Solicitor General of the United States, 1938–1940; Robert A. Taft, Republican, U.S. Senator from Ohio, 1939–1953; Thomas E. Dewey, Republican, District Attorney of New York county, 1937–1938.

[17] Mark Sullivan, author and columnist for the New York *Herald Tribune*; Arthur Krock, Washington correspondent of the *New York Times* since 1932; Robert L. O'Brien, retired newspaper publisher, and former chairman of the United States Tariff Commission, 1931–1937.

[18] Taylor had been appointed personal representative of the President to the Vatican and served from 1939–1950.

[19] Howard H. Tittmann, Jr., foreign service officer, American consul general at Geneva, 1939–1940.

And I have got to find out *just* what is in the President's mind, try to let Taylor pay his own expenses, except clerk hire and cable rates—and go to Florence to stay.

Represented the Secretary at the Fort Myer cavalry drill and show—lunch, show, tea—took the salute, inspected troops, etc. It was a bully show. Those boys are real horsemen. Afterward was received by Mrs. Roosevelt at the White House at her request to talk about the students not permitted to return to Scotland and to pursue their study of medicine. It is very unfortunate for them. There are several hundred and most of them from New York. I talked to 72 of them ten days ago. Naturally they are anxious, and they certainly are persistent. Mrs. Roosevelt wants me to get up a committee—Mt. Sinai Hospital, Johns Hopkins Medical School, Public Health Service—get a committee of the students to appear before them—circularize the medical schools of the United States and try to get them admitted over here. So I said I would try.

Welles has left Germany and is now in Paris. He is there simultaneously with the Italian reaction toward Germany because of the coal blockade and with the peace negotiations going on about Finland. It may complicate his mission, and it may facilitate it. What reactions he has we do not know. For obvious reasons he is not cabling any report of any conversations and will make his complete report to the President on his return. However, they seem to know little about the Finnish situation in Europe, for he telegraphed to us to send him news about it, and I expect the news we had, which has not appeared in the press, is probably not available to the Governments of Western Europe.

March 11, 1940

... Another conference about Myron Taylor and his status and preparation of a telegram to serve as the basis of my conversation with the President. He is sick with a slight cold and in bed. Appointment was to have been tomorrow but probably postponed because of the general confusion caused by breaking his appointments today. There are details about allowances to Taylor which will raise the question of his actual status. There are also deep political questions which may be raised if we pay his expenses and give him authority to do even certain little things, such as to use stationery. For instance, what would he have on his stationery? I am proposing he use his own stationery and start his letters "As the personal representative of the President of the United States, I have the honor . . ." and to sign it "Myron C. Taylor." All the authorizations have to be gone into very carefully and gradually in order to prevent assumption arising as to his status and also to prevent severe criticism on a religious issue, which is very apt to be raised in the Congress. It might even take the form of a rider to one of the appropriation bills to the effect that no funds appropriated shall be spent to pay any of the expenses of his mission. . . .

March 12, 1940

Saw the President today in his study where he was confined with a slight cold. I went to take up with him the question of Myron Taylor and his exact status as the President's special representative in Rome in contact with the Vatican and also to make inquiry about the expenditure of funds in connection with that mission. Suppose members of the Congress who have showed some disposition to be hyper-critical of it wanted to make a religious issue of it—which it is very easy to do in this country?

Before I started into it, however, . . . he launched on a history of Welles' visit. The President said that the idea of Welles' trip came to him as an impulse. He figured it could not do any harm and it might do good. He conceived the idea that the Germans might launch a spring offensive about now. If Welles' visit would delay that offensive or possibly prevent it, it would be worth a great deal. If it prevented it altogether, that would be fine. If it delayed it a month, that would be so much. Even a week would mean a lot, because it would help England and France to get additional supplies during that week. He feared that Germany would attack either in Roumania or in Luxembourg or along the Channel ports. It might even have been a bombardment of English ports and the resultant attack on cities. He had viewed the prospect with horror. He wanted the British to have an opportunity to withstand the attack. Each week they were getting additional supplies. However, their maximum deliveries in airplanes would not commence until September. Raw materials were still badly needed there. He wanted them to have as much time as they could have before the German attack commenced in all its ferocity in order that they might be in a better position to defend themselves. The only other reason he sent Welles abroad was to find out what he could from Mussolini and from Hitler. He already knew what the British and French thought. Welles' visit to Paris and London was just "window dressing." He had to go there to balance the picture. What he had gone to Europe for really was to get the low-down on Hitler and get Mussolini's point of view. . . .[20]

[20] In his account of his mission, Welles wrote that Roosevelt sent him abroad to see "whether there still remained any step which he, as President of the United States, could take to avert the dangers that would so clearly confront the people of this country, as well as the civilized world, if the European war continued." Although no peace negotiations resulted from the mission, Welles did furnish the President with valuable information pointing to an ominous end to the "phony war" and a renewal of hostilities. Welles returned on March 28. The German campaign against Denmark and Norway began on April 9. See Sumner Welles, *The Time for Decision* (New York: Harper, 1944), pp. 73–147.

March 13, 1940

The terms of the peace between Russia and Finland are announced. Finland really wins the war. She paid a price in men and territory, but she retains her political integrity and her independence.[21] In addition to that, she has dissipated the specter of Russian power. A little country of 2,800,000 or thereabouts stood at bay a great country of 160,000,000 people, wrought enormous damage upon them measured in many scores of thousand dead, enormous losses in materiel, great numbers of tanks and airplanes. Russia, as a matter of fact, withdrew from the Bessarabian front and other places the best troops she could find and sent them against the little Finnish army.

The political consequences of this may be very far reaching. In the first place it has been a very great help to Germany. At least the peace has. In addition to that, the specter of Russian power disappearing has been a great help. Germany no longer fears for her eastern front. She figures she can take care of that at any time. But more—Germany can count upon some help from Russia in the way of supplies now that Russia is no longer engaged with Finland. But the morale of Germany has been increased. To them it seems like a victory for their ally. The victory is interpreted as being at the expense of Germany's enemies because England and France did send some help and to my mind made the foolish mistake of announcing at the very end that they would send enormous supplies in armies and men, thereby giving to the peace—though they had withheld that impression during the war— the appearance of an allied help to the technically defeated power—the power that had to sue for terms. . . .

March 15, 1940

I had a long talk with the Secretary this morning. He seemed considerably discouraged at the outlook abroad. He thinks the British and the French are bungling their affairs and are making it very difficult for public opinion in this country to continue to support them. The interests of the American people were antagonistic to the success of Germany, but the sentiment of the American people was gradually drifting against England. The isolationists here who are always opposed to any leadership in international affairs form the basis for a considerable sentiment to the effect that whatever happens in Europe can have no effect upon us and that we are not interested in it and that we should keep entirely aloof. In addition to that, public

---

[21] The peace terms imposed upon the Finns gave the Soviet Union all of the Mannerheim Line fortifications in the Karelian Isthmus; the Finnish shores of Lake Ladoga; a substantial slice of territory in east central Finland bisected by the Arctic Circle; and small sections of the Finnish Arctic coast giving the Russians control of the Finnish warm water port of Petsamo, Finland's only major port city on the Arctic Sea. Although Finland lost important agricultural land and although her sea approaches now were dominated by the Soviet Union, the country was left independent.

sentiment was drifting away from the allies. The betting in New York was 60 to 40 that Germany would win; the Republican leadership was just in opposition to the Administration and were taking positions which added their weight to the general drift; England was very inept in her pronouncements—even this morning there appeared in the press the statement that because of their war regulations and in order to conserve their exchange they were putting even canned foods into the category which required permits for their importation —which would mean that there would be no importations, because the permits would not be issued; so that England is adding to the general sentiment in this country. I said that if Lothian's attention were specifically brought to this matter he would be able to inform his Government that the inept announcements and lack of coordination of the various authorities engaged in prosecuting the war, such as the announcement about canned foods this morning, might be brought to the attention of the British Government with the idea that they would regulate the situation and make their announcements in a way which would be palatable to the American people. He said he thought it inadvisable to discuss the matter with Lothian pointedly.

The Secretary considered it a very serious situation from two points of view. First, there was the possibility that it might react against aid to the allies and would certainly withhold from them the support of American public sentiment—at least for the time being, because the American did not look very far in the future and did not see the unfortunate consequences to America, to its institutions, its industry and commerce if Germany should win; second, he feared very much that the political situation was becoming dangerous, even to the extent that the Democratic chances in November are jeopardized. He recalled an up-state election in New York in 1911 when we won and watched the straws that drifted in the wind drift until we elected Wilson in 1912. He saw now the bi-elections in Ohio particularly interpreted as an indication of lack of public confidence; that he saw in the New Hampshire national delegate election a very large falling off of Democratic votes as an indication of the same thing. He was afraid that these were simply preliminary straws; that they were distinct warnings that we would have hard enough sledding in November. He was altogether too pessimistic and mingled the political and the foreign situations. I agreed with him except that I do not place the same interpretations upon the elections. They are isolated incidents, and there is certainly a reason to explain the New Hampshire situation even though there was a 30% falling off in votes cast in the Democratic primary.[22] I told him that it was the time for the public to be

[22] On February 27, 1940, Republicans won two special congressional elections in Ohio. In one district no Republican had been elected during the previous ten years. On March 12 New Hampshire held the first 1940 presidential primary. Although delegates pledged to vote for Roosevelt at the Democratic National Convention were elected, their margin of

educated and that they needed leadership. He agreed to that but thought it would be very unpopular at the present moment to advocate a policy which would be at variance with public sentiment. He thought the Rockefeller Foundation might devote some of its energy and funds to explaining to the public reasons why they should be interested, and he hoped public sentiment would be roused. . . . He thought that we might have done something in the case of Finland. Personally I do not see just how that could have been done unless we had sent naval units to Petsamo on the Arctic just to be there, and that action it seems to me would have been just as futile as England's promises and France's tardy announcement. What the Finns needed were guns, airplanes and fighting units, but nobody could get them there. The presence of our Navy at Petsamo, or even off the northwest Norwegian coast, could not have contributed much to the help of the Finns. Anyhow, Cordell was very much discouraged. . . .

He took me into his confidence about the personnel situation in the Department. He is very fond of Welles and appreciates his ability. However, Welles thinks so fast and moves so rapidly that he gets way out in front and leaves no trace of the positions he has taken or the commitments he has made, and the Department is sometimes left in the dark as to his meanings and actions. He acts independently and forgets to tell the Secretary. At least that is what Cordell said. It worries him, because he likes Welles. Welles sees the President rather frequently, and Cordell seems to think that Berle plays ball with Welles. The Chief of the Latin American Division seems to be out of the picture, because Welles handles many Latin American matters without telling Duggan.[23] There are several persons in the Department in key positions whose presence is due to Welles and who act as if they were part of his organization as opposed to the regular establishment. He said, however, that he had not surrendered to anybody his control of the Far Eastern situation, and he did not want anybody to do anything in that except with his consent and after consultation with him. He said that Welles had had a large experience in Latin America and was thoroughly capable of doing that and had a general utility but that he was not a specialist in European matters or in Far Eastern matters and it was those fields which now occupied the public thought and in which he thought he should be in entire control subject only to the President. He felt that there should be a united front by the Department and an agreement here before things went to the President. He spoke to me in entire confidence and for my enlightenment. I was very

victory amounted to less than two to one over candidates pledged to Postmaster General James Farley and to Vice President John Garner. The campaign and final tabulation indicated a strong anti-third term sentiment among the state's Democrats.

[23] Laurence Duggan, chief of the State Department Division of the American Republics, 1937–1940.

attentive but entirely non-communicative, except at the end I told him I always tried to "play ball" and that I had no inordinate desire to go to the White House or to talk to the President just to talk to the President because he was President and that if he wanted me to take any matters up with the President I would be glad to do so and that he could be the judge as to what should be taken up; that I naturally assumed that I would present things through him. . . .

The reactions throughout the world as reported by our cables are rather clouded as regards the cessation of the Finnish-Russian war. There is fear in the Scandinavian countries, pessimism amongst the allies, jubilation amongst the Germans, and a nondescript feeling in South America. I am afraid the psychological reaction is going to affect seriously the allies, and it will take some definite military success to reestablish them in public confidence. That certainly is the case here. It is also probable that the reaction against England and France undoubtedly existing in this country today will soften and pass in the next few months.

March 16, 1940

Long talk with Cordell this morning. First, British stoppage of our mails and complications being created for us by private agreements between the Scandinavian countries and England about taking their ships into Kirkwall and putting all mail on American ships bound for Bergen and their insistence upon a program to take our ships into Kirkwall or Halifax. Second, about trade agreements. . . .

He then got on the subject of politics, his own availability as a nominee and the contemplated cabal against him in his own state by Senator McKellar and Krump [*sic*],[24] the boss of Memphis. They are calling hurriedly a meeting of the State Committee, which will set an early date for the State Convention with the idea of taking advantage of the present situation, which is he has declared he was not a candidate and had no present or prospective intention of engaging in political activity; he could not do that and keep foreign affairs out of politics. Their use of that to oppose him by getting a delegation instructed for Roosevelt simply as a slap at him and to indicate that he has no support in his own state. We discussed various angles of it, and my reaction was that unless he had some prominent member of his state who would have influence in either the Committee of the State Convention and who would make a stand for him that it was too late to do anything about it considering that the Committee meeting is to be held day after tomorrow. He discarded that idea and said that he would not attempt it. I told him that

[24] Kenneth McKellar, Democrat, U.S. Senator from Tennessee, 1917–1953; Edward Crump, Democrat, former U.S. Representative from Tennessee, 1931–1935, and Tennessee Democratic party leader.

I thought it would make no difference anyhow; that if the delegation did not vote for Roosevelt and his name was before the Convention, that they would be morally bound to vote for him; that his position would be reinforced because it would be a plain indication to the country that he was in practice maintaining the same position he had announced, whereas if the Convention instructed for him or sent an uninstructed delegation that position might be subject to reconsideration by the public. . . .

March 18, 1940

I lunched yesterday at the Swedish Legation. The Duke of Saxe-Coburg was there. . . . While at luncheon one of the house servants approached Thomsen[25] and handed him a memorandum which seemed to excite him somewhat in spite of his ordinary calm demeanor. Immediately after luncheon was ended he asked if he might use the telephone, and he had the Secretary of his own Embassy use the telephone. On his return after a few minutes he held a whispered conversation with Thomsen and very shortly thereafter approached the Duke and said it was time for them to go, and they departed rather hurriedly.

Very few of those present I think noticed this little byplay, but I naturally wondered what it could have meant. The only inference to my mind was that something unusual and important had happened in connection with the German Embassy, but it was not until after dinner last night when I was sitting chatting with Stanley Reed that a nephew of his came in with the early editions of the morning paper with the announcement that Hitler and Mussolini were to meet. This morning it seems that Mussolini has caused the *Conte de Savoia,* on which Welles is to return, to delay her departure for another day.

To my mind, and without knowing anything about it, it looks like the beginning of the German peace offensive with Welles as the instrumentality and Mussolini as the advocate of Hitler. If that turns out to be so, it will place Mussolini even more definitely in the German group and may make his neutral position one of the levers to be used in placing England and France in a very bad position. There is local trouble in England and in France. Chamberlain is under serious fire, and Daladier is faced with the advisability of considering changes in his Cabinet. There are many implications of political difficulties at home too. If Welles should be unfortunately implicated, it might have serious political repercussions at home.

This is the beginning of the German peace offensive. . . .[26]

[25] Dr. Hans Thomsen, German chargé d'affaires in Washington, 1940–1941.

[26] Long's observations here were erroneous. On March 17, Hitler and Mussolini met near the Brenner Pass, not to begin a peace offensive, but to agree on joint Italo-German action to promote their common interests in the Balkans. Mussolini promised diplomatic support of the forthcoming German military offensives in western Europe.

March 19, 1940

The points of a peace proposal—eleven in number—are published in this morning's press and rumored and corroborated over the radio. However, there is nothing official yet. The press seems to think they are mostly Hitler's points, but a careful reading would indicate that the Four Power Pact, the Danubian Basin Pact, the status quo in the Balkans, the provision the Czechs, Slovaks and Magyars constitute a tripartite separate state, the provision for free customs transit for Italian goods at Djibouti, and general disarmament at least were Mussolini's.[27]

Conversation with the Secretary about the rumored peace terms. I told him that I thought that the terms as reported this morning in the press and by radio were more Mussolini's terms than they were Hitler's terms. He said that nobody had any confirmation of these terms or any knowledge of the point of origin and asked me to contact the National Broadcasting Company, which made the announcement here, and see what I could find out about it. . . .

March 20, 1940

. . . Lunched with Leon Henderson.[28] He has an idea that the New Dealers and the old line Democrats ought to get together. He knows the New Dealers better than the Old Timers, and I know the Old Timers better than the New Dealers. So we decided to collaborate and get them together and at least make it possible for them to have a common understanding. He seems to be for Hull for President and for Robert Jackson for Vice President —provided Roosevelt does not run.

Daladier resigned. There is considerable dissatisfaction in France at the conduct of the war. The same applies to England. The Germans have outsmarted them in publicity and in coordination. The chances are Daladier will return at the head of a new Cabinet consisting largely of the present members but with a different set-up. Three hundred persons abstained from voting on the question proposed, which necessitated a resignation and has precipitated what might be a real dilemma.

[27] Reference here is to a dispatch from the *New York Times* correspondent in Rome, Herbert L. Matthews. On March 19, the *Times* published a Matthews article detailing a peace proposal that Germany and Italy would "shortly make." The major points called for a four-power pact between Great Britain, France, Germany, and Italy which would divide Europe into zones of "influence." Each power would then inaugurate an anti-bolshevist policy with the idea of "liberating" Russia from communism, by arms if necessary. The second main item would be a Danubian Federation consisting of Germany, Italy, Yugoslavia, Rumania, Bohemia, Slovakia, and Hungary, which would attempt "to equalize" the area. The minority problems would be solved by a vast transmigration of peoples. As Long noted, Matthews' source proved to be unreliable and the major powers denied knowledge of such a plan.

[28] Member of the Securities and Exchange Commission, 1939–1941, and economic adviser to President Roosevelt.

The eleven points of peace which came out of somewhere in Italy yesterday
and was published in the papers seems to have fallen down. Welles could not
corroborate them and our efforts to trace the story have resulted only in
being informed by Saltzberger [*sic*] [29] in New York (who acted at my
request yesterday) that his correspondent Matthews in Rome received the
information "from the office of the Secretary of State of the Vatican"—
which is anything but definite.

March 22, 1940

The fall of the Daladier Government has created difficulties. The repercussions are not yet sufficiently clear to indicate the possibilities. In Italy they
seem to be the possible cause of an estrangement by reason of the antagonism
to Reynaud.[30] Russia lays responsibility for the fall to the treatment of
French Communists. Reaction in England is not yet audible here. However,
in England it turns out now that the dramatic announcement of Chamberlain
that the minute he was speaking English planes were bombing Sylt and the
press stories which followed the next day announcing damage to Sylt are
without foundation it having been demonstrated that only one building was
destroyed and no material damage done. This in connection with the fall of
the Daladier Government is apt to have a rather sobering effect on English
public opinion. Circumstances like that and the large number of sinkings by
German ships yesterday and the day before, together with the possible lack
of confidence in the new government in France, may have far-reaching
effects. . . .

March 23, 1940

Berle came in this morning for a talk. He envisages the possible victory of
Germany and the consequences upon our own military and naval defenses,
including that of industrial organization for purposes of defense—not so
much as to our immediate territory but as to our interests in Latin America.
He thinks there ought to be a movement of education to prepare the people
for the eventualities which he sees the possibility of developing. . . . Berle
has probably got definitely in his mind that Germany is going to win this
war. It may be the immediate reflex of the French Cabinet difficulties in
France. Reynaud is the new Prime Minister, and he got a majority of one

[29] Arthur Hays Sulzberger, publisher of the *New York Times*, 1935–1961.

[30] When Édouard Daladier became premier of France in April 1938, the immediate
issues and incidents which culminated in the Second World War were already in evidence.
Daladier's policy at the time of the Munich crisis (September 1938) was opposed by the
Communists and not supported by the Socialists. After the outbreak of war, the Communist party was officially dissolved, its members expelled from the Chamber of Deputies,
and its leaders arrested. Paul Reynaud succeeded Daladier and promised a more aggressive
prosecution of the war. The German victory over France led to his resignation (June 16,
1940) and the appointment of Marshal Henri-Philippe Pétain as his successor.

vote yesterday. The chances are he will not last very long. The British raid on Sylt was a flop. The German raid on Scapa Flow seems to have been more productive of damage than the British are willing to admit.[31] The Cabinet situation in England is not very satisfactory and it is certainly not stable in France. All of this is interpreted in various neutral countries as being of advantage to Germany. There is no doubt from the telegrams that we are receiving that that opinion is reflected in all neutral capitals. Berle's mind may be affected by these rumors. My own reaction is that the British cause is not proceeding as well as it might. They have used very bad judgment in taking actions which have alienated a large part of American public opinion. As usual they are blundering their way along. Their capacity for resistance is very great and they have not lost the war.

Nevertheless, I think that we do have to take into consideration the possibility of a German victory. In case of one and the destruction of the British Fleet along with it, we are not even then confronted with a military difficulty. It will take Germany a long time to mop up in Europe, and our Fleet would be able to take care of any two Fleets Germany could muster, but it will be a long time before we will have to cross that bridge. There would, however, be an immediate economic effect here. Our markets in Europe would fall off and political activities against our interest in Latin America would be intensified. That it would make enormous changes in American political life must be taken for granted. In the meantime, we should be making plans for the eventuality, but in my thought the first thing to do is to get the Fleet mobile by making additional water-ways across the Isthmus. . . .

March 25, 1940

Homer[32] had recently had a talk with the Chief. . . . The reason for the conversation was to talk over with Homer his availability as Temporary Chairman of the Convention and to explore his relations with Farley in that connection. During the course of the general conversation Jackson and Douglas[33] were each barred as nominees for the first place on the ticket. There was no mention of McNutt, the inference being that he was not considered eligible. However, Jackson was mentioned as rather acceptable and promising for second place on the ticket. The question was how that would complicate the situation vis-à-vis Farley. . . . Out of it all, Hull's name was

---

[31] Sylt is a German island in the North Sea off the coast of Schleswig-Holstein and was one of the earliest air targets of the British during World War II. Scapa Flow, an area of water off the northern coast of Scotland, was Britain's main naval base during both world wars.

[32] Homer Cummings, former U.S. Attorney General, 1933–1939.

[33] William O. Douglas, Associate Justice of the Supreme Court since 1939, and former chairman of the Securities and Exchange Commission, 1936–1939.

mentioned as being the most available and the best equipped. Much was made of his service in the Spanish War and his long contact in official life and the fact that he is more progressive mentally and philosophically than most people considered him. All pointed to the thought that the Chief was going to be for Hull and Jackson—at least for the time being—but that he was himself still in the picture. He made no remark which could be construed in any way by Homer as indicating that he would or would not eliminate himself as a possible candidate for the third term. That is the policy he has pursued consistently, and I think very wisely.

March 27, 1940

Trade Agreements Act passed its first hurdle in the Senate by a close vote. The Pittman Amendment which would have required ratification of the Senate for each Agreement and would have practically killed the Act was defeated by a close vote of 44 to 41.[34]

Germany released a White Book consisting of a lot of papers alleged to have been taken from the files of the Polish Foreign Office when the Polish Government was overcome last fall. These papers contain reports by Polish Ambassadors of conversations with Bullitt and Kennedy. The Secretary, Norman Davis and I considered what position the Department should take.

Cordell had already consulted the President, who said he would like some categorical statement. Cordell drafted the first part of the statement subsequently issued which stated that he could not put the "slightest credence" in the reports and to which I added that they had not represented at any time the policy or the thought of the American Government. The statements are not so important in themselves, but coming on the heels of Jimmie Cromwell's recent effulgence in Ottawa[35]—which was subsequently stated to have been submitted to the President and to have received his approval for delivery but which statement was also denied by the White House—these new statements about Bullitt and Kennedy have accumulative effect, as they both involve from time to time the President's name and attribute to him agreement with the ideas allegedly expressed. The danger is not an international one but a local political one. The Republicans are looking for some issue which would indicate that the Administration is edging into this war. Consequently I thought it particularly important that any statement which we issued should be definite and just as positive as we could make it.

[34] Senator Key Pittman claimed that trade agreements were really treaties and required, therefore, a two-thirds Senate majority vote. Pittman's amendment to this effect was defeated on March 27.

[35] James Cromwell, U.S. minister to Canada, January–May 1940, had publicly declared that the United States planned all-out assistance to Great Britain.

Cordell was more definitely of that opinion than Norman [Davis]. The trouble with Norman is that he always wants to compromise his position and qualify his remarks. There are times when I think you have to be blunt, and this seems to be one of them. There is just a sneaking suspicion in our minds that there is more truth than fiction in some of the reported conversations. Not only do they have the ear-marks of authenticity but they indicate actions which are characteristic of both Bullitt and Kennedy. Cordell is very much concerned about it. He has not liked the actions of either of them for a long time. They have a custom of going over his head and talking to the President, and he has found it necessary to secure agreement with the President about his intended instructions to them before they are issued in order that he and the President will find themselves in perfect agreement and that the President will stand hitched. Cordell said this afternoon that Bullitt had been drinking rather freely for the last year and had been rather unorthodox in some of his conduct not only diplomatically but otherwise and that he feared very much that there were other things in the files which might be even more disconcerting than the present revelations.

I talked to both Bullitt and Kennedy about the inadvisability of their using the telephone in their communications with the President and in their communications amongst themselves. Bullitt told me that Kennedy called up two or three times a day and discussed questions of policy and procedure over the telephone between London and Paris. Bullitt has also had one former experience when one of his conversations with Biddle was intercepted over the telephone and subsequently published by the German Government. That was last fall. Norman [Davis] remarked this afternoon that he was indiscreet on one occasion to the extent of trying to accompany [Jozef] Beck, the Polish Prime Minister, on his voyage from Warsaw to London. He even asked permission of the Department to accompany him and was refused but did ride with him on his train from Paris part of the way. This was one of Beck's preliminary conversations prior to the downfall, and Bullitt should have disconnected himself with the activity.

April 4, 1940

It has developed that certain information has been leaking. Just where the leak is nobody knows. How recently there has been leakage is not known. We do not know that there has been any leakage since the actual outbreak of the war. The reason we do know there was leakage prior to that time is that we have now been confidentially informed from British sources that certain American news is known at Berlin. It must have got to Berlin out of London through some form of secret communication. How it was obtained in the first instance for transmission to Germany is not known. On the theory that it may have been a leakage from somewhere over here I called a secret conference consisting of Berle, Dunn, Berle's Assistant Warren, and Mr. Frank,[36] my assistant. We decided to make a thorough check of the whole line of communication, physical and otherwise, from the time it leaves the desk until it leaves the boundaries of the United States on the wires. Also it will be a two-way check and will cover the wires of incoming messages and the whole distribution system within the Department. No one else is to know about it. . . .

April 5, 1940

. . . Kirk is coming home. Welles found him very tired and depressed and thinks he ought to have a vacation. He is being requested to apply for leave so it will not give an official color to his return. But Welles wants him to talk with the President and wants the President to appoint him as Minister to the first good available post. I telegraphed Kirk to come and stay with me in the country. He has done a great job in Berlin, but I am afraid he may be a little mystified about his request to return. However, it will be quite natural. Kennedy and Bullitt have been here from London and Paris, and it is very simple for him to come from Berlin. . . .

There is no apparent prospect of a peace of any kind nor is there any prospect in my mind of an intensification of the war. It looks like dragging along for the next few months until the next crop comes in and that will keep the people comparatively well fed and content until about this time next year. So it looks like holding the lines and having this thing drag on and keeping the world upset with further restrictions being imposed upon trade and commerce and a gradual suffocation of all individualistic activities whether they be trade, commerce, manufacture or political activities. Altogether it is an unpleasant picture, and it is sure to have its adverse effect upon industry in the United States and to produce additional unemployment and falling off of production—with the exception that a few lines of activity engaged in manufacturing military supplies will continue to enjoy an artificial stimulus resulting in a profit.

April 9, 1940

The Germans yesterday occupied Denmark, including Copenhagen. There was no resistance. There was considerable activity in the Kattegat, one German transport being sunk by a British submarine. There was another report of aerial and naval action but no details available, reports coming from shore. It now appears that German transports and battleships evaded

[36] Fletcher Warren, foreign service officer, executive assistant to Assistant Secretary Adolf A. Berle, Jr., 1938–1942; Laurence Frank, foreign service officer, Long's assistant, 1941–1944.

the British naval units and landed occupying forces at Bergen, Trondheim and Kristiansand,[37] these three places now reported to be under German occupation. An attempt to occupy Oslo was prevented temporarily at least by shore batteries in Oslofjord repelling a squadron of German ships. The Royal Family and the Court have left Oslo for the interior.

The British Navy must have been asleep, and the consequences would seem to hold a dire prospect. The occupation of Bergen brings Germany within easy striking distance of Scapa Flow. Her bombers can be accompanied from Bergen by pursuit planes. What the British answer will be to the German move does not appear, unless it be the landing of an expeditionary force to recapture the occupied cities and drive out the Germans and hold them under British occupation. The British stupidly brought the whole thing on [because they laid mines in Norwegian territorial waters] and were not sufficiently vigilant to protect themselves from the consequences.

The Secretary was away for a few days at Atlantic City and is returning at 11:30. Welles is much concerned but agrees with me that no announcement of any kind should be made by this Government. He and I consider the British have brought this situation on by their invasion of Norwegian waters and that their action is hard to justify. Also the consequences of their action are hard to reconcile with British vigilance. Both of us are agreed that this Government should remain perfectly quiet. . . .

Conference in Secretary's office: Welles, Berle, Hackworth, several others, on defining State Department's attitude toward extension of proscribed areas for American ships under the provisions of the Neutrality Law and in view of the developments of yesterday and today. We decided to run the line up well north of the North Cape of Norway and eastward to a line and down that line to the easternmost extremity of Norway on the Arctic Ocean. I advocated the extension of the line north of and to include the waters around Spitzbergen [sic]. Spitzbergen is Norwegian territory.[38]

The question is also raised as to the status of Iceland and Greenland. Greenland is also territory of Denmark and is in the Western Hemisphere not far from the eastern shore of Canada. It is hardly habitable but susceptible of use for naval and possibly air bases. Also Iceland is a subject of jurisdictional inquiry. Iceland does not belong to Denmark but is allied to Denmark through the personal connections of the King. The King being King of each. With Denmark under German occupation the question is not necessarily raised that Iceland is under German occupation, but as the King

[37] Kattegat, a strait between Sweden and Denmark connecting the North Sea with the Baltic Sea; Trondheim, one of the largest cities of Norway; Kristiansand, a seaport and shipping center in southern Norway.

[38] Spitsbergen is an archipelago in the Arctic Ocean about four hundred miles north of the Norwegian mainland. By a 1920 treaty, Sweden and the Soviet Union agreed to relinquish their claims and awarded it to Norway.

of Denmark has submitted to the occupation by Germany the question is raised as to what he might do in case Iceland were occupied.

Started the arrangements for the evacuation of American citizens in Scandinavia. Two boats now in port; a third one has been in and out of Bergen but has been unable to obtain docking facilities to unload. Their combined emergency passenger capacity is 300. Other evacuees will have to proceed through Germany to an Italian port. Women and children of the American staffs have been evacuated from Oslo and Goteburg, and Stockholm has been advised to evacuate and to repatriate women and children. Norway, Sweden and Denmark have been authorized to evacuate or repatriate families of other officers in other countries who were there for safety.

April 10, 1940

Long conference with the Secretary, Welles, Berle and others about the attitude of the American Government toward Danish and Norwegian credits and deposits in this country—both governmental and private. Defined Department's attitude and authorized consultations with Treasury, Commerce, etc. to draft proper papers for recommendations to the President.

Reports of heavy naval engagements in the Skagerrak.[39] The Germans seem to have accomplished landings in seven or eight points in Norway. British are attempting to dislodge them and prevent further troop shipments. Germany has demanded Norway set up a puppet government, agent of the Nazis, to be recognized by the King. The King has refused and Norway is resisting with military efforts.

Communications with Oslo interrupted and also with Copenhagen. The British and French ask us for welfare and whereabouts of their Minister at Copenhagen. British Minister reported confined and will be repatriated.

Secretary called me again to discuss politics. He is much discouraged over bi-elections. One yesterday in Nebraska for Congress indicates Republican victory.[40] The deceased member was a Republican. The Secretary complains that no organization of any kind is being effected by the Democratic elements; that there is no leadership and no coordination. Farley's units, Morgenthau's units and Wallace's appointees not organized or active. Foresees defeat in the fall unless things change. He is much concerned. He asked me to take some interest in the lack of organization.

April 11, 1940

I talked to the Secretary and Norman Davis. Norman was advising him that some announcement should be made condemning Germany for her

[39] A strait between Norway and Denmark.

[40] In a special Nebraska congressional election held on April 9, Hyde Sweet, Republican, an opponent of the New Deal farm program, defeated Charles Dafoe, the Democratic contender.

actions in Denmark and Norway. I councilled [*sic*] extreme caution on the grounds, first that it looked as if Danish authorities had voluntarily submitted to German demands and had permitted German forces to operate, and that second as to Norway the issue was clouded and was not clear. The British had laid mines in territorial waters and the impression was implanted in the minds of the American for several days that the British had taken the initiative in violation of neutrality; that the German violation was also a violation of sovereignty and a more flagrant one than the British but nevertheless the issue was not clear; that I preferred to see the United States exercise its influence through public expressions upholding right and denouncing wrong in cases where the issue was clear and where there could be no doubt of the good judgment of the Administration.

I also advocated that the United States Navy send units to Greenland to exercise our function under the Monroe Doctrine; no public announcement to be made of it but the British Ambassador should be informed orally; that the action could be taken as an incident of our patrol of American waters, which now extended way down into the South Atlantic and would be in keeping with American tradition; that it would gradually become known and that it would be approved by the American people as being a step in accordance with the Monroe Doctrine.[41] The Secretary was a little hesitant about following that advice. ·

It seems that Berle advocated that the Danish Minister be informed by the Secretary and the President that he would be recognized no matter what happened to his Government. I am surprised to learn this, because his Government seems to have acted in entire submission and to have waived some of its rights to recognition of its Ambassador if they are not willing to maintain the integrity of their own political function, at least to the point of having made a show of resistance against demands for its subordination. I am afraid this step, if taken, was done hurriedly and without thought and was due largely to the close personal relationship existing between Berle and the Dane. . . .

April 12, 1940

The Secretary this morning said that he agreed with me about Greenland. He has asked Hackworth to fortify him on the legal points concerned, particularly as regards the Monroe Doctrine and is calling in Lothian this afternoon to tell him that the United States considers Greenland within the

---

[41] One intent of the Monroe Doctrine was to prevent European powers from interfering in the affairs of the "new world" nations. Since Greenland is considered part of the western hemisphere and, therefore, technically within the "new world," Long thought that the United States should take action under the Doctrine to prevent German occupation.

Monroe Doctrine and will include it within the neutrality patrol. I am quite satisfied with the development. . . .

Talked with the Secretary about the Greenland situation just before he received Lothian to read to him the text of a statement outlining our position in regard to Greenland. I want to implement it and notify the Latin American Republics, but I have not taken that up yet but will do so tomorrow. I also want to be sure that naval units include those waters in their patrol which is not yet accepted.

Sent a cable to London, Paris and Oslo via Stockholm to inform the respective Governments of the presence in those waters of the three American ships and that the Captains respectively had orders to leave in their discretion for the United States and stating that the American Government expected that every facility would be given to the American ships to be led through mine fields and that they would not be molested by any naval units and stating that they would fly the American flag prominently and proceed under full lights at night.

Also engaged with additional evacuation activities and instructions for Americans in Scandinavia. King Haakon,[42] with Mrs. Harriman[43] trailing him has had an exciting hegira but has so far apparently succeeded in eluding the pursuing Germans.

April 13, 1940

Two long conferences with the Secretary about Greenland—He not only notified Lothian but is to receive the Canadian Minister at noon and tell him the same thing. They have agreed also to notify the Latin American countries. Decided to base the action squarely on the Monroe Doctrine but not to use that phraseology in notifying the American Republics. It is gradually working around to the sending of ships, and I think that will happen shortly, but it is the President's wish that this be treated confidentially for the time being. . . .

Farley saw the Secretary and then came in and had a chat with me. It is very apparent that he thinks Cordell can be nominated and elected and that he thinks he will be nominated for Vice President. I talked to Michelson yesterday about the subject, and Charlie has some doubts as to Farley's availability and thinks that the men who talked to Farley also talked to the President and others in a different vein. Anyhow, Farley thinks he can be nominated and that Hull and he can be elected. He is a little disturbed at the President's policy, but I told him I thought it was not only wise but the best he could pursue and it would all straighten out eventually. Farley is still devoted to the President and will do what the President wants in the last analysis and

[42] Haakon VII, king of Norway, 1905–1957.
[43] Mrs. Florence Jaffray Harriman, American minister to Norway, 1937–1940.

told me that he would not get peeved and would play ball under any circumstances. He has some antagonism and feeling against Bob Jackson. This is natural and of some long standing. They are both able, fine fellows, but Farley is more active and a better organizer and probably just as smart, but Jackson has a great intellectual capacity and is a deeper thinker than Jim but not nearly as efficient in political activity.

After Farley's visit I talked to Cordell again about my conversation with him. He told me that he had told Farley that he was not a candidate for any office and wouldn't be. Farley certainly got the impression, however, that Cordell would not hesitate to accept the nomination. They are really great friends and like each other very much. Cordell reiterated the position he has held all along. He is still concerned about the drift against the Democratic ticket and is not so sure that he or anybody else but Roosevelt could be elected. I told him about my conversation with Charlie Michelson and Charlie's optimism, but he said frankly that Charlie was mistaken.

Talked to the President about noon. . . . We discussed the Greenland status. One of his concerns was to what purpose it might be put by Danish and Norwegian ships in their efforts to reach Norway under orders from German sources. He thought they would proceed up the middle of the Atlantic, up the Greenland Straits between Greenland and Iceland, up to Spitzbergen and then down some coast either of Norway or Russia. He did not want that to happen or Greenland to be used as a port of refuge or as a fueling base. He did not know to what extent we might be able to prevent that in case we were protecting Danish sovereignty. He also expressed concern that the British and French did not land in full force and with a considerable speed in their efforts to take the highlands back of the fjords and move down the coast so as to cut off the Germans and to retake the fjords as far down as Stavengerfjord [sic],[44] if not farther. . . .

April 15, 1940

The situation seems to have worsened over the week-end. I spent yesterday quietly at home. This morning it appears the British are landing troops in Norway. The Germans are having a hard fight with the Norwegians in various fronts and the Norwegians are doing very well. However, the Germans are in complete control in the whole Oslo district and at Kristiansand and at Bergen and Trondheim. Sweden is taking preventive measures so as to defend herself against an invasion from Norway and is placing great rocks on aviation fields so as to make them useless for landing purposes and is also concentrating her land forces in the south. On the other hand, Germany has concentrated troops in Austria, and it looks like a suggestion

[44] Stavanger Fjord is a commercial and industrial area in southwest Norway which the Germans occupied on the first day of their invasion of Norway (April 9, 1940).

on the part of Hitler that Mussolini conform more regularly to the provisions of the Axis. Gibraltar advises that they are preparing against the possibility of an attack on Gibraltar from Spain and that two airplane carriers arrived last night at the Rock to supplement the air forces. . . .

The Secretary had me in for a long private chat. Japan has given every indication that she will resent British or American occupation of the Dutch East Indies in case the Netherlands is attacked by Germany and has left the intimation that she would occupy the islands. Almost all of our tin and most of our rubber come from there. The trade routes of the United States would be seriously crippled, and industry in America would be most importantly affected by the occupation of those islands by Japan. The Secretary has in mind to do something to prevent it. We discussed all the pros and cons. Amongst the ideas discussed were sending the Fleet on a courtesy visit to Singapore. This I said was impossible as long as England was at war with a country with which Japan was nearly an ally. It was then proposed to pay a courtesy visit to the Dutch East Indies. The answer is that the courtesy visit would end very shortly and that the American Fleet would soon be away from there and then occupation could then proceed. Another question to be considered in connection therewith was whether the American Fleet would be ready and prepared to act or would it be like the British Fleet when it went into the Mediterranean at the time of the Ethiopian venture?

Another question presented was how would the American Fleet get to either Singapore or to Java on a courtesy visit unless it went all the way around Australia, and in that case it would have to refuel at Australia.

The American Fleet is now on a cruise west of Hawaii. It will be returning in a few weeks to Hawaii. Would it be possible for it to have another practice cruise out toward the coast of Japan? If so, what could the Fleet do if it got there? Would it be in the position the British Fleet was in in the Mediterranean? Would not it all go back to the purposes of the American people and the temper of the country? Writing notes to Japan and telling them that we looked with disfavor upon their occupation would do no good. Public professions of displeasure would be of no avail. If we called the Japanese Ambassador in and told him that we considered these islands very important to the continuation of American trade and industry would only emphasize in the Japanese mind the importance which they were to us but would not deter the Japanese or put any effective obstacles in their way as regards their occupation but would even increase in their minds the importance of the islands as regards the United States and the advantage that would accrue to Japan vis-à-vis the United States in case they should occupy those islands. If we put an embargo on Japan and they occupied those islands, they could place an embargo on tin and rubber against us.

There are so many angles and the countries are so far away and our ships have such a definite limitation—great as their range of operations is—to fighting an engagement that far from base, that it seems almost impractical to do anything unless this country is willing to shoot. If we are willing to shoot, then the place to shoot is in Japanese waters—in my opinion. However, we are not willing to shoot, and I am unwilling to go that far or to take any steps which we could not back up.

Cordell thinks of calling in Stimson and Dawes,[45] who will be in Washington in a few days, and several other Republicans and just placing upon them the responsibility of lining up their politicians in the Congress to show a united support in favor of whatever steps the Administration may have to take in the premises. I warned him that he would be laying himself open to be shot at by them and that they might use the information to embarrass the Administration.

He asked me to think the problem over very seriously and to talk to him again. . . .

April 16, 1940

. . . The fervor in the Mediterranean seems to have died down, but there are still possibilities for action. I seriously doubt if Italy is going to move or change her position, but Mussolini keeps her in the limelight and blows hot one minute and cold the next and keeps his people guessing and the world uncertain. . . .

Talked again to the Secretary about the Far Eastern situation. He now is thinking over the possibility of issuing a statement calling attention to the fact that England, France, Japan and the United States signed the Treaty of Washington [1922] which guaranteed the integrity and peace of the Dutch East Indies and indicating that it was assumed that the Dutch East Indies consequently had nothing to fear of any of the signatory powers. That is about the only thing I see that could be done.[46]

April 23, 1940

A lengthy conference with the Secretary this morning about Greenland and about Danish ships; Welles, Moore, Berle, Feis[47] and Moffat being

[45] Henry Stimson, Republican, former Secretary of State, 1929–1933, supported many of Roosevelt's foreign policy measures. Named Secretary of War in July 1940, he served until September 1945; Charles Dawes, Republican, Vice President of the United States, 1925–1929.

[46] On April 16, the Japanese foreign office issued a statement declaring that "the Japanese Government cannot but be deeply concerned over any development accompanying the aggravation of the war in Europe that might affect the *status quo* of the Netherlands East Indies." The statement implied that Japan might intervene in the Indies if European events "give rise to an undesirable situation from the standpoint of stability in East Asia." On the following day, Secretary Hull warned Japan that any alteration of the *status quo* would jeopardize peace "in the entire Pacific area."

[47] Herbert Feis, State Department Adviser on International Economic Affairs, 1931–1943.

present. They all were in favor of sending a Consul to Greenland. Everybody present spoke in favor of it. I was the last one asked. Berle had spoken to me earlier this morning on the subject, and I expressed some doubts. I had then called in one of the legal advisors and asked him to write a memorandum on the legal status of Greenland under the present circumstances with the mother country occupied by a superior military force; and also as to what authority we would look to to issue an exequatur. So that when I was called upon I said I seemed to be the only one who had any doubts but I did not feel in a position to agree until we had more deeply explored the legal questions involved. I called attention to the fact that the Consul would be perfectly isolated. There were no means of communication around Greenland and he would not know what was going on anywhere except in the particular little locality in which he was situated. I again advocated the dispatch of destroyers and include those waters in the sphere of our neutrality patrol. This Mr. Welles objected to on the ground that it might serve as a precedent for Japan in regard to the Netherlands East Indies. The wisdom of that I conceded and said I was perfectly willing to withdraw as far as ships were concerned, but we would have Coast Guard boats which had the general function every year of patroling those waters as an ice patrol and warning ships of icebergs and that additional such vessels might be sent up there. They could cruise around on the east coast and the west coast and would know what was going on, whereas a Consul would know only what was going on in one little spot. In addition to that was the question as to what authority was going to agree to receive him as a Consul. Mr. Berle suggested that the Danish Minister here had been asked by the people in Greenland to serve their interests and that he would agree to accept a Consul. I remarked that I thought he had no authority which we could recognize to issue an exequatur or to do any other act of the Government of Greenland or for any Government which might exist in Greenland unless they wanted to set themselves up as an independent Government and we should render them *de facto* recognition. Moffat suggested that there might be a commercial agent instead of a Consul or some other arrangement which would not carry such official significance. I quite agreed that that might be done but I insisted that I thought we ought to await the study of the legal points involved, particularly in as much as the Legal Advisor's office was at present engaged upon that undertaking. That point finally prevailed.

I am conscious of finding myself rather frequently in disagreement with some of my colleagues on questions of procedure. This Greenland matter is just one of them. I cannot but view these questions in their long-range significance, and I am convinced that we have to proceed carefully and with full knowledge of the consequences of our acts. Berle is apt to jump at conclusions and then to justify or find ways of justifying his arrival at those conclusions. Of the persons this morning in conference none but Cordell (Berle?) and I are lawyers. He is very reluctant to take the opposite position when there is any dispute amongst his advisors and likes to postpone the issue for further study and eventual agreement. . . .

I said above that Cordell and I were the only lawyers. I am mistaken. Judge Moore is a lawyer. However, his mind does not seem to grasp the fine points of many things presented to him. He is a sweet old character and a fine old man, but his eighty-three years have slowed him down. Sometimes I think he is supporting me and I am sure his mind agrees and goes along with mine, only to find that I have been mistaken when it comes to a conference in which some other points of view are expressed. It is hard to tell what his decisions are.

In the seclusion of one's own mind I suppose one is free to have thoughts which are critical of one's colleagues. I do not mean to be critical, but I cannot but find my mind committed to the thought that an orderly procedure, and even a slow procedure, is at times necessary to arrive at a conclusion. Things change so fast in this world today that we have to look all around each of these changes and see how they are going to affect us and what the long-term implications of our actions and decisions may be. Under those circumstances if I find myself in disagreement with colleagues, I shall be sorry but shall have to continue along my line of thought. At the same time I am quite conscious that they will get the impression that I do not go along with their thoughts and that I am out of tune with the music they play and that they will try to arrive at policies without consulting me. That will be the natural consequence. But as long as I am here I shall have to continue to do things in the way which I think proper.

April 24, 1940

Norwegian shipping has been taken over by the British with the consent of the Norwegian Government and is operated as British shipping. We discussed all phases of it and the American interests concerned, trade routes, cargoes aboard ship, charter rights and all phases of the question. It is understood that the British have control of the ships and that they are in a category by themselves. . . . Looking to the future and the possibilities that would follow English victory, and also the situation that would result from German victory, I suggested that from a long-range point of view that we should begin to consider a question of high policy as to whether the United States Government should not enlarge its shipbuilding program so as to provide bottoms for necessary American sea routes. This was left on the table for future consideration. I am now advised informally by the Solicitor's office that we have a treaty with Denmark which probably precludes the sending of a Consul to Greenland. That matter is still open, but I am going to be sure that as far as I am concerned we shall act according to treaty obligations and under international law.

April 26, 1940

... Today—Greenland again. I finally succumbed to agree to sending a consular officer—somewhat reluctant because of our treaty of 1826 with Denmark and partly because just last summer Denmark refused to agree to our request to include Greenland in the Consular District of our Consul General at Copenhagen. Together with Berle and Hackworth it was thrashed out and I consented on Hackworth's argument that our treaty with Denmark was superseded by German military occupation and control over Denmark—that the treaty did not prevent our establishing a Consul in Greenland but made that conditional upon the consent of the Danish Government—that under present conditions that Government could not even entertain a request to it to give permission—that the Danish Minister here is as yet unrepudiated by his Government and in addition is requested to act by the local authorities in Greenland as their representative here—and that he assures they are willing to receive a Consul, provisionally. . . .

April 27, 1940

The *American White Book* [*sic*] is out. I read it today, an interesting account well dramatized by Alsop and his collaborator.[48] It was taken, I understand, from Berle's diary or papers. He is the actual author but not the titular one. Alsop spent days in Berle's office working on "personal" matters. Also started [Sir Nevile] Henderson's *Failure of a Mission: Berlin 1937–1939*. They are each echoes of a past age. The war is here. Also I put my radio address on Foreign Policy into practically finished form.

Stayed away from the Department—at home—alone—wandered around the farm—talked about vegetable garden, sowing two more fields—harrowing one—inspected horses and fruit trees. A peaceful day of needed rest. A deluded female cardinal has for a week been trying to get in through the glass of the library windows—first one window, then another. Intermittently today every fifteen or twenty minutes she has been at it—apparently undiscouraged and continuingly deluded with the thought that if there are trees and bushes outside there probably are within the window which she mistakes for a nice dark nook to build a nest.

April 28, 1940

The Germans formally accuse England of the invasion of Norway and submit documentary proof garnered from prisoners and files in the British Legation in Oslo and elsewhere. The evidence is not convincing. My own

[48] Joseph Alsop and Robert Kinter, *American White Paper* (New York: Simon and Schuster, 1940).

reaction is that they should have known ahead of the German plan to invade and made substantial efforts to prevent its success instead of the picayunish efforts for the first slow two weeks' action.

Germany is trying to placate the United States. She goes out of her way to make a show of friendliness. Her policy, however, is for the good of Germany and not for the good of the United States. Profiting by the experience of 1917–18, she tried *not* to antagonize us. She will go a long way on the road of conciliation to keep us from getting involved. First she wants to crush England—and I mean *crush*—and after consolidating her position there to turn to America, beginning with Argentina, Chile and the Panama region so as to weaken our position. They have long-sighted plans.

Sentiment in this country is gradually changing. From "stay out of war at any price" it is turning to "help the Allies in every way short of war." That has been the President's policy from the beginning—but not publicly announced as such. The country is now beginning to catch up with him. The sentiment is not yet congealed but it is definitely forming. The next change will be for more definite help to the Allies but not "men over-seas." The possibility of that is fast vanishing. They have plenty of men and the practical destruction of the German Navy renders unnecessary the thought of sending our Navy. Even with the losses they have suffered the British Navy can handle European waters. But the question of extending credit instead of requiring cash will be up at the next session of Congress if not before. The ban of American ships from belligerent and danger areas will be up contemporaneously—so that the prohibition will be removed against our transporting food and munitions produced here. The bankers will want to lend, the manufacturers will want to make, the shippers and railroads here will want to carry and the cotton, tobacco, corn, cattle and wheat farmers will want to sell—on credit, because they will see the end of cash. And with the end of cash will come the end of the Allies. So the sentiment is in the making —and when it is congealed formulated policy will change—perhaps not entirely open and honestly expressed—but nevertheless existent.

Germany sees that and is trying to prevent its rapid development by placating us in small ways. When it comes we will have internal trouble. Every Communist agent will join with the German sympathizers and the "peace at any price" element to foment discord and social disorder on top of sabotage. It will be a troublesome difficulty to handle.

My coming short but succinct radio address is based on *present* policy. There are no "ifs" in it. I think we must emphasize our peace policy at this time. This is a political year. The Republicans are trying to base their campaign on a fear that we will lead the country into war. We actually do not want to. However, the Allies must win if we are to be spared years of intensive worry and a gradual lowering of the standards of life in this country.

But the approach to helping the Allies is subject to political misrepresentation. We must not be open to the charge. Consequently I emphasize Peace—the policy to stay out of war—the hope of a reconstructed commerce and happy and contented peoples.

The cardinal is still trying to get into my window—like the vain hope of our generation to find a little quiet, a secluded quiet, a peaceful nook—even for a while.

May 2, 1940

The President sent a message to Mussolini through Phillips in which he reflected the report arriving from various places that Italy is ready and about to assume belligerency—which I do not believe. His message ended with a statement to the effect that if Italy did jump in the whole Mediterranean area would be involved, the Balkans brought in and a situation created which might impel a neutral Government to reconsider its neutral status and participate in the activities even though its decision to do so might be very reluctantly arrived at. He meant that if Italy did the United States might do something too.

I have from the beginning of the war thought that Italy would stay out at least until the decision was clear that Germany would win. I feel so now. I do not think Italy is about to enter the war, but I do think the Allies are trying to give the impression she is about to do so. Their object in creating that impression is not yet clear to me.

May 6, 1940

The British have left Norway, and the Germans are in full control of the south. The Norwegians have capitulated as has one small detachment of English left pocketed. The Germans now are pounding away to reach Narvik, and the military elements there are still holding out in the city in spite of British attempts to rout them. The British failed to notify the Norwegian military authorities that they were leaving them and failed to notify the French Government of their intention. Consequently they are receiving a great deal of criticism. If the Germans can repeat around Narvik their activities at Andalsnes and at Namos [*sic*], the British will be driven out of Narvik and the Germans will be in complete control of the entire stretch of Norway.[49] The poor King will probably have to take refuge in Sweden. . . .

May 8, 1940

Cables today indicate the possibility of an immediate attack on Belgium, Holland and Luxemburg. Even Kirk telegraphs that his information is that the attack may be imminent. Personally I think it is a smoke screen. . . .

[49] Narvik is an ice-free port in northwestern Norway. Andalsnes and Namsos are cities in western Norway which the Germans occupied after heavy aerial bombardments.

At the request of the President, Welles called a few of us this morning to consider ways and means of preventing the further inflow of German and Russian propagandists and agents and of attempting to attend to those who had filtered through. About 16,000 aliens have forfeited their bonds at the end of their period of temporary domicile. Amongst these are known to be a number of German agents. The Department of Labor is very non-cooperative. Our Department's Visa Section and Passport Division and the F.B.I. have been quite cooperative and active, but no help is received from Labor except through the Commissioner of Immigration,[50] who happens to be under that Department and who is himself in sympathy with the movement now under contemplation. Avra Warren[51] in charge of the Visa Section is very well versed in it, and he is preparing the letter directed to the President after the conference outlining the situation and proposing to him possible remedies. It is a matter to which I have given considerable attention for three or four months, but very little of it comes under my official jurisdiction. I consider it very important, and apparently now the President does, and probably something will happen in the way of coordination, because Navy, Justice, Post Office and Labor can cooperate with the Department very effectively, and also Treasury with their Coast Guard and their Customs staff, and the Post Office through their Intelligence Service. To my mind it is certain that if we have any trouble with Germany every Russian agent will become a German agent, and it is now time to begin the steps to offset the effects of our laxity. . . .

May 10, 1940

Last night I dined at a large dinner given by the Assistant Secretary of the Treasury and Mrs. Basil Harris. The Belgian Ambassador was there.[52] In the middle of dinner he was called to the telephone. When he returned he said quietly that General Watson had spoken to him for the President to advise him that the Belgian Cabinet was in night session and that they were expecting an attack by Germany. The Ambassador was not particularly perturbed and did not take it too seriously. He said to me that German troop movements and changes of troops in Westwall positions necessitated their movements along the frontier of Belgium and that there had been many such movements each of which had been interpreted as plans to attack Belgium. I had never thought they were going to attack Belgium and Holland because of the military danger involved by the exposure of their flank.

The dinner was late, and I left about half past eleven or quarter to twelve.

[50] James H. Houghteling, U.S. Commissioner of Immigration and Naturalization, 1937–1940.
[51] Foreign service officer, chief of the Department of State Visa Division, 1938–1941.
[52] Count Robert van der Straten-Ponthoz.

Fortunately I was planning to stay in town for the night, having dined in town the night before also and expecting to have to be in town this evening as well and thinking of breaking the inconvenience of having to return to the country late each night and arriving back in Washington early each morning.

Having had the conversation with the Belgian Ambassador at dinner, on my return to the hotel I called the Department of State and was informed the Secretary was in his office. I spoke to him on the telephone. He said he did not know that I could help but that several officers were there with him and he would be very glad to have me if I felt it would not be inconvenient. I immediately drove to the Department, and he told me that he had talked with Cudahy[53] in Brussels about eleven o'clock and that Cudahy had told him that there was much air activity and the German troops were being landed from parachutes and the air fields were being bombed. He also understood that an offensive was on against Luxembourg. He was to call again within an hour.

From then until 5:30 in the morning we sat in the Secretary's office. Hull, Welles, Berle, Dunn, Moffat and McDermott,[54] beside myself. Welles arrived late, having been asleep and not realizing developments until the Secretary telephoned him about half past one. The Secretary left about half past two, after having had a number of conversations with our representatives in Brussels, London and Paris. It was difficult to get messages through. After the fact became plainly demonstrated that Germany had invaded the three countries and that Holland had declared war against Germany and that Belgium had called for military assistance from England and France and had been granted it, the Secretary went home to get some sleep and Welles continued. Dunn and I stayed with Welles. I left at 5:30 in broad daylight in my evening clothes.

During the course of the evening through conversations, arriving cables and press despatches, which were remarkably efficient, and radio broadcasts the fact of invasion was unfolded. Electric mines have been laid at the outlet of all Dutch harbors; German troops have been landed from ships; all the air fields in the three territories have been bombed; and the general military activity followed the opening of the air attack which occurred at 5:15 a.m. Brussels time. The Government of Luxembourg had fled, leaving only the Foreign Minister. The Crown Princess of Holland was supposed to have left to accept a refuge in the United States with her German-born husband as the guests of the President, and the children of the King of Belgium were expected to be got out of Belgium in order to fulfill their previously made engagement for refuge in the United States also as guests of the President.

[53] John Cudahy replaced Joseph Davies as ambassador to Belgium during January 1940.
[54] Michael McDermott, foreign service officer, chief of the State Department Division of Current Information, 1927–1953.

Hull talked to the President half a dozen times, until the President finally decided to go to bed about two o'clock. Up to that time he had talked to Morgenthau and had directed the blocking of all Dutch and Belgian funds in the United States and Morgenthau had talked to Hull on the subject and after advice had issued an order to the Federal Reserve Bank to take the necessary steps before the opening of the banks and the market this morning, their acts to be subsequently confirmed or the orders countermanded, depending on the developments. It was later decided that the order would not be countermanded.

Cudahy said a bomb had dropped in the immediate vicinity of the American Embassy and destroyed one of the houses next to it and that on his way to the Foreign Office he had seen several other houses demolished by bombs. There was also loss of life, but he did not know the details. The explosion was so close to the Embassy that some of the windows were shattered.

At Amsterdam all was reported quiet, but from there it was reported there was heavy fighting at Rotterdam. Brussels reported fighting on the outskirts of the town between German parachute troops and Belgian army units. At the Hague Gordon reported over the telephone that he could hardly hear Welles' voice because of the noise of machine guns in his immediate vicinity.
. . .

During the first part of this period Kennedy reported that he knew nothing and his contacts in England had reported nothing. Apparently England was oblivious to the development. He immediately busied himself and talked to Paris, Brussels and the Hague. We had been unable to reach Paris prior to that time and had on our second attempt failed to reach Brussels or the Hague. However, shortly after he reported to us his conversation with them each of them received connections with us and each of them reported.

All the Americans are reported safe in the Hague district and in the Rotterdam district. In the Hague all were accounted for but one family, then in the outskirts of the city, after whom the Military Attaché had been dispatched to bring them to safety. Brussels had no detailed report about Americans. However, most of the Americans have left both Holland and Belgium, only about 400 remaining, and most of them in Holland being Dutch-Americans. Kirk had left Berlin and was en route to the United States on leave (under orders). When he learned of the development he returned and arrived back in Berlin before noon today. . . .

The Blitzkrieg has started. . . . After an emotional and highly interesting night I got to bed towards six o'clock and got two hours' sleep.

On returning to the Department I found the Secretary already here. The President had him, Welles, the Attorney General and the heads of the Military and Naval establishments in conference at the White House for drafting [and] promulgating another Neutrality Proclamation which must cover Holland and which may have to include Belgium. We do not want to include them, but the declaration of war by Holland makes it necessary under the terms of the Neutrality Act. Belgium has not declared war, but it is going to be very difficult to differentiate between Belgium and Holland even on those technical grounds. We thought last night it *could* be done and that the American public would probably understand and appreciate the distinction because of the American affection and admiration for Belgium. It seems just too bad that this young King will have to suffer like his father did.[55] . . .

[Later in the morning] Cordell called me in and went over several things and then took the opportunity that was afforded by the absence of other ranking officers from the Department to revert to the political aspect which has recently invested his prospects for the Presidency with real importance. It has developed to the point where he now recognizes that there is a practical unanimity of unofficial agreement upon him as the person to be nominated in case Roosevelt is not. . . . Cordell then referred to the so-called *American White Book*. He said that from the very inception of his incumbency in office he had been saddled first with one and then with another person who tried to give the impression that he was an insignificant figure and that all the important phases of the Department were attended to by the persons who were foisted upon him. Foisted is hardly the proper word. It is not at the design of the President that this situation exists, but it results from the fact that persons are appointed who have certain ideas of their own and who maintain close contacts with the entourage of the President and who have access to the President themselves. Cordell referred to the *Book* as an unintentional portrayal of him in the light of a simple country boy with a certain limited amount of common sense but who needed guidance and who was quite incapable of taking action on his own account or making decisions on official matters. There is no doubt but that he resents it, but he said that he had seen before the development—referring specifically to [Raymond] Moley—and that he found when they were given plenty of opportunity that they finally got themselves into difficulty. He had no objection to efficiency or to help and counsel and advice, which he was always glad to have, but he had no knowledge of the intended publication of the *White Book* and resented the fact that it had been published. He said Berle had referred to it one day in an offhand way just as McDermott would refer to an ordinary press release which might not have concerned any particular policy and would have been routine in character. . . .

In the midst of all the bad news last night when everyone's nerves were somewhat upset I related for the purpose of relieving the tension the situation which had just developed in our own service. The scene was at the American Consulate at Bahia in Brazil. It seems that the Vice Consul had been gambling and had lost more than he could afford. He borrowed some money from a

[55] Reference here is to Leopold III, king of Belgium, 1934–1951. His father Albert I, 1909–1934, was king during World War I and led the Belgian army in a disastrous retreat from the Germans, August–October 1914.

person resident in Washington. When pressed for payment he gave a check which was worthless. It then came to the attention of the Department, the matter being referred to his superior, the Consul. That officer said he would assume responsibility and lend the junior officer enough money to square his obligations. The sum needed was $250. He went to the bank and withdrew the $250 and placed it in the safe at the Consulate. Then he promptly went off for the week-end. On his return he found the safe had been opened and $250 had been taken. When confronted with the accusation the Vice Consul admitted the theft and immediately proceeded to jump in the river and attempt suicide. Some one thoughtlessly rescued him. In the midst of that excitement it was discovered by the Consul that during his absence from the city over the week-end an English resident of the community had attempted to rape his wife. The Consul resented the acts and telegraphed the Department requesting that he be immediately transferred and said that he would not be responsible for his actions if he should meet the gentleman in question. Before that was disposed of it developed that a Brazilian resident of the community had filed suit for divorce against his wife naming the Consul as the guilty party and immediately there appeared in the picture another Englishman who claimed that the Consul had been unduly attentive to his wife, and he made threats that if he should meet the Consul he would dispose of him instantly.

The drama unfolded to that point and we decided to telegraph the Consul General in Rio to fly to Bahia and to make an investigation and appropriate recommendations. The story seemed to relieve the tension somewhat and divert the thoughts of some of those present, including the Secretary, and I suggested that when the file is complete that the papers all be sent to me and I would bundle them up and send them to Hollywood where it would form the basis for a most interesting melodrama.

Chamberlain has resigned. Churchill is slated to succeed him. Herriot[56] has been asked to form a Cabinet to succeed Reynaud.

May 13, 1940

. . . Hull thinks now the President has decided to accept the nomination himself. He has been talking with Jackson, and Jackson told him that the President had so decided. Jackson spent yesterday on the boat with the President. . . . The Secretary today reverted again to the *White Book*. He is very resentful that it should have been written and is severely critical of Berle for his participation even though he had apparently some encouragement from across the street amongst the entourage of the President. The Secretary feels that if the high officers of the Department do not treat in confidence the confidential matters in the Department it can hardly be expected that those lower down in the scale will not have a very bad example set to them.

[56] Édouard Herriot, president of the French Chamber of Deputies, 1936–1940, and former premier, 1924–1925, 1932.

May 14, 1940

A telegram from Phillips reporting a conversation he had with Ciano indicates Italy's immediate entrance into the war. He was told that Mussolini had made up his mind that the progress of the campaign in Belgium and Holland was so indicative of German military superiority as to be convincing and referring to the war-like manifestations throughout Italy and antagonism to the Allies he said he did not know when Italy would do it and that there was still a chance she would not but that there was about one chance in ten that she would not.

Had a conference with the Secretary. Present Davies, Moffat, Dunn, Hackworth and myself. We decided to tell Phillips, who had already warned Americans quietly, to do it effectively; that they should leave Italy while the opportunity existed for travel on the Mediterranean. If the war spreads to the Mediterranean we will be unable to repatriate them except from Atlantic coast ports of Spain and Portugal. We discussed the possibility of sending a ship to Bordeaux. Paris was to be notified not to send any more people to embark from Italy and to send them to southwestern France to await transportation facilities which we would arrange. After the war breaks, persons in Switzerland or in Italy will have to be evacuated through Istanbul and by rail down to below Suez and brought around Africa. I am to arrange matters with the Maritime Commission, but they are not to act on the presumption that Italy is at war. We cannot make that assumption until it happens, but we can plan with the event in view. There are nineteen American ships in the Mediterranean, one in the Black Sea, two in the Red Sea bound toward the Mediterranean, one at a Spanish-Italian port, and eight on the Atlantic en route to the Mediterranean. . . .

May 17, 1940

Yesterday was a rather hectic day. The early despatches indicated that things were going rather badly for the Allies. I went in to talk to Cordell about the general situation, and just as I arrived Sumner [Welles] came in, and just as Sumner came in Kennedy called him on the telephone and said the situation was very bad in England; that airplanes had all stopped; ferries had stopped; the French were withholding visas from Americans passing through France; and there was no way which Americans in England could get out. In a cable he had recommended ships to a west coast English port but was ready now to recommend that they proceed to Ireland and that we send a ship to the Irish west coast. Sumner told him we would let him know, and we then discussed it. The Secretary did not want to assume responsibility for giving Americans permission to travel on belligerent ships through that area unless it was urgently necessary. He thought the responsibility was too great. That had been Kennedy's former recommendation. They asked me to contact the Navy and see what the mine situation was along the English west coast. I talked to the Hydrographic Office, and Captain Bryan said that as far as they knew it was safe; that there were no reports of mines, but that that did not mean there were no mines. He thought it was as safe as any place over there under the circumstances existing now. I drafted a cable to Kennedy authorizing him to evacuate the citizens to Ireland and wait in that country and we would consider the possibilities of sending a ship. We then telegraphed to Dublin what we had done and told Dublin to look out for them and to advise us how many and where they were.

. . . Shortly thereafter came in a telegram from Bullitt saying that Reynaud had told him that they had no assurance they could hold Paris and advising him to burn his confidential documents and that the British Ambassador had asked him to assume British interests in France. He said he was then burning his codes, cipher texts and confidential papers. This looked pretty bad. What the situation actually is regarding Bullitt nobody knows, but it seems as if he had sort of lost his head. Paris has been declared under military law, but the Germans cannot be closer than Rheims, and most of the fighting is up along the Belgian border and in Belgium. The Germans do seem to be making headway up there, but the British are putting up a pretty tough resistance. What Bullitt is going to do without codes and how he is going to communicate with us or we with him I do not know.

The President made a bully speech for preparedness in the air and asked for 50,000 planes and a capacity of 50,000 planes a year. The Congress received it uproariously and will vote everything he asked. It means nearly nine hundred million dollars of appropriations and one hundred and eighty million dollars in contract authority and all for military, naval and air defense. . . .

Yesterday was my birthday, and I hardly had a minute to realize it. I was 59 years old and didn't remember it until late in the day.

The Germans continue to sweep through France. They have occupied Brussels, and they are on the outskirts of Antwerp. In the west they proceeded north of the Marne in a big wedge almost to Amiens and up through Laon and St. Quentin. They have demolished all lines of communication and all traffic points. A report from one of our officers who accompanied the wives and children of our Foreign Service officers out of Belgium stated that every railroad station on the route had been bombed; in various places the tracks had been demolished and that great difficulty was encountered. The train suffered bombing in the near vicinity, and altogether demoralization of communications existed all the way to Paris. Unless the Allies pull themselves together there would appear to be serious danger of a capture of the British forces with their backs on the Channel as well as of Paris farther south.

In the Department we have been busy in trying to evacuate Americans. Our big ships sailing in the Mediterranean are booked up with foreigners proceeding to the United States in such quantities that they have practically absorbed all available passages so that our own citizens are going to have great difficulty getting aboard. We had a long conference with the Maritime Commission's legal advisors in an effort to discover some authority in the Secretary under the Neutrality Law to cancel the passages, but we were unable to discover such authority. The *Manhattan* sails from New York tomorrow for Genoa, and on her return trip she is sold out to refugees. I may look for some opportunity to divert her to Lisbon so that she can load Americans from the Bordeaux area and let the rest of them take their chances on another boat.

We are also proceeding with protective measures for our national defense. I had passed by Welles and the Secretary a proposed bill for the Congress for the registration of all aliens now in the country and all aliens in the future arriving and requiring them to report and authorizing their deportation if illegally entered or illegally over-staying. Justice will have supervision of the cards; the Post Office Department will do the registration; and Treasury will help the State Department in its activities at the ports, and we will tighten up on our visas from abroad and require additional information with authority to grant visas centered in Washington instead of designated to our Consuls. There are many thousands of aliens, some of them known to be active German agents, and many of them illegally in this country. We have to be very careful in keeping within the provisions of the Constitution, but it is a necessary requirement that we have authority to handle any "fourth army" or "fifth army" there may be in the United States. And the way this thing is going abroad it is possible, but highly improbable, that Germany might acquire both the French and the British fleets. . . .

May 18, 1940

The news early this morning continued to be bad. Antwerp is in the hands of the Germans and the British are in a more perilous position. Mussolini answered the President's plea to the effect that he would be going into the war. I still doubt it and consider that Mussolini is fulfilling his more useful service to Germany by keeping out of the war by maintaining a threatening position. He immobilizes about thirty French divisions on the French-Italian front. He has the British fleet in the Mediterranean, and as long as the Balkans are out of the war it is not necessary for Germany to engage in any activities there, as she would have to engage if Italy should get into it. In spite of Mussolini's answer I think it is unnecessary for him to get into the war now the way it is going. However, if Germany should not succeed in reaching Paris or in cutting up the British army in the north, then Mussolini's participation might be looked for, because that would give France and England more to do and would relieve the opposition to Germany. . . .

May 20, 1940

This has been another rather hectic day in the Department. It is now seven o'clock and I have been here since nine except for a long absence at luncheon at the Press Club to which I was invited as a guest. The Belgian Ambassador [Van der Straten-Ponthoz] and Dutch Minister[57] spoke for nearly an hour. Neither of them were impassioned. Each was realistic and each apparently on the defensive, for they spent most of their time explaining why certain German accusations of their respective countries were not true. The length of the luncheon taught me one lesson, and that is that I cannot spend the time at luncheons from now on. . . .

I had to interrupt my duties in the Department to go out to a meeting of the Merchant Library Association at the request of Betty Land to present to Mrs. Howard, the President of the Association, a book which the President had autographed and was presenting to them. It was a copy of his own book. This consumed about forty-five minutes. On my return Sumner sent for me and told me about the unfortunate occurrence in London which involved one of our code clerks in work of espionage and his arrest by the British authorities. It may mean that our own communication system is no longer secret. It is a very serious matter and we are considering now what steps to take, which would involve inspections in our Embassies in at least the four European capitals. Ways and means will be found tomorrow to do it. . . .

May 21, 1940

. . . Lindberg [*sic*] talked on the radio the other night, and it was sort of a pacifist talk. Lindberg's father was a pacifist and voted against the war in 1917 as a member of the Congress.[58] I did not hear Lindberg because I was on the air at exactly the same time. If he would stick to flying he would be the world's best, but when he gets out of his particular field and into a larger one he shows his lack of knowledge of subjects. . . .

I am enormously concerned today about the situation developed in London and about the further fact that Bullitt when he burned his own codes burned some secret devices which were intended for communication and directed to three or four other of our Missions in southern and southeastern Europe and Ankara. I am now considering the possibility of sending a courier on the first Clipper to Portugal and having one of the naval ships there go to Ireland with the devices to get it to London to supplant the one which is now gone and to have another naval ship take the others to Rome for transmission to points east to replace the ones Bullitt destroyed. Bullitt must have had a real holiday when he started that fire. . . .

[57] Dr. Alexander Louden, the Netherlands minister to the U.S., 1938–1947.

[58] During 1940 and 1941, Charles A. Lindbergh, Jr., made many speeches urging the United States to remain neutral in the European war. Charles A. Lindbergh, Sr., Republican, served as U.S. Representative from Minnesota, 1907–1917.

May 22, 1940

... We have some further ramifications in connection with the member of the staff in London. It now seems that he had photographic copies of some of the confidential messages. Amongst them were the texts of the messages sent by the President to Churchill and Churchill's response back in January and February—while Churchill was First Lord—and which concerned the passage of American ships without being taken into danger zones. These photographs were on plates. He says he got the plates with the camera of a similar employee who has now been transferred to Madrid. So we had to send a secret telegram to Madrid for two purposes, first to check up on the man in Madrid and second to get information to corroborate or deny the story of the man in London, who is now in the hands of the British police and whose immunity we have waived. We have told the British that they could prosecute him under British law. It is one of those distressing accidents. He comes from an old Virginia family, was recommended by Harry Byrd,[59] had been in the Service for some time, was stationed in Moscow and apparently there came under the lure of some monetary consideration and made a connection which when he was transferred to London (which was done on the recommendation of Steinhart [*sic*])[60] he found profitable to continue. He had not a very good reputation for efficiency and was once denied admission to the Diplomatic Career Service. This may have made him mad. The man in Spain was transferred from London to Madrid recently, and he had been reduced as to his salary because of inefficiency and a bad rating.

I have come to the conclusion that it is necessary for us to establish a career service for clerks and pay them higher salaries and to protect particularly the code clerks. This one incident involves our whole system of communications, and it just shows how dependent the Government is upon a comparatively few confidential key positions. For instance, we could not telegraph the Embassy in Madrid on this subject without the expectation that the very man who was the subject of the telegram would himself decode the message. And he might have answered it without the knowledge of the Chargé d'Affaires. So we sent a "pilot message" to the Embassy telling him that the other message was coming and that he was to decode the long message himself and to answer himself and to encipher it himself. However, it has conclusively demonstrated to my mind the necessity for a trustworthy, well paid corps of clerks to handle communications and to deal with the codes. It seems that it can be done within the law as it now exists and steps are already under way to set up such a plan for consideration and with the idea of very shortly establishing such a service—just as quickly as may be commensurate with safety.

[59] Democrat, U.S. Senator from Virginia since 1933.
[60] Laurence A. Steinhardt, U.S. Ambassador to the Soviet Union, 1939–1941.

May 28, 1940

Today starts rather hectically. The King of Belgium surrendered with his army. The conditions under which he surrendered are not known, but he has been severely criticized by the remnant of his Government sitting safely in France. The War Department thinks, and so reported to the Secretary this morning while I was there, that he was suffering from a case of "nerves" coming into play because of the terrible situation in which he found himself with machine gunning and bombing of remnants of his population which is huddled near his army in the small section of his country. His surrender takes about 300,000 soldiers. The War Department estimates there are only about 300,000 in the British army remaining in the entrenched area. They are based on the Channel and have two possible ports from which they may be evacuated. The War Department doubts they will be able to maintain their position and to hold their lines. . . .

I am still of the opinion Italy will not enter the war for four reasons I have continued to hold and all based on the thought that she is at present, as she has been all along, fulfilling her function. First, she is holding immobilized thirty divisions of the French Army on her border. Second, she is holding immobilized a large part of the British fleet in the Mediterranean. Third, she has the Balkans at bay, as they would not be otherwise, so that Germany does not have a war at her back door or another front to defend. And fourth, she is not requiring from Germany, as she would in case she were a belligerent, personnel and materiel.

However, Italy is now under the domination of Hitler and is in a position where Mussolini must take orders from him. If the French army stiffens in northern France, it is probable that Hitler will demand that he proceed. However, if the war in northern France proceeds as Hitler desires, there will be no necessity for Italy to come in. Mussolini must also be fearful that in case he does not obey the orders of Hitler from now on the same fate will overtake him which has been experienced by the countries which have been over-run.

The stock market has broken all to pieces here. As I related in my speech to the Business Advisory Council a few nights ago, if Germany wins this war and subordinates Europe, every commercial order will be routed to Berlin and filled under its orders somewhere in Europe rather than in the United States. Furthermore, our manufacturers and producers of agricultural goods will have to compete against slave labor of Europe in the world market. That will mean falling prices and declining profits here and a lowering of our standard of living with the consequent social and political disturbances. . . .

[Long was summoned to the White House to discuss evacuation of Americans from Europe. The President reaffirmed his intention to protect American citizens "whatever that might mean and wherever they might be." He left the matter entirely to Long who was] "authorized to do whatever was necessary in the way of sending ships and asking the war ships to move around and to do whatever might be necessary to gather the people and get them home." . . .

May 30, 1940

Had a deep sleep laṡt night—from 9:30 p.m. to 9:30 a.m. Feel entirely refreshed. Drove myself to Department, met with Secretary in informal conference at 10:45 till 12:45. Discussed question of Italian entry. Ciano told Sir Percy Loraine[61]—in keeping with a promise to notify him ahead of time— that Italy would enter war in a very few days. I still think it may be part of the bluff and Italy's part in fulfilling her function as an ally to keep the opponents fearful and guessing and immobilized. She is not internally prepared for immediate action though her fleet is ready and her air force well placed and ready.

Also discussed the economic consequences of a possible British collapse— American securities owned in England, the gold supply, and related questions. What would happen to them? Would Germany obtain ownership of those items and of the merchant fleets of England, Holland, Denmark, Norway? But particularly as to securities of American companies and gold—we should promptly make plans and be ready, with power in the Executive, to act before a collapse and to offset the value of such securities against the English debt to the United States and obtain title to those securities by cancellation of present ownership and resale to American interests of the properties in question—as well as Bermuda, Bahamas and all other foreign-owned territory in America. This to apply also to France and French possessions and French debt to the United States.

This is Decoration Day but not much holiday. The President is holding the first meeting of the Council of National Defense he appointed the other day.

Welles advises he and Jackson did not have a full coverage of the immigration question with the President but enough of an understanding for Jackson to proceed immediately to draft the necessary legislation and clear it directly with the President. Jackson will proceed along the line of our understanding.

It is quiet in the Department today. No clerks, no typewriting, very few telephones. One can think easier. Cordell, Welles, Feis, Moffat (now Minister to Canada [May, 1940–January, 1943] and about to proceed to his post and a *good* selection), Hackworth, Dunn, Berle before lunch, and a few others.

May 31, 1940

Bad attack of intestinal influenza last night. Very weak this morning. Went to town on time. Conference with Welles and geographic division chiefs on Continental and Hemisphere defense plans—potentials. Received Portuguese

[61] British ambassador to Italy.

Minister[62]—re: naval ships to Lisbon—O.K. with his Government—and why do they go? Any sign of trouble in immediate neighborhood soon? Answered "no." Said German Minister at Lisbon had propounded various questions to Portuguese Government about United States Naval units— Occupation of Azores? Coaling station at Lisbon? Etc. About noon felt so sick I went to our apartment at hotel and called doctor.

June 4, 1940

Still engaged in preparation of papers, consultations with Justice and Labor and arranging final draft executive orders and telegrams to restrict the granting of visas and to stop up the holes of unauthorized immigrants into the United States. Provided the President signs the Executive Order we will dispatch a long telegram which will tighten up our Consular examinations of persons requesting visas all along the line, institute border controls along Canadian and Mexican borders and tighten up the restrictions as regards Puerto Rico, Cuba and the Caribbean countries and will cause to be referred to Washington for approval any application of a journalist of any category, lecturer, propagandists and any persons suspected or possibly engaged in propaganda of any kind and from anywhere.

Also devoted considerable time to discussions individually with Welles, Hull and General Sherman Miles, the new head of the Military Intelligence concerning an inspection which we now feel we have to make of the personnel in our Foreign Service. The arrest of [Tyler] Kent in London and the disclosure of his activities in our Embassy, coupled with known leaks of information which we have been unable to account for but which concerned our correspondence with London and which had appeared at Copenhagen, Berlin and Bucharest—all have made it apparent that he may have accomplices and confederates or that there may be other cells of an aggressive diplomacy of another Government representing their interests in our own offices abroad. I tried to find a way to do the work within the Service, but that seems impractical. Consequently and regretfully I have come to the conclusion that we will have to get people from the outside and send them abroad in capacities which will permit them to have very close and rather intimate contacts with the personnel of our various offices. After discussing it with Welles and getting his approval and later obtaining the Secretary's consent to the general plan, I have adopted the procedure of appointing persons to serve as couriers. Their activities will give them a legitimate reason to be within the premises, and we can arrange for them a sort of leisure time at each end of their run. Funds will be transferred out of the Emergency Fund into the regular funds so they can be paid out of the regular funds and no suspicion will attach on that account. They will be men specifically chosen, and General Miles will help

[62] Dr. João Antonio de Bianchi, Portuguese minister to the U.S.

select a half dozen men whom he can thoroughly recommend. One to go each to London, Paris, Rome, Berlin and Moscow and will stay in and travel out of those places and cover the whole European field.

June 5, 1940

A long and final conference with the Secretary, Welles and Avra Warren approving the final drafts of the alien control activities. This does everything the Department can do without additional legislation and additional legislation pending before the Congress will take care of aliens within the United States. Our present efforts are to stop the entry of any undesirables. The Secretary asked me to present the matter to the President for his signature of the two Executive Orders.

The second phase of the war in France started this morning early. The German drive from the Channel to the Aisne[63] commenced with a movement which looks as if it might develop into an attempt to encircle Paris. Within the next twenty-four or forty-eight hours they ought to have a pretty good idea of how it will develop. . . .

June 6, 1940

Talked with J. Edgar Hoover of the F.B.I. about the personnel for the work I had been discussing with General Miles. Miles thought he could not guarantee service. Hoover is sure he can and will cooperate fully. The Germans seem to have broken through, and it may be the portent of a large opening.

June 7, 1940

Alexander Kirk came in this morning. He arrived yesterday afternoon by Clipper. He looks thin but well. He is very pessimistic about the Allied cause and very positive in the opinion that the United States should do everything in its power in connection with the Allies. He says nothing on earth will stop Hitler in the prosecution of his intentions in the United States in case he is successful in Europe and that the fight there now is unqualifiedly a fight for the things which America means and believes and lives by. He thinks we should send every bit of military help we can. Granted that we have no army and that the navy is not needed, he thinks every possible help by air should be rendered the Allies. He fears that it will be over suddenly on the continent of Europe. There is only one hope and that is to drag it out and prevent the sudden termination of the war in favor of Germany so that a process of attrition will eventually cause Germany to fail. However, in that event the process of political and social degeneration would set in in Europe and Stalin, in his opinion, would be the ultimate victor. That would have a retroactive effect

[63] A river in northeastern France.

here as well, except that it would be infinitely better than to have Hitler rampant on a prostrate Europe and ready to make trouble in Latin America and oppose the United States. He says they are arrogant, drunk with power, intense in their hatreds, determined to achieve their objectives and in control of an inconceivably strong machine. He was quite voluble on the subject and most intense and with every indication of thorough conviction.

He thinks the President should make a peace offer without consulting with anybody and to make it to all belligerents. If it offers the basis of a reasonable settlement and gives Germany a reasonable place in the scheme of Europe and in the world it might have a chance of being accepted. If it is not accepted, it would be Germany which would decline. If Germany accepted, the Allies could be brought to accept. If the Germans declined, the onus would be on them, and the United States should then, on the basis of an America united behind an effort to bring peace in the world and which had failed, should take a stand to help the Allies in every conceivable and possible way in order to postpone the sudden victory of Germany and the almost immediate consequences which would appear here.

His forecast of the future agrees entirely with my own thought and is very much along the line of my speech a week or so ago before the Business Advisory Council. However, I do not see that we are able to send any material help and the little we could send would be of no real material assistance. I doubt whether sending it or not would make any difference as regards the relations of Germany toward the United States in case she is victorious in Europe.

Kirk is going off with the President tomorrow afternoon on his boat and will have a full opportunity to discuss the matter with him. I told him that a year ago I was near being his Ambassador. He deplores the fact that there was none sent and that there is none now but is convinced that we cannot now send one.

He is very anxious to return as quickly as possible. . . .

Bullitt telegraphed urgently wanting to put a model French airplane aboard the *Washington* together with assembly plans. He said the Captain had orders not to accept it aboard but that unless ordered to the contrary he would put it on as mail. I reached the Secretary and discussed it over the telephone, and he agreed with me that it should not be accepted; that to do so would endanger the lives of American citizens because we would be unable in honesty to make the representations to belligerent Governments that the ship carried only American passengers and that it would be necessary to notify those Governments again because the ship was to proceed from Lisbon again into the danger zone to Galway, Ireland, and thence to New York. The model is a plane which the French want built in this country for military use. Bullitt said it was on the dock waiting to be loaded. Of course the secret agents of

Germany know it is there, and would know it was aboard the ship, but even if they did not know it it would be a violation of representations we must make to those Governments. Consequently I telegraphed Bullitt urgently that under no conditions was the thing to be placed aboard the ship.

June 8, 1940

Cudahy has arrived from Brussels in Berlin and wants to come home under the theory that there is no work for him to do there. Welles, Moffat and I discussed the matter this morning and decided he should return to his post and stay there and try and perform the function that Brand Whitlock did in 1914–17, take care of American interests and do what he can to lend American aid to the people there. We felt it would be a psychological disadvantage, considering American activities in the last war under Brand Whitlock, to desert Brussels under the present conditions and certainly it was too soon to come to that conclusion.

Berle and Hoover's No. 1 man came in, and we straightened out the conflict of jurisdiction between Berle's office and mine in regard to Secret Service activities. The one person whom I am having investigated because of his known misstatements and his membership in the Communist Party was also being investigated by two other agencies, one of them the F.B.I. This developed when my man made the contact and discovered other people already on the job. Hereafter all investigation work concerning any personnel in the Department of State or concerning any personnel abroad is to be exclusively within my jurisdiction, and the F.B.I. and other agencies will not act unless or until I ask their cooperation. No other arrangement could possibly work, because there would necessarily be conflicts and crossed wires.

June 12, 1940

[Italy declared war on France and Great Britain on June 10 and Italian forces penetrated southern France.] The French army is still falling back. The Germans are reported twelve miles from Paris, and Bullitt has wired which begins "As this may be my last communication to you." It looks as if Paris were about to go. If Paris goes there is very little behind that line to keep the French going. Their munitions plants and industrial areas are gone, and the big communications center at Lyons will probably be disorganized. . . .

We have gone as far as we probably can to be of assistance to the Allies by releasing a lot of airplanes which are not of the latest model but at a considerable quantity by returning them to the manufacturers for credit and the manufacturers to sell them immediately to the Allies and to be flown by the Allies across the North Atlantic. The trouble is that if we should give them about a thousand airplanes it would only be about a week's supply.

I am arranging to have five extra couriers in Europe to do very confidential inspection work and to have four or five more. The first five are being furnished by the F.B.I. and particularly chosen. The other five are to be selected by the Navy from the Marine Corps and will be placed on the Clipper and upon vessels of British registry proceeding to England. Two on the Clipper run and three on the ship run, so that pouches can go each week.

Early Tuesday morning [June 11] we had a special conclave in the Secretary's office to discuss the proscribed area following Italy's entry into the war. A line was drawn from Portugal to a point on the African coast below Casablanca, and the Red Sea was blocked off to the east and south of Aden so that no American ships can go into the Mediterranean or the approach to the Mediterranean from the south. There are 18 or 20 vessels already in the Mediterranean who may come out after completing the voyages upon which they now find themselves. We also blocked off the entrance to the Bosporus, leaving the Black Sea free and open for the passage of American citizens from Bulgaria or Rumania across to ports from which Basra would be accessible so that they might proceed through the Indian Ocean to the United States. . . . I had rather a hectic day yesterday and took friends out to dinner, to be joined later by Kirk and Bill McAdoo[64] and Doris. I was so tired after dinner that they all thought I ought to go right away. I certainly was exhausted.

June 13, 1940

Lunched with Anne O'Hare McCormick[65] and listened to her views, which are rather blue. I told her, and subsequently told the Secretary, a matter which has been disturbing my mind for some days, ever since the President used the phrase of the "hand that holds the dagger" in his Charlottesville speech. Incidentally the phrase first read "Brutus' attack on Caesar"—or words to that effect. It was cut out and the copy prepared without it, and this other phrase was interjected over the air.[66] In my opinion we have gone a little farther than we should go—not only in attacking the heads of other Governments but in making gestures to the Allies. If we are not very careful we are going to find ourselves the champions of a defeated cause. Today Paris is occupied by the Germans, the French army disorganized and in retreat, and millions of refugees along the roads of southern France in various states of

[64] William G. McAdoo, Democrat, U.S. Senator from California, 1933–1938, and former Secretary of the Treasury, 1913–1918.

[65] Writer and member of the editorial board of the *New York Times.*

[66] On June 10, 1940, in an address delivered at the University of Virginia, President Roosevelt severely criticized the Italian government for invading France. "In so doing it has manifested disregard for the rights and security of other nations, disregard for the lives of the peoples of those nations which are directly threatened by the spread of the war. . . . On this the tenth day of June, 1940, the hand that held the dagger has struck it into the back of its neighbor." (*The Public Papers and Addresses of Franklin D. Roosevelt,* compiled by Samuel I. Rosennam, [New York: Macmillan, 1940] pp. 259–264.)

despair and destitution. France has utterly collapsed. It may not be but a few weeks before England collapses and Hitler stands rampant across the continent of Europe. The United States must not put herself in a position of antagonizing that military power until it is ready to meet it. It will take us two years to be ready to meet it. To oppose it today is not only rash, but it seems to be oblivious to the fact that it only takes one power to make a war. We may have war thrust upon us if we antagonize the military machine which is about to assume control of the whole continent of Europe.

But further than that, there are implications of a political nature which are pregnant with infinite possibilities. The Democratic Convention is scheduled to meet in just about a month—July 15—and this is June 13. Suppose England collapses within thirty days and Roosevelt appears as a candidate for renomination before the Convention as an individual who has antagonized the only two powers in Europe and as the champion of the lost cause. It is quite possible that there might be serious opposition to his nomination. If he should be nominated, as he probably would anyhow, there would probably be raised by the Republicans the cry that we had tried to put the country into the war; that we had jeopardized the neutrality of the United States by supplying arms and ammunition to the losing belligerents; and that we had by personal invective antagonized the two powers to be supreme on the continent of Europe. It is quite conceivable that the country would rally to the Republican cause. It is certain that all the German elements, the Italian elements, and many of the foreign elements, and every subversive agent and every Russian activist and all the Communists, and all the Socialists, and most assuredly all the Republicans, and there are a lot of them, would be aligned against us, and we would probably be defeated in November.

Of course I look upon Bill Bullitt and Harry Hopkins[67] as the closest to the throne. Kirk has now walked into the picture with an offer of peace and then a declaration of war, and that has thrown additional fuel on the same fire. What reason have we to offer peace? And with what grace can we approach the men we have just denounced—leaders of victorious armies who have saved expression of their opposition to the United States until they have finished the job they are now bent upon, but either one of them could force the United States into war.

It would be a calamity if Roosevelt were defeated for the third term after he had been nominated, and it would do untold harm to the democratic institutions and to the political set-up of the United States if he were defeated, because he would be succeeded by those who necessarily would be in favor of playing gently in front of and acceding to the demands of the successful military powers in Europe. In our unprepared state there would be nothing else to do, because a change of Administration would bring an enormous

[67] Secretary of Commerce, 1938–1940, and adviser to President Roosevelt.

change in the organization and production of the country in its preparations to meet a possible military emergency, and it would be a calamity for the country.

I subsequently talked to Cordell Hull on the same basis, and he is in thorough accord and wanted me to talk to the President. I told him I couldn't talk to the President unless I was asked to do so or unless he, Cordell, would ask the President to talk to me. He said that he couldn't do that, because the President never discussed political questions with him. So I have determined to talk to the President's advisors, and I am starting with Leon Henderson, and I am going to his Annapolis home to have dinner with him tonight and see if I can't put a little understanding of practical politics in the minds of some gentlemen who are trying to run the American Government but who have had no political training.

June 14, 1940

Last night I went home with Leon Henderson to his summer place near Annapolis and talked to him on the way over along the line of my conversation with Cordell. He was not intimately acquainted with politics or political issues but apparently understood.

This morning I had an opportunity to talk with Berle. From his conversation I understand that he was talking with the Secretary last night and that the Secretary discussed with him and whoever else was present the subject matter of my conversation with the Secretary before that. Apparently he did not indicate that he had talked to me.

They both seemed to understand the political significance and both of them agreed with me that we should tend to our knitting and keep our mouths shut—that we ought to do everything we can to get this country in a position to do a little talking but that until we get in that position we ought not be too vocal. Berle asked me if I referred directly to the President's reference to the "hand that held the dagger." I said I did. He remarked that it had been very popular according to responses this morning to the White House. I replied I had no doubt it was popular in this country and that political movements in this country were psychological but that nobody knew what the reaction would be sixty days from now or two months from now; that if you had a virulent opposition with the Republican party taking advantage of a situation and a whole lot of elements that did not want to get this country into war that they would have a serious situation on their hands. My argument is only that we should not permit that situation to arise and that the Republican party should not have that issue, for if it did and should elect a President on that issue, we would be in a hell of a mess after January 20 next, and he would be there for four years. . . . In the meantime Paris has fallen and occupied by the Germans. The French army seems to be in almost precipitate retreat. The

British claim that they are breaking up communication lines behind the German front. The French Government has moved to Bordeaux and Hitler has announced that he will proceed against England just as soon as he clears the way in France. . . .

June 16, 1940 – Sunday

Reached Department at ten o'clock and met the Secretary. . . . Welles came in, and the three of us carried on. It was the most important conference I have sat in for a long time. France is confronted with the alternative of surrender or ask for an armistice. The Reynaud Government wants an armistice—the Generals want to surrender. The French are trying to secure the acquiescence of the British to make a separate peace. The decision is to be tomorrow. The questions for us are immediate and far reaching. Surrender will include the fleet—even an armistice may. If Germany gets the French fleet the fate of England is soon to be sealed. It involves immediately possession and control of French possessions in the Americas. I proposed a mandate to us while the French Government is an autonomous agency. Sumner amended it by having it a trusteeship to the 21 American Republics. The British possessions are in the same category. The British are in actual control of Aruba and Curacao, which complicates the situation and offers an excuse to a successful Germany with a fleet to go to Curacao and Aruba and gain a foothold in America. Our fleet is at Hawaii. I propose it be sent to the Atlantic seaboard—at least half of it—even if the movement is piece-meal and clandestine. Berle and Grady are now in and Hackworth and Hornbeck are sent for. The last named opposes the transfer. He has a private war on with Japan and argues that to divide the fleet is to announce we do not mean business anywhere and to transfer it to the Atlantic is to turn the Pacific over to Japan and invite occupation by Japan of the Dutch East Indies. Welles agrees with me. He is to draft telegrams to Germany and Italy announcing that irrespective of terms of settlement no transfer of sovereignty of American territory is to be considered as valid to any foreign power—and to France and England that we expect them to establish trusteeships for American Republics over French possessions. We must also envisage possible transfers of Portuguese possessions of Azores and Canaries. . . .

June 17, 1940

This morning the French have practically surrendered. They have ceased fighting and asked for an armistice. . . . A conference in the Secretary's office this morning. The Military Liaison reported the demoralization of the French and the probable invasion of England from Ireland with parachute troops and an intensive extension of warfare against England. But that of course does not need a military expert to predict. The fate of the British fleet will be next.

After all, it is not the fleet of the British Empire but the fleet of little England. It is the people of England itself that own it, pay for it, maintain it, man it and control it. It is controlled in the interests of the people of England. They look down upon the Canadians and Australians and South Africans. They call them "colonials," and assume that they are in a different scale of life and belong to a different scheme of things. Only England is foremost in their minds, and if the sacrificing of the fleet will save England, they will sacrifice it. They will be so mad at us for not having come to their assistance that when they sacrifice it they will probably hope the Germans will come after us with it and will wish them bon voyage. By all that I mean simply that the fleet is theirs, for their own protection, and for their own use, and if they can sacrifice it to save themselves, they will do it irrespective of what happens to Canada, Australia and other things.

At the moment it looks like 30 or 60 days as a lease of life for England. She will fight, and there will be a scrap, and if she can delay it, Germany will be eventually licked, but anybody who would predict that today would have to draw a long bow to his imagination. . . .

I understand there is talk among some of the Senators that under the present circumstances they are not as enthusiastic for Roosevelt to be renominated. It probably will not eventuate, but movements develop so quickly under present conditions that they are almost spasmodic and cannot be predicted.

Conference at the Secretary's request this afternoon in my office; representatives of European and Near Eastern Divisions and Pell[68] representing the refugees, together with Hackworth and Dunn on the question of who, how many, what categories, why and when we should have refugees, political and otherwise, and how to transport them if any and where to draw the line. The problem of refugees is getting to be enormous. France was filled with political refugees from Belgium, Holland, Poland, Germany and a lot from Italy beginning with Count Sforza, Negrín and Azaña,[69] the Cabinet of Poland and of Belgium. Wilhelmina[70] has arrived in England. The English propose to take a number of refugees to Canada. Without passport requirements, which we are now working on, they could simply walk right into the United States. Our regulation is to become effective July first, and there are multitudinous requests for delay in its operations, which cannot be granted. But to return to refugees, it was decided after full consideration that each would have to be considered on its individual case and that there were no ships to bring them in. Furthermore, if they have transit visas to go through the United States to Mexico we ought to be very careful in order that they do not con-

[68] Robert Pell, assistant chief of the Division of European Affairs, 1939–1941.
[69] Count Carlo Sforza, Italian statesman and opponent of Mussolini; Dr. Juan Negrín, prime minister of Spain, 1937–1939; Manuel Azaña y Diez, president of Spain, 1936–1939.
[70] Queen of the Netherlands, 1890–1948.

tinue their political activities in Mexico and any that do come are to understand that they come as private individuals to save their lives and not as politicians to find a safe spot from which to carry on a prolonged and renewed revolutionary activity.

June 18, 1940

. . . The invitation for the International Labor Office to come to the United States appeared. The International Labor Office was a part of the League of Nations and is now a separate organization. Winant[71] telegraphed suggesting it. Department officials, including myself, were opposed to it. Perkins[72] got the President last night to approve it, and this morning dictated a telegram for us to send. At a meeting in my office the matter was discussed, and it was decided that I was to take the matter up with the Secretary and present the case in the negative. The Secretary agreed and got in communication with the President, who approved, and so the International Labor Office is not to be invited. Amongst its personnel were some dozen names that were objectionable to the United States and whom we would have to keep constant track of if they were admitted even as members of that committee. Furthermore, it was bad politically, because inviting it would hold out the promise of inviting the political sections of the League next. In addition to that they would be confronted with a situation in the United States with very little to do; so they would immediately turn to investigation of our own labor conditions and no doubt with a little more time on their hands would begin investigating matters in Latin America and stirring up trouble there just at a time when we are trying to keep our relations with those countries on very cordial terms. Those were the objections against the extension of the invitation.

Mussolini and Hitler met in Munich and parted. There is no word yet as to what they decided or what terms they will offer to France. The conjecture is that it will be for unconditional surrender. There is also no word about the French fleet or what will become of it.

June 19, 1940

The Secretary asked me to handle the evacuation of children out of England to this country. Under our laws we are limited. The British quota is 6500 a month for ten months and has not been filled. Each case has to be handled individually and places found for the children before they are given visas. We do not want the Department responsible or the Government in it except in so far as the granting of visas exercises a control over the situation in compliance with the law. Mrs. Roosevelt is much interested. The Quaker organization

[71] John Winant, director of the International Labor Office, Geneva, 1939–1941, and former, Republican, governor of New Hampshire, 1925–1926, 1931–1934.

[72] Frances Perkins, Secretary of Labor, 1933–1945.

has been acting for her. The British want to send all the children here, and of course that cannot be done, as there are estimated between one and two hundred thousand of them. They could send them to Canada, and we could take up to our quota limit from Canada each month. There is a lot of sentiment about it and sentimentality, but the enthusiasm is liable to wane at the end of a long period, and it would be cruel to the children and a failure to discharge our obligations if we got them in here and then failed to take care of them. . . .

The condition of the French is pretty desperate. They have nominated delegates to talk to the Germans and receive terms, but the indications are the terms will demand the surrender of the fleet. This they probably will not do, as the fleet is already with the British, and so the war will proceed to the possible terrible detriment of France. The Germans will be ruthless in their prosecution of military activities now.

June 20, 1940

. . . Pittman and Bloom have started a personal war all because of the respective jurisdictions of their committees, the one in the Senate and the other in the House. The Red Cross amendment to the Neutrality Act is involved, and Bloom wants his name attached to the House bill. More seriously, the Monroe Doctrine resolution is involved, and the Bloom resolution is pigeonholed in Pittman's committee because Bloom refuses to use the Senate bill, which was passed first and sent to the House as the basis of House action.[73] I talked to both of them and told them it was ridiculous to have a personal war at a time like this. Bloom was easier to handle but a little arrogant and terribly ambitious for publicity. Pittman is very able but somewhat of a prima donna when he gets his dander up, and it is now up. He got mad at Bloom yesterday and talked to him straight from the shoulder. I talked to Sam Rayburn and told him the mess would have to be straightened out. He said he would straighten out the Neutrality situation this morning but he was going to have serious difficulty with the other bill.

One pleasant occurrence was the victory of Nasca in her first start. She won by eight lengths and eased up at one-fifth of a second off the track record. Baruch came in before he went to see the President for lunch, and I told him to tell them that Nasca was going to run. Later in the day Steve Early called me and said the President had bet two dollars, he had bet ten dollars and Baruch had bet fifty dollars and that they were all very happy, and I telegraphed Baruch back in New York that I was glad I could contribute to his expenses on his trip to Washington.

[73] Reference here is to an Administration proposal to amend the Neutrality Act of 1939 so that the Red Cross ships could proceed without obtaining previous safe conduct assurances from the warring powers.

The President appointed Frank Knox Secretary of the Navy[74] and Henry Stimson Secretary of War. That puts two more Republicans in the Cabinet and makes the Republicans responsible for the War Department and the Navy Department. It means there will be no politics in either of them and that the President views the present situation as national in character and nonpartisan in every respect. I am reminded that Pershing[75] was a Republican when he was placed in command by Mr. Wilson, and his father-in-law was the ranking Republican member of the Military Affairs Committee.[76]

Dispatched a destroyer from Lisbon to Casablanca, which is within the proscribed area, in order to pick up eighteen Americans who had been working for the French in aeronautical and airplane matters and whose personal safety might be jeopardized if they were caught. They will be taken to Lisbon to await a merchant ship for transportation.

June 21, 1940

The French went to meet the Germans at Compienne to receive the peace terms. Nothing known of them as yet. Sporadic fighting still continues in France. Rumania assumed a Fascist-Nazi status. Japan still pursues her way toward Cochin China. Our program proceeding as regards further cooperation with Latin America. I appeared before the Senate Committee on Appropriations and advocated an additional appropriation of one-half a million dollars for various social and political contacts with the Latin American Republics. Some of the Senators dubious as to the advisability of spending money on that account.

The clerk who was killed in an airplane flying from Tallin to Helsinki as courier seems to have been somewhat indiscreet. It may not have been as bad as the clerk in London. Examination of his effects after his death disclosed copies of some code messages in his room and a confidential letter he was not supposed to have which apparently had been opened and was addressed to Kirk in Berlin. The airplane in which he was killed probably did not explode but apparently was shot down by a submarine six miles off of a lighthouse off the Estonian coast. The airplane fell in such deep water that it is impracticable to retrieve it to determine what actually happened. The disturbing part is that this clerk from Helsinki and the one from London served together in Moscow. The one in London had a Russian woman he was associated with, and the one in Tallin seems to have had a Finnish lady friend. But we do not know that she was in Moscow. Both of them spoke Russian and were associates, and both of them at least were indiscreet.

[74] Knox, Republican vice-presidential nominee in 1936, served as Secretary of the Navy from 1940 to 1944.

[75] General John J. Pershing, Commander-in-Chief of the American Expeditionary Forces during World War I.

[76] Reference here is to Francis E. Warren, Republican, U.S. Senator from Wyoming, 1890–1893, 1895–1929.

June 22, 1940

The German peace terms are surrender—including the fleet; occupation of north coast and west coast. French control of district around Paris in size about one-third of France. No demand for colonies.[77] Italy is receiving French envoys to meet their terms which will probably mean occupation of all the Mediterranean coast. . . .

The warfare in France has driven hundreds of thousands to the Bordeaux area—St. Jean de Luz and points in southwestern France. Many Americans are there and may need *another* ship to be sent for them. We cabled Bordeaux, Lisbon and Madrid to ascertain how many in each jurisdiction desiring to return so we could estimate whether we ought send another ship and I have the *Washington,* just returned yesterday, on ice till Tuesday so we can send her if necessary. Also in England is a pocket of 300 (estimated) who would not leave before but who now are scared to death and who can not leave unless we send a ship because the Neutrality Law prohibits them from travelling in the proscribed area or on vessels of belligerent flag. They have had warning after warning and opportunity after opportunity to come on American vessels, but they did not like the vessels, or the crowded condition or were not scared enough or wanted private rooms with bath. So they stayed and are now there. . . .

The Republicans are gathering for their National Convention and preparing a platform which will try to make us the "war" party—gradually leading us into war. They want to "aid" the Allies but keep out of any war. It is possible for them to draft a dangerous platform and make an issue hard to beat. They would have all the Germans, all the Italians, all the Russians, Communists, subversive elements—all the Peace societies, the anti-war-at-any-price crowd—and a motley array which would include some Labor elements and be formidable. But if they *should* win—the one who succeeds Roosevelt will have been elected to pursue a policy of rapprochement with Hitler and be controlled by a discordant coalition the influence of which would be controlling. The result would be a calamity—for the United States and for the world. . . .

June 24, 1940

A terrible day—the hardest I remember—not only in volume but in importance of events. Italy signs armistice with France—effective this evening, this time. That makes it unanimous—all except England. And, the worst of it is, the French fleet is surrendered—200 ships of the navy. Only two escaped and they are with the British. Germany's commitment not to use them *may* be kept and may be—.

[77] Long's summary of Germany's peace terms to France is not quite correct. The unoccupied section of France did not include the Paris area.

Atherton[78] arrived to be Acting Chief of European Division. Cudahy ordered away from Bordeaux and what Hull considers to be a degenerate French Government to which he has been deputy Ambassador while Bullitt got himself foolishly locked up in his own Embassy in Paris.[79] Cudahy goes to London—if, when and how—but first out of France to Spain.

A note went to Japan to ask her to join with us in considering what disposition to be made of any European-owned territory in the Pacific area—as a predicate on which American-Japanese understanding could be reared—but it is months too late. It might have worked sixty days ago—and I advocated at one of the conferences that we take advantage of an opening presented to Grew[80] by an intermediary for the Foreign Minister—but got no sympathetic understanding or support. Now—the news crosses—as we send *our* approach—too late—Japan is taken over by the Military party and goes Nazi-Fascist.[81]

A dispatch from London catalogues the papers found in [Embassy code clerk] Kent's rooms. They are a complete history of our diplomatic correspondence since 1938. It is appalling. Hundreds of copies—true readings—of despatches, cables, messages. Some months every single message going into and out from the London Embassy were copied and the copies found in his room. It means not only that our codes are cracked a dozen ways but that our every diplomatic maneuver was exposed to Germany and Russia. His girl friend was a Russian. She was in his rooms when he was arrested. She had accomplices—one another Russian woman—and the spread from there on ran the gamut of spies, agents, dangerous characters—who are now rather fully disclosed. It is a terrible blow—almost a major catastrophe. No doubt the Germans will publish another White Book during our political campaign which will have as its purpose the defeat of Roosevelt and the election of a ticket opposed to him and presumably in sympathy with Hitler—an appeasement ticket—an administration to succeed ours which will play ball with

[78] Ray Atherton, foreign service officer, chief of the European Affairs Division of the State Department, 1940–1943.

[79] When the French government evacuated Paris on June 10, Ambassador Bullitt decided to remain behind until June 30. This decision was severely criticized by Secretary Hull who wrote that "it deprived Bullitt of all contact with the French Government during the crucial week between June 10, when it left Paris, and June 17, when it asked for an armistice."

[80] Joseph C. Grew, ambassador to Japan, 1932–1941. Grew recorded in his diary several friendly conciliatory conversations that he had with members of the Japanese Foreign Office between December 1939 and April 1940. See Joseph C. Grew, *Ten Years in Japan* (New York: Simon and Schuster, 1944), pp. 305–318.

[81] With the collapse of France, the Japanese military-Fascist clique led by War Minister General Shunroku Hata decided to dispense with the moderate policies of Premier Mitsumasa Yonai. On June 24, Hata declared that posterity would never forgive them if they failed to seize the opportunities presented by the international situation. The policies of the new government formed on July 22, were framed by the army and navy chiefs determined on "a new order in Greater East Asia" along totalitarian lines.

Germany or surrender America. . . . One of the knotty problems was our assent to [the] request of the British to allow access to certain documents found in Kent's possession so he [they?] can prove it at the trial and establish the chain of evidence. We agreed to some but could not implicate the Chief by consenting to correspondence between him and Churchill before Churchill became Premier—and Churchill's letter was a plea and a confession of defeat. The President did *not* accede to his request but the very correspondence might be hurtful. So we withheld permission to see or to use on the theory they had enough to convict without them.

The fortunes of war change fast. Churchill criticized the French for deserting England. The new French Government, which signed the armistice, was quick to react. They criticized Churchill and England and the psychological reaction was so quick and so severe that now France, in her papers, her statesmen and her populace condemn the criticism of Churchill so severely that they become advocates for Germany! Oh, fickle Fortune. "Consistency – !" And so ends.[82]

June 26, 1940

Discussed further restriction of immigration, including those who have visas. It is very apparent that the Germans are using visitor's visas to send agents and documents through the United States and are using their Consulates in the United States as headquarters for their nationals who enter on transit permits and who are carrying confidential documents but who are not notified to this Government and are not certified members of the German Foreign Service. . . .

June 27, 1940

Learned this morning that the French navy is in a brighter picture. England has three out of seven battleships and has a majority of the cruisers. Most all the destroyers and all the 102 submarines are either in German hands or in French colonial ports.

Proposed to the Secretary and Welles in regard to the tri-partite conference[83] the strengthening of our border controls and exercising additional

[82] On June 16, the cabinet of French Premier Paul Reynaud voted 13 to 11 to conclude a separate peace with Germany and a new government headed by Marshal Henri Pétain was formed to sue for peace. This violated an agreement with England which obligated France not to open peace negotiations without Great Britain's consent. British officials rushed to Bordeaux to remind the new Pétain government of the condition on which Britain agreed to release France from her alliance obligations—the dispatch of the French fleet to British ports. But the Pétain government proceeded to sign the armistice (June 22) which provided among other hard conditions that the French fleet should be demobilized and disarmed under German or Italian control.

[83] Throughout World War II, the refugee and alien problem proved to be thorny mainly because of overlapping jurisdictions. The Departments of State, Justice, and Interior each claimed some authority. Long's reference here is to an interdepartment conference which attempted to clarify the issue.

authority over both non-immigrant and immigrant visas, such as visitors permits, reentry permits and transit permits as well as regular immigration control. After explaining the needs for it and going into the matter thoroughly they both agreed as to principle and subsequently in conference with Berle, Warren and the head of the Immigration Service we decided upon very drastic orders and the appropriate telegrams are being prepared. . . . Just as an example of the necessity for this, we now know that Germany sends secret instructions by two different couriers, on different ships, traveling independently, each securing a transit visa and each carrying packages. Those in the possession of one are meaningless until they are matched with the contents of the package of the other. This practice violates our law and our extension of Diplomatic and Consular privileges to the Germans. We have one man, allegedly a merchant and traveling as such, in custody but only were able to secure two of his packages. He had five. The other three are at a German Consulate which we know. The opposite one of this man who carries the other messages left a port of the United States on the west coast the same night we captured our man but just before we captured him. However, there is a man on his ship watching him and able to identify him, and we know what baggage he has and where it is. He is traveling on a Japanese ship headed for South America. We would like to get the packages which he has in his possession in order to put them with the others and get the full story. We are going to need something like that to publish, because the Germans are in full possession of the information which Kent had in documentary form, and Kent had practically everything the Department has done of a confidential nature, and they are liable to publish some of it in the form of a White Book at the psychological moment during the campaign so that it will be as harmful as possible to the Democratic nominee. Of course they will want the Republican elected.

The Secretary asked me this morning what I thought of the postponement of the date of the Democratic National Convention from July 15 to September. I told him I didn't think it would make much difference. The issue in the campaign is foreign policy, and we are running it. If the nomination was to be late in September, it would be difficult to organize the mechanics of the campaign, but I thought if it was held the latter part of August or the first of September, it would make little difference. . . .

June 28, 1940

Events follow one another so fast in this world it is hard to really appreciate the rate of speed at which we are proceeding. The known world has been overrun a few times in history, but it took years and years and years. Alexander did it in his world, small as it was, and he had an army of a stupendous size of a million men on foot. Caesar did it two thousand years ago. Genghis

Khan overran his world, which was another one from the one our ancestors had lived in. Napoleon did a good job in Europe but failed to conquer all of Europe. But those all were processes of years. Today Hitler has placed himself more or less supreme in continental Europe outside of Russia. Yesterday Russia started again, and it looks as if she would occupy Finland, and she has been conceded the right to occupy Bessarabia. Rumania loses Bessarabia, and she is now afraid she will lose the Dobrudja[84] to Hungary. Turkey is afraid she will lose her strip in continental Europe, and it looks as if she was about to have a movement made against it. England is preparing against the onslaught by Germany to defeat her own island. The British navy has deserted Hong Kong and left it undefended. The French are about to lose Indo China to Japan. The islands of the seas are wondering which of them will be taken next. The colonial possessions in Africa are in a quandary, and South Africa is showing distinct signs of rebelling against the rule of England. In South America, Argentina and Uruguay and Chile are showing other signs of having within their midst strong adherents to the Nazi cause. The whole world seems to be in movement. It is kaleidoscopic. The picture is never the same for more than a few minutes. As I sit at my desk and read the telegrams that come through the day from every part of the world I am conscious of the astonishing fact that when I have digested a situation as reported from one part of the world before the day goes by a development will upset the concept upon which that information was based. No one knows what will happen next. Of all the epochs of history to be alive this seems to be the most exciting and the most conducive to an appalled interest. It takes a cool mind and a solid foundation to project the present happenings against the pattern of past developments, for with the wide-spread activity in the world and the political and social implications of it all not only is our immediate future involved but the long-range trend of our political existence depends upon the policies evolved out of the muddled scheme of affairs today.

Willkie,[85] an ex-Democrat as recently as '36, nominated for President by the Republicans last night—an able man with little public experience. His nomination shows the paucity of men of ability and reputation in the Republican party as of today. . . .

June 30, 1940

So there is war in Africa—where Hannibal was; and in Italy and France—where Caesar was; and in Scandinavia and Germany and Spain where

[84] A region in southeast Rumania.

[85] During 1940, Wendell Willkie, president of the Commonwealth and Southern Corporation, 1933–1940, became a leading and outspoken antagonist of the New Deal. His internationalist views on foreign policy enabled him to win the support of moderate and liberal Republicans who successfully worked for his nomination.

Napoleon was; and in Finland and Russia where Peter the Great was; and in Palestine and Syria near whence Mohammed inspired his fanatical followers with the zeal to conquer; and in the land of the Pharohs [*sic*]; and in the battle fields where Xerxes marched and fought, armies stand at attention, ready to go; and in Manchuria, China and Japan whence came Genghis Khan; and in the far flung islands of the seas, Haipong, Hong Kong—perhaps Maylasia [*sic*], who knows.

Genghis Khan over-ran a world we knew not but he brought changes of politics and economics and set up an enormous empire. Xerxes instituted a new order—but it soon relapsed. Caesar changed boundaries, institutions, laws, customs, trade and political institutions, and laid the basis for what we call civilization. Mahomet's followers wielded power measured by the scimitar and held it in a strong hand, overthrowing religions—those things men believe in, are aroused by and fight for—as well as customs, boundaries, allegiances and traditions. Napoleon toppled crowns—only to fit them to new heads, and ended an outcast—without lasting result.

In my early manhood I read—of course—the *Bible*—but after, the *Koran* and scanned well its import; and the *Zend Avesta*; through the *Flight of a Tartar Tribe* [?] I have visualized the hordes of Genghis Khan; through the Greek histories I labored through the tales of their conquests—and the Medes and the Persians; through Caesar's *Gallic Wars* I followed the spreading empire of Rome; Napoleonic battles, Austerlitz and all the rest, including his egotistic replacement of one of the disciples on the cathedral at Milan with a statue of himself—if one can call that victory.

Many times in my life have I thought of the things I have read, of their effect on later ages, of the suffering by their contemporaries; of the dead men and women, of the uprooted lives, of the changed fortunes of whole sections of the world, of the overthrown governments, of the seeming end of peace and happiness to millions of people at various periods of the world's history. Each of these seemed astonishing in its implications, each has stirred me to a deep realization of what those events meant to men of those days.

And now—they are all on the march again—Genghis Khan, the Pharohs [*sic*], Cyrus and Xerxes, Caesar, Mahomet, Napoleon, Peter the Great and the Hohenzollern type as well. Here am I *looking*—actually experiencing—the greatest moment in all history. It moves under my very eyes. All the emotions, the settled convictions, the boundaries of half the world, the governments of a score of nations, the peoples of three great continents, the fealties and allegiances, the concepts of a world, stability, laws, customs, trade, wealth, freedom, beliefs, religions—all jumbled up and destroyed—in the process of destruction, of change, of alteration, of subjugation.

To see the future is denied. To guess about it a waste of time. But what a moment to live!

July 4, 1940

Between the Polish Campaign and the Norwegian fight this looked like a funny war. But it doesn't look like that now. And today developed one of its most peculiar phases. The British fleet took over the French fleet by force. At Oran—near Gibraltar—the French refused to turn over and the British opened fire and destroyed most of them. A few escaped to France. So the Allies are fighting among themselves in a sideshow war with the probable result that France will be lined up against England and aligned with Germany —her present conqueror—if not actually helping her.

I hear through Stanley [Reed] that Hull declines to run for President—because he does not wish to submit his wife to severe attacks because she is Jewish—and now I hear Roosevelt feels it necessary for him to run and will take Hull for Vice President. It will be a strong ticket if so. Hull has always been interested and I think has had from time to time strong predilections toward the Presidency, but he has consistently steered away from conversations which would connect him definitely with the campaign for the office. He has been meticulous in his efforts to avoid connecting his name definitely with the campaign and has on several occasions recently said to me that he wanted to retire from public life in January but to leave to his credit an unimpeachable record of consistency and performance while in charge of the State Department, and let his reputation for the future stand on that.

July 12, 1940

I am just on the eve of leaving for Chicago for the Convention. The last ten days have been very busy and heavy days. There has developed in this country an enormous psychosis about British refugee children and wanting to get them over here. The enthusiasm operates through every class of society and all over the United States. It is one of those peculiar phenomena that appear sometimes, and I attribute it to a repressed emotion about this war. Every individual has had many feelings to which he has been unable to give expression. They are feelings of antagonism to Germany and of sympathy for Poles, Dutch, Norwegians, Finns and more latterly for the people of France and other invaded countries. But there has been nothing to *do* about anything. Now all of a sudden there was a suggestion that British children be taken out of the area of danger and brought to the United States. They talked of 100,000, of 200,000, of any number. Of course we were sympathetic to the suggestion and have done everything we could to pave the way for the immigration— within the limitations of the law. All the red tape that is set up by regulation in addition to the law has been brushed aside and every facility has been extended. There is the quota which permits 6,500 a month for ten months, but there immediately developed a clamor for more spaces than were provided by the quota. They wanted to get them all out immediately. Of course that could not physically be done. Then the British began sending over enemy aliens whom they had interned in England so that they could be got out of England and held in Canada. This utilizes a good deal of shipping space. Instead of making it available to children, they have put enemy aliens aboard these vessels and have transported 6700 of them up to this date—at least those are our estimates from Canada—and there are still thousands to come. Of course you cannot explain that to the public without being critical of England, and we cannot do that. So we have had to handle the thing very delicately and carefully and deal with a great many of emotional people—people temporarily emotional and who ordinarily are hard-headed, common-sensed individuals. Three or four of these newspaper columnists have been hyper-critical of the Department and its attitude not realizing and being unable to understand when it was explained to them that the Department's regulations had nothing whatever to do with the situation. They were British children to be transported by England and we were perfectly willing to facilitate their departure and given them visas under the quota. Only about 3000 have developed in the last four weeks. There is a possibility to take 1300 between now and the first of August. But there is still the clamor for giving them visitors visas instead of immigrant visas. I have talked to Kennedy on the telephone, and I have telegraphed back and forth to him, but many of them do not want to be separated from their children, and the British Government will not give them passports until they secure passage on a vessel, and there are no vessels on which England is willing to accommodate them and they then send out the suggestion that we send American ships for them. The British Ambassador made that suggestion to Hull. It is a perilous thought. The very surest way to get America into this war would be to send an American ship to England and put 2000 babies on it and then have it sunk by a German torpedo. That would shove us right into the middle of the war, and that cannot be done. I have been firm with all of these people and just as polite as I know how to be and as considerate and have fairly well got away with it. The Secretary made a statement yesterday which I drafted and which epitomizes our policy. . . .

I just had a very significant talk with Cordell. In the last week the Presidential situation has developed to the point where it is now certain that Roosevelt will be nominated by acclamation. In the last few days has emerged the figure of Hull to be nominated for Vice President. At his press conference at noon today he was questioned on the subject, and his answer was rather facetious and to the effect that it was a poor fellow that couldn't get his name in the paper somehow these days. I told him I thought I could have improvised a little better reply for him to make. He retorted that he couldn't take it seriously and would have felt like a fool if he had straightened up and put on a solemn face and made a solemn declaration. Norman Davis and I were sitting in his office. I told him that I thought he was going to be nominated by acclamation and that it was his duty to accept it. He said there were various reasons why he should not do it. His field was foreign affairs. He wanted to be at least an advisor on foreign affairs; that as Vice President he would be in a pocket. He would have no function. He could not envisage the Vice President suggesting to another Secretary of State what he should do. The whole idea was displeasing to him. He said that it wouldn't make any difference who was nominated for Vice President; that the fight would be for or against Roosevelt. I agreed with the latter but said that it made a great deal of difference who was nominated for Vice President and that certain persons whose names had been mentioned would be a detriment and that while the person nominated did not as a matter of actual practice carry a great deal of positive force, still the presence of an acceptable person on the ticket performed a very useful and serviceable political function. He said that he was not satisfied with the thought and that he was going to the President and tell him that he did not want him to use his name or to propose him for Vice President. He is going off to Havana on Thursday of next week, the 18th.[86] The nomination will probably not be made by that time. He will probably be incommunicado as far as the Convention is concerned because he will be either on the train or on a boat or in a session of the delegates at the Pan American Conference. The chances are it will be thrust upon him and he will not have an opportunity to decline. He asked me to help him not to be nominated, but I withheld any comment. As I left he asked me to come back to see him before I took the train, but I think I shall probably not do it and will not go unless he specifically calls me again. He feels that he has been largely responsible for the nomination of the President the first time; that he has served him faithfully for eight years, sometimes under very discouraging circumstances, and that he is entitled to have his real desires considered in this important matter.

July 28, 1940 – Nantucket

Have been here for a week. For the week preceding I was in Chicago at the Democratic National Convention. It was a foregone conclusion Roosevelt would be nominated. Farley let his name go before the Convention—I think largely out of pride that he should be recorded as mentioned for the office. He was also hurt that he was not running the show for Roosevelt but as he was a technical competitor and a little out of humor he naturally could not be.

[86] At Havana, delegates of twenty-one republics of the Pan American Union gathered for an Inter-American Conference. On July 30, they signed the Act of Havana which provided that the American republics, collectively or individually, might, in the interest of common defense, take over and administer any European possession in the New World endangered by aggression. This measure was designed to prevent the transfer to Germany of European colonies in the western hemisphere.

Instead Wallace and Ickes were running the show. For a while it looked as if they were going to make a mess of it—and they did as far as the Resolutions Committee was concerned. They let it be stacked against us by the "isolation" group and that group prevailed on Bob Wagner[87] to appoint a subcommittee to draft the platform whereon sat a very substantial representation, so they were able to write the foreign affairs platform to suit themselves or carry a hard fight to the floor. The result was they wrote that plank as desired. I did not see the resolutions before they were presented to the Convention, though Hull had asked me to try and get it softened to the point where it would not preclude our use of naval or air forces abroad if necessary—not that he wanted to use them but for the effect on Germany and Japan he did not want a commitment which would announce to them in advance that they could do as they pleased with American rights in their jurisdictions and areas without fear of forceful objection by us. We were all agreed "no army" should be sent anywhere—but he wanted mobility of action as regards the fleet and air units. However, I was unable to do anything. Wagner twice said I might discuss the matter when it was drafted but that it was not then even in the rough. As it turned out I never did see it—nor anyone else outside the Committee except Hopkins, Ickes and Frank Walker, and the telephone to the White House.

The rest of the Convention proceeded smoothly and regularly enough and was well managed. I was an observer. I had less to do with it than any Convention I have attended since 1912. 1916, 1924, 1928, and 1932 I was very active—though I was a member only in 1928. 1920 I was the nominee for the Senate and stayed in Missouri. 1936 I was in the hospital. But I did have a number of conferences with Farley in an effort to soften his humor and keep him in line. He and I have been good friends since 1932. He was determined to quit *all* political activity then and there. My conversations with him were not controlling by any means but I am sure they helped. He wants to go into business and make some money—and he has less than none—but he will stay as Chairman for a while and will continue in New York as State Chairman and with his hand at the throttle.

The President's desire to have Wallace on his ticket produced quite a stir.[88] There was lots of solid opposition because Wallace is not considered a Democrat. I could not see the merit in the opposition. We were a minority party in '32 and needed lots of Republican votes. We got them—and recognized them by the appointment to the Cabinet of Wallace and Ickes—representing respectively the middle-of-the-road Republican and the radicals. He has played our game—has accepted our philosophy—has become a Democrat—and I think

[87] Robert Wagner, Democrat, U.S. Senator from New York, 1927–1949. For Long's clarification of "the 'isolationist' group" see below, p. 124.

[88] At Roosevelt's urging, the Democratic Convention chose Henry Wallace as the vice-presidential nominee.

is a good nominee—and I am a partisan and a life-long member of the party.
The opposition was partly opposition to Roosevelt and partly organization
resentment at the nomination of anything but a regular machine-made Democrat.

One other function I had was at Hull's request and as his representative
to keep him from being nominated for Vice President. We had several long
talks before I went out and I talked with him several times a day on the long
distance phone till he left for Havana on Thursday of that week. He went to
the President and talked two and a half hours with him and took the determined position his role was foreign affairs and that he would be side-tracked
as Vice President. He let the President realize he was adamant. Up to that
conversation the President wanted him. The sentiment at Chicago was for
him. He would have been nominated easily. But when he told me of his conversation with the President I told Farley, Cummings—who wanted Barkley
—and other leaders there—and it looked for twenty-four hours as if the field
was open and lightning might strike anyone. But the next day Wallace's
name was put out and that night (or the next) he was nominated.

The Convention adjourned peacefully and in good humor and it looks as if
the nominees would win.

August 8, 1940

Cudahy went to London recently and has unburdened himself of a highly
questionable press interview in which he advocates feeding the starving Belgians and the starving people of Europe, generally praising the Germans and
comparing them most generously with the American troops. We ordered him
home immediately, but the reverberations of his indiscretion will be rumbling
around for some time. . . .

August 13, 1940

. . . Lunched with Bullitt. He says Petain is not Fascist or Nazi but simply
the administrator of an estate in bankruptcy—trying to save what he can. He
thinks France will continue long under German influence if not control because of the fear of further punishment. He thinks this country alarmingly
calm and disinterested about its fate; that Hitler will be here through South
America "before Christmas"; that sentiment should be aroused; that the
President told him to get movements started and he is doing it. He quoted the
President as saying he himself could not be alarming because the people would
think he was playing politics—with which I quite agree. . . .

England is experiencing a serious bombardment. It looks like the beginning of the long expected drive. There are many losses on each side but the
British cannot replace their lost men. That is the neck of the bottle. The implications are serious for us. If England is forced to submit—which I easily

envisage and somewhat expect—though I see a hard struggle with possible victory—we may look for the British fleet to get to German hands—or at least what may be left of it. In that case we have a fight on our hands—with the Atlantic and Pacific to guard—and South America not only to protect but to prevent the establishment there of even local armies armed and trained by Germans. They would have air bases there as a matter of course—and refuelling ports—and we could not permit that. If we did it would be our turn next. . . .

August 16, 1940

Phillips was in yesterday. I did not ask him whether he is resigning— though I know he wants to. He has family difficulties. He looks very well— says all his information is Germany will win—control all Central, Western, Eastern Europe, let Italy run Balkans, North Africa, Mediterranean. Ciano confident. He (Phillips) thinks there should be no more provocative statements. Wants to rest in Maine woods.

Cudahy was in today. He is sure Germany will win—if by a miracle England can hold out it will be a "30 years war" and Europe destroyed—all to our own disadvantage—and Communism win—more or less my own thesis. He sees no disadvantage to us if Germany wins—I disagree—and thinks the Monroe Doctrine an egotistic monstrosity—to which I violently disagreed, citing its successful history and the necessity of our own defense.

There is a plan now to lease British Naval and Air bases in this Hemisphere (except islands off Argentina?) for 99 years and pay for it in old destroyers. It would work if England wins or the destroyers were sunk—but would not be so good if Germany got the destroyers. . . .

August 22, 1940

. . . Germany announces she will not give safe conduct to ships to evacuate British children—just as the Congress passes the bill. I had not considered she would—and that would block the movement for safe conduct from belligerents is a pre-requisite in the bill.

The President in conference Saturday night at Ogdensburg with McKenzie King[89] told him he was so glad there was practically speaking no "border" between the United States and Canada to which the Prime Minister rejoined "Well, you are doing your best to make one." This floored the President. He was not intimately familiar with the operation of our immigration restrictions, particularly on the Canadian border. Considering the larger aspects of our

[89] On August 18, Canadian Prime Minister Mackenzie King met President Roosevelt near Ogdensburg, New York, for a conference of historic significance. They agreed to establish a Permanent Joint Board on Defense to "consider in the broad sense the defense of the north half of the Western Hemisphere" and "commence immediate studies relating to sea, land, and air problems including personnel and material."

relations with Canada now he became much interested and somewhat exercised. As a consequence he told Sumner today to do something to lessen the irritation. Sumner passed it on to me. I called Bob Jackson and asked him to send representatives to a conference in my office. They came, met with our men, decided something could be done. So I got off a wire to Ottawa advising that our people and Justice would be in Ottawa day after tomorrow and to arrange a meeting for them with the Canadian officials and we were disposed to do all we could within the requirements of our law.

August 24, 1940

Trotsky is dead—murdered by an alleged member of the O.G.P.U. and agent of Stalin—a violent end to a life of violence.[90] The request is made to have funeral and burial in this country but we ruled against it.

The Canadian border question is up in Ottawa where I sent a delegation to talk with the Canadians. They practically accept our modification of regulations but do not want compulsory finger-printing and ask for "finger print or photograph." . . .

August 27, 1940

Had a long talk with Cordell this morning. He is very much concerned about the vote of the Senate yesterday in limiting the persons taken in the draft to do service in this Hemisphere. It is not that he wants to send an army abroad—and I quite agree with him—but it is the effect on Germany and on Japan at the present moment of notifying them officially and positively that they may do as they please anywhere in Europe or in Asia with American rights and that they will have no interference whatsoever from the Government of the United States and no threat be possible to hold them in line. . . . In an election year these questions are always like dynamite. They are liable to explode and do damage at the most unexpected time and in the most unexpected places. As it stands today the isolationist block consists in its leadership of Clark, Wheeler, Nye[91] and a few highly vocalized gentlemen, and they lead the Republicans who are in opposition to the President and who vote solidly against this and that which he advocates, and they gather up enough space in the newspapers and enough scattering votes in each House to make very embarrassing situations for the President. And Mr. Willkie, who is supposed to be the leader of the Republicans expresses opinions in agreement with the President's policies but is unable to control the Republicans in his

[90] After Lenin's death in 1924, Trotsky, advocating world revolution, came into increasing conflict with Stalin's plans for "socialism in one country." In 1926, Trotsky was expelled from the Politburo and, in 1929, ordered to leave Russia. In exile, Trotsky repeatedly attacked the Stalinist regime in his voluminous writings. Trotsky's assassin was thought to be an agent of the Soviet secret police (O.G.P.U.).

[91] Gerald P. Nye, Republican, U.S. Senator from North Dakota, 1925–1945.

party. And he is very little of a leader if he can't control the political element of his own political organization. What he would do if he were put in control of the Government can only be inferred from the lack of influence he has with his own party.

August 28, 1940

Long conference this morning with the Secretary. Prior to discussion with me he discussed in my presence with Hackworth certain phases of the redraft of the memoranda and communications concerning the acquisition of naval bases from England in this Hemisphere. The Secretary has been in the thick of the drafting with the President and the Secretaries of War and Navy and with the British Ambassador. It has all been kept very confidential and even certain phases of it in the Department have not been typewritten but have been drafted and carried in longhand.

We agreed that the transfer of fifty destroyers to England would be a violation of international law and that Germany might take umbrage at it. We are not so much worried on that account, because we have approached the subject from the point of view of national defense. We have tried to distinguish between strict neutrality and that necessary latitude which must exist in any independent government to permit it to defend itself. He spoke of the situation in Belgium before the attack upon Belgium. Belgium proclaimed her neutrality. In the strict practice of her neutrality she was overwhelmed and destroyed because she was isolated by virtue of her strict construction of neutrality, thereby being prevented from consulting the military authorities of France and of England to determine what might be done *in case she was attacked.* The consequence was that by the observance of her strict neutrality Belgium was overwhelmed.

The very same philosophy applies to Holland. The Dutch Government was so meticulous in their efforts not to offend Germany that they adopted the strictest interpretation of neutrality and would permit their military authorities to consult only with the little Kingdom of Belgium and not with either France or England, and in consequence Holland was overwhelmed.

On the same philosophy, if we consider our neutrality as a thing apart, we will be prevented from employing measures necessary to our self-defense because we too will in the practice of a meticulously strict neutrality be prevented from buying certain bases now belonging to England and paying for them in the manner agreeable to us.

There is one other small detail that has to be cleared up on the record. Churchill in one of his off-hand speeches in the Parliament offered to give these bases to the United States. We feel there must be a *quid pro quo,* and England wants destroyers. England is actually giving to us two bases in Canada, and that will appear on the record, and the other bases are to be purchased and our right and title in each of them will run for 99 years—a consideration far more valuable to us today than the fifty destroyers and of infinite value as compared to the value of the destroyers for the next hundred years. Furthermore, my mind goes back to the Louisiana Purchase and the same precedent and the same reasons that existed for that and the similar situation in Europe which existed at the time of the Louisiana Purchase with dictatorial power attempting to overrun Europe.

The agreement will probably be arrived at before very long, and there is certain to be a howl from certain of the political elements in this country, but I am sure that when presented along the lines indicated that we will have the support of the great majority of the people for the very simple reason that we are gaining very greatly in our abilities to defend ourselves. . . .

August 31, 1940

Hull has been working all week on the "Bases for Destroyers" deal. I have not been engaged on it but he has talked it over with me several times—that last at noon today. When he got back it was in the shape that England would "give" us bases and we give her destroyers. Churchill has stated in Parliament he would give us bases in their American possessions—and they must be pretty desperate to even think of it. In their eyes it is probably a step to wean us into the war. Cordell thought it ought to be a bona-fide sale and purchase. He so convinced the President. England submitted memoranda through Lothian to him and to the President. He re-formulated and redrafted—re-submitted—etc.—until today he had the final draft. Hackworth and Judge Townsend[92] of Justice worked with him and this morning they and Berle sat with him. He was all preoccupied with it and dispatched his covering note to the President at Hyde Park. They will be announced Tuesday.

Considering Churchill's statement about "gift" there had to be some "gift" in it. So they are to give us two bases in Canada. We buy eight others—Bermuda, Bahamas, Trinidad, British Guiana—both land bases for air and sea bases—and others. We transfer to them destroyers—fifty of them—and gloss over the value of the *quid pro quo*. The value of the destroyers is inconsequential when compared to that of ten bases—eight of them for Caribbean defense—for 100 years. The destroyers will be gone in ten. It is an enormous step in Continental defense.

Of course it is a violation of international law as far as destroyers are concerned. Germany may take violent exception to it and declare war on us. Cordell realizes that—specifically said he did, and says the President does too.[93] It is a violation of the strict interpretation of international law but that

[92] Newman A. Townsend, acting Assistant Solicitor General, Department of Justice.

[93] With the rapid German victories in western Europe during the spring of 1940, President Roosevelt made the decision to take the lead in declaring peril and to act against it. All aid was now given to England—short of participation.

concept has to be modified by modern circumstances and merged with the border-line of neutral conduct. To get the bases we have to pay something. We cannot with dignity accept a gift. We must pay something. That "something" would be credits, or gold or articles of value. We choose destroyers. The consideration moving to us is vastly important to our national defense— to our larger aspect of national defense which must be expanded to include Continental defense—perhaps Hemisphere defense. Bombers in the air have changed many situations and caused re-appraisement of many others. And if our liberty of action as a neutral is to be restricted by the concepts prevailing in Holland and Belgium, we and any other nation would be so restricted in our action and in our policy that we would be isolated, would be held isolated until Germany had polished off the others one by one and could arrange to give us her undivided attention.

That of course is inacceptable to America.

This may be the most important move in American Foreign Policy since Jefferson purchased the Louisiana Territory—to which it is not dissimilar. John Breckinridge helped him in that deal and I would like to help Roosevelt in this one.

These are momentous days we are living in. All the things we have used as fundamentals are challenged. A revolution is on which attempts to throw over our political, financial, social and economic structures. Potent new concepts based on force threaten the whole framework. Some one of these days the crisis will appear. The grand moment will arrive which will decide history for the future—and I wonder if we will recognize it as it passes? Will we appreciate the drama and feel the thrill of world decision? Or will the sun set inconspicuously below the horizon and only future generations be wise enough to point back to it and say "On September 3rd, 1940 . . . How I would love to have lived that moment" and not know that those who did were unable to distinguish that moment from any other in a period of years?

Charlemagne, Genghis Khan, Julius Caesar, and the developments they represent—did their contemporaries have that thrill? And will we?

For years I thought I have lived through such a moment November 11, 1918—but I was mistaken. For years after Waterloo people thought so—duly to discover after all that Napoleon was only a local character. Jefferson created an age—but when was the moment it began? The Declaration of Independence had to be implemented. Its drafting nor its pronouncement, neither were sufficient to institute an age modelled on his philosophy.

Anyhow, I hope I will be in the middle of it, will be part of it and be conscious of it. And may the decision insure that form of government for all the world which allows free men and women a decent freedom of action in life.

September 2, 1940

Today one year ago I returned to the State Department. The war began the day before. It has been a year of hard work, as well as of momentous development. From a comparative tranquility we have developed into a war-sensitive status. We appropriated large sums for the Navy and spurred on our building; we have revamped our internal economy; we have appropriated large sums for the Army; we have called out the National Guard; we have solidified our relations with other American Republics—and even closer with Canada; we have practically arranged to take over outposts of defense in the form of naval and air bases; and we are about to invoke conscription for an armed force. Our relations with Germany, Italy, Russia and Japan have worsened, and we move little by little to the point of rupture of relations.

September 9, 1940

London suffering terrific bombardments—day after day. Many pictures publicized—apparently by design—to bring the havoc to every mind. England retaliating by bombing Hamburg, Berlin, etc., but no pictures of damage available from there and reports of damage minimized. Reports of German planes downed point to ineffectual opposition. The real meaning of it all is not yet clear.

Meantime here—huge Navy contracts signed—billions for ships and planes. Maine votes today, the first election of the campaign. Willkie falls in stature and importance and loses strength, while Roosevelt gains—The destroyers for bases deal is almost universally applauded—The Duchess of Windsor applied for an American passport and I authorized it to be sent her at Nassau after conferring with the Secretary, a forerunner of *their* residence here is my guess. Cordell talked to Lothian at my suggestion to the effect that it was not opportune for them to come here now and Lothian said they would not come "till after election"—A refugee ship from Lisbon at Vera Cruz refused permission to land its passengers there and putting in at Norfolk for coal on its way back to Portugal, and the refugees want to land. Rabbi Wise[94] pleads, as many others do—Sol Bloom and many more—but to do so would be a violation of the spirit of the law if not the letter. We have been generous—but there are limitations. . . .

September 14, 1940

The attack on England continues and London is under almost continuous bombardment, and England is retaliating and Germany is being badly bombed in various centers.

The new French Ambassador, Henry-Haye,[95] arrived and presented his

[94] Rabbi Stephen Wise, often president of the American Jewish Congress and of the World Jewish Congress, between 1917 and 1949.
[95] Gaston Henry-Haye, French (Vichy) ambassador to the United States, 1940–1942.

credentials to the President. He was received very coldly and was told rather bluntly that as long as the present French Government continued its attitude toward the Hitler Government it would be advisable for the French Embassy in Washington to have little public comment and to issue few statements to the press. If that suggestion were followed it would not be necessary for the American Government to issue any statements on the subject. The Ambassador emerged from the audience with his face very red and in a considerable state of perturbation. . . .

It is planned to move Kirk from Berlin to Rome as Chargé d'Affaires, and Phillips will resign and Kirk will become Chargé. I cabled him privately that his name was being considered in order to break it gradually and to relieve his mind of any thought that his transfer was related to any other matter except his own efficiency and former experience. . . .

I talked to the Secretary again this morning about our Far Eastern policy, and I told him that I agreed that it had been necessary to be firm and considering the coordination between Germany and Japan that our policy had no doubt been correct up to date. However, when it came to taking an irrevocable stand we were liable to be very much embarrassed. In the first place we could not fight a war in the western Pacific, and in the second place we might have to submit to indignities because of our inability to do that, particularly at this time. I thought the people would not understand the nature of our interests in the Far East, which was insignificant compared to our interests both commercial and political in South America and in Europe. I asked him if I interpreted in the same light that he did the telegrams which Grew has been sending and indicating that Grew felt that we had approached the point where only force would be understood. He said that he understood Grew and me and that he had come to the end of the road and that nothing would be understood by the Japanese except a show of force. . . . I now understand that it has been discussed as a matter of high policy and that the Administration has made up its mind to deal very firmly with Japan and that no steps will be spared and that those steps may even lead to war. . . .

I want to be firm with Japan and want to preserve our own rights in the Far East, and I want to see the general principles of peaceful and orderly law and order proceed out there. Of course Japan is doing everything in her power to upset the regular and peaceful procedure. Nevertheless, if we get in difficulties with Japan today it will enormously complicate the situation in the world. Germany can have a pretty free hand in Latin America—much more free than she could otherwise—and our steps toward a preparedness in anticipation of a German attack will be threatened and our resources will be drained or to a certain extent diminished as far as Germany is concerned by having a serious controversy with Japan in the Far East.

September 18, 1940

A number of developments in our procedure in granting visas in excess of the quota have troubled me recently. It was brought to a head by the visit of a vessel named the *Quanza* to Norfolk. It had eighty-odd persons aboard who left Portugal on the ninth of August in an effort to get to some country in the Americas. They were all Jewish. They all had money. The vessel got to Vera Cruz, Mexico, and the Mexican Government refused to permit them to land. Nicaragua refused them permission. Their travel documents were repudiated by the Governments there. It seems there is a prevailing habit for the Consuls and other officers of some South American and Central American countries to accept from $100 to $500 for the privilege of granting visas and other papers. These people all had visas to go to some third country, but they are repudiated by the Governments in Central America. Unable to land there they proceeded ostensibly for Portugal and then conveniently discovered that they would have to put into Norfolk for coal. As soon as it became known that they were to arrive at Norfolk I was flooded with pressure groups and telegrams and telephones and personal visits to permit the landing of persons off of the boat. I consistently declined to deviate from the procedure which we had adopted and said that the fact that the people were on the boat and were nearing the American shores did not constitute an emergency of any kind.

Mrs. Roosevelt called me up and expressed her interest in the children and a few other categories. She talked to the President, and the President asked me to call him the next day. They were then in Hyde Park, and he was about to return to Washington. I called the next day, but it was apparent that he did not want to talk to me on the subject, and I inferred—and it now seems correctly so—that he would leave the matter entirely in my hands.

The boat landed, and an attorney down there swore out writs of habeas corpus for two persons aboard. Another writ was filed against the ship in the form of a lible. The vessel was delayed more than twenty-four hours, which was permitted for the coaling, so it was necessary for them to make a formal entry. Apparently there was every effort to delay the vessel from sailing and a concerted effort by persons on shore cooperating in the interests of persons aboard.

The President's Advisory Committee [for Political Refugees] representative, Mr. Patrick Malin, proceeded to Norfolk to represent the President's Committee. I had agreed with the Department of Justice to treat the passengers on the ship on the same basis that we treated persons in Europe, which was: first, we would recognize the recommendations of the President's Advisory Committee for Political Refugees who were in imminent danger and who were of the leading intellectuals of the liberal movement in Europe; second, recognize the Marshal Field Committee for the Saving of British Children by taking their recommendation for children aboard, provided they complied with the requirements; and third, to let off the boat for purposes of transit across or through the United States any persons whose travel documents were corroborated to us as authentic.

After various conversations there I was finally called up on Saturday night by Mr. Malin and told that they had found three children and two mothers, making five; that they had found thirty-five persons who had valid travel documents entitled to travel across the United States—which was greatly to my surprise and far in excess of the number I anticipated and I am sure now was due to a very generous interpretation of the validity of the documents in question; and that he had construed everybody else on the boat to be a political refugee and that they could come ashore.

I remonstrated violently; said that I thought it was a violation of the law; that it was not in accord with my understanding with them; that it was not a proper interpretation of my agreement; that I would not be party to it; that I would not give my consent; that I would have no responsibility for it; and that if they did that I would have to take the matter up some other way.

I laid it before the Secretary, and he authorized me to present the whole matter to the attention of the President. I did this today in the form of a letter which reviewed the situation and asked his consent to change the procedure, which would place in our Consuls abroad rather than in the President's Committee in New York the final determination as to whether the person was entitled to entry into the United States. We have been very generous in offering hospitality in the United States to persons who have been in imminent danger there who have been leaders of public thought there in the form of Rabbis in Germany, Poland and near-by territories and who were leaders of Rabbinical schools and colleges; and also to a category of leaders in the labor union movement in Europe who were recommended by William Green and a committee of the American Federation of Labor; and also to certain intellectuals who were guaranteed by the President's Advisory Committee. The list of Rabbis has been closed and the list of labor leaders has been closed. And now it remains for the President's Committee to be curbed in its activities so that the laws again can operate in their normal course.

I have felt that the procedure of extending visas to persons in the categories indicated was a perfectly legitimate practice provided the bars were not thrown down to the extent that the categories were expanded and a lot of persons admitted to the United States in contravention of the law. I have been very careful to limit the authorization of visas to the end that the law be observed, and in my opinion a departure from this practice would be in effect to render the immigration laws nugatory.

September 25, 1940

The Secretary is in another jam. This time Henry Morgenthau has taken over the negotiation and arrangement of a loan originally intended for China.

The Secretary wanted to announce the loan the day Japan invaded China. As it stands now it seems that the matter was brought up in Cabinet at the last meeting and Henry Morgenthau was authorized by the President to pursue a plan which meant the purchase of manganese from Russia with the understanding that Russia would buy tungsten from China and with the proceeds of that China could buy military supplies. It sort of threw a monkey wrench into Welles' negotiations with the Russian Ambassador which have been going on here for six weeks in an effort to straighten out the relations between the two Governments. Welles was upset about it. The Secretary tried to stop the initial meeting of the Committee Morgenthau called on the matter but was unsuccessful. He is all wrought up and provoked again. He said that continual interference within the sphere of his own function greatly irritated him and caused him to lose sleep. He said he hadn't slept for five nights. He said it was a drain on his physical resources and he felt as if he could not continue long and for that reason he had sometime since determined that he would resign in January. He said he was sure the President did not desire to interfere with him but it was just one of the ways the President has of doing business. He feels there is nothing personal in it but that it is nevertheless a serious handicap to the functioning of his office and to the carrying out of policy which nowadays is so ramified that it gets into every part of the world. . . .

September 28, 1940

Cordell had his way. The Morgenthau activity in re: China via Russia is out and we make a direct loan to China—twenty-five million. The next day we announced an embargo on scrap iron and steel. Each measure directed against Japan. The next day, which was yesterday, Japan signs in the axis with Germany and Italy, warning us.[96] And so we go—more and more—farther and farther along the road to war. But we are not ready to fight any war now—to say nothing of a war on two oceans at once—and that is what the Berlin-Rome-Tokyo agreement means. Nor will we be ready to fight any war for eighteen months in the future.

Martin Dies[97] has unearthed a lot of evidence that Germany is extending her Nazi activities in this country. He promptly went to Texas so he would not be bedevilled by other members of his committee and telegraphed the President whom to talk to. The President told him to talk to me and notified

[96] On September 27, Japan, Germany, and Italy transformed their working political understanding under the Anti-Comintern Pact of 1936 into a military alliance. It provided, in effect, that if the United States should participate in either the Far Eastern or the European wars to an extent found by the signatories to extend beyond "short of war" action, the participants in the other conflict would establish a state of war with the United States. It was under the terms of this agreement that, on December 11, 1941, Germany and Italy declared war on the United States.

[97] Democrat, U.S. Representative from Texas, 1931–1945, and chairman of the House Committee to Investigate Un-American Activities, 1938–1944.

Hull. I sent two men to study the evidence and report. They are still studying —have turned up a lot Dies did not know about and will not be ready to report for four or five days yet. Dies phoned me, said he would do anything we wanted—have an open hearing or turn the stuff over to us and let us handle it. I told him we would have to study it all and digest it before deciding. He said he would stay in Texas until the decision.

There are many papers involving the German Embassy and the Consular officers directly with one or the other or all of three propaganda and organization agencies in New York. It looks on the face of it that we will be under the necessity to close a number of German Consulates and perhaps send home some of the members of the Embassy staff—for improper activity—and that will invite reprisals—and we will go closer and closer to what looks to be the inevitable unless this war is finished soon; and I don't see any chance for that. In the meantime I am tightening up on immigrants and visitors. I have the support of the Attorney General but not the support I would like from some of his subordinates, who, for sentiment or for sympathy, are inclined to be soft-hearted. This is no time for that. . . .

The newly announced alliance—Germany, Italy, Japan—is only formally new. It has been apparent to us for a long time that the three Governments were acting concertedly with the idea of harassing us in the Pacific while Germany and Italy master Europe. My objection to our aggressive response to pin pricks has been based on the knowledge that we cannot fight a war in Asiatic waters—at any time—and that to crawl into it now when we may be engaged in the Atlantic theater, even against our will, is too dangerous a program.

We cannot always shape our policies independently. We cannot permit German agents to organize subversive projects. But we can let Japan run her course in Asia without getting involved ourselves—and attend to that later when we are free in the Atlantic. The situation at Shanghai alone may involve us.[98] It may explode at any instant—and we would be powerless in the face of predictable events. . . .

October 1, 1940

I am waiting still for the report of the man I sent to go over the evidence in the Dies Committee but do not expect him to be ready to report until Thursday of this week, and maybe later. I know enough about it now to know that there is enough evidence to inflame the country. The question will have to be determined as to how to use the information in the most effective way but with the least harmful results to our sentimental equilibrium. Anticipating that they will be ready for a report by Thursday I have called a tentative

[98] Since the 1840's the International settlement at Shanghai had been governed by a municipal council elected by the foreign taxpayers. A small detachment of U.S. marines had been stationed there since 1937. See below, p. 138.

meeting for three o'clock that afternoon at which will be present [J. Edgar] Hoover of the F.B.I., General [Sherman] Miles of M.I.D. [Military Intelligence] and Admiral [Walter] Anderson of O.N.I. [Naval Intelligence], the idea being that the information contained in the report may be such as to require some immediate steps for supervision and possibly for taking in custody certain individuals and which ought to be done, if it is to be done, before any public use is made of the information on which the action is based. . . .

October 3, 1940

About noon I had a long satisfactory conversation with the President on the subject of refugees. McDonald, Chairman of the President's Advisory Committee on Refugees [1940–1945], has developed a very definite and violent antagonism to me. He thinks I have been non-cooperative and obstructive and has given evidence of his personal animosity. In a recent conversation in Mr. Welles' office he indicated that I had a superlative ego and a vindicative [*sic*] mentality added to his disregard, to put it lightly, of me. During that conversation I responded enthusiastically to the thought that he lay the matter before the President. He did not do so at the time but apparently approached Mrs. Roosevelt and she got a wrong impression. As a matter of fact we had been more generous with the President's Advisory Committee than we had with any of the other groups which have been active in arranging for refugees to leave Europe, and that has been the case because he was Chairman of the President's Advisory Committee. Nevertheless, he presented the matter in a very sorry light and made several misstatements of fact in his conversation with Mrs. Roosevelt. She wrote the President; the President talked to Welles; and Welles suggested the President see me and talk it over.

So when I saw him this morning the whole subject of immigration, visas, safety of the United States, procedures to be followed; and all that sort of thing was on the table. I found that he was 100% in accord with my ideas. He said that when Myron Taylor had returned from Europe recently the only thing which they discussed outside of Vatican matters was the visa and refugee situation and the manner in which our Consulates were being deprived of a certain amount of discretion by the rulings of the Department. It was these very things which created the recent difficulty between McDonald and myself, because we had reinvested the Consuls with their legitimate authority after having noted from our experiences in the other and more lax administration that we were admitting persons who should not properly come into the United States. The President expressed himself as in entire accord with the policy which would exclude persons about whom there was any suspicion that they would be inimical to the welfare of the United States no matter who had vouchsafed for them and irrespective of their financial or other standing. I left him with the satisfactory thought that he was whole-heartedly in support of the policy which would resolve in favor of the United States any doubts about admissability of any individual. I specifically presented to him the case Rabbi Wise had been urging upon me. They were a man and his wife who had represented the Rabbi's organization but who professed to a long series of political activities in Europe and an intention to follow a course in the United States irrespective of the desires of the American Government but to take orders from the World Jewish Congress. They professed to have been responsible for the overthrow of one Rumanian government and to have been very active in politics in Europe for years. The President agreed that those persons ought not be admitted to the United States in spite of the fact that Rabbi Wise in all sincerity desired them here. We discussed several other individual matters as illustrative of policy, and I found him in entire agreement in every single instance. He said he would call for Mr. McDonald and have a talk with him. . . .

October 4, 1940

Had a meeting in my office with the heads of F.B.I., M.I.D., O.N.I. and the Dies Committee. The Dies Committee submitted a list of some two thousand odd names. There was apparent jealousy and friction between the F.B.I. and the Dies Committee. I did my best to keep it all on an even keel and to place the interests of the country above the pride and special interests of any branch of the Government. To a large measure I was successful and the lists were finally turned over to F.B.I.

Almost immediately it became apparent that the labor situation in the United States might militate against action being taken against names on the list. A number of these people belong to various unions and some of them are prominent persons in the unions—even names on this list. The unions might call all their members out in case some of them were arrested. This develops a matter of high policy which will have to be settled by the White House. It will not arise today or tomorrow. The meeting adjourned until next Thursday at three o'clock. Prior to that time, however, I think the matter may have to be submitted to the White House for its guidance in case trouble does happen in case activity should start because of these lists. These lists are only part of the general names. The F.B.I. already has a considerable list which it has been working on for some years and has kept current with the Army and Navy files.

On the whole it is one of the most important things we have on hand, because it runs to sabotage not only of our own ships but of the aircraft we are sending to England, and there have been several incidents recently, one in the Bath Ship Yard and one in the complete destruction of a brand new airplane in the air, the loss of which cannot be explained, and both of which are directly attributable to subversive activities.

October 7, 1940

Early this morning I went to see the Secretary. He said he had not disturbed me yesterday but that he wanted to advise me about the developments in relation to the Far East. It had been decided to direct the wives and children of Naval and Army officers and Americans in general to leave the Far East and to do so as soon as practicable; the accommodations on the regular liners were booked up until the first of December. Chances were about 50–50 as to whether the Japanese would proceed on through Cochin-China and Thailand and attack Singapore. In that development it would be a question of policy as to what our Navy should do. In order that they might be ready for any eventuality they had decided to concentrate the fleet again at Honolulu and prepare it for instant action. The first step had been the recall to colors on Saturday of the entire Naval Reserve, both officers and enlisted men. Preparations were under way for supplies and ammunition. They would be ready for any eventuality. It did not mean that the eventuality would develop. Under the circumstances, however, it became advisable to get Americans out of the Far East. As soon as they were removed and as the rear guard of the movement the Marines stationed at Tientsin and Shanghai would be withdrawn. He asked me to proceed with the plans for evacuation.

I am also advised by Berle's office that from a reliable source they have learned that the Gestapo is contemplating the arrest of two members of the American Consulate at Prague as having been engaged in activities inimical to the Reich.

I can see very plainly the fearful trend of present events. England is going to announce the opening of the Burma Road. Japan will say that that is a hostile act and directed against her in her war against China. Japan will very probably declare war upon England. She will enlist through the government at Vichy the entire cooperation of Indo-China to carry on operations against the Burma Road. If Indo-China shows any disinclination, Japan will move into Indo-China in force, and Thailand, the old Siam, will immediately move to reoccupy certain of the provinces contiguous to her borders which France took from Siam and annexed to Indo-China. This puts Thailand and Japan in coordination and practically as allies. Thailand, under the Japanese urge, will attempt to move across to Penang and help the Japanese in an encircling movement aimed at Singapore. Singapore is the objective of Japan. As long as England holds it Japan's trade with the Netherlands East Indies is jeopardized and her use of her merchant ships to carry oil and other supplies north from Java are subject to momentary interruption by the British from Singapore. Consequently, Singapore is its objective, and Singapore is thinly held because Britain's navy is largely engaged other places, particularly in the eastern Mediterranean, in the neighborhood of Gibraltar and around the British Isles. There are several wounded ducks at a British port on the west coast of

Africa. Two of her big ships were damaged in the fight at Dakar. So that Singapore is thinly held and the Japanese think they would have an easier time investing it now than they would in the future.

From Bangkok we get advice that the government there is a military dictatorship and that the Prime Minister is either a tool in their hands or a willing collaborator and that they are ready to cooperate with Japan to the fullest extent.

From Moscow we get the information that the British Ambassador there talked to Molotov[99] on Friday and said things to him from which Molotov should very plainly infer that the United States and Great Britain were collaborating in the Pacific and that the United States would support the British Navy in the protection of Singapore. The British Ambassador subsequently talked to Steinhardt and Steinhardt inferred that the British Ambassador had over-stated his case with the idea of impressing Molotov. The British are trying to persuade the Russians to join with England against the tri-partite agreement,[100] but Molotov winced at the suggestion of cooperation with England, but he recovered somewhat when he understood that the cooperation was intended only in the support of China.

I cannot see how Russia can cooperate with England under the present circumstances. If she did she would invite war on two fronts. Of course if she had war on two fronts it would relieve the Straits Settlements as well as the British Isles from the pressure under which they now are.

But the point of it all is that our Navy is standing ready, and British Ambassadors are giving intimations that the United States is going to cooperate with Great Britain. If I could only work it out so that Russia would take some reckless step and cause both Germany and Japan to close in on it, we might be in a better position to help mop up. But if that does not happen, it looks to me as if little by little we were going to be faced with a situation which will bring us into conflict with Japan, and if the Japanese declare war on England within the next week or two we will face a decision of policy at that time.

October 8, 1940

. . . Cordell today gave more evidence of extreme understanding of the implications involved than in my recent conversations with him. He does not desire war with Japan. At the same time conversations are proceeding

[99] Vyacheslav Molotov, Soviet Minister for Foreign Affairs, 1939–1949, and premier of the U.S.S.R., 1930–1941.
[100] Although the Tri-partite Alliance between Japan, Germany, and Italy of September 27 affirmed that its terms did not apply to the Soviet Union, as the Soviet-German non-aggression pact of 1939 was still in effect, it in fact provided the basis for a new series of Axis political agreements in eastern Europe. What amounted to an anti-Soviet bloc of states was formed under German sanction.

between Welles and the Russian Ambassador in continuation of the conversations they have held but necessarily involving today Russia's position since the Tri-partite agreement and what she can or will do. I have not been consulted about that phase of it, but I have distinct impressions that no definitive arrangement should be made with Russia for the reason that she is incapable of being of any effective assistance to anybody and for the additional reason that she would do whatever is best to save her own skin for the time being.

Preliminary to the general conference on the Far East I was alone with the Secretary and took up again with him the general situation out there and the prospect of an unfortunate incident unless we straightened out the Shanghai situation. There are two delicate situations there, one having arisen because of the entrance into the American Sector of a number of Japanese marines in plain clothes. They were arrested and it caused a situation which has not yet been straightened out. The other situation concerns the territory evacuated by the British and the insistence of the Japanese of occupying that area.

As far as the first is concerned, a telegram came in which indicates that on the basis of a new phraseology for an exchange of notes between the respective military authorities at Shanghai the incident might be settled, and I suggested that that be removed as a point of irritation by trying to settle on the basis of the new proposal. The Secretary's reply was that we were going to withdraw from Shanghai and that as soon as the Marines were out that would settle the whole question. I remarked that the Marines couldn't get out for two or three months and that there might be irritating complications and that if we pushed this one out of the way there would be one less to dispose of. He said that the Japanese were so disposed that they would create another situation and reiterated that the withdrawal of the Marines would settle the whole question. So that's that.

October 9, 1940

I took up again with the Secretary the Far Eastern situation. I told him that it was apparent to my mind that England was making statements which led to the direct inference that the United States was to cooperate with England in the Far East. The British Ambassador in Moscow reported to Steinhardt the former's conversation with Molotov and made statements which could only lead to that inference. Lothian has permitted the impression to gain currency that the United States is to be allied with England. Churchill and other public characters in London have given the same impression. I asked him point blank whether he was aware of any understanding. He replied in the negative and said that not only was there no understanding as far as his knowledge went but there was no predicate for an understanding. Lothian had approached him on several occasions in discussions of Singapore and other available bases, and he had always replied that it was not necessary to discuss matters of that character; that everybody knew those places existed; that the British people and the American people were on friendly terms; and if the desirability or necessity for any such activity on the part of the United States for the use of any such ports should in the future develop that those matters could be settled then.

Hull said that he had absolutely no knowledge of any agreement for the use of Singapore and had only yesterday talked to the President and the President had said to him, "You don't think we ought to occupy Singapore, do you?" And he had replied, "No, Mr. President, I have no idea we ought to use Singapore." He said that unless the President had given some specific statement, which he felt he couldn't and wouldn't have done without advising the Secretary of State; that there was no other way for an understanding to be arrived at; and that to the best of his knowledge and belief there was no understanding of any kind with any foreign Government and specifically not with England. He looks upon the Navy's activities as regards Hawaii and their reenforcement of personnel there and the acquisition of ships for those purposes as being simply a measure of preparedness. He thinks the time may come when the question will have to be decided as to whether or not they shall move from Hawaii to the west, but I am satisfied today that he is definitely of the opinion that we are not proceeding towards war with Japan and that no commitment of any kind has been made with England to cooperate in the Pacific or anywhere else.[101]

I also took the occasion to warn him about Hornbeck. He realizes the antipathy which Hornbeck holds for Japan and the lengths to which his rather violent mentality will lead him. He said that he realized that and was taking steps to circumvent Hornbeck by talking directly to [Maxwell] Hamilton, who is Chief of the Far Eastern Division [1937–1943]. I said that that was all right within the Department but Hornbeck should not be entrusted as a spokesman for the Department, as he was yesterday when he was told to take up some matters with the Chief of Staff. He accepted the suggestion and said he agreed with me thoroughly and would arrange that in the future. My knowledge of Hornbeck runs back to more than twenty years ago. When I was in the Department during the last war he tried to get a position in the Department and was unsuccessful. His temperament and all were unsatisfactory to us at that time. However, during the Harding regime he was taken in and has been here ever since. And he is rather a dangerous man, in my opinion, when delicate matters are concerned in connection with which he has a violent prejudice.

---

[101] With the fall of the Netherlands, Japan increased diplomatic pressure to obtain economic control of the Netherlands East Indies while avoiding the risk of direct conflict with the Western nations. American policy attempted to bring economic and diplomatic pressure on Japan in order to keep the *status quo*.

One encouraging development is indicated from Tokyo. Grew was called hurriedly and urgently to the Foreign Office. He was told that the Japanese Government had noticed with some surprise that the United States was to place an entire embargo on Japan and that Americans were being "ordered" out of Japan and China and Indo-China. They wanted to know what it all meant. Grew replied that in the first place he knew of no general embargo, and in the second place that Americans had not been "ordered" out but it had been suggested that they might want to leave because of general hostilities. He added that the American Government was peacefully inclined and was not an aggressive military organization. The Japanese replied that Japan was very peacefully inclined and had no intention of fighting the United States and going to war. The perturbation which they showed and the urgency of the call all indicate that the Japanese are considerably worried. The trouble is, however, that the army does not take orders from the Foreign Office. . . .

October 10, 1940

. . . There came up several other questions [at a meeting with Roosevelt attended by Hull, Welles and Long], among them that of partial embargoes against Japan. The President's position was that we were not to shut off oil from Japan or machine tools from Japan and thereby force her into a military expedition against the Dutch East Indies but that we were to withhold from Japan only such things as we vitally needed ourselves, such as high test gas and certain machine tools and certain machinery which we absolutely now needed ourselves; that there was to be no prodding of Japan and that we were not going to get into any war by forcing Japan into a position where she was going to fight for some reason or other.

The Dies Committee matter he [Roosevelt] suggested be turned over to the Attorney General in the ordinary course and that he be confronted with the evidence which we had secured from the Dies Committee in order that he might bring deportation proceedings or whatever other proceedings might be justified against persons who had been acting improperly in this country; and that subsequently we should take up with the German Embassy the question of cancellation of exequaturs of any members of the German Consulate staffs who had been engaged in extra-Consular and improper functions.

That takes the thing out of the hands of the Dies Committee and puts it in the hands of the Department of Justice and dispenses with the idea of a public hearing before the Dies Committee. . . .

I thought the President looked very well, though his face was somewhat drawn. A lot of little lines are developing around the larger ones. He is carrying an enormous load, but he seems to have it all at his finger tips. He was right "on the ball" in each of the varied different subjects we presented this afternoon.

I called up Dies down in Texas and told him that the President had decided
to submit the documents he had furnished to the Attorney General in order
that he institute proceedings if he found them justified against the Trans-
Ocean group, headed by Zapp, and the other irregularities in connection with
their enterprise in this country.[102] I suggested to him that under the circumstances it would not be possible to hold the public hearing until after the
Attorney General had instituted proceedings or come to some other conclusion and that that would probably take some weeks. Dies said that he was perfectly willing and he was willing to play ball and that he was going to extend
his investigations against some private business concerns and he thought he
was going to raid one of them tomorrow. He said it might raise a flurry in
public opinion but he felt it justified because he found there was a group of
important American business men who were cooperating with German,
Italian and Japanese interests in an "appeasement" program. I asked him if
the name of one of the gentlemen began with the letter "M" (meaning Jim
Mooney[103] of General Motors). He said it did begin with "M."

He said he had a list of more than 100,000 names which he was going to
submit to me and that he was going to submit to me copies of all the documents he found. I could not refuse to accept them, nor could I side-step the
offer, but I don't know what in the world I can do with 100,000 names or
with a constant stream of documents, but I will do the best I can if and when
they develop. During the conversation I told him it would probably be some
weeks before he could start his public hearings but that by that time he might
want to extend the scope of them.

October 11, 1940

The President commented very adversely and critically yesterday about
Bullitt, Phillips, Kennedy, Cudahy and other Ambassadors who felt they had
been so over-worked they had to come home and go on a long rest cure. I
reminded him that I "flopped" on him once. He replied that that was different
because I was really an ill man; that that didn't count; but these other fellows
seemed to think that since a few bombs had missed them that they were nervous wrecks and candidates for rest cures. Welles reported he had a telephone
conversation with Kennedy yesterday morning and Kennedy was in a very
bad humor and was coming home. He would rather have orders to come, but
if he did not get orders he was coming anyhow and resign. The President did
not want him to come. He looks upon him as a trouble-maker and as a person
entirely out of hand and out of sympathy. Welles insisted upon recommenda-

[102] The Transocean News Service, a German agency for the dissemination of Nazi
propaganda in the United States, was accused by the House Un-American Activities
Committee of being engaged in espionage activities. Manfred Zapp was the head of the
agency in America.
[103] James D. Mooney, vice president of General Motors, in charge of overseas operations.

tion and he finally compromised by saying he could come home the latter part of this month and that he would himself send him a personal letter, which Welles was to draft, giving him instructions about his conversation and conduct when he got here.

The only reference to politics during the whole conversation of more than an hour was his [Welles] expressed thought that Kennedy might come out for Willkie. He realizes Kennedy is in a terrible blue funk about England would give that impression here and would advise the public probably that England was about to collapse. The President thought that would be very unfortunate. He also thought Kennedy's resentment would carry him so far as to urge the election of Willkie. The President also gradually got to the point of stating that we are no nearer war now than we had been for six years and he was going to make an opportunity on his train today or tomorrow to talk to newspaper men and to give that definite impression. I told him that the Hearst press was starting on a campaign in New York today to give the definite impression that Roosevelt was headed for war and Willkie for peace. He said that he was not headed for war and that he was going to call the newspaper correspondents aboard his train and give a direct talk to them and emphasize the fact that we were trying to steer clear of war and doing everything possible to keep away from war and were no nearer war now than we were since the war started. . . .

October 16, 1940

The war gets more complicated. Germany is now in Rumania. The British very stupidly conducted sabotage activities there that were traced to the British diplomatic mission. The facts were not disclosed to the public but they resulted in a complete disfavor for the English, which made the German task easier. Russia is still undecided, apparently, as to what to do or when to do it. There are 150,000 to 200,000 Russian troops on the Rumanian border, but Rumania is now under the control of Germany. Turkey and Russia show signs of collaboration, and I assume Russia would rather have Turkey in charge of the Dardanelles than Germany. Germany is apparently headed toward the Dardanelles, and Italy is prepared to attack Greece with the prospect of a battle on the part of the Greeks. There are now ten Italian divisions in Albania, and they can be moved either against Yugoslavia or against Greece.

The Axis is apparently moving in three directions, outside of the British Isles: down through the Balkans to close Suez with Italy working across the Libyan desert with the same objective, down through Spain to control Gibraltar and with the Japanese down through Indo-China and Thailand to control Singapore.

It is all a fantastic procedure. It would be incredible if it were not true. The developments of the last fifteen months have been almost incredible, and the principal item of it all was the complete collapse of France, which nobody foresaw—not even the Germans.

In conversation with General Marshall[104] at lunch today with the Chiefs of Staff of the Pan American states, but in private conversation, he said that the Germans must have discovered some new principle, for they were not attacking England in mass formation. They tried the mass formation at first and lost so heavily that they were forced to use their lighter planes and forego the formation. Now, however, they are back with the heavier planes in formation and the British are not able, as yet at least, to stop them. Consequently, London is having the worst time of the war. He does not know what the principle involved may be. It may be the adjustment or replacement of a gun in the rear cockpit, or it may be some new armor device, or it may be something else. Whatever the new idea developed it remains as yet unknown, but he assumes that some prisoner will talk and sooner or later the development may be known.

The political campaign at home proceeds largely with activity on the part of the Republicans. Willkie *seems* to have made some gains in the last week. Whether the gains are actual or vocal it is hard to determine. The Republicans have a great deal of money, and they have practically all of the press. They are able to get headlines and to give wide publicity to Willkie's utterances. But his utterances are inadequate and misleading, but that is what one must expect in a political campaign.

We have asked Germany if she would give us a safe conduct for another ship to go to Ireland to repatriate Americans. Heretofore we have not asked for a safe conduct for any ship except the *American Legion*, and that was a Government-owned vessel. Since then, however, the Germans have declared a blockade of the British Isles and adjoining waters, so we have come to the conclusion we would ask Germany whether she would grant a safe conduct in case we asked for it and indicated we would ask for it in case the answer were in the affirmative. There are about 700 Americans in England that Kennedy is crazy to get home, and we may feel that we owe them the obligation to send a boat for them even though practically all the boats we have sent have come back with accommodations vacant and these people were notified and refused to come. . . .

October 19, 1940

Finally finished the negotiations for the voyage of the *Washington*. The letter was signed this morning, and it left this morning on its way to the Far East to evacuate Americans. Two other boats of our line to Australia are already on the way.

[104] George C. Marshall, Army chief of staff, 1939–1945.

Had a long conference yesterday at luncheon with Welles, Solicitor General Biddle and Hart[105] about the functions of the President's Advisory Committee [on Political Refugees]. We came to an understanding which is definite as to the extent of the functions of the Consuls abroad. They have entire authority even though the names are recommended to them by the President's Committee to withhold visas if in their discretion the persons are not as represented or if their presence in the United States would be inimical to the interests of the United States. . . .

October 21, 1940

Another very busy day. Kirk here from Berlin. He consents to go to Rome and will take over the Villa Taverna. He goes back under protest and thinks there ought to be an Ambassador. That is not possible under our present policy.

The French fleet has been manned by an extra call of 43,000 men and has left Toulon "on maneuvers." It looks as if the French and the Italian fleets were going to join up and tackle the British in the Eastern Mediterranean. The British fleet has incurred some losses which have not been advertised, and it is not at top fighting strength. In my opinion the British are in a rather serious situation in the Mediterranean.

Another long session on the Defense Communications Board, which was from 12:45 to three o'clock, including lunch there; so that since my arrival this morning until now, something after six o'clock, I have not had a free instant, and I am catching a seven o'clock train to New York.

October 25, 1940

This is the 25th. The 23rd I spent at Democratic Headquarters in New York. Was in conference with Flynn, Michelson, Wayne Johnson, etc. They seem to think that the campaign is in very good shape. Some of them have doubts about New York, but Vincent Daley [*sic*][106] is rather definite in his statements that he will hold the up-State majority down to three or four hundred thousand and that New York City will pile up seven to nine hundred thousand. They will leave a leeway of somewhere in the neighborhood of half a million. A large registration does not seem to worry them.

There are several weak spots that we might lose, such as Massachusetts, Connecticut, New Jersey, Ohio, Michigan, Illinois and Wisconsin. There are certain States that Willkie probably will carry: the two Dakotas, Kansas, Nebraska, Maine and Vermont. The others mentioned are more or less

[105] Francis Biddle, U.S. Solicitor General, 1940–1941; David A. Hart, Assistant United States Attorney.

[106] Edward J. Flynn, National Chairman of the Democratic party, 1940–1942; Wayne Johnson, chairman of the Democratic National Finance Committee; Vincent Dailey, assistant chairman of the New York State Democratic party.

doubtful. The chances are that he will get some and we will get some. Those not mentioned seem to be safe for Roosevelt, which would give him a safe majority.

Went down to Princeton that night and attended a Trustees' meeting the next day. There came up the question of University supervision and control of the upper-class clubs and all of its implications concerning student social life. I could not accede to the proposals and spoke briefly against them before the Board. I had seen the proposals only two days before and took my position largely on the fact that owing to the lack of time I had been unable to convince myself it was the right thing to do. The Board was very largely in favor of it and so the resolution was passed. . . .

October 28, 1940

The war spreads farther. Italy attacked Greece this morning, and England has come to the assistance of Greece, which will probably pull Germany down on Yugoslavia and Turkey. Anyhow Greece is in. The objective of course is the Suez Canal. The King of Egypt[107] is leaning away from the British. . . .

November 3, 1940

All week I have been awfully busy—politics piled on top of foreign affairs —probably to the detriment of each. The campaign is in its closing days and is hectic—as always they are at this stage. I think Roosevelt will win by a comfortable margin—perhaps 100 electoral votes. New York State seems to be *very* close—considering the size of the vote. Our people figure we can carry it by some 25,000 to 300,000—bottom and top estimate. That is close. We do not *need* it—but it would be better to have it. There is disaffection there with the Italian vote (because of the "dagger" speech) and naturally with the Germans. And there are many thousand of each.

I have been instrumental in getting Kennedy to speak right—and in getting Bennett Clark on the radio—have telephoned for money contributions and have probably got around $25,000 into the coffers—and we need it badly. The Republicans have millions. We are having trouble paying for radio time.

Tonight I have talked to Dr. Dixon[108] at Mayo's about "Socialized Medicine" and the reports circulated to our disadvantage that we favor it— which we do not. Talked to Dr. McIntire[109] at the White House to get a repetition into the President's speech tomorrow night of his speech on the subject at the Cancer Research hospital—which hardly anyone heard because it was at four in the afternoon.

[107] Farouk I, king of Egypt, 1936–1952.
[108] Dr. Claude F. Dixon, head of surgery, Mayo Clinic, Rochester, Minnesota.
[109] Ross McIntire, personal physician to the President.

November 6, 1940

Yesterday was Election Day. I voted early and came to the Department and left early. Spent the evening at home by the radio taking down the returns. I had been very confident of the election and had thought that Roosevelt would win by a large majority. A few days ago at the Club I participated in a pool, which I apparently won. I gave Roosevelt 486 electoral votes as my estimate in the pool. He has 470 up to noon today and probably will get more. There have been no great shifts in sentiment or public opinion. None of the groups which have been backing Roosevelt have left him. Individuals have differed with him and some of the soi-disant leaders like Al Smith, John Davis[110] and John L. Lewis and others have opposed him, but they have not carried their followers with them nor have they induced their groups to oppose Roosevelt. The consequence is Roosevelt continued to represent the hopes, the beliefs, the aspirations, the judgments of that great body of Americans who lie between ultra-conservatives on the extreme right and ultra-radicals on the extreme left. It is a great thing for America that he has been re-elected. It is hard to conceive what would have developed in the international situation if Roosevelt had been repudiated by the American people, with Germany on the rampage in one part of the world and Japan rampant in the other. Each would have felt that the opportunity was ripe for further aggression, and the situation confronting the United States would have been more complicated.

I was up late last night, so slept somewhat late this morning and arrived late at the Department. Kennedy came down, and I sat in for a long talk with him, the Secretary and Welles. He is quite a realist, and he sees England gone. I think he is probably somewhat influenced by the situation he has been in. It could hardly be otherwise. Bombs dropping around, industry paralyzed and communication lines being gradually disrupted must bring with them a sense of defeatism.

Anyway, Kennedy thinks that England is broke; that she will have about two hundred million dollars in gold; that she can spend that here but if she does she will have to go off the gold standard; that if she goes off the gold standard her obligation to us cannot be met; that in any case she cannot continue to buy from us for cash and that she must have money. He said that they were just waiting until the present moment, after the election, to present to us their requests for credits. Without credits they cannot continue. He warned them that changing our system was a question of changing our laws and that change could not be easily done and would require a great deal of consideration and possible delay in action, if there was to be any action.

He thinks we ought to be realists in our policy; that we ought to realize

[110] Alfred E. Smith, Democrat, governor of New York, 1919–1920, 1923–1928, and Democratic presidential nominee in 1928, joined with John W. Davis, Democratic presidential nominee in 1924, in denouncing Roosevelt for seeking an unprecedented third term.

that the British Empire is gone; that the British Navy may be gone. Even with the British Navy afloat they have won only one victory and that at Montevideo. Every time they have gone in range of a shore battery or an air field on land they have been defeated. They are unable to clear the seas of raiders. If Italy is successful in Greece and Germany goes on into Turkey, the British bases in the Mediterranean will have to be abandoned, and they will be forced out of the Mediterranean, if they can get out. He sees the Empire crumbling.

On the other hand, he sees Hitler rampant on European soil, dominant even over England. He sees a new philosophy, both political and economic, with the United States excluded from European markets and from Far Eastern markets and from South American markets, for he feels that we are not able to absorb the products of South America except for gold and that we would soon be transferring our gold to South America and that the process could not last very long.

Consequently he thinks that we ought to take some steps to implement a realistic policy and make some approach to Germany and to Japan which would result in an economic collaboration. He does not see how or what. He has no suggestion to make. He only feels that what we are doing is wrong but does not know how to do it right.

He says we are sending Generals and Admirals to England and instead we ought also to be sending economic experts. He says England is just as much of a socialistic state today as is Germany or Italy. He is sure that England cannot hold out unless America will just take over the airplane production and furnish England thousands and thousands and thousands of planes. She will not be able to make planes much longer. Even when she does receive them from America she has to put them in the factories and supplement them with armor. He said she had not received from the United States, up to the time he left, one single fighting plane. English planes were superior to the Germans and the English fighting flying men were superior to the Germans. He has seen three English fighting planes drive off and bring down twenty Germans, but the Germans have now adopted a new technique in maneuvers, and now they do get through to London, and they have very great explosives. He has seen twenty houses collapsed by one. They now do penetrate, and they allow seven minutes to get from the coast to London. He thinks the English will soon be battered into a desire for some understanding with Germany and that Churchill will go and that Lloyd George will take his place.

Furthermore, he thinks that the spirit and the morale of the world is broken; that people have lost their faith in God. He cited an example of a little church in Horta which was holding a vesper service and that there was a crowd of men on the other side of the street. Upon being approached the men said there was no use in going to church, that men could no longer believe in

God, that the situations which were developing in the world could never happen if there was a God; that they were disillusioned; they were without hope.

He is going to take a short vacation and use up his leave for a month or more and then he is going to return to Washington and see the President. He is going to say that if there is something real to be done in England and if a policy can be worked out that will insure the winning of this war that he will go back to England, but if there is not that he will tell the President that there is nothing for him to do in England and that he will resign. He does not believe in our present policy. He does not believe in the continuing of democracy. He thinks that we will have to assume a Fascist form of government here or something similar to it if we are to survive in a world of concentrated and centralized power.

After the interview I spoke to him at some length and he expanded somewhat more upon his political and economic theories. He said he was going to the west coast and would see Hearst and try and set him right and see other publishers like McCormick. I told him he ought not to talk to the press or to talk in a way that would scare the American people or scare them; that the American people needed education in foreign affairs and that to thrust it upon them too suddenly would be disastrous. He agreed and said that he would not do that.

I will have a chance to talk with him again after he comes back to Washington.

November 7, 1940

As one of the crowd I saw the President come up Pennsylvania Avenue and enter the White House grounds on his triumphal return to the capital. A real lot of enthusiasm for Washington to manifest.

Later I saw him for a few minutes at his desk and congratulated him. He looks pretty well—and not as tired as one would think. He said he was going off on his yacht for a few days away from the telephone. . . .

Kennedy told me Hitler had twice sent him a message asking him to go to Germany for a conference—which he of course refused. Hitler must have got the impression Kennedy had views which Hitler might use as an approach to us. As a matter of fact Kennedy thinks we ought to lay the basis for some cooperation. He does not go to the extent of appeasing—but the extent to which he would go is undefined. His ideas as to what should be done are nebulous—but he is positive in the thought something should be done—some uncharted way found. He sees nothing else to trade with and fears the consequences of industrial competition. He also holds to the idea what we need is bigger, faster and more airplanes—bombers, fighters, etc.; no navy is useful in competition with planes; more and bigger warships are useless; planes are the masters of the vessels within 250 miles of an air base.

November 12, 1940

Beginning last Thursday I have each day except Sunday had long talks with the Secretary about general policy. That would be the mornings of the 7th, 8th, 9th and 11th. Welles was there two or three times; Norman Davis on the Saturday morning conference. And I wish I had made memoranda contemporaneously with the conversations, but the crush of things has just prevented taking the time necessary to make memoranda until late in the evening, and each evening I was so tired that I just could not do it.

It started off on Thursday [November 7] with Cordell and myself. He opened the conversation by remarking that the election had continued the Roosevelt policies in force and effect but that the road ahead was awfully hard. We then got into a discussion of the domestic situation with the necessity for very heavy expenditures and higher taxes. He was afraid that there would be a tendency toward regimentation. He was afraid that we were moving toward inflation. In argument I suggested that it was not a question of what the debt limit should be; that it had to go above forty-five billion because we were engaged in a work of buying armament which could not be paid for unless it did. I expressed the thought that this country could stand a debt of one hundred billion. We had 250% coverage for our circulation, and our national debt was to be measured not by the gold we had on hand but by the resources of our soil and our subsoil and the energy and ingenuity of our people; that the national income was now seventy billions of dollars; and that no important country on earth had a smaller per capita debt or a higher per capita coverage for its monetary need. Norman Davis had come in, and he more or less agreed with me. Cordell said that the first time he had heard those theories expressed in a general way was in 1892—meaning the campaign of Cleveland when he was confronted with the silver question and when the taxation program of Henry George was a political issue.

We then went into the foreign field and discussed generally the deterioration abroad, Italy's campaign against Greece and the probable position of Russia, the difficulty of the British maintaining their fleet at Crete, and the gloomy side of the eastern Mediterranean picture, and the economic effect on the United States of Hitler's control of Europe. . . .

We then got into the situation of the Far East. I was just thinking aloud—not making any proposals or making any concrete suggestions, but simply to use the situations that existed in order to be useful in evolving a policy.

As the basic thought that it was necessary for England to win, and with the terrible damage she is sustaining to her convoys and merchant shipping at the present time, it was my thought that if our fleet could be in the Atlantic, Germany would be at a great disadvantage and would hesitate to do many things. It would certainly strengthen the hand of England. However, for the fleet to be in the Atlantic it had to be taken out of the Pacific. If it is taken out of the Pacific Japan will have an entirely free hand and will be urged by Germany to proceed on her campaign of expansion. To prevent that we have got to do one or the other of two things. First, we have got to lick Japan in the Pacific before we can take our fleet out—and if we started to do that we would have war in the Atlantic too—or second, we have got to come to some understanding with Japan. Concentrating for the moment on what understanding was possible with Japan, I thought it was a good omen that they were sending us a new Ambassador who had standing at home and real influence in Japan. Through his reasonable attitude toward the United States we might find an opening. If we shut off oil from Japan it would force her to go to the Dutch East Indies, because she had to have oil. Being unable to get it here she would have to get it there. However, to get to the Dutch East Indies she would be gambling terribly, because Singapore would be on her line of communication, and with even a modicum of British Naval units at Singapore she would be taking a chance on every shipment of oil she sent out and would have a very long extended line of communications. Japan would not want to go to the Dutch East Indies without eliminating Singapore, and that seems impossible at the moment. Consequently it becomes a matter of policy for us to continue to sell oil to Japan and to sell her other things.

I questioned the embargo on scrap iron. Japan does not *need* the scrap iron. She can use it and can get a better quality of steel, but Japan has two million tons of iron ore a year available to her in Japan proper, Korea, Manchuria and northern China. So that she does not actually need the scrap iron, though she would prefer to have it. So the shutting off of scrap iron becomes simply an irritant, and various other little things we have done, like withholding the issuing of exequaturs for two additional Japanese Consulates, in this country, are only additional irritants. They do no effective good, and they do act as obstacles to the bettering of relations. Whether it will be possible to come to an understanding with Japan is another thing. It might not be, but I thought we ought not put little petty obstacles in the path of an understanding. If we could come to an understanding with Japan, even for the duration of the war, without sacrificing any principle on our part, we would then be in a position to move the fleet out of the Pacific and bolster up the situation in the Atlantic so that Germany would hesitate, and the time might come when it would be infinitely useful to have our fleet concentrated and mobile.

The Secretary said that he had done every reasonable thing to bring Japan to an understanding and that he had worried and thought and tried every expedient but that Japan made it impossible to proceed with any order. He did not throw out the possibility of an understanding but did not know how to proceed to attain it without sacrificing principle and felt that every time we relaxed in our rigorous attitude toward Japan she took advantage of the relaxation in the misconception that we were weak or were willing to permit her to carry out her designs to establish a "new order" in Asia and in the islands of the sea. He felt that once she got to Singapore she would be around to the Red Sea and the Gulf of Arabia. Of course that is a pretty long distance for Japan to move. It is more probable that Russia would edge her way down or that Germany would push her way through. . . .

For hours and hours, probably five or six hours, during these days we have sat and quietly discussed all the phases of international activity. In the meantime Pittman died. I have lost an intimate friend, and the Senate has lost its ablest member. He had one of the keenest intellects and was one of the most resourceful men I have ever known. Right after his reelection to the Senate on Tuesday he became weaker and his heart gave out on Saturday. I could not go to the funeral. They wanted me to go, but it is impossible for me to be away for a week, and it would take a week to get to Reno and return. [Walter] George of Georgia will succeed to the Foreign Relations Chairmanship, but he is not in sympathy with our foreign relations, and he is one of the men that the President tried to purge; so that both politically and from his international point of view he will be a more difficult man to deal with than Pittman. However, he is a man of fine honor and a very able citizen. He is an excellent lawyer and a high type of American.

In our conversations we also decided to send somebody, probably Robert Murphy[111] to North Africa on a tour to contact the French Governor and Generals there to see what could be done in the way of bolstering up and coordinating the French Colonial Empire in friendly cooperation with the United States as compared with the Vichy Government and incidentally as a means of promoting the cause against Germany. Murphy knows the men and talks the language well and has been our Chargé in Vichy. He seems to be the logical person to send.

November 13, 1940

Yesterday was a tough day. Amongst the other difficulties it developed late in the afternoon that the Governor of the Virgin Islands, [Lawrence W.] Cramer by name, under the guidance of the Solicitor in the Department of the Interior[112] and a Mr. Hart in the Department of Justice, had issued a proclamation admitting refugees to the Virgin Islands on their appearance at the port of entry. After a short period of residence in the Virgin Islands and an affidavit that they are bona fide residents they may proceed without visas or other formalities to the United States. There is no consular investigation of the individuals prior to their arrival in the Virgin Islands. There are twelve

---

[111] Counselor and chargé d'affaires of the American embassy, Vichy, France, 1940–1942. For Robert Murphy's account of his North African mission see his *Diplomat Among Warriors* (New York: Doubleday, 1964), pp. 66 ff.

[112] Nathan R. Margold, who held that office from 1933 to 1942.

thousand refugees in Portugal and the only practical limitation upon their proceeding to the Virgin Islands is that they have enough money so that they will not become public charges. Amongst the twelve thousand are many German agents. . . . The proclamation had been issued on the seventh and became effective yesterday and was to be published today. It constituted a pipe line to siphon refugees out of Portugal into the United States without the precautionary steps of investigation and checking and is part of a program which Mr. Hart has indulged in in connection with the President's Advisory Committee. Biddle, the Solicitor General, has been associated with him, but I think he has not quite understood the purposes and objectives.

As soon as I could see Hull I laid the matter before him. Prior to that I had tried to reach the President, but he was in his swimming pool. Hull authorized me to talk to the President, and I had the opportunity over the telephone at nine o'clock last night. When I explained the matter to him he was a little perturbed and asked me to talk to Ickes immediately and to call him back. I talked to Ickes and found that he knew of the order and had authorized it and that he was an advocate of the whole scheme. He said that he would send his Solicitor around to talk to me in the morning. I told him that our consular activities served as a sieve through which we could strain the applicants. His reply was that the holes in the sieve were too small and that they ought to be bigger and perhaps now we could negotiate and get them bigger. The inference was very plain that he was trying to take into the United States persons whom he thought the Department of State would not admit. He was rather obdurate and a little sarcastic.

At the end of the conversation I called the President again and told him the situation. He was still more provoked and said that he would send an order over there suspending the proclamation and authorized me to proceed with the scheme within the lines of his policy, which he has laid down and which I think I thoroughly understand.

November 14, 1940

. . . Lunched with [Bernard] Baruch. Louis Johnson[113] sat with us for most of the time, and through him and Baruch I got in touch with their airplane production activities. Johnson thinks we ought to have two billion dollars more in order to be effective, the principal part of which would be spent in plant expansion. He is satisfied with the progress of production in so far as the funds available permit. He disclosed to me that we were building stratosphere flying fortresses which cruise at a 38,000 foot level at three hundred miles an hour and are consequently above the reach of any anti-aircraft projectiles and above the range of all air machines with the exception that a few

[113] Former Assistant Secretary of War, 1937–1940.

of the fighters can reach that level but cannot stay there. Some of these are being made available to England. They descend to the 20,000 foot level for bombing purposes and are equipped with bombing sights which at that height are appallingly exact. They have a capacity for 4500 miles. We have made available to England the bombing sight developed by the Army, which is very effective, but it is not comparable to the secret bombing sight of the Navy. American genius in mechanized instrumentalities is so far superior to that of any country in the world that it is only a question of necessity for it which will produce whatever may be needed to have an instrument superior to that which any other Government can produce.

Louis Johnson was let out as Assistant Secretary of War and was not made Secretary as he hoped for. He has been somewhat provoked by it but has tried to play the game. He still hopes the President will give him some authoritative position in connection with production and principally with airplanes and that he will have with him a colleague of a business type. . . .

Molotov has been in Berlin for two days. The result of the conferences, we do not know.[114] We get reports. But they are all speculative. It is reasonable to suppose that Finland and Turkey are the two principal fields of discussion. They have rival ambitions in Finland—which may incidentally save the independence of Finland—and they have conflicting ambitions as regards Turkey because of the Dardanelles. Generally speaking, however, Russia will have to side with Germany for the time being. Cripps,[115] the British Ambassador in Moscow, was rather disillusioned by the visit of Molotov to Berlin because he had got the impression he was making some headway with the Russians and had so advised his Government. It stands to reason that Russia cannot play the British game under the present circumstances or cooperate in any way with England. To antagonize Germany at the present time might lead to almost immediate reprisals and is certain to lay the basis for future military activity against Russia on the part of Germany—if it were necessary to reinforce that intention on the part of Germany for future execution.

We are trying to keep Spain out, but we don't want to make any mistake, and we have authorized Weddell[116] to say to Franco that if the Spanish Government will make an open public declaration of its policy that we will be prepared to consider further the possibility of our making loans to Spain and to proceed with reasonable expedition.

---

[114] The Germans proposed that the Soviet Union associate with the Tri-partite Alliance (Germany, Italy, and Japan) and accept Iran and India as its sphere of influence. If this were acceptable, a separate agreement would be concluded with Turkey providing preferred treatment for Soviet vessels in the Straits. This did not satisfy the Soviet requirement that Germany should not have exclusive influence in the Balkans. Since this objection challenged German predominance in that area, Hitler carried the negotiations no further.

[115] Sir Stafford Cripps, British ambassador to the Soviet Union, 1940–1942.

[116] Alexander Weddell, ambassador to Spain, 1939–1942.

November 20, 1940

The situation in Europe gets a little thicker. Hungary signed up this morning as a member of the Rome, Berlin, Tokyo axis, and it looks as if Rumania and Jugoslavia and Bulgaria would do the same thing. That more or less opens the way for Germany to proceed against Turkey or against the Thrace end of Greece. They have a considerable number of troops and equipment already in Rumanian territory, and it looks now as if they would have to come to the help of Italy, which seems to have got a bear by the tail. The Greeks have inflicted severe losses on the Italians and have driven them back across the frontier and have done a great deal of damage to their lines of communication. . . .

The situation in Spain has deteriorated as well. No assurances can be obtained from the Spanish Government that they will not cooperate with the Axis powers, and there is every indication that they are gradually moving the line up against England and to either act themselves or to permit the Germans to act in the rear of Gibraltar.

In the meantime I am still having a good deal of trouble with refugees. With every desire in the world to save out of Europe intellectuals and outstanding persons who have made contributions to the arts, sciences, literature, etc., it seems difficult to draw the line and to get the other agencies of the Government to cooperate. We are still in negotiations with the Department of Justice on the subject of procedure. We have been admitting persons recommended by the President's Committee and recommended by various other individuals and organizations. However, mistakes are made from time to time and persons whom they recommend turn out to be different. The Committees making the recommendations are entirely sincere in the matter, but it is to be expected that they will make mistakes and that they are not entirely informed of other persons. A good example appeared the other day when one of our agents abroad was notified that a certain individual who had been given a visa and who had departed for the United States had now developed to be an expert dynamiter with subversive intent. His name was turned over to F.B.I., but that does not operate to prevent his entrance into the United States.

There are thousands and thousands of people in Europe trying to get to this country. There are many additional thousands at Haiti, Santo Domingo, Nicaragua, Mexico, Brazil and various other of the Republics in South America, and numbers of them now are appearing at Shanghai, having fled eastward out of Europe. The problem is to admit outside the quota persons who really ought to be admitted and to hold over for the regular quota immigration those who should come in the ordinary way under the ordinary processes of quota distribution. Our negotiations are continuing today, and it is expected that during the course of this day the Department of Justice will come to accept the line which we have been holding.

November 24, 1940

The Secretary returned this morning from his vacation after a ten days' rest. I went to the Department and sat in with him, Welles, Grady, Hackworth, Green[117] and Hamilton of the Far Eastern Division, and Feis. The Secretary took up the question of further restrictions upon exports to Japan. Before the conference began he showed me a memorandum of a conversation that he had made after some conversations with the British Ambassador prior to the latter's departure for England, in which memorandum the Secretary reviewed the world situation and took the position that you could not operate in the Far East without repercussions in Europe and that American policy had to be based upon the world situation rather than on the facts in any particular locality.

The National Defense Council and the Army and the Navy have been recommending that certain additional prohibitions should be placed upon exports to Japan. These additions would include about thirty different types of machine tools and certain ingredients used in the manufacture of the tetraethyl mixture which is injected into gasoline gas and which gives it its high octane quality. Having prohibited the export of high grade gas to Japan, the Treasury and the authorities mentioned were considering the extension of the prohibition to the materials which go into the manufacture of the ingredient to be added to gasoline.

There was a long interesting and involved discussion which was participated in by everyone present except myself. There was a difference of opinion as to whether or not the particular machine tools were of particular value to Japan. There was a difference of opinion as to whether or not they were necessary to us at this stage of our national defense. The Secretary continued to bring back the discussion to the broad plane of world conditions. It finally ended by authorizing Green to extend the list of certain machine tools which it was considered were necessary for our national defense; to withhold the ingredients for high octane gas for further consideration; and to call a conference tomorrow morning of the Chief of Staff and the Chief of Naval Operations with the Secretary of State in order that he might determine how far Navy was prepared to go in case the activities of the State Department in placing further embargoes upon Japan would cause a situation with Japan which would precipitate war. The movements of Japanese troops recently and their concentration on the coast were considered. Our attitude toward Japan and the possibility of Japanese movements southward from their present positions was considered. It developed that six submarines had left Honolulu for Manila and that six additional submarines were leaving this week.

[117] Joseph Green, chief of the State Department Office of Arms and Munition Controls, 1935–1941.

The whole movement is rather austere in its aspects. The Secretary was very loathe [sic] to do anything that would aggravate Japan to the point of war. He assumed they did not want a war with us, and he was sure we did not want a war with them. He wanted to be very careful lest the acts of the American Government should precipitate a war with Japan, and he wanted to know just how far the Navy was prepared to go before any steps were taken which might precipitate hostilities. After talking with the Chiefs of the Army and the Navy he was to see the President tomorrow afternoon and discuss the whole matter with him in order that the policy of the United States Government might be expressed as that of the whole Government and not as the independent action of any of the effective branches of the Government.

November 25, 1940

This morning the [Washington] *Post* carried a story very critical about me by one of the columnists. The origin of it goes back to the same as the other criticisms which have appeared heretofore but by different columnists. They find their source in the opposition of various groups to the policy which I have personified officially for the exclusion from the United States of undesirable persons and a very careful scrutiny of all who are permitted to come in. The pressure that has been brought to bear on me the last two months has been astonishing. The opposition is now using me as the fulcrum to pry open the door. I antagonized Ickes irreparably by opposing his Virgin Islands scheme, and he is aligned with certain persons in the Department of Justice and in other branches of the Government in an effort to unseat me officially.
. . .[118]

November 27, 1940

. . . I have talked several times recently with the Secretary and to Welles about persons in this Government who are working at cross purposes with the Administration. There are several in the Department of Justice collaborating with several in the Department of Interior and have their colleagues in various of the other Departments of the Government. They are radical and have peculiar ideas—at least the ideas to me are radical and some of them inadmissable and unacceptable. For instance, there is a clique in the Department of Justice under Biddle who take the tenuous ground and proclaim it as a constitutional fact that an intending immigrant somewhere abroad and an alien who applies for a visa to come to the United States is immediately blanketed in under the constitutional provision of free speech. They claim that there attaches to him something of the constitutional guarantees so that if he wants to come to the United States as an immigrant for permanent resi-

[118] As Secretary of the Interior, Harold Ickes supervised the administration of the Virgin Islands. Ickes planned to allow an unlimited number of financially solvent refugees to settle in the islands. Long bitterly opposed the plan. See above, pp. 151 f.

dence and intends to engage in political activity which may be against the interest of the United States the constitutional guarantee of free speech protects him to the extent that that characteristic of his will not be held against him as a ground for his exclusion from the United States. Six months ago we submitted to the Department of Justice the text of a proposed law which would place immigrants on the same basis as visitors to the United States in respect to political activities which they would engage upon after admission to the United States. In the case of visitors we are authorized by law to withhold visas if the person applying for a visa intends to engage in political activity in the United States which might be against the interests of the United States. We wanted that same authority to refuse a visa to a person who was coming to the United States to live permanently. The Department of Justice blocked it on the theory I have above outlined. We tried to agree upon a compromise in phraseology. The text of the compromise has remained in a pigeon hole in the Department of Justice, and we are unable to get any agreement on it.

Jackson himself does not subscribe to that theory. I have discussed the matter with him, and he has taken the definite position orally that we can exclude from the United States any person because we do not like the color of his eyes or for any other reason and that the exercise of the authority to admit persons to the United States is a manifestation of sovereign power. But Jackson has under him a number of persons who have peculiar ideas and radical tendencies and sympathies toward forces which are inadmissable and unacceptable to my mind. And it is these persons and some others whom I do not know or know of whom Dies has investigated and about whom he has files which I understand are highly explosive and which he may release to the detriment of the Administration and particularly to the Department of Justice if he and Jackson get into a fight. They have been very near a fight, and each has issued a diatribe against the other. The President is the only person who can handle it, and it is now planned that he have this meeting with Dies. I am sure he can straighten the matter out, and I hope he can arrange that there will be coordination between the two Departments.

The Secretary is very much concerned that we be kept out. That has been my idea also, and I have tried in all my contacts with the Department of Justice and with the Dies Committee, as well as in the telegrams I have drafted for the Secretary to be sent to Dies to assume the position of cooperation with both of them but have not got involved with either of them. We have received evidence from Dies and thanked him for it and have transmitted that evidence to the Department of Justice for legal advice upon it.

November 28, 1940

The President has asked for the resignations of all Chiefs of Missions, career officers and others. He feels that the ending of the second term and the beginning of a third term creates a situation which is similar to a change of administration, and I think he feels that in order to continue the vitality it is necessary to make changes. I hope he carries the same policy into the domestic office-holding field. As far as I am concerned I am going to submit my resignation. I talked it over with Welles some days ago, and he was rather inclined against the suggestion. In a subsequent conversation, however, he agreed to it. I then discussed it with the Secretary. He will submit his resignation, with some reference to the thought that during the period of trouble his services will be at the disposal of the President in any capacity that may be desirable either officially or unofficially, and he agreed that it would be proper for me to submit my resignation if I cared to do so. The telegram was sent to the Chief of each Mission stating that at the direction of the President it had been dispatched. Letters were written to those who were in the United States. Bullitt having already had his successor appointed, was automatically out and did not receive a letter. Admiral Leahy[119] will succeed him at Vichy.

November 29, 1940

. . . Resignations are coming in already as the result of yesterday's telegram. I wrote my letter of resignation to the President and signed it, saying that it was not that I wanted to leave the Government under his leadership but that I did feel he was entitled to an entirely free hand from now on and that if my resignation could make it easier for him that I would be derelict if I didn't submit it. At the end of a day like this, which has just been another one of those awful days when you have to make decisions every few minutes and things pile in so fast you can hardly attend to them, I almost hope he will accept it. I am just tired out and still have to go out to dinner and be polite when I feel like lying down and going to sleep right now.

December 9, 1940

I have been away for some days. I went to the University of North Carolina to make an address and from there spent a day with my sister and then went down and shot a few duck with Bernie Baruch in South Carolina and arrived this morning rested and with a clearer point of view.

The attacks in the newspapers still seem to continue against me little by little and indicate that the wild-eyed elements have marked me out as their objective.

I find myself with a very full desk, the important part of which is the German Consular activities. There is an analysis of them which may serve as the basis for the withdrawal of the exaquaturs of some of them. I have to get into that and come to some decision about it. And there are the extra-curricular activities of the Germans, like the Trans-Ocean News Service and the Ger-

[119] Admiral William Leahy served as ambassador to Vichy, France, 1941–1942.

man Library of Information. There is another file on that, and I shall have to come to some decision on it too.

Have not yet seen the Secretary, who was absent this afternoon, nor Welles. We are all somewhat worried about a leak to one of the columnists about the mission of Murphy to North Africa. Mr. Berle, who is a friend of Alsop, is a little concerned about the possible attribution to him of the leak.

While I was away with no telephone on the island [Nantucket] and a perfect quiet my mind got working over the situation as regards England and the enormous losses she is suffering in tonnage. In conformity with our policy to help England as far as we can and to take every step we can to aid her short of war, it seemed the best thing we could do for her for the time being would be to make available to her tonnage. There are in our ports fifty-seven old ships left out of the old emergency fleet corporation, boats which we can make available to her. In addition there are an unknown number of vessels flying the flag of Norway, Denmark, Holland, Belgium, France, Poland and now Greece somewhere in our Atlantic and Pacific ports and in those of our insular possessions, like Honolulu, the Philippines, Panama, etc. It seemed to me that we could possibly take some steps to gain possession of those vessels and make them available to England. I have thought it out in pretty general terms—necessarily—but formed the basic belief that it might be done and that all we needed was some justification for it.

Upon my return this morning one of the first things I did was to direct a compilation of each of the countries mentioned above of vessels of their flag in our ports, indicating the name, the tonnage, the character of vessel, whether passenger, freight or tanker, and the American interest therein, if any, to total them by countries and then to get a grand total of all that tonnage. When that is compiled in the next few days I will send it to the Legal Advisor for him to search the treaties and the law and see what, if anything, we can do, with the thought that we will do the maximum possible and will try and justify our actions in law.

December 10, 1940

Today I saw the Secretary about noon and took up with him the question of the ships of the countries which have been over-run by Germany and which are now lying in our ports. He approved heartily of the thought and wanted only to be sure that we were on safe legal ground. I told him that when the list was completed I would go over it very carefully and submit it to Hackworth for his legal attention.

This morning also I had up the question of the German Consuls. We have enough evidence to justify the withdrawal of exequaturs from Dr. Dräger[120]

[120] Friedhelm Dräger, German vice consul, New York City.

and one of his associates. Dräger has acted as party leader in the United States and has carried on activities beyond his proper function as a Consul.

As a double-barrel of the gun I also had up the official German activities, such as the German Library of Information and the German Railroad Office. They are acting within legislative authority. They do not have to do anything but register with us and say that they are going to engage in propaganda. The Department has no control over them, cannot withdraw any license, because no license is given, and is not furnished even with copies of the alleged information which they distribute and some of which has been highly offensive, particularly one publication which used Hitler's speech at the Party Congress after the President's message in which he tried to ridicule the President. The publication in question was set up in sort of question and answer form. While they are not amenable to judicial process or to the administrative authority of the Department of State, it seems that they are amenable to control through the exercise by the President of his Constitutional prerogative to control foreign affairs and on the theory that activities of that kind at this time are not to the best interests of the United States in that they tend to break up the public opinion and to disorganize public thought and to bring the official acts of the United States into question and to scatter a point of view which is not to the best interests of this country. However, it is improbable we can operate on the Germans alone. It may be that if we do it with the Germans we shall do it with the British, French, Italian and Japanese as well, and the Russians also. My thought is that if they were all suppressed we would be better off. The only danger is that now they are registered and the names of persons active in those organizations are certified to us, whereas they would probably be driven underground or carry on with sympathetic American citizens in case they were suppressed.

December 11, 1940

Last evening had a long conference in the Secretary's office, four or five of us, on the subject of relief and the food situation in Europe. Norman Davis and Welles among the conferees. The question of the food situation as it actually existed was clouded. I had asked Mr. Geist[121] three months ago to keep the run of it and to make a careful study of the actual food situation in Europe by countries. He has been doing this, but he is now out of the city and will not return until Friday. Herbert Hoover has been very insistent about feeding all the stricken people in Europe and now has a dispute with the British Embassy on the subject. The British do not want food helpful to Germany to get into Europe and intend to maintain their blockade. We want to

[121] Raymond Geist, foreign service officer, chief of the State Department Division of Commercial Affairs, 1940–1943.

see food of some kind got to Europe in Spain and southern France—that is, in the unoccupied territories—provided it does not get into the hands of the Germans and to consist largely of milk for children. Consequently our position is between the Hoover activities and the British position.

Today I have been engaged with three present difficulties, the refugee question, which is again the subject of some bitter comment in the morning press, the relief problem in Europe generally, and the German agents and their activities in this country. Each of them are moving forward to a definite position, and we probably will be ready to make some definite statement on the subject of the refugees. . . .

December 12, 1940

My inquiry about ships for England has developed quite a number. Fifteen of our laid-up ships were sold to the British yesterday—the highest bidder—and twenty-four more are to be offered tomorrow. There are also a number of ships owned by the countries which have been over-run by Germany. I discussed the legal phases of it with Hackworth, and he is trying to find a legal basis for some action.

As regards refugees, which is a continuing and complicated problem, Rabbi Wise and Rabbi Teitelbaum[122] headed a delegation and asked me to accept 3,800 additional names from Lithuania and that part of the present Russian jurisdiction. After a long conversation I was noncommittal as to what the Department would do but feel it is just a part of the movement to place me and the Department in general in an embarrassing position.

The attacks against the Department continue. [New York] *PM* this afternoon reprints an editorial from the [Louisville] *Courier Journal* in which it condemns the whole Department underneath Hull and suggests we all ought to be kicked out and even damns Hull himself with faint praise. The Secretary is considerably worried about the entire business and spoke to me again about the memorandum which I have in preparation. The continuing attacks on the Department are unpleasant and indicative of a determined effort on the part of some groups to undermine the work of the Department and to interfere with the continuation of its general policies.

December 16, 1940

The President returned this afternoon from his Caribbean cruise. Saturday the Secretary said he would like to present him with a memorandum reviewing the refugee problem. I worked it out rather thoroughly and took it in to the Secretary just before he went to keep his first engagement with the

---

[122] Aaron Teitelbaum, formerly executive secretary of the Central Relief Committee to aid Jews suffering as a result of World War I.

President within an hour of the latter's return. The attacks on the Department and the unpleasant situation in the press over the refugee matter seems to continue. It is more widespread than it was and seems to be joined up with the small element in this country which wants to push us into this war. Those persons are largely concentrated along the Atlantic seaboard, and principally around New York. There are elements of them in the Government here. They are all woven together in the barrage of opposition against the State Department which makes me the bull's eye. . . .

The *Western Prince* was sunk and on it twenty-eight bags of our mail in charge of a courier. Unfortunately it was largely Christmas packages to our officers abroad from their friends and families at home. There was also one confidential pouch in the personal charge of the courier, who was responsible for all the mail. Whether he was lost we do not know, as the list of survivors has not reached port. It is the fifth accident we have had to our couriers in the Atlantic service. Three of them are traveling on British ships direct to England and two of them on the Clipper to Lisbon and return.

The Department is considering, but without my being party to the conference, the dispatch of Red Cross foodstuffs to Spain and Southern France. There is going to be a good deal of opposition to the granting of food supplies to Spain because the elements in this country that backed the Republican Government in Spain are particularly opposed to it and think Franco is hooked up as part and parcel of the German-Italian block. Our effort is directed particularly to keeping Spain from being hooked up. I only know of it incidentally through my casual conversation with Norman Davis in the Secretary's anteroom as he and the Secretary were bound over to see the President on the subject and get his final approval. But even in spite of my lack of contact with it, I am sure to be attacked in the papers as having been the one. That line of attack just seems to suit the columnists and propagandists who are pursuing their attack upon me these days.

December 18, 1940

The President sent over early this morning his approval of the statement I drew in connection with the refugee problem and his authorization to release the statement for publication as a press release. He has approved our entire policy.

I am now engaged on reviewing the food situation in Europe for his information and enclosing to him a memorandum on the subject of the general food situation and which study is divided into countries and shows the actual food situation in each country, grouped in sections of the Continent, and which is compilation of the figures we started to obtain last summer and which give a very comprehensive picture of the supply of each staple food item in each country.

December 19, 1940

The Secretary for the first time in my hearing called attention to the fact that we were getting very close to this war [and] that within ten days or six weeks or six months we might be in this war. It depended upon Hitler and not upon us. Of course in my opinion it depends partly upon what we do which might give Hitler a reason. As to what we will do from time to time depends on our attitude toward England and the belief we have that it will be necessary to support England more and more.

The shipping situation throws things in very definite relief. There are 615,000 tons of foreign-flag shipping in our ports. That includes Danish, Dutch, Norwegian, Belgian, French, German and Italian ships. The French *Normandie* alone accounts for 80,000 of those tons. These vessels have diverse kinds of engines of foreign make, spare parts for which are impossible to get and the intricacies of which are not known to our certified engineers who under the law alone are permitted to take charge of the engine rooms. Some of these ships are very small and are not useful to us. Some of the ships would be useful to us. But if we took these ships and gave England some of ours, it would displace American crews off of the ships we gave away, and under our laws they could not be employed on vessels built abroad coming under the American flag, and they would be displaced by foreigners, which would cause labor troubles. . . .

We are building vessels at the rate of one a week. These vessels average about 10,000 tons each. There are about fifty of them to be produced in the next year under our regular program. That means that within a year we would produce 500,000 tons, or that we would be replacing the present losses on the North Atlantic routes which are sustained in five weeks. It would take us a year at the present rate to compensate for the present losses on the North Atlantic.

If we let England have the Allied fleet in our waters and let her have all of our World War over-age fleet, where will *we* be in case we should have to get into this war? That is the question that worries me. I am quite reconciled to the thought that we have got to help England, in every way possible, and I am in every way trying to follow out the President's policy in that respect, but I am sure he has in contemplation the actual needs of the United States. . . .

The President has declined to accept my resignation. He sent me a note this morning.

December 23, 1940

The shipping question leaked. Who talked I do not know, but it has been in the press and it almost established a world's record in getting to London. It has been a subject very much publicized for the last three days. The German

Government has taken note of the remarks of Cross[123] of the British Shipping Commission on the floor of the Parliament, and Cross in his speech reflected to such an extent the considerations which had been the subject of conversation in our meetings that the thought is almost inescapable that he must have had some communication on the subject and that communication could only have come from the British Embassy here. How the British Embassy got advised of it is a perfect mystery to me. It is too accurate to have been a coincidence. Nevertheless the whole matter has been aired in the press to an astonishing extent. This morning I was called upon by Mr. Gould Lincoln of the staff of the *Washington Star* who had somehow discovered that I had a good deal to do with it. I was entirely noncommittal in my statements to him and tried to step out of the picture and to leave the whole thing in a nebulous state as far as his impressions were concerned. Whether I succeeded will probably appear later in the press.

I presented to the Secretary and to Welles separately today the situation in which I find myself at my desk. The flow of work is almost impossible to attempt. I am doing practically a two-man job. The consequence is I don't get to do either part of it quite properly. I have all the administrative work in the Department and all of the administrative work of the Foreign Service throughout the world, which in times of stress like this is multiplied. It includes extra couriers and the movement of mails. It includes changes of personnel for this reason or that reason. It includes certain phases of Secret Service activity; and it includes also all the legislative and budgetary and fiscal affairs and the securing from the legislative branch the funds necessary to run the Foreign Service and the administration of those funds after they have been provided. If anybody wants a clerk or an Assistant Chief or wants to expand their Division it necessarily comes to me, and they come so fast and there are so many different phases of administrative activity as to require the attention of one man in any normal working day.

But in addition to that I have the Division of International Communication, which has now as one phase of it this shipping question and which has as another phase the radio and telegraphic communications. Because of that I am on this Communications Defense Board, which requires about five hours a week away from my desk, to say nothing of other times at my desk. And then there is the Visa Division, which encompasses the whole refugee problem. And there is the Special Division with its representation of interests and its relief problems. And there is the Passport Division and its problems and various of the other Divisions which I have to supervise from the point of view of policy to say nothing of the supervisory phases of every one of them, including the safety of the codes, the soundness of the trunk lines from the

[123] Sir Ronald Cross, British Minister of Shipping, 1940–1941.

Department to the international cables, the personnel in the telegraph room and the confidential file room and the production of new codes.

I just told the Secretary and Welles it was a two-man job and that I thought somebody ought to have the administrative phases and I ought to have the other phases of it. I asked them to consider the necessities of the situation and the future of the Department. They both understand it, but I wanted to impress upon them that there was a volume of work that in justice to the future of the Department ought to be so distributed as to be properly attended to, and at the present time it is not so distributed.

I received again the delegation of Rabbis with their spokesman Mr. Schenkolewski and two other gentlemen. I have received them on a number of occasions. They had another list of persons to whom we should grant visas. I explained to them the policy of the Department as it now existed and that immigrant visas were now available to these persons and that they should be approached with the idea of applying for immigrant visas rather than asking us to start again the issuance of visitor's visas when the emergency was not as it had been when we had instituted the practice.

December 29, 1940

Another year draws to a close—a hectic, sombre year of trouble. The "phoney" war came suddenly to an end with the invasion of the Low Countries. Till then it had seemed unreal—since then very real, though it is a different kind of military activity than its predecessors. There has been no large loss of life—no big battles except for the battle of Flanders. The tragedy of it was the collapse of France—as yet not entirely explained. Since the collapse and the occupation of northern France and the Low Countries there has been waged a continuous air battle with England the sufferer and on the defensive. The terrors of night raids continues and the destruction of towns, residences, docks, factories and churches goes on indiscriminately, though it is possible the danger is ancillary to a warfare on military objectives. Germany has received its share of bombing but it could not be as much in danger because London is just across the Channel from the fields of Northern France but Berlin is still the long distance from England.

Sinking by submarine is the other warfare—and England's line of ships from Canada afford a continuing target for the U-boats. More than four million tons have been sunk and that much tonnage of food, supplies and materiel has gone to Davey Jones.

Italy's almost surreptitious and certainly opportunistic entrance into the war has ended in disaster on two fronts—Albania and Egypt with the result that the threat of Germany to the Mediterranean has been temporarily halted.

But the war has spread, distrust is more widely felt, fear is almost universal and dislocation of trade and commerce as well as peacetime pursuits is almost ubiquitous. Hungary and Rumania have fallen into the German orbit of influence and activity while the danger of enmeshing Bulgaria, Turkey and Russia is constant. Russia stands like the proverbial ox—awaiting the slaughter—if ever Germany and Japan are freed of the distraction presently offered by England to the one and by China to the other. Meanwhile Stalin is cheering on both sides with the fond hope each will wear out itself in efforts to destroy the other, thus preparing fertility for the seeds of Communism to take root in the chaos he hopes will follow in the wake of 1940.

Japan, having joined the Axis Powers, has worked in unison with them, extending her clutches over Southern China, into Indo-China, to the doors of old Siam—now known as Thailand—and fingering the Dutch East Indies. Japan's attitude toward us has been threatening—disdainful, almost challenging. Germany sicks her on to further aggravations with the hope we will be so engaged in the Pacific we could not be effective in the Eastern Atlantic.

Meanwhile we face very heavy taxes for 1941—with a draft army in the making, battleships building, fighting aircraft in quantity production and guns and explosives in the making. Industry is booming but profits are recaptured by the Government so no runaway prices or stock booms are here or in sight. The statutory limit to the national debt is bulging and will have to be expanded.

All this means centralization of power, expanded Government activity and artificial stimulus to industry and employment—and all of it necessary and proper for the national defense. The trouble will come at the time of adjustment.

I have sat at the keyhole of the world during these last twelve months and have seen it all unfold and have had a small part in the formation of policy at each stage.

The effort to help England—short of war—to stave off a break with Japan without stepping backward, and to handle the large and troublesome problems which developed out of it all have been part of my task and my task part of the picture. Repatriation was concluded—including the exodus from the Far East. Relief has continued a debated subject with complications created by ambitious minded and misguided persons. Refugees have been and continue to be a tragic and difficult problem. In each of these I have had the major part and have been the policy making officer and the executive agent of the Government. . . .

We come to the end of the year with a three-pronged foreign policy—to help England as much as we can without becoming involved in the war; to checkmate Japan in her aggressions; to cement our friendships with South America—and with one big domestic policy—to prepare our defenses against any possible attack, a policy which is bound to have a long-range effect upon our political philosophy for it will mean regularization of our policies toward

Labor and toward Industry as well as adjustments in our financial and economic practices.

So we come to the end of this bad year—with a world in confusion, in sorrow, in suffering but with a wholesome political structure at home, a clear vision and a full competence to face the unknown storms ahead.

Preparing to Participate

... Yesterday I telephoned to Harold Dodds and told him I thought Princeton ought to offer an honorary degree to Roosevelt. The partisan, political and personal sentiments which exist among the members of the Board at Princeton, all of them opposed to Roosevelt, ought not to stand in the way of an expression by Princeton. Harvard and Yale have conferred degrees on him in years gone by, and when I suggested it a year ago there was definite opposition. I attributed that to the campaign and political considerations. I told him that I had voted for honorary degrees for persons that were not particularly pleasing to me and whose philosophy I was not in sympathy with but I recognized them as strong, outstanding persons. I saw no reason why the other members of the Board should not adopt the same attitude and recognize Roosevelt as a great force in the world and as a master mind of his political school and age. Dodds accepted the idea and said he would present it and recommend it to the Committee. I told him I was sorry I could not attend the Committee, but I had two Board meetings here, but that I would be at the Board meeting.

Started the New Year with the relief problem again active. Norman Davis talked to me at length about the difficulties that he is in and that the British Embassy is in because of the multiplicity of the efforts to aid Britain. One organization has collected as much as four hundred thousand dollars and is unable to do anything. There are many organizations active on account of aid to Britain, and none of them are able to do anything. . . .

Late in the afternoon the Secretary sent for me and handed me a little pencilled memorandum written on a White House memorandum pad and signed "F.D.R." It read that the President wanted Judge Moore's feelings to be assuaged and wanted me to take his place as Counselor and that he wanted Dean Acheson to fill the vacancy Grady left. Grady left this afternoon. It is very gratifying to me to feel that I shall be relieved of some of the excessive work that has crowded my desk and made broader thinking very difficult. Naturally I am gratified that the President and the Secretary want me to engage upon a work which is much more appealing than the tense detailed executive activity I have been confronted with for a year. And it is also odd that the appointment as Counselor will be in January and my appointment as Assistant Secretary in this term was in January (1940). My first appointment to the Department as Assistant Secretary was in January (1917). They all turn out to be about the 25th to 27th of the month, and if this proceeds on its normal course it will probably be about that same time. It was just twenty-four years ago that I entered on my first tour in the Department.

January 10, 1941

Today all day with the Personnel Board in examinations. At 5:30 joined the Secretary in his office in a conference on payment by the British and the psychological effect of the possible statement they were not to pay for anything in the way of arms and ammunition. He thought they ought to make a statement that they had a couple of billion dollars that they were putting into the pot and were helping as much as they could. He is afraid of the psychological reaction of persons who would feel that England was already defeated and already bankrupt and that we were taking over a war and would pick up a defeated nation and a bankrupt nation and carry on for them. He thought there would be a distinct reaction against the President's program for lending aid and the reaction would come from the very people who had been supporting it. Norman Davis was present and he agreed, and I certainly agree. . . .

January 13, 1941

Sat in this morning with the Secretary, Norman Davis, Welles and Berle on the subject matter of his [Hull's] testimony before the Committee of the Congress tomorrow. The purpose of the conference was to outline and advise on the general policy for a statement which he would be ready to release to the press so that they would not be left to draw their own conclusions from an executive hearing.

Shortly after I returned to my office the Secretary called me in and said he was very much embarrassed by the attitude Berle had taken over my proposed appointment as Counselor. He said that Berle felt that he should be appointed Counselor and that he was very much embarrassed amongst his friends and associates by not being appointed and that he had been here ahead of me. There were various other comments the Secretary made, all running to the same point. He repeated several times that he was very much embarrassed and that he wanted me in that post.

I said that I understood the situation and that I thought Mr. Berle would do that. As a matter of fact he had on a former occasion told me he would leave the Department if anyone other than he were appointed to that post and had acted in very bad manners and had lost his temper. I had reprimanded him. I was not surprised nor was I inclined to embarrass the Secretary or the President or anybody else. It is not my particular ambition to be an Assistant Secretary. I was Assistant Secretary twenty-five years ago. In length of service with the Department, if that was any ground at all, I was far in front of Mr. Berle, but I had no desire to embarrass the Secretary or anybody and I would readily adjust myself to any plan that would be for the best interests of the Department and the Administration.

The Secretary then suggested that instead of appointing a Counselor that they might appoint another Assistant Secretary and leave the post of Counselor vacant and that I could take over the work, other than the administrative work, and leave that to Shaw,[1] who would be appointed Assistant Secretary. I said that I would be very glad; that of course I felt that I would like to be something besides an Assistant Secretary; but that was purely a matter of personal satisfaction and I could very readily accede to the suggestion he made.

January 23, 1941

Have been ill with the flu and confined to the room at the hotel. I came back yesterday for the first time. I missed all the Inaugural ceremonies.

Dean Acheson's name was sent to the Senate today.[2] Mine did not go. I have said nothing more, done nothing more and heard nothing more about my proposed appointment as Counselor. I suppose the President will have to be consulted and agree to the Secretary's idea. So that the omission of my name today may and may not be significant.

The Italians have been driven farther into Libya, and the British have penetrated Eritrea. There has been a lessening of the intensity of the bombing of England and of submarine sinkings. Rumania has exploded in a revolution. There are probably 150,000 German troops in Rumania, but it looks like a silent threat against Bulgaria. Bulgaria has about made up its mind it will put up a verbal resistance, which means that Germany will be able to occupy that country without any bloodshed if they can scare up a few "incidents," like the killing of a few Germans or alleged atrocities of any kind.

Leahy arrived in Vichy and has had a long interview with Admiral Darlan[3] which shows very plainly the intentions of the Vichy Government as regards the French fleet and antagonism toward England.

The refugee problem still continues but not in quite such intensified form. I now have the problem of alien enemies interned in Canada which they want to release if we will take them here. A Mr. Alexander Patterson, the representative of the British Home Office, came to the Department some weeks ago and talked to Welles and me and has now submitted a list of those whom they might release if we would agree to accept them.

[1] G. Howland Shaw, foreign service officer, chief of the State Department Division of Foreign Service Personnel, 1937–1941.
[2] Acheson was appointed Assistant Secretary of State, a post he held from 1941 to 1945.
[3] Admiral Jean François Darlan, vice premier of the Vichy government, 1941–1942.

January 26, 1941

Did not give myself a chance to recover from the flu and in consequence have been half sick. Went to the farm yesterday afternoon, had a restful night—fourteen hours in bed and most of the time asleep. So today feel much better. But I weighed only 128 pounds stripped this A.M.—down ten pounds. . . .

Italy seems to be getting pretty low in morale—after Albania and Egypt. Unconfirmed reports come that riots and trouble have appeared in Turin and Milan. It might help Germany and it might hurt Germany—depending on the development. The falling away of Italy from the Axis might make Japan look on it with different eyes.

January 27, 1941

I asked the Italian Ambassador[4] and Donna Elly to lunch en famille at the hotel today in order that I might have a chance to chat with him and see what he knew about the reports of social disorders in Italy and what he had on his mind. It was the first time I have had a talk with him for a long time. I found him very apprehensive but entirely uninformed of disorders, though it was apparent that he feared almost anything. He spoke of the unwillingness of the Italians to enter the present conflict and the effect upon them of the military defeats in Africa and in Albania and of the short rations existing in Italy. He also spoke of the unfortunate timing of their entrance into the war. I remarked that the timing looked very bad, which he admitted. He said that he supposed that Italy had been forced into it by "the other end," meaning Hitler. He had not heard that any Germans were in Italy. I told him that our reports indicated that there were Germans in Italy in the Turin district and that a number of Germans had crossed the Brenner Pass on their way south, but we did not know where they were; that I heard some were headed for Albania, but we had not heard that any had arrived there; it was reported some were to go to Africa, but we had not heard that any had arrived there. He interjected that he did not see how they could be transported there. I said there were some at Sicily in the air fields, and he asked if I meant at Catania, and I said yes, at Catania and also on the southwest field.

His first remark to me, rather immediately, was "Have you heard anything to confirm the reports about the riots in Milan and Turin?" I replied that I had not, and he asked if I did hear anything if I would let him know. Later in the afternoon we did receive from Rome a cable denying the reports about Milan. I met Donna Elly still at the apartment playing bridge when I returned about 6:30 and sent word to him through her that there was no basis for the report about Milan.

I told him that I wanted him to feel free to come and talk to me at any time

[4] Don Ascanio dei principi Colonna.

and that it was possible that circumstances would develop so it would be to everybody's advantage for the Government of Italy to have an opportunity to talk to a person whom she could trust and that Mussolini and Ciano both knew me well and that if there ever came an opportunity for him to have a helpful conversation with me, he would find me ready to listen to him. He said that he would remember it very gratefully and that if the opportunity came he would be very glad to take advantage of it. He is such a timid person, however, that I doubt that he will ever take the initiative.

January 28, 1941

There is in the making a possibility for a good deal of publicity about the refugee problem. There is a report published this morning and put on the radio by I.N.S. to the effect that the German Government and the American Government have had some communication as regards the exit from Germany of so-called refugees. Rabbi Wise heard it and called the Department from New York. He was told that there was no such communication between the two Governments. The Secretary denied the press story at his conference, but the denial went only so far as the two Governments are concerned.

For a week I have been trying to talk to the Secretary on the general situation. I talked to Welles, and he thought we ought to talk to the President and lay the situation before him. The situation is just this, briefly: Our quota with Germany is 37,000 a year. That many emigrants can leave Germany. That many can be given visas. Under our law the Consul gives visas to persons who are not excludable under the law. One of our regulations is that they must have exit permits before they get the visas. The exit permit and the police character record are furnished the emigrant by the Gestapo. Germany is now sending two trainloads a week, 500 on each train, out of Germany, through France and Spain to Portugal. Passage for these persons is paid by Jewish aid societies and friends in the United States. The cost is $485 per person. Of this sum Germany gets $325 for railroad fare and expenses and the balance goes to the steamship company from Portugal to the United States. That means that Germany is getting $235,000 foreign exchange a week, there being two trains with 500 persons on each train each week. A travel agency run by a man named [Paul] Tausig in New York is acting for the Hebrew societies and sympathetic persons on this side. The payments are made in this country. The United States Lines is contemplating running the *Manhattan* and the *Washington* between New York and Vigo. They came to discuss the matter with me last week in company with Truitt of the Maritime Commission. I tried to discourage it but could not be specific. Today Bill Stanley,[5] who represents them, came to ask about it and inadvertently told me that the United States Lines' agent in Spain had been

[5] William Stanley, former Assistant to the Attorney General, 1933–1935.

spoken to by the agent of the German Government and advised that the German Government could furnish them with a great many passengers bound for the United States.

While no arrangement exists between the two Governments, there is no doubt in operation a systematic traffic in private hands with the connivance of the German Government. It is sinister, because the German Government only gives permits to the persons they want to come to the United States. It is a perfect opening for Germany to load the United States with agents.

Several members of Congress are very much interested. One of them has written to me and telegraphed to me. That was Beckworth [6] of Texas. I telephoned to him this morning and promised to give him the information he requested, but that only applies to non-quota visas, that is the visitors recommended by the President's Advisory and other Committees. His inquiry does not go to the meat of the problem. The press story now current may develop the practice, and it may lead to a Congressional investigation. I have tried to keep the thing on an even keel and am now hopeful that the Department will stay on an even keel. We are quite in the clear in the matter so far. I have been condemned by one side, and it looks as if I might now be condemned by the other, but I have tried to be just as careful as I possibly could.

January 29, 1941

Nasca won a nice race in California yesterday. She is back in form again.

The Lend-Lease bill proceeds on its way. There will be limitations as to time but it is hoped there will be no prohibition of "convoy." It is not that we want to convoy British ships—there is no intention of doing so—but to specifically prohibit it in the law would be to announce to Germany and Japan the definite limitations to our policy and announce to them they can go as far as they like and suffer no opposition from us.

The immigration of refugees question proceeds in full vigor and complexity.

This afternoon went with the Secretary to the Appropriations Committee of the House. He made a very effective opening statement and found the members in sympathetic mood. After today I shall carry on till the hearings are closed.

Passports to travel to England on British vessels is again to the fore. Red Cross asks it and a Harvard Medical unit. It opens the question again and concerns the same privilege for 2000 Americans there who want to come home. I am very hesitant. It will vitiate the prohibition of the Neutrality Act and open the way for untold pressure and many groups.

[6] Lindley Beckworth, Democrat, U.S. Representative from Texas since 1939.

February 3, 1941

Pallbearer for [William G.] McAdoo—one of the ablest men I have ever known—a close friend of twenty-five years standing. Then to the Appropriations Committee—then Spanish, Russian and German refugee question and "retirement of officers" bill to get rid of "dead wood"—appointments in diplomatic service—Kirk to Cairo, which I suggested and advocated— Winant[7] Ambassador to London—and various others—mostly shifts. . . .

February 6, 1941

This afternoon had a conference with the Secretary on the general subject of immigration, present Berle for a while, Acheson, Atherton, Avra Warren and Hackworth. I set out the situation existing in Russia and in Germany in showing that we no longer had control of the choice as to who should come into the United States but that the Governments of Germany and Russia respectively were choosing in their jurisdictions persons that we should receive. Then the subject of the Spanish refugees in southern France— 85,000 remaining there—and the groups collecting in Portugal, Shanghai, Yokohama and other points as well as the Canadian, Cuban, South American and Caribbean islands—pockets of persons who had escaped Europe and who were applying for immigration to this country. The Secretary was interested but had no direct decision. . . . So the whole thing goes over for another conference to be called sometime next week. . . .

February 7, 1941

. . . This evening had a long talk with Hull—the first individual conversation in weeks. He is much worried about the British—thinks they are in a *very* bad way and are *very* stupid. They are alienating the French more and more by their policies—giving the French no inducement to resist German pressure—nor any reason to be even sympathetic. Very stupid also in the Far East—and in Russia. Their man in Moscow has held aloof from the Government—as a sign of British superiority—and had not seen Molotov for weeks, till he was sent for and then Molotov wouldn't even discuss questions with him. They criticize us for trading with Russia and holding the lines open when their own policies have driven Russia into German arms. Hull talked to Halifax,[8] whom I have not yet seen, and remonstrated with him about France and their policy and said he would proceed on other lines—including their superior attitude toward us and their failure to bring cooperation in some ways to play in their dealings with us while expecting everything from us to help them.

The Secretary then launched into the White House attitude and treatment

[7] Alexander Kirk, now ambassador to Egypt, 1941–1944; John Winant, now ambassador to Great Britain, 1941–1946.

[8] Lord Halifax, now British ambassador to the United States, 1941–1946.

of the Department and encroachment in Foreign Affairs; criticized the appointment of Winant as being entirely unacquainted with the operations of Foreign Affairs, though a "fine young man" as he expressed it; then for relying on Hopkins and some others for advice as to policy; then of the criticisms and opposition toward Wheeler, which is just helping Wheeler and making him a powerful leader as the residuary legatee of the forces recently supporting Roosevelt but now opposing the Lend Lease bill; and then Mrs. Roosevelt for encouraging persons to strike, as she is reported to have done yesterday.

He was in a sombre mood and very communicative—and it seems to be my fate to receive confidences of Secretaries of State in disagreement with their Presidents—but this is child's play compared to the Lansing situation.

Hull feels he has diminishing influence. He said he had sought out Bob Jackson as one who had real influence with the President and asked him to investigate the situation, satisfy himself—and if he corroborated it all to go to the President and warn him—for Hull feared the possible defeat of the Lend Lease bill or emasculation to the point it would amount to defeat.

February 10, 1941

Judge Moore died Saturday and was buried this afternoon. I had to be before the House Committee [on Appropriations] at the time and so could not attend the funeral.

The Japanese are preparing for a southward movement and it looks very much as if they would cross the Malay Peninsula and attack Rangoon, Saigon and Penang. Rangoon controls the southern lead to the Burma Road, and Penang controls the northern end of the Straits of Malakka which lead to Singapore. We considered on Saturday the advisability of warning Americans out of that whole area, but it seemed not quite timely. Americans in Rangoon and in the neighboring parts of Burma are numerous, being there largely on oil and rubber business. It is also true of Singapore, and there are many in the Sumatra and Java area. It seems improbable that they would go to Java before Singapore is attacked, but it looks as if they were preparing seriously to hedge around Singapore by crossing the narrow strip of land and to make this move simultaneously with the German move against England which is expected in April at the latest. . . .

I have read today despatches written in December about the terrible destruction at Coventry, Southampton, Liverpool, Birmingham and other places in England—mail reports of our Consuls to the Consulate General and forwarded by London—mail despatches which come slow but which give a good picture of the destruction.

Had a long talk for an hour with the Danish Minister[9] on the question of

[9] Henrik De Kauffmann.

Danish ships. It was inconclusive and just part of the picture of the foreign vessels lying idle in our ports. It is slowly moving to some decision, but what the decision will be I do not know, except that I am sure that either we or the British or both of us will get the use of the ships.

February 11, 1941

... The President held a high council yesterday with the Secretaries of State, War, Navy and the Chiefs of the Military and Naval staffs and the Commission for National Defense. They decided to again warn Americans out of Japan and China and to seek information from Singapore, Batavia and Rangoon as to the number of dependents of American citizens, that is women and children, who were there. On receipt of that information we will probably suggest the evacuation of dependents in the Rangoon area and possibly the Singapore area—possibly the whole area—and my personal feeling is that Rangoon is a dangerous spot. Japan could prosecute a campaign there without exciting the public opinion of the United States. Burma means little to the man on the street. Nobody knows what Burma is or what its significance is in the present geography of the Far East. I happen to know it very well. I have been in Rangoon, and I have tramped the country north and west of it looking for tiger and hippopotamus. It is almost in Siam. It is only fifteen minutes by air from Siam. The railroad has its southern terminus at Rangoon and its northern terminus at the beginning of the Burma Road. Here the Irrowaddy River bears freight north to Mandalay, paralleling the railroad, and from there leads to the Burma Road. There is no other way to get to the Burma Road on the southern or western end. To control Rangoon would be to control the Burma Road and stop the roll of supplies to the Chinese military forces.

This all has real significance for us. My mind has long encompassed the possibilities of the present developing circumstances, but there is nothing we can do about it unless we are prepared to fight an enormous and extended naval war and to attack Japan proper by air in order that she will be forced to recall her expeditionary forces—and that of course is in the future for decision, but it may not be long before some kind of a decision has to be made. Grew feels the same way. He has advised us that he feels the time is fast approaching when we will have to make a decision to take a stand or not to take a stand, but I know it would be a difficult thing to convince the American people that a Japanese expedition against Burma and bombing of a place called Rangoon had any significant relationship to world events.

February 13, 1941

... Shaw[10] has been notified that he will be appointed and steps are being

[10] G. Howland Shaw served as Assistant Secretary of State from 1941 to 1945.

taken to expedite it. I have given orders that no papers are to be prepared for my signature next week. I have just come to the end of the rope as far as my labors are concerned. In going over the assignments of work with Shaw it develops that I have twenty-three of the forty-one divisions in the Department under my direct supervision. The administrative Divisions are thirteen in number. The ten other Divisions are Passports, Visa, Special Division work, International Communications, Cultural Relations, International Conferences and a few more, and there is plenty of work in at least half of them, particularly with the Special Division, which includes relief, the Visa Division, which includes refugees, and the Division of International Communications, which includes not only the work of the Defense Communications Board but all the foreign ships and questions concerning them.

February 15, 1941

It is 1:30 Saturday afternoon, and I have done all I could to extricate myself from the multiplicity of work in this office. I have given orders that no papers are to be prepared for my signature next week. Since last November I have been trying to get a division of labor in this office and an equable distribution of work among Assistant Secretaries. In various conversations recently with Mr. Welles and others I have secured their agreement, but no positive steps have actually been taken. The nomination of Shaw has not been sent to the Senate. When I first spoke of it last fall I was asked to wait till the first of the year. The first of the year I was asked to wait till Inauguration. At Inauguration I was asked to wait till the first of February and to carry on at each of these intervals. All of this I assented to do, though the drain on me has been terrific. My physical and nervous resources have been taxed to the point of exhaustion, and on several occasions as I have retired at night I have felt so exhausted I have felt I was uncertain as to whether I would be able to get out of bed in the morning. Under those circumstances I cannot do justice to any one item of the hundreds which pass before me each day. There is necessarily a hasty and a less than full consideration. Under the circumstances I notified them during the early part of this week that some arrangement would have to be made.

During the period of my incumbency I have kept the machinery of the Department of State working both in the Department at home and in the offices abroad at top speed. The communicating system which links the Department of State with its offices abroad has been very much hampered by reason of the breaking communications, telegraphic, telephonic and postal, and supplemental steps have been taken to have the mails carried by hand by couriers throughout the continent of Europe and in two different parts of Asia. No break-down has occurred, and the whole machinery has moved. Even in the Department we have had more than 150,000 hours overtime work. The last six months shows that we have been working on that basis at a rate of about 200,000 hours of overtime for the current fiscal year which will end June 30. My office has put in more than its share of that overtime.

In addition to the mechanics of the Department and the Foreign Service I have had supervision and control of various and important works. In a resumé of the allocation to my office for the purpose of considering redistribution it has developed that I have 23 of the 42 Divisions in the Department of State. Mr. Berle has had one, with parts of two more, one concerning Greenland and its contacts with Denmark, and the other being general supervision of matters in the Near East.

The Office of Counselor, most of which I have done, has had two Divisions, one of them the Legal Division in cooperation with the Secretary. Mr. Berle also had supervision of two others in normal cooperation with the Secretary, but each of them depended directly from the Secretary and he had very little to do with them. Mr. Grady had three Divisions. Mr. Welles carries a very large responsibility, because he has the ultimate decision in some of the matters which I have directly under my control, and he has practically all the conversations with Ambassadors and Ministers as well as important secret liaison work with the Army and Navy and contacts with the White House. He is carrying a very heavy load. The Secretary has carried a very heavy load, because he has supervision over the whole show, and he knows what is going on in most all of its aspects, certainly in all the important phases, but Welles' office and my office have carried the big loads, he in matters largely of policy and my office largely in matters of mechanical operation together with certain important elements of policy. Twenty-three Divisions is just too much for any one person to supervise and control, particularly when ten or twelve of them are active every minute and need decisions not once a day but three, four, five or ten times a day, and as an adjunct of my occupation I have been Chairman of the Personnel Board, which is a considerable work in itself, have been the custodian of the Emergency Funds, which have run to nearly two million dollars, and have been responsible for the Budget and obtaining appropriations from the Congress, requiring attendance at protracted hearings which takes one away from attention to Department matters, and as a member of the Defense Communications Board, which is growing in importance and which takes a great deal of time. The combination is just too much, and it will get worse. So Shaw is to take over just the administrative Divisions, thirteen of them. Some of the others will be distributed, and I will take over the work which Judge Moore had, but which he had been unable to attend to for some months past and which I have had in some important aspects during his disability.

This morning, for instance, I have had a conference with the Secretary and Hackworth on Belgian ships, approving a draft of a reply to the Belgian Embassy on the four Gulf oil boats under libel by the Belgians, and have dictated a letter to Mr. Butler, Counselor of the British Embassy, along the same lines as the Belgian note. Discussed with Winant his mission to London and details of it, including Ben Cohen.[11] Have discussed with the White House Administrative Assistant to the President the status of Cohen and the payment of his salary; and a passport case which required a lot of time because it would have established a precedent if it had stood as recommended and would have been a violation of our regulations to permit a Mrs. Florence[12] to go to London in connection with Winant's mission; and with the Department of Justice on the extent and quantity of investigations and character of investigations which the F.B.I. is to make about certain foreign personnel and in addition the allocation of one of our officers in Switzerland to continue certain observations for the benefit of F.B.I.'s investigation; and with Dr. Feis as to the policy of sending, at the request of the Commission for National Defense, an Army transport from Manila to Singapore to load rubber, which I decided in the affirmative, fully realizing the possible danger in that area and the unusual nature of the voyage as a Government-owned vessel and part of the armed forces.

Mr. Delano,[13] apparently with knowledge of the White House, came with a Mr. Florence to ask for a passport for Mrs. Florence to accompany her husband and to work with him as an unintegrated part of Winant's mission to London—labor, economics, production. I told them the justification would have to be clear and the record straight—else it would be a departure from our practice and get the Department in an inconsistent and untenable position. They submitted a letter from Winant. It was not sufficient in justification. Then Winant telephoned from New York and expressed his sincere desire—that she was part of a team, very capable; that the work was important; that Bevin[14] was close to him and these people to Bevin and to him and it all had to do with Labor and production and politics and post-war conditions. I asked him about Ben Cohen going with him and what capacity and said the President had O.K.ed the expenses for his going but had not advised me as to what capacity or anything else. Winant did not know "capacity"; he would do drafting and he thought "legal advisor" would be satisfactory. Hull knew nothing about it and referred me to the White House, with the result as indicated.

[11] Benjamin V. Cohen, lawyer, and adviser to Ambassador John Winant, 1941.

[12] Philip Florence, British economist, served as consultant to the United States National Resources Planning Board, 1940–1941. His wife, an American citizen, required special approval to travel to England.

[13] Frederic Delano, chairman of the National Resources Planning Board, 1934–1943.

[14] Ernest Bevin, British Minister of Labor and National Service, 1940–1945.

Out of it all, and with my other understanding as background, I now believe Roosevelt is playing the other end of the game with Winant. Roosevelt had his own contacts with Churchill and has the formal and customary contacts with the old style British Government and important people through our formal diplomatic establishment. However he sees the possibility (even probability) of a "new order" in England. The Country Gentleman type, the landed and industrial aristocracy of England are being jolted out of position. If Churchill should fall, a new Government would be drafted from a new type—not the McDonald[15] type but more wholly composed of popular interests and definitely labor groups, among whom would be persons now considered radical and with Bevin as the possible head of the Government. In other words, a Government out of sympathy with the present and past influences in controlling groups—a new set-up. Roosevelt sees this possibility and is establishing contacts with what may be the Government in the future. Consequently there is going to London an "unorthodox" group—Winant, an intense, melodramatic theorist with a philosophy imbedded in humanitarianism and directed by sympathy for labor as such; Ben Cohen, a very able protege of Felix Frankfurter[16] and a representative of his racial group and philosophy who will do the reporting for the mission in its extra-curricular activities; the Florences, who will be unofficial contacts (he is a professor in England) and will continue the I.L.O. contacts for Winant, tying the British Labor groups to the International Labor Organization (now in Canada) and its various workings.

It looks as if F.D.R. was starting two horses in the race.

February 17, 1941

. . . The new Japanese Ambassador[17] called the other day for a very short formal call. He had a long conference with the President. The President approached him in a very friendly manner and said he was going to call him "Admiral" and not "Ambassador" and that he could always come to see him and talk things over, and then started on a long and serious dissertation about the difficulties between the two countries and then picked out one and then another incident, including the *Panay* and ending with the southward movement.[18] The Ambassador gave every indication that he was sincerely

[15] J. Ramsay MacDonald, Prime Minister of Great Britain, 1923–1924, 1929–1935. MacDonald had begun his career as a Socialist and had been one of the founders of the Labor party, but during his last years as Prime Minister, Laborites accused him of having betrayed his lifelong convictions.

[16] Associate Justice of the Supreme Court, 1939–1962.

[17] Admiral Kichisaburo Nomura, formerly the Japanese foreign minister, 1939–1940, conducted the "peace" negotiations with the United States which were interrupted by the Japanese attack on southern French Indo-China in July.

[18] On December 12, 1937, Japanese planes had bombed the American gunboat *Panay* on the Yangtze River. The vessel sank with a loss of two persons killed and thirty wounded.

interested in reestablishing the two Governments on a close and friendly basis. At the same time we are considering warning our people out of Indo-China, Siam, Burma and Malay, which includes the Dutch East Indies, Borneo and the Singapore areas. I have slowed it down, partly because I thought it very untimely considering the arrival of the new Ambassador, and partly because I think Americans will not be much in danger anywhere but at Rangoon and Penang. Besides, there are no special ships available to send for them, and there is an extreme paucity of vessels on the run out of Singapore for those parts.

February 18, 1941

Lunch with Senator Russell[19] of Georgia. He will introduce bill to exclude immigrants who are considered to be inimical to our welfare. Now they are not excludable if they come for permanent residence—only if visitors or in transit. We have tried to get the bill agreed to by Justice for six months— just succeeded. Hatton Sumners[20] of Texas agrees to introduce in House. Worried about reference to Immigration Committee as composed and suggest reference to Judiciary Committee. Sumners thinks reference should be arranged before introduction. So I saw Rayburn.[21] He was not sure of parliamentary procedure—border-line case—or overlapping jurisdictions. Will arrange for Sumners to talk with Rayburn and decide.

Hull is sick—temperature, congestion in head and nose—trained nurse— not thought serious.

Arranged with Welles redistribution of work. I will take over Counselor's work, including all legislation and appearance before Legislative Committees and coordination with the Legal Advisor, as well as carry three Divisions—Special Division, with its extra war works—Visa Division, with the refugees—and International Communications, with its shipping problems and radio activities, including the protective work of the Communications Defense Board. Shaw will have all the purely administrative duties and the other seven Divisions I have carried are to be divided between Berle and Acheson so that those two officers will have to shoulder a fair proportion of the work.

February 21, 1941

Received today a document in German, the source of which I will not

---

The Japanese government declared that this was a mistake, apologized, and agreed to pay the United States $2,214,007.36 as an indemnification.

[19] Richard Russell, Democrat, U.S. Senator from Georgia since 1933.

[20] Hatton Sumners, Democrat, U.S. Representative from Texas, 1913–1947.

[21] Sam Rayburn was elected Speaker of the House of Representatives on September 16, 1940. With the exception of the years during the Eightieth Congress (1947–1949), he held that position until his death in 1961.

record.[22] It is probably the most important document that has arrived in the Department of State, certainly since the war began. It discloses the economic and financial condition of Germany. It is authoritative. It indicates that Germany's condition will be precarious in the fall of 1941 and that she will not last until the fall of 1941 if serious damage is done to her oil supplies and to her manufacturing plants before that time. A good deal of damage has been done but not enough to prevent effective military operations. However, economic chaos and disaster are predicted if the British destructive bombing raids should interfere with their production.

All I have had translated is the summary and recapitulation. The rest of the document will be translated over the holiday. It is shown that the plan is to make war on Russia as soon as a war against England can be finished. I will know more about it on Monday when I have had a chance to read the full translation. It will go to the President Monday afternoon, and I am recommending that we advise the British and that we do everything possible to give them long-range bombers immediately. The document is stated to have been submitted to Hitler at Berchtesgaden at a war council the first part of January 1941—about January fifth to seventh. It is a report in two parts—economic and financial—envisaging the future. The financial is not of immediate importance, as it is assumed Germany can continue to finance herself, and so the translation of that part is postponed till next week. The economic part is of especial importance—particularly as to the metals situation and Germany's ability to produce or acquire essential and strategic materials *and* to manufacture them into war materials. . . .

The whole document will be translated by two foreign service officers tomorrow, dictating to Miss Aderton and her assistant in my office—working throughout the holiday—Washington's Birthday—so it can be submitted to the President in good English on his return Monday from Hyde Park.

Then it must be verified. There is one man in this country who can do so because of his former connections, and he will be asked to come here to examine it.[23]

If authentic (and I have no real doubt of it—because of the manner of its acquisition) it will point to policy. First to acquaint the British so they can direct their air attacks with increased and more discerning accuracy, and second, to get them just as many long-range bombers as possible and as quickly as possible.

It also discloses the German intention to fight Russia as soon as England can be conquered— Consequently it might be used to incite Russia against Germany. That however is not a very hopeful development as much as it

[22] Long received the documents from Sam Woods, the commercial attaché to the American embassy, Berlin, 1939–1941.

[23] Heinrich Bruening, former German chancellor, 1930–1932.

might be helpful, for Russia is fearfully awaiting the slaughter and too afraid as well as too helpless to take the offensive even for reasons of preventing the future slaughter. Nevertheless, it can be tried. . . .

February 26, 1941

The Secretary approves the plan for distribution of Departmental work I proposèd. Acheson gets economic, Berle financial, Shaw administrative and I the legal and legislative as well as three of the Divisions—Special, Visa and Communications, except aviation. All the other twenty Divisions are scattered among the other three. My life will be less hectic and others will have enough to keep them busy.

Arranged with Martin Dies to support a commutation of sentence by Justice in the case of a convicted Communist agent provided he leave the United States immediately and in order to save the life of two convicted United States citizens in Russia and repatriation of at least one more, with chance to get out six wives of Americans. He and Jackson are at dagger points and cannot even meet to discuss questions. So I was hauled into it to do the arranging.

England breaks relations with Bulgaria—and we take over their interests. Turkey advises MacMurray[24] they mean to fight if Bulgaria is attacked or occupied and they consent to England bolstering the courage of Yugoslavia to do the same. Japan awaits the replies of France and Thailand—for the renewed peace proposal—ready to take over control in Indo-China in either event. A German warship reported by Batavia to be in Indian Ocean—about 68° E–20° S—bound east for Japanese mandated Islands and seven British cruisers looking for her.

March 11, 1941

A week ago yesterday the readjustment of labors in the Department became effective, and I transferred my seat from the desk I have occupied into the room Judge Moore occupied, and I have become charged with legislative liaison work with the House and with the Senate and with appearances before the Committees of the Congress on matters affecting Bills in which the Department may be interested. I have picked up the Philippine Islands and the Fisheries and an indefinable sphere of activity in the phases of belligerency and neutrality, and I have brought along the refugees with the Visa Division, the Defense Communications activity with the Division of International Communications as well as our interests in all the foreign ships under that Division, and my old Special Division with the prisoners of war and relief to Americans and repatriation and representation of the interests of other Governments, which is gradually expanding and covers about

[24] John V. MacMurray, U.S. ambassador to Turkey, 1936–1942.

half of Europe today, including Bulgaria, and it looks as if it would soon increase to Greece and Turkey about which we have been already approached.

Since then things have moved rather rapidly. The opposition to the Lend Lease Bill collapsed in the Senate, and it was passed by that body, and today will pass the House, with the unexpected opposition of only about 25 or 30 votes.[25] It creates an entirely new situation and one somewhat anomalous for this Government and new in our history. We have *ipso facto* passed out of the sphere of neutrality. We are certainly no longer neutral. We are giving all aid to England short of war. Just how far you can go and keep out of war is the general problem, and into that general category will come many, many questions. There are certain persons in Washington who want this Government to get into the war immediately. There are certain others that want to do things that would lead us into the war. I want to do everything that we ought to do to help to beat Germany, if possible, and to save England, but I do not want to do anything which would get us into this war now. In the first place, we are not prepared to fight. In the second place, as I understand the directives of the President and the American people, they do not want to get into the war. But there will be constant pressure on the part of certain officials to do this and to do that which if done would place us in the position of being almost a belligerent, or at least within the sphere in which we could be charged with participating in the war.

I see signs that the War Department wants to pick up the ball and carry it. Stimson is of the mind to go to war. His whole organization will probably develop that psychology, as was possibly indicated by an incident this morning. Last night the Secretary [Hull] asked me to find out what was meant by a telegram which Winant sent and which referred to some activities under General Arnold.[26] I asked the liaison officer to take the matter up with General Arnold and to have somebody come over who could discuss it. He asked General Arnold to come this morning. Instead of General Arnold arriving, General Marshall telephoned and said that Arnold was very busy and wanted to know what it was all about. I told him that I assumed they were all busy but that the Secretary of State had asked for certain information stating that we had had a telegram. He said that the Secretary of War had not seen the telegram and that the Secretary of War considered that he was attending to that himself. He reluctantly said that he would send Arnold over, whereupon I said not to send him; that we would do it in a way that was

[25] Lend-lease enabled any country whose defense the President deemed vital to that of the United States to receive arms, supplies, and other equipment by sale, transfer, exchange, or lease. The measure passed the Senate, 60–31, and the House 317–71. Total lend-lease aid during the course of the war amounted to more than fifty billion dollars.

[26] General Henry H. "Hap" Arnold, chief of the Army Air Forces, 1941–1946.

easiest for everybody and that I would send somebody over to see General Arnold.

When it was all washed out it developed that it concerned the sending of about eighty civilians and members of the armed force and the aviation branch to England to help put in shape certain of the planes which we were furnishing them, some of which had got damaged on landing, and to be instructors. They were to go in civilian clothes, were not to fly in combat and were to confine their flights to England. So that was entirely satisfactory, but it was General Marshall's attitude and his references to the Secretary of War's exclusive interest in the matter which indicated that from now on the War Department thought that they were taking the lead. Of course it becomes necessary for the Department of State to be party to a lot of decisions, because the policy of the Government is involved, and the policy is somewhat molded by the requirements of international law and by the practice of other Governments, and I expect that we will find various renewals of this same attitude as it develops.

However, I want to be a sort of cylinder in the engine rather than a brake on the wheel, except that I do not want to get to the point where we get into this war; and that is a definite conclusion of mind deliberately arrived at and will continue at least until the time that we are ready to fight. If after we are ready to fight and the German activity is a menace to the United States and its future, and all of the terrible implications of the German victory appear on the horizon to be inescapable unless we fight, than I will be in the forefront of those trying to defeat Germany by whatsoever means may be necessary. But that is in the future and is dependent upon our ability to prepare ourselves properly, effectively, from a military point of view. . . .

March 12, 1941

Most of the day has been devoted to the question of exploring possibilities for taking over the neutral ships in our ports and trying to find some authority in the Government to do so. Admiral [Emory "Jerry"] Land of the Maritime Commission had a proposal for legislation which stopped short of confiscation or requisition. That was before the conference in the Secretary's office several days ago. This morning's session was composed of the same persons except Admiral Land. It was decided that that legislation would be inopportune for several reasons. . . . The consensus was that unless the Attorney General did specifically hold that the President had authority under the Export Control Act to list ships by Executive Proclamation and then draft regulations as to how vessels should be treated, there was no power existing in the Government, and it would be necessary to resort to negotiation with the British. It is necessary to consult them, because they have tenaciously held to the policy of capturing all vessels of foreign flags if they are found out of port in the open waters, and if we came to an agreement, it would be with the owners of the vessels to operate them under their own flags. . . .

My interest in this has been intense since the first part of December, and I have continuously tried to bring about some arrangement whereby these vessels could be acquired by the United States. There are more than a million tons of shipping in this Hemisphere of foreign flag. They are all lying idle in various ports. Tonnage is scarce, and the British have suffered material losses. I would like to see as much of it as possible made available to the British either directly or as substitute tonnage taking the place of vessels now in operation on other routes which could be diverted to the North Atlantic run. Of course no vessels under the American flag can make that run.

My mind is also clarified a good deal in regard to the matters which have been troubling me for some days and which concern the extent to which we could go under the Lend Lease Bill. As I now see it, there is a mandate to do everything we can to help Britain short of war. "Short of war" means to abstain from military activities. It does not mean that we shall abstain from repairing airplanes or instructing them in flying airplanes or equipping airplanes or sending mechanics and helpers and workers and airplane experts to instruct them—anywhere except on fields of combat. Consequently we can send crews to England to help to condition planes we ship to England, to help assemble them, to repair them and to instruct aviators in regard to flying—provided the persons are not in military uniform. It follows from that that persons shall be permitted to sail in belligerent bottoms through the proscribed zone. Otherwise they will never be able to get to England, because the air transportation is too limited. So that it results in a situation whereby the Lend Lease Bill is superimposed upon the Neutrality Law, and the authority which the Secretary has sparingly used to validate passports for travel on belligerent vessels and in the proscribed zone should now properly be used more generously in order to effectuate the purposes of the Lend Lease Bill to permit the travel to England of persons of the type indicated. So that my mind is rapidly clarifying. . . .

March 13, 1941

The Attorney General decided in the negative on the shipping matter which was the subject of our conference yesterday. That leaves only negotiation as a process. He left one opening and that was in case of dire necessity that he would construe the general powers of the President in the time of an emergency to include the power to take over such vessels but hoped we would approach that very cautiously and hold it only as a last reserve. Of course that situation does not exist and is not envisaged. . . .

March 15, 1941

The Italian Ambassador called on me at my apartment at my request to receive the answer, which I gave him orally, to his request that we reconsider the closing of the Italian Consulates in Newark and Detroit. I told him we could not reconsider the decision, which was based on national policy and was simply an expression of it, as the Lease-Lend Bill is, and that there might be further expressions of that policy. From his questions and his general conversation I inferred that he was somewhat fearful lest this lead to a movement on our part which would result in a breach of relations with Italy.

March 24, 1941

Have been very inattentive to keeping the record of activities during the last few weeks.

Last week there arrived the fourth document from Germany.[27] It is unlike the others in that it is probably not a copy of a document but a relation of information of a military character as to present naval, land and air warfare plans, and in the second part it is a resumé of the present psychological condition and state of morale in Germany.

As soon as the first few pages concerning the war plans were translated it developed to be a very important communication. It envisages very definitely war against Russia and records the report of a new floating mine for which they have a manufacturing capacity of 4000 a month. It also has a sinister reference to a report on poison gas. On the surface it looked as if it might have been placed in our hands with design. It was open to the possible suspicion that the other three documents having been known to have been acquired by us this one was planted upon us with the idea of frightening, because the implication about the poison gas and the inference upon the widespread use of this new mine, the description of which was terrible, might be calculated to deter any activities on our part.

On the other hand some of the statements were subject to rather accurate check and were reasonable.

Nevertheless and in order to be sure, I called in the F.B.I. and handed them all four documents in order that the one last received, dated February 19, should be compared in physical body to the three preceding. This was done very efficiently. The paper was all identified as being the same and the typewriters used in typing the reports were identified as being the same typewriters. Three different typewriters were used in typing the first three reports, and two of the same three typewriters were used on the fourth report. That proves rather definitely that all four documents came from the same hand, though the hand is unknown here. I have not had the chance to

[27] See above, pp. 182–184.

check up the fourth with the same person with whom I checked the first three [Bruening], but I have arranged for an invitation to be extended to him to a conference on the subject. When I gave the fourth copy to General Miles of the Army and when he read it he said he thought it was the most important document that had been received by the Army from the State Department in his recollection.

Ten days ago the House passed a Bill with a proviso that none of the money appropriated in the Bill should be spent for food outside of the United States. This Appropriation Bill was for the Navy. It went to the Senate unnoticed and was reported out by the Committee of the Senate. On the floor of the Senate a motion was made to eliminate that section. It ended in a tie, 32 to 32, with Wallace[28] at lunch and not in the chair and absent so that he could not vote to break the tie, and consequently the motion to delete was lost—on the count. However, it developed later that Senator Russell had voted to delete and had then left the room and had not checked the calling of his name.

The clause meant a great deal to us in our relations with Latin America, because the question of beef from the Argentine was immediately presented. We are doing everything in our power to develop economic ties with the countries in the South so as to strengthen our political ties and our national defense cooperation. With this proviso in the Bill exception was taken to it in Argentina and probably very properly. It also served as the basis for German and Italian diplomatic maneuvers throughout Latin America and for the agents of Germany and Italy down there to use as an example of the bad faith of the United States in their dealings with those countries and as indications of our selfishness in our attitude toward them.

To add to the difficulties, on the same day that the tie vote was had in the Senate the House passed a supplemental deficiency bill for national defense in which the same proviso was inserted, except that it was broader and included clothes as well as food.

This morning I took the matter up, the Congress having been recessed since Friday. I went to the Capitol and talked to Senator George[29] of the Foreign Relations Committee and with several of the other Senators and with Senator [James] Byrnes and with Senator Alva Adams[30] of Colorado, who is Chairman of the Sub-Committee of the Senate Committee considering the bill.

When the Senate met today they corrected the record to show that Senator Russell had voted to delete, and the motion thereby was carried. This laid

[28] Henry Wallace, now Vice President of the United States, 1941–1945.

[29] Walter George, Democrat, U.S. Senator from Georgia, 1922–1957, and chairman of the Foreign Relations Committee, 1941.

[30] Democrat, U.S. Senator from Colorado, 1923–1924, 1933–1941.

the basis for a similar position in regard to the other bill which was just presented from the House to the Senate today. Then I went over and talked to Sam Rayburn, the Speaker, and found him surprised that the clause had been in the second bill and positive in his statement that he and McCormack [31] would do whatever was necessary to get the House to adopt the Senate attitude. He was very positive in his statements that the Administration's plans as regards Latin America should not be jeopardized by the action of a minority of members in the House. So I think the thing probably will get straightened away, and I hope in the future the appropriations committee will be under Rayburn's guidance and refrain from making any such exclusions in the bills which they report.

We have decided to send two ships to France with wheat. The purpose is political. The British were very loathe [sic] to agree to it, but the Secretary had insisted upon England's taking some steps to indicate that she was not hostile to all the French people, particularly those in unoccupied France, more or less as a means of preventing them from relying entirely upon Germany and being forced to side with Germany even to the extent of using their fleet to oppose England and to allow Germany to occupy North African possessions. These were not conditions in the gift, but they were presented separately to the French Government. The British were just told that it was necessary from the point of view of political expediency that this help be sent to France and that they were to allow it to go through the British blockade. . . .

The Dutch Minister and the Minister of Foreign Affairs of the Netherlands on his way to Batavia called a few days ago, and we had a considerable discussion on vessels. Also the Danish Minister has been in for several very long conferences. It all has to do with foreign-flag ships in our ports. We have no authority to deal with them, though a bill is pending in the Congress, having been introduced without Administration support, which would give us authority to purchase any of these vessels. The difficulty in advocating it as an Administration measure is that each Government to the south of us will interpret that as a green light to go ahead and take such of these vessels as they find in their own ports. In the meantime there are negotiations between private American parties and the German Government for the sale of all the German ships in this Hemisphere and the same negotiator plans subsequently and provided he is successful with the German Government to proceed to Italy and continue negotiations there for the purchase of all the Italian vessels in this Hemisphere. This is a transaction different from the one that Congressman Boykin [32] was interested in, which contemplated the purchase of Italian ships with foodstuffs and the transport of those foodstuffs to Italy.

[31] John W. McCormack, Democrat, U.S. Representative from Massachusetts since 1928.
[32] Frank Boykin, Democrat, U.S. Representative from Alabama, 1935–1963.

Also discussed unofficially and quite personally with the Dutch Minister and the Minister of Foreign Affairs the question of an LL.D. Degree from Princeton for Her Royal Highness Princess Julianna. Dodds had written several letters but had got no response, and they telephoned me to see if I could get some action. They said that they thought they would be very glad to do it but would have to get confirmation from London.

March 28, 1941

The British last evening informally proposed a plan to put the Danish flag ships in this hemisphere—about 60 of them—200,000 gross tons—to work. The British were to get 75%—we to use 25% under their warrants and with British permission in hemisphere trade—all insured in England—charters to be arranged with the Danish owners at our insistence. It is not satisfactory, of course. There seems no reason why we should do the negotiating and take the onus instead of Britain doing so. Anyhow—it is probably dead. The President is now considering a plan of expropriation, authority for which will be asked of Congress. Cooperation of the other American Governments will be asked in advance and as much secrecy as possible will be maintained until the resolution is introduced. That will supersede this British proposal and all others and clear the way for getting not only Danish but all foreign flag idle ships in the hemisphere—except those of the belligerents, Germany and Italy. Expropriation is the only effective and practical plan.

French flag ships to carry mercy food to France for the Red Cross also up for discussion reassurances in writing from England and for the other belligerents. As the vessels are not American flag ships we cannot ask safe conduct—but we will notify them and it will be to the same effect.

March 30, 1941

This morning early the Department got me out of bed to the telephone and advised me that we had taken over the Italian and German ships, which came as a perfect surprise. I telephoned Welles. He had not heard of it. We agreed for a conference about ten o'clock at the Department. I then got Gaston [33] after considerable delay, as he was telephoning on his own line, and he told me that there had been sabotage by the Italians and Germans, some by lighting fires under dry boilers, some by boring cylinders, some by removing parts and some by smashing machinery and that the vessels had already been boarded and taken into protective control. I called and notified the Department to call several officers for consultation, got some breakfast and went by the Bowie track, where I had engaged to meet to see my horses work, to tell them that I would not be there, and hurried on to town.

[33] Herbert E. Gaston, Assistant Secretary of the Treasury in Charge of Customs, Coast Guard, Narcotics, and Secret Service.

Conference with Welles, Hackworth, Bonsal, Saugstad,[34] and Atherton.

I argued that the incident be taken advantage of for the purpose of taking over all the foreign flag ships. There were various conferences by Mr. Welles at the conference with Gaston and Admiral Stark,[35] each of them several times. It was finally decided that we would not be justified in taking over the French ships on the basis of our present information and that to do so might jeopardize the delicate arrangements we had been building up with France so as to get confidence with the Petain Government; that to take the ships would jeopardize that and that the confidence was not worth 150,000 tons of shipping in trade. The Belgian ships were considered not to be in danger. However, the Danish ships were a different matter, and it was decided to recommend to the President that the Danish ships also be taken into custody. The question then arose as to what to do with the crews and as to whether there was legislation and authority for confining them. That was passed on to a conference with Treasury tomorrow morning.

The action of sabotage is sinister. It means that the German Government is about to take some aggressive action as regards the United States—in my opinion. One Italian vessel left the port of Recife ostensibly for Oslo with full cargo, leaving last night. Another Italian vessel left another port with a load of fuel oil. Each of them probably have a rendezvous with several other German ships which have left Brazilian and Argentine ports in the last few days and with the German battleships known to be in the Atlantic. This act of sabotage here is no doubt connected with that operation and is probably indicative of Germany's hostile intentions.

Anyhow we get, even in damaged shape, all of the German and Italian ships now here, and we will ask the Congress for authority, which will no doubt be forthcoming, to seize the ships to our own use. The same will apply to the Danish vessels. Consequently our fleet will be enhanced by some three or four hundred thousand tons and efforts will have to be made immediately to repair the damage done to the machinery.

The conference broke up about noon.

We sent a telegram, triple priority, to each of the Latin American countries advising them of the action taken. Only yesterday we had advised some of them that we had no settled policy in regard to foreign flag vessels and suggested to them that they withhold any action there pending clarification here. So the news must have come as a distinct surprise to them, and it is hoped the telegram will sufficiently explain the situation.

[34] Philip Bonsal, acting chief of the State Department Division of American Republics, 1940, and chief, 1941–1944; Jesse Saugstad, assistant chief, State Department Division of International Communications, 1938–1944.

[35] Harold Stark, chief of Naval Operations, 1939–1942. Stark commanded U.S. naval forces in Europe, 1942–1945.

March 31, 1941

A busy day. The press is full of the ship "seizures" and the office full of diplomats in consequence thereof. Arrangements not yet complete for dealing with the crews taken in custody, some of whom spent the night in jail because there was no public place to keep them.

The Danish Minister almost thanked me for taking his vessels. It relieved him of a real problem. The Italian Ambassador came to protest—but there was little punch in it. There were too many answers to his faint complaints. The Swiss Minister wanted us to help him buy some vessels to sail under the Swiss flag—60,000 tons. I told him if he could find any ships to buy we would give him our blessing provided it did not contravene an American interest.

The Treasury has got a copy of a telegram to the Captain of one of the Italian ships ordering the Captain to destroy the engine—and another to the same man to transmit orders to two other Captains to destroy the engines of those vessels. Each message was signed "Adetto Navale"—but without name, each is *en claire* in Italian and uses language which does not read "to destroy" but which was the signal to be read and to mean "to destroy"—according to the Captain addressed. One is dated March 19. The "Adetto Navale" is Admiral Lais [36] with whom we dined only last Thursday—the 27th. He will have to be sent home—*persona non grata*. He was most effusive the night we were there—and worried about his son who had graduated prematurely from the Italian Naval Academy and had joined the fleet. I expect he is even more worried now since the British have administered a severe defeat to the Italian Navy in the Ionian Sea—a loss of three destroyers and two cruisers and a 35,000 ton battleship damaged. Between the British at sea and in Africa and the Greeks on land the Italians are having a poor time—and now to lose 28 ships in our ports—two they destroyed in Punta Arenas and one the Cubans may take in Havana tonight—as well as five lost to Chile and one to Peru. . . .

April 1, 1941

The evidence in the form of photostats of two telegrams sent by the Italian Naval Attaché to the Captain of one ship in Norfolk was furnished by the Treasury. Upon further inquiry at the telegraph office I was able to substantiate the fact that fifteen different telegrams had been sent, some of them on the 19th of March and some on the 28th of March. Each of them ended with the words "Inviarmi situazione graduale numerica personale di bordo" and signed "Adetto Navale." This is now understood to be the signal to destroy the engine in the vessel. I was engaged during the afternoon with Hackworth and Savage drafting a notice to the Italian Ambassador declaring the Naval Attaché *persona non grata*. There is sufficient evidence to indicate that he was the agent responsible, and he will have to go. I have looked up

[36] Vice Admiral Alberto Lais, Italian naval attaché in Washington.

the precedent in the Von Papen case in 1915, and we are following that procedure.[37]

April 2, 1941

The psychological situation in the world has changed enormously in the past four or five days. The Yugoslav resistance to the demands of Germany and the coup d'état there, the British victory in the Ionian over the Italian fleet, further losses in Abyssinia on the part of the Italians, and the reaction in the United States and Central and South America to the acts of sabotage committed by the Italians and Germans on their vessels have changed the whole temper of the world. For the moment it seems to presage a Germany on the defensive. The experience of watching this change since Friday of last week, and this is now Wednesday of this week, and to watch it from the intimate point of view of the confidential cables and conversations in the Department has been an unusual experience. All of the countries opposed to Germany seem to have taken heart anew, and even countries under the yoke of Germany or in her immediate jurisdiction have indicated by popular expressions their sympathies with the United States and inferentially [*sic*] their opposition to Germany. In Geneva there has been a demonstration almost of affection before the American Consulate, and in several parts of France there have been demonstrations, particularly at Lyon.

The German acts of sabotage appear to be reckless. At Tampico and in ports of Peru, Ecuador, Costa Rica and other ports in Mexico they have been reckless in the destruction of valuable vessels. And the mystery of it all is that there is no real reason for it. No country in South America, except Chile, and Peru, had undertaken steps to control German or Italian shipping, and those two countries were more or less blocked in their efforts. In the United States we had no intention of taking over German or Italian vessels because they were in different categories, being active belligerents, and were different from the other foreign flag vessels because they were not active belligerents. Upon them we looked with covetous eyes and tried in every possible way to get control of them by legal means, but we were apparently up against a blind wall with the only opening being that of private purchase. Strangely enough the German Government and the Italian Government were each in negotiation with private parties for the disposal of their vessels in the Americas. One American individual still believed after our assumption of control over the German vessels in the United States that he was still negotiating with the German Government and that the German Government was assenting. There has been no apparent reason for their action. I am sure

[37] Franz von Papen, German military attaché in Washington during 1915, was accused by the United States of working to promote strikes in American industrial plants. He was recalled at the request of the State Department in December 1915.

from what I know of the whole situation in the two Americas that no Government except Chile and Peru had any intention whatsoever of moving against those vessels and we certainly had none until they committed the acts of sabotage. . . .

April 4, 1941

. . . The Italians have complained bitterly about the treatment of their seamen in certain places. In Panama their consular agent was arrested; in Baltimore their men were held incommunicado; in Mobile they were placed in jails. I have had each of the matters up with the appropriate Department, which was the Department of Justice in all instances except the War Department which had control over the Panama situation.

My new car was delivered at five o'clock, but I have been detained until now it is seven and I am bound for home. I am taking tomorrow and next week as a vacation, having had two weeks last summer and two days duck shooting last December, but that is all except an occasional half holiday Saturday since the first of September 1939, and I need a change both to my mind and my nerves.

April 12, 1941

I have been away for a week. One day I went to New Jersey to attend a testimonial to Leon Henderson by his home town—Millville. He is a fine able fellow who has fought his way up from the truck garden and the newsboy. Each other day I have rested, been out of doors, seen the spring commence. Since I have been on leave Germany has overrun Yugoslavia, penetrated Greece, recovered the Italian losses in Tripoli and Cirenaica; England has bombed Berlin heavily; the President has asked for legislation to permit him to take Italian and German ships here—and other foreign flag vessels— has taken over the Danish ships, has taken over Greenland for defense by arrangement with Kauffmann;[38] strikes have threatened the flow of defense articles—some have been settled, some others broken out. My office has been finished up with new paint. At least something will look brighter when I return tomorrow. The situation abroad had deteriorated—but it looks better here than it did a week ago.

April 17, 1941

. . . I should have recorded a conversation with Hull several weeks ago— [April 1] he asked me to talk to him. He asked me what I thought of the proposal to convoy. I answered that when we did we were in the war; that if convoying itself were not to be considered an act of war certainly our vessels would be engaged by Germany and we would have to consider that

[38] Danish minister to the United States.

an act of war against us; that we were not ready for war and I did not want us to get into it at least until we were ready. He is not apt to be specifically committal but from his conversation I am sure he held the same opinion. He went to the President's conference and I understand he and the President were of the same mind—and that others were not.

Acheson yesterday to me advocated we get into the war—*in order* to speed up our defense program. He thought if we were at war, labor would be easier managed. I told him he had the cart before the horse—we had to have our defense program before we got into the war.

April 22, 1941

This morning appeared before the [House] Merchant Marine and Fisheries Committee in an animated hearing and presented the Department's attitude to support the President's request for authority to take over the foreign flag ships. Considerable objection on the part of the minority members and one majority member, a former National Commander of the American Legion. Admiral Land also presented the case from the point of view of operation.

Lunched with Captain Kirk [39] and I suggested to him that the Navy make a "restricted area" of the Virgin Islands to prevent the raising of the political questions involved in this refugee and undesirable citizen traffic which is going on. Ickes and the pressure of his friends to get in persons like Beogler, Lamm, Tittel [?] and various others and the appearance down there of a man who we supposed was named Gumble but who turns out to be somebody else who has already appeared at the port of the Virgin Islands—and the cooperation of certain persons in the Department of Interior and the Immigration Bureaus and Robert Morse Lovett [40] in the government of the Virgin Islands itself—all makes it very difficult, but if the Navy could declare it a restricted area for strictly naval reasons, we would have no more trouble. Kirk took well to the idea and would see if he could put it through. . . .

April 24, 1941

Took the afternoon off yesterday and went to see Equipet run in the Aberdeen Stakes at Havre de Grace. She ran a good race and came in third.

The Greeks are still fighting but falling back, and the British are finding themselves in a bad spot. Evacuation is proceeding as far as practicable. I refused to agree to a proposal that Americans be evacuated on British convoyed boats. We have given them every warning to evacuate months ago.

In Egypt the Germans have three divisions; about twice as many tanks as the British have. When the Germans move down to the Dodecanese Islands, and no doubt into Syria, a pincers movement will begin against the Suez

[39] Alan G. Kirk, chief of Naval Intelligence Division, 1941.
[40] Government Secretary of the Virgin Islands, 1939–1943.

Breckinridge Long and Representative Champ Clark of Missouri, January 1920.

Long at William McAdoo's pre-convention headquarters, New York, June 1924, conferring with Clyde L. Herring, Democratic National Committeeman (left) and David L. Rockwell, McAdoo's national campaign manager (center)

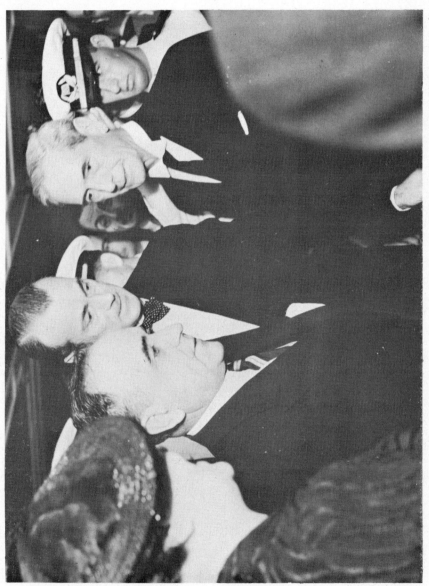

Long with President Getulio Vargas of Brazil and Jefferson Caffrey, American Ambassador to Brazil, 1938.

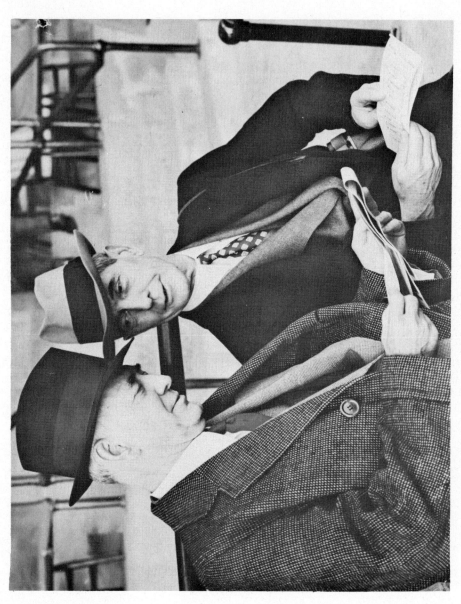

Long with Senator Key Pittman of Nevada at Laurel (Maryland) Race

The Department of State in 1942. From the left, Secretary of State Cordell Hull; Under Secretary of State Sumner Welles; Assistant Secretaries of State Breckinridge Long, G. Howland Shaw, and Adolf A. Berle, Jr.; Legal Adviser Green H. Hackworth; and Assistant Secretary of State Dean Acheson.

Long and other members of the Department of State with General Isaias Medina, President of Venezuela, January, 1944. From the left, Dean Acheson, Long, General Medina, Edward Stettinius, Jr., and

The Dumbarton Oaks delegation, August 1944. Long is second from left, seated.

incidents very closely kept and others of greater importance. Most them mentioned this nasty rumor and said his informant had told him that Hull had made certain remarks which he repeated verbatim about the person in question and concerning these rumors. I was astonished - and immediately realized that the informant could be the source of the leaks Hull had mentioned. Thinking that Hull could identify the few persons he had talked to in such an intimate way and that by a process of elimination he might identify the actual leak to the informer I went to him and told the Kroock story - but not mentioning the scandal or the person concerned. I did tell him I thought he should see Kroock and get from him if possible a first hand account of the whole picture of the possible leak. He agreed to do that and intended to do it soon.
During our conversation he made some critical remarks of a personal nature to elucidate some of the difficulties he labored under officially and then hinted at this scandal in such a way I knew he knew of it. So today it came out matedly into the open but never specifically named - and all because Kroock was the recipient of leaky rumor of an entirely different variety. When he brought that subject up and Kroock had already used that same unpleasant subject to emphasize that he had a direct line to Hull's own confidential conversation I thought it well to tie the two together and to impress upon Hull the advisability of his having a personal talk with Kroock to explore the source of the leak.

9/12. How carried about this scandal rumor and decided I would do - in our attempt to discourage any use and prevent an outbreak. So I went to Hull's apartment after - very busy day and 3rd cabinet lunch. In analysis I presented the thought = It was very dangerous to pic = men at bay, when charged with infamy, were vicious and that any moral without proof was ill-advised = that any proof once existing might not now be in existence = that one named - a two possible named - utterances would not be of weight if there was no evidence = or if Ross and denials from substantial third parties = that I could not believe the tale = that one high official of the White House was stated to have suppressed any conversation from certain persons = that under suppression substantiation even if true was impractical = that the key person was that particular White House official = that any further conversation should be discontinued = if and that then the W.H. official should be approached directly. That argument, expanded and amplified, was accepted and the definite statement made that it was not the truth of the story which concerned him as much as the general contemporary currency, which might involve the President and the whole Administration if it proceeded - and that if anything was ever done it would be to approach the W.H. official. That ended it I hope - for he will not approach that official. I called attention to the unreliable reputation of one of the principle purveyors of the gossip - who had first approached Hull - but he countered by relating it was the death-bed statement which was made

A page from the Breckinridge Long diary.

Canal, and it begins to look like very serious trouble for the British in the Eastern Mediterranean and in that area. It is a development of what I foresaw in 1935 when the Italians were on the edge of Egypt during the Ethiopian war. It must not be forgotten that the Italians then were in far better morale and far better equipped with fighting material in comparison to the British than the Italians are today. There Germans today are proving what the Italians might have done if the British had started to fight in 1935, for the British were totally unprepared to stop any advance at that time. Nevertheless, the desert is a formidable barrier to any army, German or other kind.

Defense Communications Board all morning.

Received the Italian Ambassador this afternoon and presented him with our reply to his protest about seizing the Italian ships. He took a very serious view of the situation, and I made a memo of the conversation.

April 25, 1941

The President has approved the proposal to concentrate visa control in Washington and has directed the allocation of space near the Department for that purpose. I took it up with the Secretary this morning, and he said to go ahead. The President also recommends that we take some steps to make some arrangement to prevent the entrance into this country illegally of alien seamen—a flagrant abuse of our laws in which we are not receiving cooperation from the Bureau of Immigration. We have tried to get legislation on the subject, but we have not received cooperation. We have agreed with Justice on the text, but their influence is against legislation on the subject.

Simultaneously with the President's approval there came a proposal from the Secretary of War transmitting a copy of recommendation to the President by the chiefs of M.I.D., O.N.I. and F.B.I. to control all immigration into the United States through visas, diplomatic as well as others, and to institute an exit permit system. I have gradually been moving in that direction for a year. On several occasions in the past when I have discussed it I have been unable to get the cooperation needed. Now the Secretary has approved it, and I am hopeful that legislation can be passed to effectuate it. . . .

The German Chargé d'Affaires, Dr. Thomsen, came in at my request and discussed the administrative difficulties we were having in getting mail out of Paris. There is a very large congestion and no help from the German authorities. Amongst it all the representation of the interests of other Governments in that area. There are nearly 100 bags of mail accumulated at Paris intended for the Department.

He then took up the question of the German Consulate in San Francisco and its inability to find a place in which to do business. They are unable to lease any premises. The present lease runs out on the first of May and will not be renewed, and they have now bought a house which they have now been advised they will be unable to use because of zoning restrictions. But there is nothing we can do about it, and it will have to appear in the Courts out there unless they can arrange it satisfactorily with the local authorities.

My visit to the Senate disclosed that Martin of West Virginia is liable to be seated in the vacancy left by Neeley. There has been the question as to who had the authority to fill the vacancy. Neeley's appointee [Joseph Rosier] [41] is the Administration choice; the other appointee, that of the retiring Governor, is Martin. Martin has been to see me to secure my help with the White House, but I have withheld. It now develops Martin is liable to be seated. All the Republicans, practically all the disgruntled Democrats and a few personal associates banded together are about enough to seat him. I saw Sherman Minton [42] there. He is the liaison between the White House and the Congress. He is somewhat ineffectual because certain commitments in the way of appointments made to certain members have not been observed. I have been very successful in my movements on the Hill so far as liaison between the Department of State and the Congress is concerned, but I cannot continue to be successful if the Senators and Members of the Congress are alienated. I tried to talk it over with Steve Early this afternoon, but we could not get together, so he will see me tomorrow morning.

The British continue their withdrawal, and difficulties pile up in Africa. The Germans are accumulating in West Africa. Our policy is to let supplies go there, and I told the Treasury this morning to let the *Scherazade* load 12,000 tons of gas (not high octane) and 6,000 gallons of kerosene. Regular runs are being made between New York and Casablanca with ordinary supplies, but not war materials, and sugar, bananas and tobacco are going from Martinique to Casablanca. This is all in the hope that the French forces in Africa will resent the presence of the Germans there and will band together and cooperate with the British. I am beginning to suspect they will expect us to send an army there, but that seems impractical and entirely out of the question. What is not impractical, however, and what is being arranged, is an air base in Brazil at Natal. With a big air base there we will be as close to Africa and the Germans at Dakar as they are to America. If the Germans move down into Spain, and it looks as if they were preparing to do so, they will overrun Portugal and we will then have to occupy the Azores and the Canary Islands. Of course the Germans will say that is a violation of international law. Under the circumstances it will be quite logical with them and quite within the law if they should occupy them—from their point of view.

[41] Retiring West Virginia Governor Homer Holt appointed Clarence Martin, a lawyer, to fill the Senate seat vacated by Mathew Neely, the newly elected governor. Neely, after being sworn in as governor, appointed Joseph Rosier to the Senate seat. After a prolonged dispute, the Senate on May 13 agreed to admit Rosier.

[42] Democrat, former U.S. Senator from Indiana, 1935–1941, and special administrative assistant to the President during 1941.

I talked with the Secretary this morning. He is quite provoked at the speech Frank Knox made last night. Knox made statements which were rather definite as far as our foreign policy is concerned and were more advanced than any the Secretary felt justified in saying. Knox made the statement that the President had O.K.'d his speech. The Secretary constantly has his feelings hurt that way and every once in a while he unburdens his soul to me. They spoke almost simultaneously, he in Washington and Knox in New York. The Secretary thinks that the implications from Knox's speech are that we are going ahead as far as it is necessary to go while he feels that we can't turn backwards, but the question of convoys and expeditionary forces are considerations which are not dictated by present developments.

My very definite feeling is that as soon as we convoy we are in the war, and it will be assumed by Germany to be an aggressive act. That will be understood in Japan as an obligation on her part to become active in the Pacific. If, however, Germany can be construed the aggressor, Japan will feel no obligation to anyone. I would rather see us fight one war at a time, but not to fight any until we are ready to fight. We are not ready now. In the meantime we ought to establish a big base in Brazil and be prepared to do instantaneously what may be necessary in the Azores and the Cape Verde Islands. If England relinquishes command of the seas we have got to pick it up without hesitation or an instant's lapse. And the British naval forces in the Eastern Mediterranean are in serious danger.

Except for the fact that the sun is shining brightly and the day has been a beautiful spring day, there doesn't seem to be anything else that is encouraging or agreeable to think about.

April 28, 1941

... Meeting: Secretary, Norman Davis, Atherton, Dunn, Hamilton, Hornbeck, and myself. Subject—aid to North West Africa, Unoccupied France, Spain—to keep alive sentiment for us, to make it easier for them to resist German demands, to pave the way for *possible* resistance to Germany. It is hopeless in my opinion, but the only thing for us to do. Milk for babies, bread until July (when a new crop will come in) and supplies for the industrial and economic life of Morocco—so their light and power plants can run —oil, gas—and regular food supplies. We have to do it I suppose—but it will not impress them like the German victories in the Balkans have. Germany now has *25 divisions* in Tripoli. When they find that out they will be impressed. German troops are appearing in small but increasing numbers in Morocco. German "civilians" are appearing by the trainload in Spain—with machine- and small anti-air guns as "baggage." It is pretty hopeless to oppose that with milk for babies and a little free bread.

April 30, 1941

Spent all morning before the Appropriations Committee of the Senate. This afternoon had a long conference with the Attorney General on the general subject of control of immigration and emigration in all its phases, including seamen.

May 5, 1941

I should have gone yesterday to Staunton to the dedication of the Woodrow Wilson Birthplace. I contributed $500 toward it. I have been interested in it and felt that I should go and fully intended to go. The President and the Secretary were both there, and I should have been there, but I was so tired on Saturday that I just could not get up Sunday morning at half past six to motor there and consequently did not go, much to my regret.

Kirk reports from Cairo the impression existing there, which certainly is reflected here—or is certainly adhered to by me and by the Secretary—that the British possession of the Canal and control of Egypt is now in imminent danger. The pincers movement can now begin from Syria and Iraq on the one side and from Libya on the other side. Turkey will be surrounded by Syria, Iraq and Russia on the south and east and with Bulgaria and Greece and Germany in the background on the north and it will probably fold up like Rumania or Hungary.

May 12, 1941

. . . In conversation with Welles tonight he showed the first signs of fear about England. He said he thought the next three months were *the* critical months. If London had many more experiences like it had last night, in which it took a terrific beating from the air, he was afraid the morale of the British people might break, and he could not but wonder that they might break. England is not able to retaliate because she has not received from us long-range bombers in sufficient quantities to really punish Berlin. They can only carry light loads. They now have our fighting planes, and they are being delivered in increased quantities. They have today a superiority in the air of fighting planes and have brought down an enormous number of German raiders in the twenty-four hours preceding this morning, but they are not able to retaliate and give Germany what England is taking from Germany. If they could do that and if the English people could feel that Germany was suffering too, their morale would be different.

May 13, 1941

Before the Appropriations Committee of the Senate and talked with Senator George to clear up possible misunderstandings as the result of a letter he wrote to the Augusta *Herald* which was quoted extensively abroad indicating that he was opposed to convoys.

I have been on the fringe of the fight for the Senatorial seat from West Virginia. Martin was appointed by Holt and Rosier appointed by Neeley when Neeley became Governor, necessarily terminating his Senate seat. The vote was very close, and I was trying to keep Martin in line in case he should be elected.

The arrival of Hess in England has created an astonishing sensation.[43] It is the most fantastic thing that has happened since the war began. He is either crazy or he jumped out just ahead of the firing squad. It is not either one of those facts, however, that is the important one. The importance comes in the reasons underlying. Nobody knows the causes of the trouble between him and Hitler, and there will be a lot of speculation as to the cause. It reminds me of Hamlet, and of the flight of McDuff.

May 22, 1941

These last days seem to indicate the doom of the British in the Eastern Mediterranean. It is being proven they cannot hold Crete. Their air force has had to leave. The Germans are arriving by the thousands by air. When I received a secret document a few weeks ago which revealed that the Germans had trailers to transport planes—and could carry 150 men fully equipped in each trailer in the air and 150 in the tug plane I was a bit skeptical. Now it is proven true. The Germans are landing by the thousand that way—via the parachute—in Crete. The British Navy cannot stay there. They are too close to the Stuker fields in Greece. Their Navy is in dire difficulty. And when Crete is lost the Nazis are close onto Port Said and the Canal. In other words they are damn near licked in the Mediterranean area.

And world opinion is that they are licked. We hear it from South America, from the Far East, from West Africa. Rochat in Africa tells Murphy so. Our missions in South Africa report the opinion of responsible statesmen there to that effect. The Turks act that way—so do the Russians—the Finns even are turning, the Swedes are impressed, the Japs are convinced. . . .

Hull told me this morning Welles had tried to induce the President to declare *Africa* within the Monroe Doctrine. He (Hull) had differed with Welles. He said he felt Welles, being somewhat in disagreement with Hull's policy of careful stepping, had, he said, gone over his head (to use his own words) to the President several times. He had just waited. The President called him and he expressed his opposition and advised against any such foolish move. He was disappointed in Welles and provoked—but said he was not entirely unaccustomed to the practice.

---

[43] Rudolf Hess, deputy leader of the Nazi party and Hitler's closest personal confidant, unexpectedly fled to Scotland on May 10. Hess claimed his mission was to make peace between England and Germany. See William L. Shirer, *The Rise and Fall of the Third Reich* (New York: Simon and Schuster, 1960), pp. 834–838.

And so we start into real summer weather—thermometer at 96° today— and the longest drought at this season I ever remember. It is getting disastrous here.

May 27, 1941

The President yesterday approved my bill—which would be a reenactment of the 1918 statute to control the exit and entry from and into the United States of all persons, including American citizens. This to be done by passport control and by the control of exit permits. I am proceeding to take it up finally with the Attorney General and then to have it introduced in the Senate and in the House. . . .

June 4, 1941

Everything seems so discouraging now. The strikes are interfering with production. They are not dealt with realistically. Besides strikes there are slow-downs. In addition to labor difficulties, some of which are subversive, there is and has been a lack of efficiency in organization and management in a number of factories and plants for which the management alone is responsible. At least that is my information. Anyhow, we are *not* prepared—not enough planes, guns, explosives, shells. Nor a sufficient supply line of those articles. We are *not* ready to fight. And yet we are racing into it. I don't see now how we can avoid it. We are planning to take over the Azores, possibly the Canaries and Cape Verdes. Ships for transport have been given the Navy —39 of them just a few days ago, in addition to their other heavy allotments. South American and Far Eastern trade routes are being divested of tonnage which is transferred to the Navy. The political repercussions of that in Latin America may be far reaching. Anyhow it is being done. The Navy has the boats. I have talked to Welles, to Jerry [Emory] Land, to Stettinius who manages Priorities, to Will Clayton.[44] They all say "Do something" but Jerry. He says, "I have my orders from the President. I think some of it is suicidal but I have to obey. I never remember a war won by a country which sacrificed its trade routes and did not keep them open. We are sacrificing ours. But orders are orders." And so we prepare to take a big leap—almost overseas—to islands in another hemisphere which *can* command the sea routes to this hemisphere. Since the islands are not German nor German-controlled it may not mean war with Germany, but it probably will lead to it. Portugal has protested the references to her insular possessions by the President in his speech. And when I tried to review the whole situation today with Hull he said the needs of the Navy were paramount and that the consequences of naval concentration of tonnage was just part of the "fog" we are now

[44] Edward Stettinius, lend-lease administrator, 1941–1943; William L. Clayton, deputy administrator of the Federal Loan Agency, 1940–1942.

entering upon—that "nobody could see through the fog to any great distance."...

If we were ready to start I would not worry so much about it all—but the combination of circumstances means we almost must face the world alone—for Japan will soon be starting on her road to oil in Java, with tin and rubber to torment us with.[45] But as a result of it all I am very depressed.

Winant is back from London. I have not seen him. I talked to the Secretary today about it, and he says that Winant doesn't know anything new and that he apparently is not in touch with the situation as much as we are and that his statements indicate only the necessities for convoys, more airplanes and greater help. Hull says that he hasn't anything like the information that we have here....

June 6, 1941

This morning was spent with the Foreign Affairs Committee of the House in executive session. I presented the necessity for reinstituting authority to control the entry into and departure from the United States over all persons, including American citizens, and the requirement that they have passports, and including all aliens and the requirement that they have exit permits before they be permitted to depart, in addition to the immigration control we already have. The Committee voted out the resolution favorably with only one opposing vote....

I had a chat with Winant. I asked him if the British realized the implications of the situation in the Near East. He said that they expect to win in the Near East and that they were going to concentrate all their forces there and hold them and that they were confident of beating the Germans. He said the British were thinking only of carrying on and that he was having success here in getting help for England. In discussing the quantity of help he said that he was satisfied with what we had done and were doing and that we had done more in the way of production than any other country in the world could have done in the same time. I mentioned the labor difficulties prevalent here now and manifested by strikes and slow-downs. I remarked that I hoped

[45] The acute economic and financial strain imposed by more than four years of fighting in China had undermined Japan's military machine. The United States and Great Britain continued to extend aid to China. This Anglo-American support encouraged the Netherlands East Indies to reject Japan's demands for peaceful incorporation into the Japanese politico-economic empire (May–June, 1941). On May 25, Japanese troops broke into sealed warehouses in Haiphong, Japanese occupied French Indo-China, and seized $10,000,000 worth of American-owned gasoline and other goods originally destined for China. Washington protested to no avail, and on May 29, cut off the export from the Philippines to Japan of raw materials needed by the Japanese war machine. Nevertheless, n`gotiations for a settlement of American-Japanese issues, which had been reopened after Ambassador Nomura's arrival in Washington during February, continued.

the subversive elements in labor would not create a situation which would cause a reaction against labor as a whole and deprive them of any advantages which we had accorded them during the last eight years. His reply was that the persons that were critical of labor today were the old-time opponents of labor and he thought that labor was doing very well.

Winant is an odd person. He is thoroughly intense. He has a fervor that is constant, and I should think it would wear him out mentally and nervously. He has a sort of dischevelled personal appearance as to hair and clothes. His features are good and his eyes are brilliant. They burn with a sort of intensity which controls his whole being even in the most casual conversation and on ordinary trivial subjects. It is so to such an extent that I always wonder whether he can have the breadth of vision necessary to form a good judgment when his mind and whole nervous system seem to be so enormously concentrated on any given subject. His intensity would seem to exclude from his vision subjects related to but not immediately part of the matter in his thought. . . .

June 13, 1941

. . . The labor situation has developed rather pointedly. An acute manifestation happened in an airplane plant in the Los Angeles area. The President eventually took over the plant and sent soldiers to open up the picket lines. The strike collapsed and the officers of the C.I.O. are now engaged in an effort to segregate the Communists and saboteurs from their ranks.

I had a long talk last Saturday with Dan Tobin. He says the labor leaders, and particularly the leaders of the A.F. of L. are laboring under difficulties which the British labor union leaders do not have. They have a homogeneous membership. Here all and every kind of nationality enters into the membership. As a consequence of it there are sentiments of national sympathies with other countries. Some of the members are extreme and some of the subordinate leaders are extremists. . . . He is an admirer of [John L.] Lewis but does not subscribe to any of his wild theories and thinks he is a dangerous man. Nevertheless he admires his ability. Lewis hurt himself materially by his political activity against Roosevelt last fall. Lewis realizes this. He is now trying to reingratiate himself with Roosevelt. Tobin told me in the greatest confidence that he and the President had talked over this situation and that the President had told him that Myron Taylor—who has been and is a friend of Lewis and who allowed Lewis to organize his steel workers when he was President of the U.S. Steel—went to the President as the agent of Lewis and proposed to him that Lewis return to the President on certain conditions. The conditions were that Miss Perkins be fired and that a man sympathetic to labor be put in her place—assumably to be approved by Lewis; second, that the President displace Hillman of the Emergency Defense Commission and put in his place Murray,[46] the President of the C.I.O., and [William] Green of the A.F. of L. Tobin said the President was disinclined to attach conditions to Lewis' support of his national defense movement and of his own leadership of the country under the present circumstances—and Tobin approved the President's stand.

June 17, 1941

I spent the week-end at Princeton. It was the termination of my term as a Trustee. Mr. Cleveland Dodge[47] was elected to fill my succession on the Board. I did not attend the last meeting of the Board because I felt I would prefer not to be actually present, though I had an opportunity to talk to various members of the Board and to discuss the business of the University. It turned out to be the largest meeting the Board had ever had and that I was the only absentee.

During my absence at Princeton the Department notified the German Government to withdraw its Consuls from the United States. I was not consulted about it and did not know the action was immediately contemplated. Had I been consulted I would have counselled a delay of a week until I could get through the Congress the legislation now pending to control the departure of aliens. The Government is without real legislative authority to prohibit the departure from the United States of aliens but probably can exercise some control in view of the fact that the funds are now frozen. I have had to arrange with Senator Byrnes and Van Nuys[48] in the Senate and with Bloom and Speaker Rayburn in the House to give consideration to the Bill in the next session of the Senate, which will be Thursday, and which they hope to pass by unanimous consent and rush it to the House in order that the House may adopt the slight Senate amendment and pass it by unanimous consent the same day so that effective control over aliens will conceivably exist by Thursday night. . . .

Personally I am committed to the program to prevent persons coming into the United States who are or who are apt to become the enemies of the United States. I cannot adopt the philosophy that some segment of our Constitutional guarantees of liberty attach to an alien outside the United States the moment he applies for a visa to come here, nor can I condone the persons of any race, religion or category who entertain the slightest doubts about the desirability of the United States and its form of Government as compared to their own or some other form and who would serve the interests of another while here, and that mental attitude is going to direct my

---

[46] Sidney Hillman, labor leader, and former vice president of the C.I.O., 1937–1939; Philip Murray, president of the C.I.O., 1940–1952.
[47] Financier and vice president of Phelps Dodge Corporation, 1924–1961.
[48] Frederick Van Nuys, Democrat, U.S. Senator from Indiana, 1933–1944.

course in the Department of State as long as I am here. I plainly foresee that following that course is going to bring on some more pointed difficulties with the Department of Justice than it has heretofore. I have always been able to straighten them out with Jackson. However I have had nothing but difficulty with Biddle[43] and his subordinates.

June 20, 1941

Yesterday the German and Italian Governments each ordered our Consuls out of all countries under their jurisdiction and control. We are today deciding to send the Italian Consuls out of the United States. Presumably they can leave contemporaneously with the Germans.

June 21, 1941

... The situation is tense in Moscow. I signed a cable authorizing Steinhardt to get American citizens out via Siberia—if possible. There are not many unofficial Americans there and the women have been sent out. Stalin is reported to be refusing Germany's demands and making counterdemands which Germany has refused. But each side works in the dark and no one really knows what is happening. We have known for some time from one of our secret documents that Germany would be prepared to wage war now against Russia unless demands were made. The armies are all ready.

Then—if Germany is successful—in either way—it looks as if she would make a proposal for peace to England.

This is Saturday afternoon—the longest day of the year—and it is just five o'clock—and I am going home—till Monday morning.

June 22, 1941

Germany invaded Russia at dawn this morning, and Hitler issued a characteristic declaration of war. He assumed to speak for Finland and Rumania as well. It is a momentous movement but one we have expected and of which we have had fairly definite information, some of it for a long time. Just what it will mean in the form of alignments and shiftings is not clear. Of course Hitler's object is threefold—first to liquidate Communism and its leaders; second to obtain food in the Ukraine and oil in the Caucasus; third to rehabilitate himself and help his cause in all so-called democratic countries and enlist the decent opinion of the world by fighting Communism.

What the effect will be here is hard to tell, but it may mean serious political complications. We cannot waver in our opposition to Hitler just because somebody else, in this case even Communistic Russia, is opposing Hitler. We cannot change our stand because he happens to have picked on another

---

[49] Francis Biddle replaced Robert Jackson as U.S. Attorney General, a position he held from 1941 to 1945.

party for which I personally have the greatest dislike. A true reading of my actual thoughts as regards both Communism and Hitlerism would not be a decoration to these pages. And there will be serious political complications here at home because a goodly number of the conservative group will waver in their opposition to Hitler and a goodly number of the ultra-radical group will want us to intensify our opposition. I can foresee no great change in American foreign policy. . . .

I talked with Welles on the phone on the general subject of America's attitude and cautioned great care and deliberation in the preparation of a statement and expressed some doubt as to the advisability of issuing a statement immediately. He agreed.

June 25, 1941

Russia and Germany are fighting in the dark as far as we are concerned. There is no information except respective official communiques in which each side more or less claims to have already won the war. It will take time to get any real facts. Finland claims not to be a belligerent. But I asked to hold clearance from Finnish vessels. The crews are proGerman. If once Finland sides actively with Germany we will take the ships. . . .

The immigration problem is very hot. The Consulates close July 15 in Germany and Italy. That is the deadline. Everyone wants their friends out *now*. Pressure is *very* bad. And Germany sees her last chance to get her agents out and our inspection is very austere.

June 30, 1941

Russia and Germany are hard at it—each still claiming a lot. Nobody in other countries really knows—for they are fighting in the dark as far as we are concerned. Cripps, the British Ambassador, returns to Moscow with a military mission and was received by Molotov who he reported to Steinhardt to be very nervous, ill at ease and essentially non-communicative. Steinhardt thinks the Government may flee without notice leaving the Diplomatic Corps there. Without stating definitely his opinion he leaves the inference to be drawn between the lines that the Stalin Government is about to fall.

From his cable and from the communiques I gather that the Russians are in a bad way—that they were taken unawares and were expecting an attack *after* some protracted negotiations during which they would have an opportunity to dispose their troops. They expected demands—which they would argue about, in the meantime arrange their placements. But now it seems there were no demands but a sudden thrust. But even if they had had a few more weeks or months it would not have made any difference. They are just incapable of efficient action. For two years now they have just been standing like the proverbial ox. Now the axe is falling. My only hope is that Hitler will become so extended and involved he will collapse too.

During these momentous movements—maybe epochal—I am so engaged with our defense arrangements I can only get glimpses of the European movement. Getting our Consuls home from Germany and Italy; and theirs to go back from here—Presidential proclamation to effectuate passport and alien control, and regulations to govern—for agreement by State and Justice before it gets to the White House— Refugees and immigrants hectically pushing to get under the wire before July 1—Foreign vessels, and the taking of those sabotaged under forfeiture statutes instead of for "just compensation," as I stated to Senate and House—keeping visiting vessels from using their radios in our ports—trying to patch up disagreements with the Department of Justice— Preparing a speech the President asked me to make at Gettysburg day after tomorrow—these and half a hundred more have kept me all day long.

July 6, 1941

This Russian-German war is complicating the situation just as I feared it would. The Sunday morning it started two weeks ago I talked with Welles on the telephone and suggested we go very slow in making any public expression of our position and take our time formulating our policy. We did not go slow enough. And I suppose the lack of any actual aid to Russia may eventually lead to a correct appreciation of our policy. But it is getting mixed up. One of Hitler's purposes was to ingratiate himself with large elements of thought in all the countries opposing him by smashing at a regime they loathed more than they hated him and his crowd. And that is happening. A large part of the people even in conquered territory are bitterly opposed to Russia under Communistic rule. Many people in the United States are confused. The great majority of our people have learned that Communism is something to be suppressed and the enemy of our law and order. They do not now understand why we can align ourselves even a little with it. The Vatican has had a clique which was not bitterly opposed to Hitler—partly because he has under his military jurisdiction the largest Catholic population in the world. They seem to have influence enough now to win others in the Vatican to their side, for while the others opposed Hitler yet they were in violent opposition to Communism as the very negation of the law and philosophy of the Church.

And now we find it in South America. Each one of the twenty Republics south of us is Catholic. In a number of them already are apparent not only a change of heart toward Hitler but a distinct wavering in the quality of their support to us. In Colombia it is very pronounced. Norman Armour[50] spoke to me of the effect in Argentina. It is becoming apparent in other

[50] Ambassador to Argentina, 1939–1944.

countries and will develop more. They just can't understand the United States supporting Stalin—and they won't go along on that basis.

In the meantime our military authorities figure the German move has been a success up to date. At its present rate they think Russia will fall by October. . . .

July 7, 1941

Our military authorities working on their maps and plotting the German position concluded that the German armies will take Moscow within a week but that they will probably try to annihilate the Russian armies in their path. Of course they may be mistaken, but we notified Steinhardt in the belief that he would not be getting that kind of information and in order he might make plans for moving if possible.

I have also had a session about German films operating in the United States—"Victory in the West" and "Bismark"—each of which is having an insidious effect. They are reported to be bold showings of the organized power and to be making a very unwholesome impression from the United States' point of view on the persons in the vicinity of the movie houses in which they are shown. We are now trying to prevent the entry into the United States of such films—which can probably be done under the tariff laws—and to prevent the showing of ones now here. But that presents a more difficult question. Perhaps it can be worked out through the President's proclamation, and I am trying to get the proclamation interpreted so as to make it possible for us to prohibit the showing of those films. Under the proclamation we can apprehend agents. Under it also we ought also to be able to apprehend the more lasting and effectual instrumentality of the agent which in this case would be the films.

August 1, 1941

Nantucket. Have been here nearly three weeks. I was tired out. It has been a long and wearing year and it has taken its toll in physical and nervous energy. Am considerably rested and after another week will be ready to return. Hull is not yet returned. He was exhausted and has been away nearly two months.

Hopkins[51] went back to London about the time I left. One of my last acts was to get him his passport. He is now in Moscow. He may find out something about the Russo-German war but it is difficult at Nantucket to do anything but surmise. The communiques are conflicting—frequently contradictory. However, it seems the Russians are holding better than expected.

---

[51] President Roosevelt sent Harry Hopkins, his close personal confidant, on several special European assignments.

Germany—as we know—expected to finish the job in six weeks. It is now in the sixth week and they have not penetrated any material distance into Russia proper though they did waltz through Poland and the Baltic States. . . .

August 11, 1941

Hull is back—looks well and says he feels so. Welles is away "for four or five days only." I did not ask but guess he has joined the probable conference with the President where Churchill is reported to be too—along with Hopkins and several other officials.[52] The Secretary seems a little put out by the intimate association of Welles with the Chief. It is discernable [*sic*] in little remarks he makes. They are of entirely different types—Welles daring, thorough, quick thinking, clear headed—but possibly a little on the too daring side in an effort to do whatever the President says even if not thoroughly considered. For instance, there was once a draft telegram the President had approved. The last sentence was ambiguous and I suggested a modification of phraseology. He stated quite definitely, "Breck, the President approved *that.*" When I explained the modification and resultant clarity he assented—but the definity in his impetuous remark was clear indication of what I mean. Hull, on the other hand, is wary, scrupulous in exploring all the ground around, slow to come to conclusion, less clear in preliminary thought, critical of any proposal which he assumes responsibility for—even the President's—and not lacking in courage to present his different advice to the President or other proposer. Sometimes his continuing scouting, while mildly aggravating, is misconstrued as either a manifestation of diffidence or as an indication that he lacks decisiveness. Neither is correct. He is far from diffident and he has sufficient capacity for decision—after he has canvassed all the possible consequences of his decision.

Naturally, two such different temperaments have some little difficulty in reconciling themselves in continuous contacts—but one would have to be very well acquainted with either *and* very observing to discover evidence of antagonism. Each is a gentleman and would respect the position of the other.

I began to pick up the threads I let loose four weeks ago. Russia seems to be losing ground now. The Germans expected to be finished in six weeks— and this is the eighth. They have had a costly trip—and there is far to go— but they are making headway now.

[52] Reference here is to the secret meetings (August 9–12) that took place between Roosevelt and Churchill aboard the United States cruiser *Augusta* and the British battleship *Prince of Wales* at Argentia Bay off Newfoundland. As a result of these meetings, the Atlantic Charter was issued, which consisted of a joint statement defining the broad postwar aims of the United States and Great Britain. By September 24, fifteen anti-Axis nations, including the Soviet Union, had endorsed the Charter.

August 12, 1941

The Secretary took up Japan today—in conversation, speaking to me and Hackworth. He had conferred with Stimson. Had suggested Japan was getting firmly entrenched in Indo-China; would probably move into Thailand. If that happened England would have to attack. She would then call for help from us. Did Stimson have a plan? He did not. Then Hull suggested he had better hurry and get one—one way or the other. Perhaps Japan would skip Thailand and move into the Dutch Indies. The British might feel they should attack—by sea. If they did, did Stimson have a plan? He had not. Then the same remark.

Then he told of his talk with Knox. Were they planning to send supplies to Vladivostok for the Russians? Yes. Why Vladivostok? It is right on the border of Japan. The vessel must proceed nearly into if not quite into Japanese waters. One small vessel, if stopped or attacked, might precipitate a war for us in Far Eastern waters. Why not send the vessel to Murmansk—past Iceland, well north of the North Cape? Shorter, quicker, delivery closer to the scene of need—no provocation in the Far East. If he did send it to Vladivostok and it got attacked, did he have a plan? He did not. Then he had better get one before he sent any vessel.

He used these incidents as he does from time to time to show his technique—his thoroughness—his effort to obtain unanimity of thought and purpose among Cabinet officers too often prone to proceed directly to the President and obtain Executive approval of a plan or an idea which has not been thoroughly explored or developed. Also I suspect he uses them a little now and then to bolster himself against the suspicion or impression that the President is favoring the dashing, quick-deciding Welles over himself and to give the counteracting impression that he is the ameliorating influence in the Cabinet and the personification of wisdom. And I write it not meanly or critically. I think that a natural human reaction and a refuge in self defense.

August 13, 1941

The conference at sea is over I hear and the announcement I hear is made the President will return Saturday. The silence still continues to permit the Prime Minister to return safely to his island before announcement is made of developments there. . . .

August 14, 1941

President and Churchill released text of their statement. Meeting carried on in mystery. Psychological effect sure to be very great. It means coordinating world sentiment and available force against Germany.

August 19, 1941

Very long day. Hull somewhat uneasy about policy which puts through a careful scrutiny all prospective immigrants who have close relatives in Germany or Russia. There is a recrudescence of criticism from radical elements and organizations interested in getting persons into the United States from the doubtful territory. Welles thought I should see the President and present him with the whole picture. I asked General Watson what he thought. He is always—and properly—trying to protect the President and save his time. To my surprise he entered in his quite outspoken way on a criticism of Welles for trying to "take over" Hull's functions; said he was continually trying to confer with the President; and then went on to say the President felt the same way. He (the General) thought Hull the best thing in the Cabinet and the greatest strength to the Administration. Also, that Hull had got very provoked and threatened to resign if things were not regulated. He had said so to Frank Walker and had used his cuss words. Pa's [Watson] mind was very definite and his speech devoid of delicate embellishment. When I returned to my office the Secretary was calling for me. Welles was there; also Atherton and Duggan. First was the question whether we should do more with the text of the Roosevelt-Churchill agreement than send it to the Latin American Governments. After some discussion that was disposed of in the negative and he excused the others but asked me to stay and suggested Sumner might stay. He then asked about the immigrant question and relatives in occupied territory. I reviewed the history of it all since my original conversation with Bob Jackson while he was Attorney General and on through the legislative phase and the dispute with Justice over the implementation of the legislation since Jackson left and Biddle became Acting Attorney General. Then I put the "relatives" phase back into that picture and related the history of it and the substance of the language (Section 11) of the regulations which Justice has agreed to. Hull was afraid the opposition might carry some political embarrassment but thought the President ought to see me because there had been a dispute between two of his important Departments. I thought the President should have a memorandum of the whole thing—as succinct as possible. That was decided. I then dictated—with the help of Warren—the memorandum.

August 22, 1941

This morning I tried to straighten out the air lines carrying mail through Panama north so that the British might have a chance to censor German mail. It had been proposed to divert all the mail on arrival at Cristobel to be sent from there to Barranquilla, thence to Jamaica where it would come into British jurisdiction and where they would go through the Italian and German mail, the other being subsequently forwarded north to Miami and to its destination. . . .

And while everybody in the United States Government is trying to help England we get a telegram from Winant saying that the British and Japanese Governments have entered into a barter trade agreement. Clearance is to be between the Yokahama Specie Bank and the Bank of England. Winant called Eden, but Eden apparently knew nothing about it. Eden put him in touch with a Mr. Waley in the British Treasury. Eventually Waley got the text of the agreement. The British just do not know how to play cricket. One of the things they proposed to sell to Japan was cotton, and one of our largest exports to Japan has been cotton, which we have embargoed. One phrase quoted by Winant as having been used by Mr. Waley is probably indicative of the whole British attitude. It reads, "We are trying not to be behind you, and we don't mind getting a little ahead of you."

August 24, 1941

Listened to Churchill but otherwise just sat around and talked and rested. Sold four calves—$126—1900 pounds—seven cents a pound. I seem unable to get even fair prices—because I suppose I have neither time nor opportunity to see to such things myself.

August 27, 1941

The President sent for me to discuss the immigration problem before he shall receive the McDonald group. I found him keen, well, in high spirits and thoroughly in accord with our policies and practices. Was with him about three-quarters of an hour, part of the time he had Fred Sterling,[53] just back from Stockholm, in and questioned him at some length about the situation in and temper and psychology of Sweden and the leaders and people.

August 29, 1941

Our association with Russia and our military supplies to Russia are the cause of many misgivings among our own people. The Church Federation is rampant at our association with such a monstrous character. Early asked me today to help get a Dr. Daniel A. Poling to London—and back—passport, place on a bomber, and return, so he could attend a meeting of the International Christian Endeavor of which he is President and help straighten out the thought—and speech—of his people and stem the tide of criticism on his return. I got his passport right away—and a place on the bomber for day after tomorrow—and a British visa—with such rapidity in fact I think the good Doctor was almost breathless. But the situation he is to help to cure is real and is playing directly into the hands of Wheeler and Lindberg [sic]—who by the way are causing all kinds of excitement in Oklahoma City

[53] Minister to Sweden, 1938–1942.

today and with their speech tonight. I talked to Josh Lee[54] on the long distance to Oklahoma City. He was all agog and was planning to answer them Sunday night.

The Japs approached the President yesterday on Far Eastern matters. It may be very significant. I do not yet know what it was about.[55]

August 31, 1941

Yesterday the Secretary talked to me alone and most frankly about Japan and his personal difficulties connected with that problem. It seems he has been in secret conference with Nomura. The Ambassador has been going to Hull's hotel apartment for long talks for three months. They have had more than twenty talks and a general approach to the whole Japanese situation has been made and distinct progress toward an understanding has resulted. The "China Affair," Manchuria, Thailand, trade, raw materials, Russia—all the phases and facets of the complicated mess were included—economics, finance, politics. It had simmered down to three broad topics—American rights, interests and economic needs; liquidation of the Chinese war; and Japan's security.

Then came the President's conference with Churchill and Hull's exclusion from it or from knowledge not only of the subject matters for discussion and commitments to be made but Hull's ignorance of the place of conference and the direction he should not know. Further—Welles' invitation to accompany the President. The implications of it all were that Hull was not in the intimate confidence of the President and had no authority to talk to Nomura or to commit the Government to a settlement of the problems. (Hull did not say he had kept the President currently advised of his talks or even informed him of the fact, to say nothing of the general import. That seems to be the very weak point of his story and detracts from any imagined grievance he may have suffered.) Anyhow, at the conference, it was agreed Churchill should make certain statements in public about Japan and was authorized to say the United States would back him up.

---

[54] Democrat, U.S. Senator from Oklahoma, 1937–1943.

[55] When the Japanese occupied southern French Indo-China in July, Washington broke off conversations with the Japanese ambassador. On July 24, Roosevelt ordered Japanese assets in the United States frozen; the British Commonwealth nations followed suit. The effect was to suspend virtually all Japanese commerce with areas that normally accounted for three-quarters of Japan's foreign trade outside of the yen bloc. On September 3, after the Japanese had suggested a meeting between Premier Konoye and Roosevelt, the President asked Japan to accept the following principles as the basis for future commercial relations: (1) respect for the territorial integrity of all nations; (2) noninterference in the internal affairs of other countries; (3) non-disturbance of the *status quo* in the Pacific except by peaceful means. Exchanges of proposals and counterproposals continued until December 7. Long's entry for August 31 indicates that Secretary Hull had been conducting his own private talks with the Japanese ambassador. See *The Memoirs of Cordell Hull* (New York: Macmillan, 1948), pp. 982 ff.

On the return to Washington he had conferred with the President and explained that his commitment to Churchill would, if carried out, upset the whole program. The President understood immediately and accepted Hull's ideas. It was too late to stop Churchill—but a cable was sent cancelling the arrangement for the President to follow it up—and Churchill's statement was allowed to stand by itself.

As to Welles' going to the Conference, Hull said if he had been asked for a suggestion he would have named Welles—but he resented not being asked for suggestions and being kept in the dark about it all—and he was mad that the incident should have come close to wrecking his work for settlement. He resents Welles' constant contacts with the President—which are over his mental objection, though he has never spoken of it, he said, except to his wife and to me. And she, he said, was constantly upset by the practice—and it kept him upset. For instance, he said, he had explained to Welles yesterday morning the latest development, and Welles was all excited about it and said he was going over in a few minutes to say "Good-bye" to the President and would tell him. Hull said, "He could hardly wait to get out of my room to rush over there and tell him something important. Of course I did not interpose an objection when he displayed such anxiety to do it."

That last picture he probably over-drew—for as long as I have known Welles I have never seen him display anxiety. I have seen him irritated and bursting from within with anger—but he carries a poker face and displays little of emotion—particularly when he is trying to conceal his emotion.

Then the Secretary lit into Ickes! What he didn't say about him! He let his vocabulary run; called him a "damn trouble maker" and a meddler. His dispatch of oil ships to Vladivostok with a defy at Japan and a public blast just put dynamite under Cordell's three-months' effort. But he thought he had solved that and still had *hopes* for a solution of the Far Eastern mess. It was a hope—distinctly—but real progress had been made on two of the points and the third was having heavy going. He did not take me more into his confidence on the points but I was left with the impression it was the withdrawal from China which was the hardest.

He also criticized Sumner for talking to the press, clandestinely, about things he should not divulge and said if he himself did not it was someone in close contact with him who knew all the developments and did talk, off the record, for the benefit of Sumner in publicity.

This is the end of the first two years of the war. Tomorrow is the anniversary of the invasion of Poland—and of my call to Washington. It seems like only a few months—and the future is unknown. It looks better now—much better. The Russians are holding pretty well—inflicting terrible losses in men and machines and causing an enormous and an unexpected effort. And the weather there will get worse and make it still more difficult for Hitler.

So it looks better for our friends—and seems Hitler cannot achieve his maximum ambitions. It does not appear to me yet he can be administered a military defeat—though it is possible to achieve over him a political victory.

September 3, 1941

Attended the meeting of the Economic Defense Board in the Vice President's office. Subjects—general export licenses to South American countries and the establishment of a system which would regularize and permit same to operate; vegetable oils—including peanut oils in West Africa and shipments of same to France—no report pending further advices as to possible British naval action in regard to same. . . . The Secretary had asked me to represent him at the meeting. Acheson, under whose jurisdiction over economic matters it normally falls, was out of town. But he suddenly appeared at the meeting—having just returned at the request not of the Secretary but of one of his understrappers who apparently was jealously guarding his prerogatives and who must have attached undue importance to the fact of attendance on the meeting of the Board. It is amusing to watch some maneuvers in protection of an assumed self importance. . . .

September 4, 1941

At the request of the President attended a conference with him, McDonald's Refugee Committee and Attorney General Biddle. They are critical of the Department's policy—consequently of me. Biddle is their advocate. Rabbi Wise and the Archbishop of New Orleans were their principal spokesmen. Various amendments to procedure were proposed. Wise always assumes such a sanctimonious air and pleads for the "intellectuals and brave spirits, refugees from the tortures of the dictators" or words to that effect. Of course only an infinitesimal fraction of the immigrants are of that category—and some are certainly German agents and others are sympathizers, the last named coming here because it is away from the scene of combat and looks like a safe place. I got a little mad and fear I betrayed it. But I did not allude to the *Navemar*—en route from Lisbon to Havana and New York—a freight boat, passenger accommodations for 15 and 1200 poor Jews above and below decks with no sanitary arrangements, no service, no kitchen facilities, at from $700 to $1500 apiece, 4 dead before reaching Bermuda, 6 hospitalized there, 1 of which died, victims of the greed of their fellows—not of Germany or the United States policy. The vessel is a menace to the health of any port where it stops and a shame to the human greed which makes it possible. But I did not allude to it in reply to Rabbi Wise. Each one of these men hates me. I am to them the embodiment of a nemesis. They each and all believe every person, everywhere, has a *right* to come to the United States. I believe *nobody,* anywhere has a *right* to enter the United

States unless the United States desires. That desire is expressed in law and effectuated by regulations. The latter are drawn with the approval of the Secretary of State and confirmed by the President. I administer them to the very best of my ability and belief, consistently, in some respects generously, and all with the welfare and public interest of the United States at heart. The exclusion of any person is objectionable to these eminent gentlemen and my system of selection is anathema to them. They would throw me to the wolves in their eagerness to destroy me—and will try in the future as they have in the past to ruin my political status.

September 11, 1941

... Russia is still holding and making the cost to Germany enormous. Leningrad still holds out. We are informed by Phillips that Hitler was duped by Stalin through the medium of false reports planted on him in lieu of authentic information and which showed Russian equipment and production at a fraction of its real efficiency and he is now raging. This leaks as a sidelight on the Hitler-Mussolini meeting at the Eastern front.

September 18, 1941

Tonight dined with Baruch. He appears before the Senate Committee tomorrow—subject Price Control. His paper was all prepared. He had tried to make it non-critical but to present a cure for the situation. He sees inflation in bad form if Price Control is not rigorously instituted—but by price control he means "cost control" really because the price of raw materials and the price of the finished product includes the cost of labor and labor is confronted with rent, heat, light and fuel costs, and prices—so it must include *all* elements if it is to be effective control. Bernie is wise and courageous— and honest. The President shies away from giving him too much credit, personally or officially. Formerly Bernie wanted recognition—officially. Now he spurns it—theoretically. He does not believe in large committees— but in one man responsibility and advisors or technicians selected and authorized by that one man. Bernie does not point to the one man. He likes Leon Henderson and trusts him and plans during his answers on cross examination to say some complimentary things about him—"that will help him with the Conservatives—where he needs it." I left him early—to retire.

September 22, 1941

Have been wrestling with the Moving Picture Producers' problem with England. They have $36,000,000 in profits tied up there and unable to get it transferred into dollars and paid to them. They also have made all their deliveries for the year under their existing contracts. They are holding up the new contract for another year pending settlement of their present impounded balances. I have had it back and forth across my desk for months. The British say they need all their dollar securities and credits to pay for war supplies here and can't afford to use those securities to pay the balance they owe for moving pictures. Hull is interested to do all he can for the Movie people for he thinks they and their pictures are a valuable—and, in our way of life, a necessary and almost indispensable link between Government action and popular psychology. So he put it in my hands. Will Hays [56] represents the Movies. He and I have had many conversations, most of them on long distance phone. I have drafted cables—some of them very definite and pretty stiff—which Hull has signed and thoroughly approved. . . . The Producers will be nearly bankrupt and unable to deliver more pictures to England— and which England says she absolutely must have. But in the end Harry Hopkins may include future films in the gifts under Lend-Lease! *Quien sabe?*

September 24, 1941

Most of the day spent in discussions on repeal or amendment of Neutrality Law. None of it would have developed if Maritime Commission, instead of arming our ships, had given the ships to England. That would be expensive but not nearly as expensive as a war—which is the consequence of our changing policy. The present situation requires change in the law. My contacts at the Capitol advise the Congress would pass a repeal bill—and more easily than an amendment. Repeal would carry away the "Danger Zones" which not only prevent access to England but which actually serve as a sort of blockade to German held territory. To throw that away would make a lot of trouble here because of pressure of various groups to send this and send that to one country or another. I have presented this and argued for amendment— which could be done by a "rider" on some bill and avoid also the delays of hearings before committees which would consider a separate bill.

September 27, 1941

Long conference this morning in the Secretary's office on the Neutrality repeal question. Welles, Berle, Hackworth, Pasvolsky, Savage and Dunn. The Secretary related the substance and tenor of his conversation with Senator George. George had told him apparently just about what I had told him about the attitude of the Congress. George has considerable weight in the Senate and has a growing importance there. His position would be adhered to by a considerable number of Senators ordinarily friendly to the Administration. Mr. Welles thought we should ask for the power to put

[56] Former chairman of the Republican National Committee, 1918–1921, and now president of the Motion Picture Producers and Distributors of America, 1922–1945.

guns aboard. The Secretary thought that would not be sufficient. When they asked what I thought I reviewed the political situation vis-à-vis the Senate and the country and took the position that the principal thing was to get supplies to England. The arming of ships was not necessary and had elements of danger in it even, because the arming of ships carrying contraband would be a justification to Germany for sinking them if destined to one of her enemies. On the other hand we were spending time, labor and money and making supplies to reach England and that it didn't make sense to have those supplies sent to the bottom of the ocean. What we really needed and the crux of the whole thing was to get supplies to England. There would be less of a fight on the part of the Congress and a better understanding on the part of the people if we eliminated the bugaboo of an expeditionary force. That was what was really the crux of the Congressional opposition and of the people's real feeling. They feel that if some authority is given by a repeal of the whole Act that it will open the way for an expeditionary force to the Continent. That is not presently in our minds and may never be. The aim then is to get supplies to England. I then read a draft of proposed new legislation which would authorize the President to send vessels to countries he considered necessary for our national defense in spite of any existing danger zones. We already have that right under our present practice except as to England itself. There seemed to be more or less agreement with my point of view but no agreement was reached and the Secretary was apparently not satisfied with a partial treatment of the matter. After about an hour the conference adjourned. I made no reference to the ancillary plan of giving the vessels to England.

September 29, 1941

Neutrality Bill Amendment or Repeal still the major business. Conferred again several times with the Secretary. Continued my contacts with the Senate. The best obtainable from the Republican side is the contact White has with the Republican Pair Clerk and with the secretary of McNary.[57] They each think the repeal can pass if the President demands it. The Democratic picture is not so rosy. They think arming our ships in "waters necessary to our defense"—whatever that means—can carry. They are afraid of delivery of goods in our ships to England. Learned of Connally's[58] speech to be delivered tonight, advocating arms but not quite definite on delivery to England. In the last conference the Secretary wants us to sleep over it and advise him early tomorrow morning before he sees the President.

[57] James A. White, assistant to Long, 1941; Charles McNary, Republican, U.S. Senator from Oregon, 1917–1944.
[58] Tom Connally, Democrat, U.S. Senator from Texas, 1929–1953, and chairman of the Senate Foreign Relations Committee, 1941–1947, 1949–1953.

September 30, 1941

Promptly at nine the Secretary asked for me. He was seeing Stimson and Marshall at 9:15—the President at 10:00. For fifteen minutes Hackworth and I refreshed his memory on the principal points—1–arming ships—and 2–a) either repeal of the section of the Act prohibiting passage to belligerent ports or, b) my alternative, enabling the passage of the proscribed zone and voyage to belligerent ports but retaining the zone for other purposes.

This afternoon he called again. Hackworth, Berle, Dunn, and Savage were there. Without saying exactly what the President desired, he left the impression the President wanted to start with placing guns and follow that with repeal of the prohibition against entry of zone and voyage to belligerent ports—but not to draft legislation—only to draft letters to the Chairman of the Senate and House committees on each subject. A long discussion followed. Various views were expressed. A proposal was made to arm ships *and* go to Halifax—now prohibited as an enemy port. I thought that inadequate. The psychological effect here would be that we were backtracking. . . .

I advocated we do *not* repeal the danger zone provision nor remove the zones but that we authorize the President to send vessels through the zone. The reasons: 1) repeal would be hard for a lot of people who thought in their ignorance—but still thought—that the Neutrality Law provided Neutrality, which it does not. Nevertheless, they thought it did and would think its repeal was practically a declaration of war. So, to leave the law on the books and amend it only for the purpose in mind would be easier. 2) The repeal of the law would open up the way for an expeditionary force, which was not now remotely in mind. But the people abhorred the thought of sending an army over seas and would oppose the movement which opened the way. My suggestion did not open the way but only applied to goods, of whatever nature. Besides repeal would open up the entire Atlantic Coast of Europe and the pressure on me for Refugee ships, Relief to stricken populations, etc., would be endless. So I preferred it in *status quo*—prohibited by law.

In general, repeal would be harder to get and a request for it would create a different psychology. Without repeal everything we wanted could be done. An expeditionary force, if ever needed, could not be sent anyhow without a declaration of war and such a declaration would *ipso facto* end any and all provisions of the so-called Neutrality Law.

Others had other views but there seemed to be general agreement with mine. I did not do all the talking; Berle did some, Hackworth some and Savage some. Of course, the Secretary did a lot but he was trying to get the views of each and get agreement on something which would appeal to him as practical and desirable. So he did a lot of listening.

The decision was finally arrived at to draft three letters for the President to send the Chairmen and to serve as the basis for his talk tomorrow morning with Congressional leaders. One would ask to arm merchant vessels; two would ask for repeal of the objectionable prohibitory sections; and three would be my substitute authorizing vessels to proceed through the zone to take Lease-Lend aid to countries "resisting aggression" or which the President thought supply was necessary for our defense.

October 29, 1941

The Secretary had a long conference with the President this afternoon. When he returned to the Department he sent for me. The object of the conference was to discuss the Far Eastern situation and policy. In connection with the Far East, and having in mind the obligation of Japan to join Germany in case the United States was considered the aggressor in our relations with Germany, the Secretary pointed out the fallacy of the speeches of Knox, Stimson and others as being belligerent in character and being personal declarations of war. However, they are high officials of the American Government and he was sure that the statements made by each of them and several other high officials could be interpreted by Hitler and passed on to Japan as indications that the United States was taking the offensive. He also alluded to the President's own speeches in which the President had discussed freedom of the seas and had made that the cardinal issue. The Secretary called attention to his own speech and read to him his statement before the House Committee which we had helped him prepare and which indicates the policy which he has followed and which he has tried to direct. Emphasis is not laid on freedom of the seas but on defense. The freedom of the seas doctrine runs to all seas and is nebulous and implies in the last analysis that Germany is entitled to freedom just as much as any other nation. However, the idea that Hitler is trying to control the seas for the purpose of using them as a pathway to the Americas and that we are placed upon the defensive to prevent him from coming to the Americas and are acting against him in a purely defensive way has been the theory which the Secretary has evolved and in which we have concurred and in which I have been one of the proponents. It negatives the idea of freedom of the seas for the time being and emphasizes the necessity of defensive action on the seas against an aggressive belligerent. Under that theory Hitler cannot point to our policy as a directive to Japan to join him in war against the United States on the theory that Japan is bound to follow Germany if Germany is attacked by the United States. The Secretary said that the President accepted the argument and approved the policy, but the Secretary is still afraid that the persons intimately associated with the President and more continually in his presence, but who do not have the same understanding of foreign relations, will in the future, as they have in the past, induce the President to make statements which may not be in conformity with that policy. He hopes the President will now adopt his suggestions.

During the course of the conversation this afternoon he took up the matter of our dispute with the Department of Justice over the control of immigration and refugees. He told the President that the two Departments had got into a sort of deadlock over the matter and that there had probably been some antagonism in the lower runs of the two Departments and that it all revolved around the question as to whether control over these matters was to be in the Department of State or the Department of Justice or whether the Department of Justice should have a part of the control. He alluded to the practice during the Wilson regime and the law of 1918 which vested in the Department of State exclusive control. The President said, "I want control in the Department of State." The Secretary accepted that as a directive as to policy, which was in entire accord with our contentions. The President irrelevantly went on to say something about some advisor from the Department of Justice having some contact with it but he did not press the matter and the Secretary understood from the manner of his conversation that he did not seriously propose it. That would seem to indicate the President still feels, as I am sure he has up to now felt, that the Department of State ought to be in charge of these matters and that my activities still have his entire approval. It now remains, however, for the Secretary to come to an understanding with Biddle. . . .

October 30, 1941

Letter received from Biddle—to the Secretary—referring to their recent conversation and making various suggestions as to how the visa and immigrant procedure should be improved and criticizing us for our lack of policy. Secretary has not seen it yet. Just another unfortunate incident in the long drawn out controversy over the question of joint or unified control.

October 31, 1941

Stopped the Maritime Commission from taking the *Brennero*—a tanker owned by the Italian Government—which the Ambassador had protested. And later told Knox, at the Secretary's request, he could not take the *Normandie*. Knox wanted it to transport 400 planes to Russia via the Arctic–White Sea route—as a substitute for a naval carrier to do that to Vladivostok. I told him the French would explode on us and make it easier for the Germans to force themselves into West Africa—with air bases and submarine bases at Casablanca, Dakar, etc., which Knox wouldn't like either. He was reconciled but not satisfied.

That sounds like a negative day—and so much of it was. We did confer with the Secretary—Welles, Hackworth, Warren and I and drafted a memorandum proposing a final offer to the Attorney General for his agreement to close our long controversy. It was agreed to and he signed a covering note I drafted enclosing it to Biddle. He is somewhat provoked—but not nearly so tired and disheartened at the long argument as I am. If Biddle does not agree Hull now intends to present it direct to the President.

November 5, 1941

The Attorney General agrees to the last proposal for control of entry of aliens! That covers the principle we have insisted upon—ultimate control here in th s Department—(or exclusively in some other Department). Of course we never proposed the alternative. Now, after more than four months of argument and discussion—since June 21—we have the agreement. Details, in conformity with the principle, remain to be formalized. The selection by the President of two members of the Board of Review to represent *his* point of view—also remains. But the principal object has been attained.

November 14, 1941

Japanese Special Ambassador on way to discuss the Far East situation with Hull and President.[59] Renewed troop movements by Japan in and northward from Harbin. The Japanese Chargé in South Africa asks Brazilian Consul to take over Japanese interests "in case" and packs his files in boxes and trunks. Peculiar movements of Japanese troops reported near Canton.

November 20, 1941

Hull has not progressed far in his talks with the Japanese. He told me yesterday he had abstained from any reference to their barrage contemporaneous with the opening of their talks and had proceeded to outline our position as if nothing had been said by them. I got from Arthur Krock a copy of a press release "for the confidential background information of the

[59] Saburo Kurusu arrived in Washington on November 20 with a program for mutual understanding. Under these proposals, the United States would supply Japan with as much oil as she required, suspend freezing monetary measures, discontinue aid to China, and cooperate with Japan in securing commodities which both countries needed from the Netherlands East Indies. In return, Japan offered to withdraw from French Indo-China "upon either the restoration of peace between Japan and China or the establishment of an equitable peace in the Pacific area." In the meanwhile, Japan offered to withdraw immediately her troops from southern French Indo-China. Finally, a mutual Japanese-American agreement would oppose any military alteration of the new *status quo*. Herbert Feis in *The Road to Pearl Harbor* (Princeton: Princeton University Press, 1950), p. 307, states that Kurusu's mission "was unpromising, even if not false. His purpose, looked at in the best light, was to persuade the American government to accept the latest Japanese terms in preference to war. Looked at in the worst light, it was to engage American interest while the assault plans were being secretly completed."

press" which had been furnished him by the "War Department." I saw a story in the morning *Washington Post* apparently based on it but not quoting it. I told the Secretary I thought it was out of harmony with his policy. He was quite provoked and took it up and later told me, still provoked, that Marshall had given it out himself. It is obvious that it played directly into the hands of the war party in Japan. The paper stated the number of planes in the Philippines, the number to be there by December 15 and the total to be there in six weeks—mentioned air bases in Siberia—possible operations in Indo-China and Maylasia [*sic*] and stated there were troops based in Australia. The paper characterized the assemblage of bombers as the greatest in the history of the world. It had every indication of being an attempt to propagate news stories which would be intimidating to Japan—and provocative. Certainly it is not in the province of the War Department to get into that field of policy—during such negotiations.

And now comes Knox to proclaim that our vessels will be armed in two weeks. They can't be—but his announcement may be held as justification by Germany for sinking our unarmed vessels.

November 25, 1941

Since yesterday when Knox phoned me, and at the request of Hull, I have been trying to get the Navy and Jerry Land of the Maritime Commission to accept our ideas about guns on merchant vessels—consequent upon the repeal of the pertinent sections of the Neutrality Act. Knox wants guns on all our ships. Land is willing to go part way. Knox made a public statement. My fears are that if they announce the arming they will strengthen the justification for attack—even though our ships will not be armed. It will take months to arm them.

Besides we may not want them all armed. Those to Portugal we do not want armed now. We have asked Portugal to broach to Germany that they be not attacked if unarmed. . . .

November 27, 1941

The conversations—highly important—with the Japanese have been proceeding for some days. Hull has carried them on himself and has taken no one into his confidence except the President. Hornbeck and Wallace Murray have of necessity been part of it, but the Secretary has had his hand on the wheel and has worked very hard. He told me yesterday he had worked sixteen hours the day before. He has talked to me several times but only in generalities. He was not much encouraged about the ultimate outcome—but felt it was worth every effort and a lot of patience to explore every possibility.

Announcements by Knox and statements by Stimson—on matters having repercussions of foreign affairs have not helped. I tried to put a stopper on

Knox in the memorandum which went to the President yesterday by having him and Land agree to the suggestion that all releases to the press having foreign relations angles should be funnelled through the White House and announced *there* or by an agency of the Government designated to do it. . . .

Our Navy is sinking subs—"plenty of them" as one Naval officer said to me today—but I have not asked for details—prefer not to know for the time being.

November 28, 1941

Had a long talk with Steinhardt—just back from Moscow via Kuibyshev. He thinks the Russians will keep on fighting and will eventually beat the Germans, have moved many of their factories eastward to positions temporarily safe and will move them farther east if necessary; that they will not have to go east as far as the Urals; that Moscow will not fall unless it should do so in the next two weeks—which he does not expect, and that Old Man Winter will beat the Germans if the Russians do not. Losses to date he figures at—German, 2 million; Russian 3 1/2 million—though that is only estimate of the intelligent, thoughtful and generally observant people with whom he conversed. There is no accurate way of ascertaining the real facts.

He left there in zero weather but no snow. The ground was frozen hard and afforded good going for tanks and trucks. But snow and 40 degrees (Fahrenheit) below zero are just around the corner and the Germans unprepared for it.

He left with Litvinov[60] but parted at Baghdad. He felt Litvinov always intended to proceed via the Pacific—as he is now doing. Litvinov is coming here as Ambassador. I saw him in Rome. He lunched with me on his way back to Moscow after exchanging notes in Washington with Roosevelt on recognition of Russia [1933].

Steinhardt is an able man and has decisiveness and courage. He took a definite stand on the immigration and refugee question and opposed the immigration in large numbers from Russia and Poland of the Eastern Europeans whom he characterizes as entirely unfit to become citizens of this country. He says they are lawless, scheming, defiant—and in many ways unassimilable. He said the general type of intending immigrant was just the same as the criminal Jews who crowd our police court dockets in New York and with whom he is acquainted and whom he feels are never to become moderately decent American citizens.

I think he is right—not as regards the Russian and Polish Jew alone but the lower level of all that Slav population of Eastern Europe and Western Asia—the Caucasus, Georgia, Ukraine, Croat, Slovene, Carpatho-Ukraine,

[60] Maxim Litvinov, former Russian Commissar for Foreign Affairs, 1930–1939, served as ambassador to the United States, 1941–1943.

Montenegro, etc. They look upon public office as a private sinecure and as an opportunity for personal enrichment—think officers of Government are to be forced or bribed to satisfy their desires—think of government and society in the light of their own unfortunate experiences abroad—in short have a philosophy entirely foreign to our standards of government and proper conduct in public and private life.

December 7, 1941

The Japanese problem is practically at a crisis. They have answered in an equivocal way the question put by the President.[61] They have not replied to the basic questions raised by Hull in the paper he handed them.[62] In the meantime they are reinforcing their troops in southern Indo-China and forwarding trucks, artillery, supplies of all kinds—bicycles, sawed-off shot-guns, etc. Their transports in flocks of twenty and thirty land at Saigon and some move west around the southern corner toward Bangkok. They plead that their moves are simply defensive against China—but they are moving away from China toward Siam. They claim Vichy authorizes their activity— but Vichy has weakly tried in spite of German pressure to relieve itself of the consequences of its earlier consent to collaboration in Indo-China.

Here Nomura and Kurusu kill time. Many of the Japanese officials here— including some of the Embassy staff—are on the way out, some to South America, some to Japan on the vessel we agreed they could send over for evacuation purposes. I gave to Welles a long list of Japanese official-diplo- matic people and otherwise—who had obtained reservations on the Clipper or aboard ships and who must get exit permits. Some go to diplomatic missions in Brazil, Chile, Peru, etc. Some bound home. I suggested the South American governments might collaborate with us by not receiving the diplomats leaving here under circumstances approximating a breach of

[61] Reports of heavy Japanese troop movements into southern French Indo-China led President Roosevelt, on December 2, to ask Tokyo the reasons for this step and "the intention of the Japanese Government." Ambassador Nomura replied on December 5 that these reports had been exaggerated and there had been no violation of the Vichy-Tokyo accord of July 23, 1941.

[62] On November 26, the State Department, after consulting and receiving the approval of the British, Dutch, Chinese, Australian, and New Zealand representatives in Washington, proposed to Japan the following mutual commitments: (1) a nonaggression pact among the governments concerned with the Pacific; (2) conclusion of an agreement with the same governments respecting the territorial integrity of Indo-China; (3) not to support any government in China other than the Chunking Government [Chiang Kai-Shek]; (4) to relinquish extraterritorial rights in China; (5) to negotiate a reciprocal trade treaty; (6) to remove monetary freezing restrictions; (7) to agree upon a stabilized dollar-yen rate; (8) to agree that no agreement previously concluded with third powers be interpreted so as to conflict with the fundamental purpose of the proposed formula. Meanwhile, on Novem- ber 25, the carrier force which would attack Pearl Harbor left the Kurile Islands. The following day, the United States warned Britain of an impending Japanese attack, most likely in the Philippines or Southeast Asia.

relations—for they would simply augment their staffs in South America to work against us there.

The President sent a communication to the Emperor of Japan—to keep the record straight and ask his help in preserving peace.[63] But the chances of peace are slim. . . .

Momentous things happen these days—and, because there are so many of them and our stake so great—we handle them without excitement, in ordinary course, and with dispatch, though any one of them a few years ago would have thrown the Foreign offices of the world into excitement and confusion.

After writing the foregoing a few people came for luncheon—the Turkish Ambassador, General Corbin, Orme Wilson,[64] Will Clayton and their wives. During luncheon Miss Aderton phoned to advise me Japan had attacked the United States at Honolulu and Manila. After the guests left I motored in through a heavy Sunday traffic to the Department where I found the Secretary, Welles, Berle, Hackworth, Atherton, Savage and several others, including Norman Davis, the only one outside the Department. The business was the drafting of a statement as a preface to the release of notes recently exchanged between Hull and the Japanese.

After that I ordered that exit permits be withheld from all Japanese till further orders; circularized all Missions abroad through their Consulate appendages to advise merchant vessels Japan had attacked the United States and to proceed in observance of regulations given them for such contingency; ordered all communications by cable or wireless stopped to Japan— except official messages; the protection by police of all Japanese Consulates in the United States and possessions as well as the Embassy; in communication with F.C.C., Navy and Maritime Commission. Also with the Treasury concerning customs and the provisions of the Trading With the Enemy Act in operation.

December 8, 1941

Sick at heart. I am so damned mad at the Navy for being asleep at the switch at Honolulu. It is the worst day in American history. They spent their lives in preparation for a supreme moment—and then were asleep when it

[63] On December 6, Roosevelt appealed to Emperor Hirohito to "give thought in this definite emergency to ways of dispelling the dark clouds." He described the alarm aroused in the United States by Japanese military preparations in Indo-China and declared that the withdrawal of Japanese troops "would result in the assurance of peace throughout the whole of the South Pacific area."

[64] Turkish Ambassador Mehmet Münir Ertegün; Brigadier General Clifford L. Corbin, Office of the Quartermaster General; Orme Wilson, foreign service officer, Department of State liaison officer with the War and Navy Departments, 1940–1944.

came. At the Defense Communications Board this morning I learned of the extent of our losses—and it is staggering.

All day we have been in hectic steps of transition from a peace basis to a war basis. There are so many things to arrange for. Started the morning with Tom Connally—a prearranged conference about a treaty now over-shadowed by yesterday's events. It was short work to brush it aside and help him go over and finish a draft resolution of war. I wanted to hear the President address the joint session but could not leave my desk. I heard Mr. Wilson in '17—and heard the Rankin [65] woman vote "No," as she did again today— the only "No" in either house. The President had used the words "Imperial Government of Germany" in one place and "Government of Imperial Germany" in another place in his message and the resolutions in the two houses each used one—and the different one from the other. They were advised unless the texts exactly conformed it would be necessary to send the House Resolution back to the Senate—and each wanted to know which appellation of Germany was correct—and everybody in the State Department had different ideas—some arguing for "Government of Germany"—others just for "Germany." I finally told them to accept the one which had already been passed—no matter which—and have the House conform to it and we would call that the official name of Germany.

December 11, 1941

A very busy day. Germany and Italy declared war on us and we on them. With the Secretary and Berle and Hackworth drafted resolutions of war— one for Germany—one for Italy—and the President's address to the Congress—and got it to the White House late. . . .

And—a hundred other things I can't remember and am too tired to record. It has been a hectic day.

December 12, 1941

. . . I have arranged for Leland Harrison, still Minister to Switzerland, but on leave, to be Assistant to me to handle the melee of representation of interests—ours abroad by Switzerland and our enemies' here through powers of their choosing. Curiously enough Switzerland represents Italy and Germany in Washington as well as United States in Germany and Italy. Who represents Japan we do not know. The Japs are under confinement in the Embassy. They can send out for food and other necessaries but are held carefully. Italy and Germany are confined to metropolitan Washington. None have telephone, telegraph or other means of communication—except through their representing power.

[65] Jeannette Rankin, Republican, U.S. Representative from Montana, 1917-1919, 1941-1943.

This has been another hectic day but from now on I think it will be better organized and more orderly.

December 13, 1941

Military Intelligence reported to us information from an alleged authoritative source that the Japanese Ambassador, Nomura, and his Naval Attaché planned hari-kiri [sic] and that the story would be made in Japan that they had been murdered. I immediately called a few officers—Hornbeck, Hamilton, Bucknell and Harrison,[66] to consider policy. The implications were patent. The result of such a story would be destruction of every American in Japanese jurisdiction. No Japanese in the United States would be safe if anything happened to our people there.

Letting the story leak to the press was considered—and discarded. My desire was to have complete understanding of the whole business by a public or a responsible official agent of another Government. It was decided to ask the Swiss Minister [67] (Switzerland represents American interests in Japan as well as in Germany and Italy) to go to Nomura and tell him we were much concerned and ask him not to do it—suggesting the possible consequences. Harrison saw the Minister and he agreed to go and did. At four Bruggmann came to see me to report. He found a strange situation at the Embassy. All doors within were closed. All was quiet and gloomy. One man met him at the door and took him to a room. Soon the Minister of the Embassy appeared and they conversed. He had some difficulty in getting the Ambassador to appear. Then the Japanese Minister insisted on staying. Finally Bruggmann made it plain he wanted to talk to Nomura quite privately and eventually succeeded. He told Nomura the story. Nomura was noncommittal, evasive. Bruggmann had difficulty following his statement. He had done his duty. He had been for peace. He had done his best. His conscience was clear. Hari-kiri was not a personal question. The decision was made under law, religion. A named (but unknown) god had ultimate responsibility for the decision. So Nomura did not know. The name of the god sounded to Bruggmann's Swiss ears and repeated by his Swiss tongue was something like "Hu Rhun." He could not be more accurate. He had some difficulty in following Nomura's English. He thought he had no present intention to do so but that the act might be decided for him later. It was mentioned the Japanese Ambassador returned from Moscow when war broke out years ago. So, the inference was it was not necessarily to be committed. So Bruggmann left with a semi-optimistic impression but still in doubt. During his private audience with Nomura on three different occasions persons entered the room to tell

[66] Howard Bucknell, Jr., Division of Current Information, 1940–1943; Wallace K. Harrison, assistant coordinator of Inter-American Affairs, 1941–1943.

[67] Charles Bruggmann.

Nomura lunch was ready for him. Bruggmann thought they were observers. He also thought the Minister was the "all seeing eye" of the Government like the "party" man in Nazi Embassies and like the Ogpu man in the Russian Embassies. Anyhow, he ended pleasantly and with a smile from Nomura and a shake of the hand. He had a thoroughly uncomfortable time of it and felt the whole experience very gruesome.

I thanked him for having performed a humanitarian service and expressed our deep appreciation for his cooperation. When he left me (and Harrison was with me) Harrison made a secret memo of his visit to Bruggmann and of Bruggman's visit to us.

So we have got it into a position from which we can operate if it should unfortunately happen. We have another Government with knowledge of the whole circumstance and we have a record of our action. We took the further precaution to send a note to Bruggmann setting out all we are doing to make the Japs decently comfortable, police protection, limited telephone, access to food and drug supplies, access to laundered clothes, etc. as well as preliminary plans for repatriation in exchange for our people. We asked him to advise the Japanese Embassy. Also we cabled the text to Bern with the request it be cabled to Tokyo. The trouble is *where* to exchange the Japs. Somebody thought of Lorenzo Marques! There must be a neutral port to do the job. There are very few outside the Americas. Lorenzo Marques in East Africa is something to have thought about!

Left Department at seven o'clock—exhausted after one of the most strenuous weeks in my life.

December 14, 1941

I wish I had had time during this past momentous week to set out at some length my part in it, my activities, my impressions, my observations of others. But I had not. These past seven days have been hectic. The blow at Pearl Harbor stunned us all—its suddenness and its real unexpectedness. But immediately the reaction was anger and a determination to take tenfold retribution. The isolationists disappeared. The country was a unit. The real damage at Honolulu has not been disclosed. Apparently Japan does not accurately know. To advise her would be foolish—as well as dangerous.[68]

Cordell Hull has been a real tough person. He held to the line of his policy throughout. His warnings to his colleagues in the Cabinet were not accepted

---

[68] The damage inflicted by the Japanese was severe indeed. Nineteen naval vessels, including eight battleships, were sunk or severely damaged. In addition, 188 United States aircraft were destroyed. Military casualties were 2,280 killed and 1,109 wounded. Sixty-eight civilians also perished.

—to, I suppose, their present regret. The State Department was ready. In my jurisdiction telegrams were all prepared in advance—1) to warn our representatives in all the Axis countries of the probability of severance of actual communication and what to do when it happened; 2) to turn over representation of the interests of other Governments to Switzerland; 3) to ask their Swiss colleagues to take over American interests and to notify the Government to which they were accredited; and various other details. It was only necessary to sign them. The supporting notes to the representatives in Washington were also ready—just for signature and delivery. In the communications field, all defense plans had been made. All they needed was the outbreak of war as the signal. Between noon and midnight of last Sunday the whole system went into operation—over the whole area under the jurisdiction of the Government. In the visa and refugee and immigration field the work was already on a war-time basis—due to my stubborn resistance to many efforts directed at discrediting me and breaking down my system of sifting out aliens desiring admission and allowing to enter only those above any suspicion. The advent of war found us in much better shape because of it and freer of Fifth Columnists and saboteurs than it would have been otherwise.

In all my jurisdiction we were ready. Only the Far Eastern Division would not cooperate to arrange either representation of our interests in Japan and Thailand and to arrange for recent repatriation. They resented our suggestions and insisted on doing things themselves when they saw fit. Consequently nothing was done. The Near East assumes a similar attitude on some matters, notably Relief. Except for those two instances our readiness was complete. Already anticipatory telegrams have gone out to North Africa, West Africa—places such as Dakar, Casablanca, Tunis, Algiers, etc.—and to Spain, Portugal, Vichy and Consulates in France, Helsinki, and Copenhagen.

Hungary, Bulgaria and Rumania—the first and second officially reported—have declared war. The President wants to ignore them—as opera boufe. We are examining the legal consequences of ignoring. Perhaps there are Constitutional obstacles to action against them unless war is declared—and action may be advisable—as in Rumania for instance to destroy the oil fields, if our fliers actively cooperate over there.

Mussolini just got an "also ran" notice in the President's message to Congress, though we had to declare separately war against Italy.

In the first part of the week I had a talk with Berle. I told him we had to cooperate to give full effectiveness to win the war—that personal animosities and antagonisms were out—for the duration; that I would take him on after the war was over but there was no place for private wars now. He agreed, I must say with apparent readiness. So that is that.

Atherton is a brick. He is a fine, able man—level-headed, cool, quick—and open and honest. I have formed a real admiration for his mental integrity and for his ability. He sees things from my point of view. His advice and counsel have been of great assistance to the Secretary and to the correctness of our policy in these past formative days.

December 16, 1941

Advices indicate the German army in full retreat from Russia. Temperature reported last Sunday 57 degrees below zero. The Germans unprepared to keep the field—inadequate clothing and no shelter. The extreme cold freezes the lubricating oil in their machines and renders them stationary. Men are freezing to death by the thousands. The Russians, appropriately clothed and with shelter in Moscow and the other cities can harass the retreating foe. In the Black Sea area the movement is reported as a rout—Germans fleeing for their lives. Hitler is reported to have been much affected. If the reports from Russia are true it may mean the biggest military catastrophe in history—all of which is valuable to us. . . .

We do not know what the Japanese are doing to our citizens or officials—except at Hanoi they arrested the Consul, took his safe, codes and files. After talking with the Secretary I sent a message to them through the Swiss asking what they were doing with our people and protesting the treatment of Clubb[69] at Hanoi. I wanted to make it stronger—to threaten to take one of their Consuls—and to take him—but the Far Eastern Division would not agree to go that far.

Honolulu was bombed again today. Singapore is seriously threatened from the land and may fall. Midway and Wake still resist continuing attempts at destruction.

A censor was appointed today to take over. The Navy had planned for three years to do the job, but at the moment of action the President decided he did not want a military censorship so put it under [J. Edgar] Hoover temporarily. Soon a civilian will take over. Perhaps some of the confusion will cease—soon. I am having drawn up a definite statement of *what* is to be done regarding *each* country—both incoming messages and outgoing messages to Governments and their representatives—and also regarding transit messages from South American Governments to Europe and return. That and the treatment accorded the various Missions here who are now enemies are problems.

December 17, 1941

. . . I have been trying to steer a careful course to protect our national interest and at the same time not to provoke harsh and improper treatment upon our representatives in enemy hands, particularly Germany and Japan. I have been pretty tough on the Japs. For six days they slept 40 in the Embassy prepared to sleep 10. They had no mattresses, no bedclothes, no clean

[69] O. Edmund Clubb, foreign service officer, consul at Hanoi, 1941.

linen. At the end of that period I allowed emissaries to get laundry, beds, mattresses and four of them to return to their accustomed places of abode where were their wives and children—under guard. This I revoked today early. But the Germans were given no notice, not allowed to take any clothes with them and found about 90 in the single building. The protecting power will certainly report it and our people will probably suffer in consequence. So I had to get out a carefully worded press release to paint the lily as best I could so the possible effect of it would be as good as possible.

Joe Grew must be suffering anyhow. The sparse message he sent through the Swiss indicates by omission he is far from comfortable or happy.

December 18, 1941

. . . I wish I had written the details of Hull's warnings to Knox, Stimson, Stark and Marshall—as of the time—two weeks before the Honolulu attack, and three or four times after—to be on guard and to expect anything—any minute. He sized up Kurusu and estimated his mission as one of delay. He saw the stalemate approaching and realized the danger. He warned our people of the element of surprise and of the adoption of it as a part of their policy. And then they followed the "business as usual" course and had all the ships in Pearl Harbor over the week-end so the men could go ashore Saturday night and the officers go to Waikiki Sunday—as usual. The result is not known, except to those in Honolulu and a few here. I do not want to know it all. I do know—second hand from an officer just returned transmitted through a General (Maj. General ———)—enough to know that Admiral Noyes[70] told me the truth the day after the attack. It is a terrible story and confronts us with great danger.

December 20, 1941

On the home front—Hull has proposed a Supreme War Council. The President has issued his order for a Censor and created a policy committee without the State Department being represented. Berle must be disappointed because his mouth has been watering for that activity. The Vice President, Attorney General, Postmaster General, Secretaries of War and Navy, Donovan (Coordinator of Information), MacLeish (Facts and Figures) and Mellett[71] form the Committee. I had proposed to the Secretary that he propose to the President the appointment of an outstanding man in whom the people have

[70] Rear Admiral Leigh Noyes, head of the Communications Division of the Office of Naval Operations.

[71] William J. Donovan, Coordinator of Information, 1941–1942; Archibald MacLeish, Librarian of Congress, 1939–1944, and assistant director of the Office of War Information, 1942–1943; Lowell Mellett, administrative assistant to the President, 1940–1944.

confidence and who has force of character and organizing ability—like Willkie
—to be practically a Minister of Information—over Donovan, MacLeish,
War, Navy, the Censor—and possibly State. He did not shy away from it—
but was thinking it over when this burst—which is my idea inverted. This is a
policy committee at the top and a man underneath. Mine was a powerful
figure at the top and the heads of the agencies underneath subject to dictation
and control by the one individual. Mine would work. This will become a mess.
The Censor will be unable to control Donovan. MacLeish will have difficulty
getting any results from his organization. The Censor will lose control of
censorship because those he is supposed to control will sit on the Committee
which fixes policy for him.

One most important thing to be controlled is Donovan. His organization
is composed largely of inexperienced people—inexperienced in so far as dealing with high powered confidential information is concerned. They get all our
information and use it ad lib. Sometimes there is a definite flare-back because
of lack of judgment in its use. For instance—the Governor of Dakar gave our
Consul some information, and expressed his hope the United States would
win the war. The Consul promptly telegraphed us. Donovan got the message
and promptly also put on the radio band to Europe just what the Governor
said! The result was Vichy got excited, the Governor got chagrined to the
point he closed communication with the Consul and Germany got busy with
pressure on Vichy to extend her military activity in West Africa. . . .

The Germans are still active in the Crimea—Sevastopol under attack—and
are trying to hold their positions along the Black Sea east coast but they are
still retreating along the whole rest of the front. They are going to try to hold
the line Riga-Smolensk-Mariupol.[72] We are advised the high command wanted
to fall back to the German-Russian border in Poland, as it was when Russia
was invaded—but Hitler said the political situation would not permit that and
they must establish a line farther east.

The Far East gets worse. Hong Kong is invaded but some parts of the
forts still hold out—and looks doomed. Singapore is being approached and
is practically unusable already. Penang has been occupied. Rangoon will be
the next Japanese objective—for who holds it controls the Burma Road.

How often do the scenes of my wanderings come into this war news and
awaken recollections of the past—Rangoon, with its wonder pagoda, the beginning and end of my abortive tiger hunt; Penang and its then sleepy, hot,
lazy town; Singapore, its rain, rain, rain and its Raffles Hotel; Hong Kong, its
embroidery and silk, its fenicula, its high rock, muggy atmosphere and great

---

[72] This German military line stretched from Rigà, capital of Latvia and a Baltic Sea port,
through Smolensk, a city in central European Russia on the upper Dnieper River, to
Mariupol (now Zhdanov), in the southeast Ukraine on the Sea of Azov.

roadstead, Shanghai and its bund; Yokohama—to say nothing of the scenes of recent activity—Moscow, Leningrad, Helsinki, Oslo—Libya, and on, and on. Strange places they were—far flung and disconnected. Now they are all tied in together and in the softening light of recollection they are all part of the same picture just as in reality this shrunken world has brought them close together. Strange scenes, strange faces, funny little people, nice little men and women in strange costumes, of different races, different customs, different philosophies—they are all now brought into our common cause because they are all attacked by the same ferocious scourge—the modern Genghis Khan. Destruction, rapine and desolation are the goals and peaceful people the victims.

But it is more than that. This is the end of an era. It is one of the great moments in history. That which has been shall be no more. A new order begins. For even when we win this war and stop the shooting, the life we knew and used to lead will be no more. Social forces have upheaved. Economic facts have changed political theory. Financial systems are being bent out of shape. The relationships of our recent memory are disrupted. A new theory of relativity will come into play. All the rules we have learned and which guided our way through our social, political and economic lives—have been broken, but the new ones have not been agreed to or announced.

A wonderful time to live—and as I do I often think of Susie Boogher's [?] desire to be present at the physical destruction of New York. This is not New York—but the world.

December 22, 1941

The Japs landing in the Philippines, sinking vessels off California coast—and one near Hawaii.

Hitler has taken over supreme command of the army—to use his "intuition" and the Germans being driven back on all fronts of Russia.

Churchill arrived to confer with Roosevelt. A Supreme War Council in the making. The pattern of 1917–18 is being followed.

December 23, 1941

My father was born 99 years ago.

Jap submarines active in our coastal waters off California.

No word from Japan, Germany or Italy about exchanging our diplomatic officers, etc. Each had a proposal—we no answer yet.

Hull read me the text of his proposed statement to Justice Roberts[73]—made at Roberts' request as part of the inquiry into Pearl Harbor. The Secre-

---

[73] Owen J. Roberts, Associate Justice of the Supreme Court, 1930–1945, was appointed by the President to head a committee of inquiry to investigate the Pearl Harbor disaster.

tary records that he specifically told the full Cabinet on November 7 to expect trouble at any time; and to the War Council on November 25 to be prepared for an aggressive act, widespread, at a number of places at any time using the element of surprise as one of their principal weapons. In addition in personal conversation with the Secretaries of War and Navy and with Stark and Marshall—together and separately he repeated his warnings time and again. These last he refuses to put in his statement. He said it would look too much like criticism of another Department—though he admitted he realized each Department must stand on its own merit in cases like this.

December 30, 1941

Held conference in my office with representatives of RCA, ITT, All America Cables and Mackay Radio. Agreed on policy of cooperation among American owners to stop radio communication by their companies in South America with Tokyo, Berlin and Rome; determined to seek British cooperation in stations jointly owned or controlled by British and American interests.

Saw Harry Hopkins at White House. He looks badly—was in bed—said he was not sick but relaxing. However a lot of medicine bottles were on tables. His mind active as ever. Presented radio problems in South America and of communications with British Empire points. He sees and agrees and will seek Churchill's help and will let me know by end of week.

Lunched at Press Club. Litvinof [sic] spoke—able man and a smart speech. He compared the German attack on Russia to a Japanese occupation of our west coast and said we would not then be sending armies to "distant points"—so Russia was not sending armies to fight Japan. He considered Hitler the world's worst enemy. Russia was busy conquering him. But do not be over-optimistic. It might not vanquish him now—only wound him so he might long continue to fight. Russia had no "exclusive" attitude about fighting Hitler—would be glad to have others join in the battle to help destroy him. To lend passive help against Japan like affording air bases would be *causus belli*—and Russia had no quarrel with Japan now—Japan had not attacked her—Russia was occupied with Germany.

The interference was easy that Russia and Japan had an understanding—"non aggression"—and Russia would take all the assistance she could get against Germany but give no help other places. And that is just about the way I figure it. Russia, with Germany crippled, is in a powerful position—more powerful than any save the U.S.A.—and intends to be just as cold, calculating and hard in the use of her power as she has always been. She is not fighting for "liberty," for "democracy," for the "freedom of others"—but only for Russia, and will use her power only to advance the selfish ambitions of the leaders of Russia.

Tonight Washington had a trial "blackout"—its first.

News of the passage through the Canal of two airplane carriers was published in Europe. We have difficulty keeping secrets.

December 31, 1941

The year goes out in a gloom. Manila is about to fall. The 11 p.m. radio announces fighting in the outskirts. Help has not arrived in time. To fight land battles it is necessary to have soldiers and tanks—each in quantities larger and more effective than the enemy. To prevent the soldiers from landing from the sea it is necessary to have superiority in the air—of bombers. (Oh, shades of Billy Mitchell!) To operate the bombers it is necessary to have fighters to protect them. That is where we have failed. There are no fighters and only a few bombers left. The things on the way are fine—but they should have been there in hidden air-domes *before* the show started. The "press release" of Stimson to Krock should have been true—but not advertised.

On other fronts (other than our own) the news is better. Russia is doing very well—on the Moscow front and also in the Crimea. The British *claim* successes in the desert. Singapore is reported resisting. But Jap U-boats are off Alaska and we are being pushed out of the Philippines. And the more we are pushed away the farther it is to get at Japan. The result is a loss of prestige on our part. The invincibility of the United States is being questioned by the world. The effect of that on the coming Rio Conference may be of the first importance. We *have* to be impressive there.

These first set-backs make the atmosphere of this year-end glum but tomorrow will dawn a new day and before that year ends our efforts will have demonstrated to Japan and the onlookers that we are masters of the situation.

In the process, however, we will have several convulsions at home. The lack of rubber threatens to create a revolution in our social and industrial lives. The taxes—1/2 of our national income for the year 1942—will cause a convulsion in social and economic life and add its effect to the industrial upheaval. The effect on labor—wages, hours, conditions—cannot now be estimated—but if income is to be taxed to an average of 50% it means that "unearned" income will be even more heavily taxed and that wages of labor will bear a charge of 1/3 its amount (with perhaps 2/3 on "unearned" income). If we are to avoid inflation, price control will be necessary over *all* the ingredients of cost—including labor. And when that commences our political system changes from a representative form to a dictatorial form—except that the change is taken by the representatives of the people. But that temporary adherence is one of the prices we have to pay for this war—and for winning it. It must be won. The alternative is the extinguishment of our political and social institutions. As the alternative is not admissable or acceptable there is only one answer—to win the war.

So the new year will start with that grim realization and irrevocable determination—and their concurrent inflexibility, do whatever may be necessary to win the war.

And so ends—looking to the New Year.

Defending Democracy

The New Year starts with a determination to do whatever may be necessary to make it end well.

The trouble over St. Pierre–Miquelon continues. The principle of change of sovereignty over possessions in the Americas makes it important to us. The British look upon it carelessly. Churchill made it worse by his speech in Canada.[1] This morning with the Secretary, Welles, Berle, Atherton, Hackworth and I carried on an effort to reduce the affair to writing. I have some hesitations about emphasizing our reasons because to do so throws in relief our obligation—as the sponsor for the Monroe Doctrine and as a party to the Inter-American convention involved—and it will be very difficult if even possible under those circumstances to discharge our obligation because our associates in the war are not in agreement with us. And yet the French West Indies, French and Dutch Guiana, British Honduras and various islands come under the same heading and this may be used as a precedent. Hull is very provoked at Churchill's expression—as is Welles.

The White House has under negotiation with Churchill the text of a joint statement on the conduct of the war.[2] During our conference this morning the Secretary called the President on the telephone, with us present. I have not been party to the preceding conversations but it was apparent this morning Hull had learned—or had just come to realize—one or the other—that Russia was not being treated as a principal partner. He told the President in his opinion it would be a fatal mistake not to bring Litvinof in on a basis of importance equal to Churchill. Just what the stage of development of the preceding concerned I did not get—because the paper had been drafted—after

[1] The State Department continued official diplomatic relations with the Vichy government of France but deplored the growing influence of Hitler. On December 24, 1941, the "Free French" seized two small French islands—St. Pierre and Miquelon—located off the southeast coast of Newfoundland. The Department strongly objected to this action, fearing that the delicate negotiations in progress with Vichy would be jeopardized. Prime Minister Churchill supported this seizure by the "Free French."

[2] Prime Minister Winston Churchill conferred in Washington with President Roosevelt (December 22, 1941—January 14, 1942) affirming the basis of joint strategy—to concentrate upon the defeat of the Axis Powers in Europe and to follow a policy of containment in the Far East until military victories in Europe or Allied resources permitted stronger action against Japan. During this conference, the Declaration of the United Nations was drafted, and the Combined Chiefs of Staff and the Munitions Assignment Board were established.

many slow stages—and was all but ready for signature. Its text had been cabled to the Governments associated with the war against Germany and Japan and it had been drafted with the thought particularly in mind that Russia was not at war with Japan. The President apparently accepted the thought. Hull was positive in the expression of his opinion.

January 3, 1942

Churchill insists that provision be made for adherence to the joint declaration by the Free French. It had to be carefully phrased so the invitation to sign and acceptance would not constitute recognition of the DeGaulle organization as a government—else we would be at war with Vichy. It was phrased in general terms so as to permit adherence by the representatives of a people whose country was under occupation or partial occupation by Germany—but it meant Free France.

As a result of the joint declaration there has been established a unified command in the Far East—army, navy and air under one command. That is what we need everywhere now.

The shortage of rubber means shortage of tires. I am finding difficulty in obtaining needed tires. The situation threatens to change our whole transportation life—and we all ride on rubber. Now motor cars will be unable to carry the private citizen. The manufacture of cars is interdicted and the sale of tires is rationed.

January 5, 1942

St. Pierre and Miquelon still consume a lot of department time.[3] There has been a deal of criticism of the Department and of Hull—as "appeasers" etc., because we disagreed about the seizure—and all largely because the Department's position was not properly publicized. I got in a conference by accident this evening. The text of the proposed paper was to my mind unsatisfactory and not to the point. It had been submitted to the British. They proposed amendments and took the position both Canada and de Gaulle should be consulted. They said Canada asked postponement and de Gaulle approval. It was apparent that nothing along that line could happen for days. So I spoke my mind—it was not to the point, no mention of the Monroe Doctrine, which is basis for our position and our responsibility—the question of leadership in the Hemisphere, Churchill or Roosevelt—the effect before the coming American Conference at Rio. Several expressed their agreement with me. The meeting ended. Tonight after dinner I have drafted a substitute based on the Monroe Doctrine and will submit it tomorrow as a new basis for discussion and drafting.

[3] Hull and Long insisted that the *status quo* of these islands be restored immediately while the British Government maintained that both Canada and Charles de Gaulle the "Free French" leader, should be consulted.

January 6, 1942

The discussion about St. Pierre–Miquelon continues still. My suggestion for a new draft has been discarded on the basis that it is not politic for us to emphasize the Monroe Doctrine in this connection because to do so would require us to act immediately to enforce it and—"the Navy is busy in other ways." I have not changed my opinion and for the reasons indicated do not agree with the proposed draft, which was the subject of another two hour conference this afternoon. I think entirely too much attention is being devoted to it and that the approach of the draft goes into unnecessary details in addition to the fact that it lacks the base, which I consider the proper base, and that is the Monroe Doctrine.

Left the Department at eight o'clock after an awfully busy day, went to dinner with Mrs. Marye[4] at a party of 54 and returned to the apartment as soon as possible thereafter and worked until midnight in reading memoranda on different phases of foreign policy so that I would be properly prepared to confront the Senate Foreign Relations Committee in the morning.

The President delivered his "State of the Nation" speech. I did not hear it and have not had time yet to read it.

January 7, 1942

Appeared before the Foreign Relations Committee of the Senate. Full discussion of foreign policy in all its phases. Some critical comment about St. Pierre–Miquelon but apparent approval and concurrence in all other matters —even on the part of the opposition. La Follette[5] particularly tried to be helpful. It was all "off the record"—supposedly in secret session.

January 10, 1942

Biddle, in phone conversation, said he had written the President criticizing the Department of State treatment of Italian diplomats here—too much liberty allowed in interest of national security. We treat them just like our people are treated in Italy—and all the others are on a reciprocal basis. It is up to F.B.I. to watch them and prevent activities inimical to our national security.

Litvinof came in. He discussed "Free People" movements and particularly some of their leaders—disparagingly—Strasser particularly offensive; Bruening an ultra-conservative; King Carol,[6] a joke in the role of a "democrat" etc. There is a movement on to glorify Russia, part of the activities of the Communists in this country who aim at control of our Government and whose

[4] Mrs. George Thomas Marye, wife of the late Ambassador to Russia, 1914–1916.

[5] Robert La Follette, Jr., Republican, U.S. Senator from Wisconsin, 1925–1947.

[6] Otto Strasser was an opponent of Hitler within the Nazi party until his expulsion in 1930; King Carol II of Rumania vacated his throne in 1940 and fled his country. In 1942 he proclaimed himself leader of the forces of a Free Rumania.

ambitions the recent developments in Europe are helping immeasurably. Litvinof's gratuitous conversation I judged to be a side-light on this and a reflection of some of his purposes. He is an able man—with a full pack of cards—and will bear close observation.

January 13, 1942

Hull is worried. His status is clouded. He is cleaning out his desk. For several days he has unostentatiously—almost secretly—been getting out, and mostly into wastebaskets, the papers accumulated through years in the drawers of his big desk. He is awfully disappointed—and expecting the worst. This St. Pierre–Miquelon affair—insignificant in itself—has served to reveal that his relationship to the President has undergone a very definite change for the worse. He tried to get the President to make a statement about the islands. The President refused. He then tried to get the President's approval to a statement Hull would release about the islands. The President in a short and preemptory "no" startled the Secretary into the realization a sudden change had occurred. He talked to me at some length today as he sat slowly pulling papers out of drawers and letting them flicker from his fingers to a copious wastebasket. He is incensed at Churchill for his Canadian speech, for his antagonistic attitude and for his apparent ascendency in Presidential favor to the extent he can control expressions of American foreign policy. But more than that and above it all he sees his world toppling. Churchill has given the official bludgeoning to the corner-stone of Hull's entire foreign policy—not St. Pierre–Miquelon and its relationship to Vichy, the French fleet and West Africa, for that was the President's own policy—but to Hull's plans for political recrudescence through trade agreements. Churchill has refused to include in the contract for our compensation for Lend-Lease the agreement to discard the Empire tariff and trade program.[7] Hull secured the President's acceptance. Churchill has got it eliminated. They dined side by side last night and Hull approached the subject only to have Churchill say he definitely refused to agree to it and would not accept it.

Of course *that* is Hull. That is his political *raison d'etre*. It is his stock in trade. His trade agreements—as expressions of his economic philosophy— are the base on which rest his whole foreign activity. Without that base the structure falls. And Churchill has kicked the base out from under—for without England's cooperation the world phase of its operation ceases.

Hull calls him selfish, vindictive, vicious. He blames Hopkins for permitting it—and comments on his lack of understanding of world affairs—his impracticability. He looks tired, thin, disheartened and has no present zest for his work. He is awaiting the blow. The blow may come—to him and to

[7] Reference here is to the preferential tariff rates and trade quotas mutually accorded to member nations of the British Commonwealth.

me, for I have incurred the enmity of various powerful and vengeful elements; the Communists, extreme radicals, Jewish professional agitators, refugee enthusiasts who blindly seek the admission of persons under the guise of refugees, and their sympathetic agents in the Government service who are their spokesmen and agents. They all hate me—and are opposed to Hull because he has supported me. Now they join openly with the pro-British who rant about the two little barren rocks in the Gulf of St. Lawrence, and with the radicals who oppose Knudson [sic],[8] Jesse Jones, and with the others who lay a smoke-screen about themselves—all to get control of these places in the Government—to control foreign policy and to admit Fifth Columnists—etc.

The President may be placed in a position where it may be easier for him to sacrifice some of us—and that is the fortune of politics. Hull expects it. He has not seen the President but once in a week—the time he got the preemptory "no"—and sent word to him today, so General Watson told me, that he had several things to talk with the President about but would wait till he finished with Churchill.

January 22, 1942

Yesterday I appeared for the second time before the Foreign Relations Committee to present them with an off the record background of foreign developments and policies. I talked about the Rio Conference,[9] the situation on the German east front, policies toward Vichy and the French African colonies, proposed acquisition of French ships in United States ports and about the Burma Road and the relation of Rangoon to it. I carefully and pointedly avoided all mention of military and naval operations or situation in the whole Far Eastern area.

After the Committee adjourned I went with Tom Connally and Senator George into the former's private office. There the three of us, but particularly those two, engaged in a conversation for fifteen or twenty minutes as to the necessity of maintaining secrecy about my appearances before the Committee and the subject matters of my conversation. They agreed it would be most unfortunate if any member of the Committee should make any statements to the press in those connections and expressed the understanding that it would be impossible for the Department of State to continue the practice of affording the Committee information if it was to find its way to the public press.

After luncheon with several others, including Mr. Herbert, the British

[8] William S. Knudsen, president of the General Motors Corporation, who served as director-general of the Office of Production Management, 1941–1945.

[9] At the Rio de Janeiro Conference (January 15–28), delegates from the twenty-one American republics voted to recommend to their respective governments a break in diplomatic relations with the Axis powers. Sumner Welles represented the United States.

Censor, and with several other Senators in Ed Halsey's[10] office I returned to the Department.

To my perfect surprise and horror about five o'clock in the afternoon there appeared a news flash to the effect that Connally had himself talked to the newspapers, had predicted the fall of Singapore, which I had not mentioned at all, and had criticized Argentina and predicted an overthrow of the President of Argentina in case he did not agree with the program of the Conference proceeding at Rio de Janeiro. The Secretary was very much excited. The President was mad. The latter called up Connally, and then Hull called him, and Connally got mad. The result can only be conjectured, but it comes just at the time when the Argentine delegation, heretofore refusing to co-operate, had just been brought into line and had agreed to sign the Resolution breaking relations with the Axis powers.[11]

It is almost incomprehensible how a person in a responsible position could make a blatant statement, as attributed to Connally, at a time when in Europe, South America, Asia and Australia, to say nothing of Africa and the islands of the sea, every nation is living at a nervous tension and liable to be upset by any ribald activity, and the statement of Connally was certainly ribald.

Of course there is an implication that the subject matters of his conversation, which were not confined to these two subjects but covered a wide range, were the matters discussed by me with the Committee and that what he said were my views as presented to the Committee.

January 23, 1942

The implementation of the agreements of the Churchill-Roosevelt conferences developed today. Pooling committees—three in number—were announced, composed of United States and British members to allocate materials, implements and ships to the associated governments. The trouble will be with governments *not* members of the committees—Russia, China, Netherlands, etc.—and the "etc." includes *all* the smaller governments which are jealous of their positions and prerogatives.

The Rio Conference hit a snag and postponed its plenary session and adjournment. Sumner was to have left by air at three o'clock tonight—but the Peru-Ecuador boundary settlement broke out again. . . .[12]

---

[10] Edwin Halsey, secretary of the U.S. Senate, 1933–1945.

[11] Argentina did not break relations with the Axis Powers until January 26, 1944.

[12] The century-old territorial controversy between Ecuador and Peru flared out in an undeclared war during 1941. In spite of attempts by the United States and Latin American nations to mediate, skirmishes continued throughout the year. The issue came before the conference of American Foreign Ministers meeting at Rio. Four mediating powers— Argentina, Brazil, Chile, and the United States—finally worked out a compromise procedure which was signed by Ecuador and Peru on January 29.

January 25, 1942

Welles has had a very successful experience at Rio. They all got together on a resolution, even though it was a compromise. Nevertheless, it represents a unanimity, and most of them will go past the point agreed upon. Argentina made the compromise necessary, but he did better than I really thought he would with Argentina.

The Pearl Harbor report is out.[13] Hull is not only exonerated but placed in a very commendable position. The naval and military officers in charge are excoriated and probably will be court martialed. There is probably one phase of the report which does not appear on the surface but which is sure to cause criticism and opposition from that element of our political body which is represented by the opposition in the Senate and House. What I have in mind is the lack of sufficient preparation and the inference to be drawn from the report that Honolulu was not properly prepared because we had been giving all our supplies to England and other countries. That is sure to cause some criticism and difficulty.

January 28, 1942

I saw the President at noon and was discouraged to see him looking tired and apparently somewhat weary.

I had to clear with him the question of vessels to make the repatriation of our diplomats for the European and Japanese diplomats in exchange. There are no vessels available unless the War Department will release them. He is the only official who could direct their release. I explained the whole situation, which involved not only the exchange of diplomats but the bringing to the United States of the representatives of the Axis powers in countries which are breaking relations with the Axis powers and the bringing to the United States of undesirable, untrustworthy aliens in those countries for internment in the United States. Those countries are not equipped to handle such a problem efficiently and effectively.

He saw the situation and expressed his particular sympathy for Joe Grew, and at my request at the end of my interview he noted on the basic memorandum that they must be exchanged and authorized me to present the matter in his name to the appropriate authorities. . . .

January 29, 1942

Dined last night at the Turkish Embassy. The dinner was for Steinhardt, now en route to his new post at Ankara. Bob Jackson[14] was there and a number of others. After dinner I had a talk with Jackson—the first one for some

[13] Presidential Commission headed by Supreme Court Justice Owen J. Roberts attributed the effectiveness of the Japanese attack to the failure of the naval and army commanders at Hawaii to adopt adequate defense measures.

[14] Robert Jackson, now Associate Justice of the Supreme Court, 1941–1954.

time. He asked me how the immigration problem was getting on. I told him about the new procedure, and I found him still entirely in accord with the thoughts that he had expressed in our various conversations while he was Attorney General. . . . I was gratified to hear this, because Berle had told me some weeks ago Jackson had changed his mind on the subject.

I told Jackson I regretted that Biddle had a very decided hostility toward me. He replied—and in doing so indicated he knew of that hostility—that it was because of a young man named Prichard[15] in whom Biddle had placed a mistaken confidence. Prichard had felt bitterly toward me and had had a distinct influence on Biddle. He was employed in immigration matters. Jackson characterized him as a man of faulty judgment, intense temperamental equipment and extreme prejudice but with a mind of brilliant flashes, negatived by his temper. Apparently Biddle had talked to Jackson about me and his antipathy toward me but I assume Jackson retired from the "conflict" behind the seclusion of his judicial robes.

I told him my impression of Biddle was that of a very able man, with reserve, courage and determination but one who had such a big undertaking that he had not time to go into the merits of many matters so he disposed of many of them hurriedly on memoranda or letters drafted by his subordinates and acted on an *ex parte* opinion. He said he thought that was a fair estimate of the situation. . . .

There is an increased and increasing criticism of England for its acquisitiveness in regard to American materials and products—not for war but for *post war* use—such as cable lines. They have received through lend lease hundreds of miles of pipe to pipe oil—*after the war*—from *yet untouched* and undeveloped oil fields south of the Caspian Sea—to Basra. And they entered into a treaty with Russia providing for the procedure of arranging with the Government of Iran to gain *title* to the lines in the post war settlement. The wells are not even to be drilled during the war, but are to serve an economic purpose after that. And *we* who *own* the pipe, *transport* the pipe and *furnish* the pipe—were not to be considered. We are trying to arrange with the Government of Iran to have a settlement for it with *Iran* in due course—but England and Russia will have the whip hand there and Iran will buy part of her liberation from English clutches by assigning her interest in the pipe to England—in spite of any arrangement we may now be able to come to with Iran. And this cable is in some way connected to the pipe program. Both envisage a *post war* activity. And we do *both* for them—in the name of military necessity—and get what? Only laughs, later, not any thanks—and deserve only derision—unless we can save it by a treaty with *Iran*.

England's policy seems to emerge. Suck the United States dry. When the peace comes ally with Russia. Let Russia have Poland, Eastern Germany,

[15] Edward F. Prichard, head attorney, Office of Economic Stabilization.

Baltic States, Finland. Hold the Mediterranean; Turkey hold the Dardenelles. Hold Iraq and Iran and India (if the Japs don't get it)—and let the United States alone politically and strangle it commercially. Raw materials from Russia and part control of the seas and Middle East and Africa will render the United States unnecessary as an ally—or even friend—even though they will owe us billions and billions of dollars for life-line goods. Russia and England· Raw materials and a manufacturing salesman.

If they would take the British business men and put them in charge of their Army and Navy they would win some battles. They are smart boys.

When I take a position to protect American interests I am conscious of creating a sentiment that I am anti-British. If we are cooperating with them for our mutual good I like to see a little cooperation from them too.

January 31, 1942

Hull has written the President about St. Pierre–Miquelon that the islands are French—of whichever faction—and as long as they are French we are not concerned—but they must stay French—and the incident might be considered closed. What reply—if any—I do not know but the President told Anne O'Hare McCormick that he thought Hull attached entirely too much importance to the incident and allowed it to be magnified out of its proportion—and that he thought it was because Hull was tired out and should go away and take a rest.

He is tired. He stayed at home three days this week—came down yesterday and attended Cabinet—but is in bed today with a slight cold.

Welles arrived back in Miami about noon—forty hours from Rio by air. Astonishing!

February 1, 1942

Went to the Department this afternoon. Cable from Singapore stated some Americans evacuated on unconvoyed vessel, many women and children unable to be taken aboard and left behind. Later two big American transports officered by the United States Navy arrived without previous announcement and under convoy, took aboard full load of English, refused transport to American women and children and left without them. We took it up with Navy and I got off a telegram reminding of our former instructions and authorizing Consul again to ask High Command for transports.

If that story should gain currency it might lose the war for England. Who could have given such orders I can not even imagine but it makes me boil.

February 3, 1942

In place of Hull I appeared before the Foreign Affairs Committee of the

House in support of the half billion financial assistance bill for China. Morgenthau, Stimson, Knox and Jones presented their Department's views—all in support. The Committee voted it out unanimously and very quickly. Bloom asked me to stay and help draft report. In consequence I was away from the Department from 10 a.m. till 3:30 p.m. Then I had to receive a writer doing an article for the *Nation*. He will no doubt criticize me. He came in belligerently antagonistic and went out only slightly less so. I was tired by seven o'clock and my desk far from cleared so I left it for tomorrow and brought all my telegrams which I read after dinner.

We have taken a crack at the Japs in their eastern islands and MacArthur[16] has cracked them again. Some planes are in action in the Java, Celebes and Singapore areas but not yet in quantity, and the Japs still are on the aggressive. The British are out of Malaya—the siege of Singapore is on, and Jap forces are backing around to threaten Rangoon. Our Consul even in Bombay is getting excited, expects an attack there and asks authority to move the Consulate to less vulnerable locality! Quivers seem to be moving along the spine of everything "east of Suez." It just shows how very thin was the veneer of British control over half a world. The "yellow peril" is a real menace but it seems impracticable for them to spread their veneer over such an area. Polynesia, Maylaysia [*sic*], I can see. India and the Bay of Bengal still seem remote for them.

February 5, 1942

The President is sick. He has been away several days—I think in his little house near Pa [Edwin] Watson's above Charlottesville. He was tired; when I saw him last week he seemed *very* tired. His mind was tired. He needed a rest —badly. In that shape he went away and picked up an infection. Today nothing is being sent him.

I went before the Senate Committee on Foreign Relations on the Chinese loan bill. The same witnesses were there. The Committee voted it out unanimously and the Senate passed it unanimously—$500,000,000—through both Committees and through both houses without a single dissenting vote.

In his statement I thought Knox gratuitously [*sic*] indiscreet. He spoke of the route of shipping to Australia, of the plans of naval operation against the easterly Japanese islands, stating that the recent operation was just the beginning of a movement of naval and air forces against other and more westerly islands with the object of deploying important elements of the Japanese naval forces; that the plan of operation envisaged progressive movement against naval and air bases in those islands; that Chinese air bases were contemplated for use against Japan for a very heavy bombing operation; that

[16] After the Japanese attack on December 7, General Douglas MacArthur commanded the defense of the Philippines until March 1942, when, under the orders of President Roosevelt, he left for Australia to take command of Allied forces in the southwest Pacific.

2000 trucks are carrying a Chinese army to fight in Burma; and allowing to be inferred that McArthur [*sic*] would get *no* reinforcements and only such help as might be caused by Japanese preoccupation in Malaya and mandated islands due to increased pressure on the enemy in those areas. None of this was pertinent to the bill—but he just has to talk. In my youth we used to have a term—"flannel-mouth."

Stimson did not come up to the standard of his testimony before the House Committee. Between the two there was painted a very black picture— lack of planes, lack of men, lack of ammunition where it was needed, lack of ships to carry men, material and ammunition as well as equipment of all sorts. It is easy to interpret that they expect (even though it be a fearful anticipation) the fall of Singapore, the loss of Java and the occupation of Australia, with the closing of the Burma Road as one of the moral certainties. They talked of "another route" as if it were this side the realm of fantasy to build now, quickly, from Calcutta to Lasio, and as if that would not be as vulnerable as the "Burma" route.

[Senator Hiram] Johnson of California asked about the defense of that coast. He got scant comfort. Knox said there were no ships available to amplify the patrol, no more planes for that work, no submarines now available, no more anti-aircraft guns. He tried to quiet his fears by saying there were more anti-air guns there than anywhere else in the United States but spoiled the effect of his attempt at pacification by saying that raids might be expected and could not be prevented. Johnson was volubly resentful—but voted for the bill.

The whole picture was pretty dark—an aggressive foe, well prepared, with a superiority of men, planes and naval support—a scattered front with a very long line of communications—and probable defeat in the western Pacific with a "long, long pull" to push the enemy out of situations it was much easier to defend than to retake.

The picture leaves China suspended in the firmament of unreality—unless she can fight alone on a nebulous "credit" without receiving guns and ammunition or tangible materiel. And with China gone—the enemy cannot be reached except directly by sea or from Siberia by air. And Russia is provoked, to say the least, that only infinitesimal substance has followed our fulsome commitments for material aid.

The truth is we are spreading our butter very thin over the world—even in the United States. To England we have given enormously—but also to the Egyptian area, the western desert, Iran, Burma, Singapore, Java, Australia, South America East Coast and South America West Coast. The attack is world wide—and we have spread world wide—and without concentration anywhere. The trouble is our enemies are concentrating in a few places —Russian front, Libya, Malaysia. Germany is reinforcing her armies against

Russia, Romel [*sic*][17] is pushing the British back in Libya—to Tobruk again—and the Japs are most efficiently and successfully spreading over the whole map of southeastern Asia and Oceania. . . .

February 7, 1942

Five British ships lying in New York because members of crews deserted—through a hole in our immigration laws. British pressure has now focussed attention on it and a move excitedly develops to have the President appoint a committee to do something about the general situation. It is not a new trouble. For eighteen months I have been trying to secure cooperation from the other agencies of government. I called it twice to the attention of the President and he wanted it stopped. Jackson and I conferred when he was Attorney General and he cooperated. After the law of June 21, 1941, we argued for five months—till November 14—with Justice about the regulations to enforce the control over arrival and departure of all aliens—including seamen. They would not consent to control by the Secretary of State over seamen, though we argued and pressed them to do so. In order to get the regulations accepted by Justice we finally agreed to let Justice control seamen and their entry, etc. Now it develops—the records show—4600 alien seamen left their ships in our ports and did not depart—a sad commentary on our "strict" control over alien entries and a travesty about our elaborate visa system designed to prevent just that thing and effectively applicable to all but seamen. 4600 a year got in anyhow because there is no enforcement. It started out to protect us against Fifth Columnists—and it ends up to man British ships. My own record in the matter is only too clear. I offered to control it in the Department of State—under the authority of the proposed regulations but had to yield that point in order to get the rest of the regulations agreed to and in operation. There is sufficient authority in law; there are agencies of the Government capable of enforcing the regulations—either the Coast Guard or the Navy—but to date there has been no adequate enforcement. And because of the present urge it may be taken up through some other channel.

February 15, 1942

Sunday—at home— Listened to Churchill speak from London. Good oratory but weak substance. He relied on Russia, on China, most of all on the United States. Apparently and by deduction very little reliance on England. No mention of the Channel escape of the three German naval ships.[18]

[17] General Erwin Rommel, Commander of German forces in North Africa, 1941–1943.
[18] On February 11–12, the German warships *Scharnhorst* and *Prinz Eugen*, with naval and air escort, escaped from Brest and fought their way up the English Channel through the Straits of Dover toward Helgoland. Forty-three British and twenty-eight German airplanes were lost during the battle.

Singapore has fallen. Sumatra under parachute attack. Rangoon still resisting. MacArthur making a wonderful stand. Our planes and ships streaming into Australia. But Australia will be cut off from the west if and when the Japs get the air bases and harbors in western Java and Sumatra. Then the only line will be to the United States up the Eastern Pacific.

Ships are the scarcest thing in the world—next to rubber tires. The question of sailors deserting in United States ports becomes poignant again because it leaves ships without crews. I have called a meeting for tomorrow a.m.—Justice, Maritime Commission and Coast Guard—and will propose an effective solution. It is not a State Department job but a shipping job.

Ship shortage has delayed the exchange of diplomats but the Cabinet on Friday acted on a memorandum of mine after the Maritime Commission finally agreed to the minimum of my requests and approved the specific program—but ships still unnamed and unallocated—though promised.

Labor troubles at the farm. The gardener quit yesterday after having caused my farm hand helper to quit earlier in the week. So now I depend on faithful Bill all alone to tide over and I have been on the phone half the day trying to get others. The Army has taken so many and high wages in industry have called away so many more that problems are many—here near Laurel and elsewhere. Miss Aderton's husband is called—and so it goes. No bright sign anywhere yet.

This country is just waking up. At first it was incredulous—then stunned. Now it is getting mad. The danger is it may turn on the administration. Pearl Harbor has passed. Press and people turned on LaGuardia and Mrs. Roosevelt.[19] The Congress may turn on the President and on some of the "fringe" in office. It just *might* be very bad—and I will do everything I can to stop it. But if it gets a good, quick start no individual can stop it. None will consider them themselves [*sic*] at fault. The truth is the administration is not to blame for our unpreparedness, for the apathy of the people, for the Lindberg [*sic*] philosophy which was so popular, for our general selfishness and softness. It was and still is, part of a national state of mind. The country is to blame and not the administration which had to be guided by the refusal of the people to believe we could ever lack anything, from soup to nuts—or from knitting yarn to rubber tires and tin cans. Now they are mad—not at their own apathy but at those who cried "wolf, wolf"—and they are going to take it out on somebody! None of which will help the war effort, and all of which will help the enemy. I hope it will be short-lived.

[19] Fiorello LaGuardia, mayor of New York City, 1934–1945, and Mrs. Franklin Roosevelt became the target of many former isolationists who claimed that, through their talks and writings, these two prominent people had incited the Axis attack upon the United States.

February 21, 1942

This week now closing has witnessed a temporary worsening of the war situation—in the Far East and in our very adjacent waters, but more particularly in its repercussions in the countries to the south of us.

In the Far East—since the surrender of Singapore—Rangoon has been evacuated by the civilian personnel, Sumatra has been occupied and Timor and Bali have been taken. Our troops and air forces have arrived there in increasing numbers but not yet in sufficient strength to stop the advances.

The Germans claim more than 500,000 tons sunk off our Atlantic Coast and in the Caribbean. We have not admitted that much. The waters of Aruba[20] were attacked, the town shelled; eight or ten ships, mostly tankers, sunk in the Caribbean—two of them in the roadstead at Trinidad; a German submarine appeared at French Martinique this morning for the announced purpose of putting ashore a hospital case but no doubt to produce a political effect.

All this is having a distinct political effect in South America. Venezuela is querulous. Brazil is experiencing a resurgence of the opposition Nazi party. Bolivia even is backing away from its ejection of Nazi diplomats. Ecuador and Peru are hesitant.

It means that all of Latin America is weighing in the balance their ideas of United States invincibility against these challenges to our authority right in our own yard. . . .

Within the country there is a lot of dissatisfaction. The Senators show signs of incipient independence. I have been up twice during the week—once on a "snooping" expedition and I found what I expected: (1) a near conviction we will lose the fall elections, and the House; (2) that the Senators are going to play safe in their own states and vote the way it will help them most at home. The other visit was to the Foreign Relations Committee of the Senate on an informal proposal to repeal the Neutrality Act.

The exchange of diplomats is coming slowly—mostly boat trouble—no vessel actually allocated yet. Communications by radio with British possessions comes slowly too.

March 8, 1942

Java has fallen to the Japs. The Burma Road is cut. The history of the last three months is far from bright.

I have had incommunicado for about five weeks the Japanese Consulate staff from Honolulu. I directed General Gullion[21] who placed them incommunicado in Hawaii, to bring them here. That was done two weeks or more ago. I then directed their detention at a camp in Arizona and held incom-

[20] Aruba is an island in the former Netherlands West Indies.
[21] Major General Allen Gullion, Office of the Provost Marshal General.

municado. This to continue until our Consul in Saigon was permitted to be contacted personally. To date we have not heard that he has been.

Negotiations for the exchange move slowly. The Treasury—and partly Acheson, the liaison—have not helped much. They want to restrict the Swiss representing Germany here to force Germany to send fresh money for representation purposes rather than use the cash and bank accounts here. The idea is it will hurt Germany to furnish new money. But, Germany allows Switzerland to use seventy to eighty thousand dollars we gave over in cash in Germany to represent our interests. The Swiss are mad and say it is infringement of their diplomatic status for us to make such restrictions—and Germany may retaliate against us. I have got provoked about it because it may seriously affect the health and comfort of the thousands of United States citizens in enemy territory—for the ministration of whose welfare I am responsible. Again, Switzerland might say it is just too much trouble to represent us— and then where would we be?—with no other Government we could find to do it satisfactorily. If we allowed them to spend all the money all of them have here it would not be one million—or six months expense—and is one million of fresh money sufficient to cause our people all the suffering they would have to undergo! . . .

England rumors that Cripps[22] will succeed Churchill—and if he does the implications are bad.

India is clamoring for independence—but can't agree on what kind—and the Tories in England can't understand that business is not quite as usual East of Suez. I am reminded of my thesis in 1908—"The Impossibility of India's Revolt from England"—for my M.A.

March 9, 1942

I am apprehensive lest we be left mostly alone to carry on this fight. Russia might easily make peace with Germany, the latter to retire to her boundaries as of June '41 and promise to stay out. Germany could then start her two incipient campaigns 1) against Egypt, from Libya where she is now heavily reinforcing Rommel and 2) against Syria based on Greece and thence against Suez through Palestine. And I have *no* confidence in Turkey's Allied cooperation. Both those campaigns might succeed—and Japanese submarines might make it very difficult to supply the Middle East from around the Cape of Good Hope.

Then—Where would we be? Russia out, Suez gone, Turkey with the enemy along with Iraq and Iran, and the British Navy emasculated! And we with a fight in two oceans against a combined navy superior to ours.

I am apprehensive about Russia—have been for weeks now—and today my fears are given some corroboration in suggestions from abroad to the

[22] Sir Stafford Cripps, now Lord Privy Seal and Deputy Prime Minister, 1942.

same effect. All the political elements are there—a tired army, a battered people, a disappointed but not defeated adversary, a vision of spring with longer fighting days to come unless an armistice can luckily be arranged. And on Germany's side—a battered army, a grumbling population, a low morale, and two easier campaigns on the program which have to wait on developments on the Russian front and could be immediately prosecuted if that were terminated.

The urge is on both sides—and I am fearful.

March 25, 1942

Had an unusual meeting in my office today. The Swiss Minister became incensed day before yesterday because he had been asked to let the F.B.I. "survey" the Italian Embassy—under his protection. He came down and told me indignantly of a series of incidents and wanted to talk to the Attorney General—the boss of the F.B.I. After exchanging memos with Welles, I asked Biddle to meet the Minister in my office. They met this afternoon. They had a difference of opinion. The Swiss maintained the premises under his protection were inviolate. Biddle said they were not; that the Cabinet had discussed the question of requisitioning them; that it was a sadistic thought that the German Embassy might become the Office for Alien Property Custodian; that our law permitted it; that the decision was delayed until our officers had made their exit from enemy territories; but the right existed. Bruggmann excitedly came back: the power might exist; but international law and custom forbade it; he must protest the thought as regards property here under his protection but his Government must deny the right and point to the difficulty Switzerland would have protecting American interests all over the world. Neither would yield.

It finally settled down to a relation by Bruggmann of certain unrelated incidents which he wrongfully but naturally correlated and built in his imagination to something real. These were explained away and Biddle promised to present any complaints so Bruggmann could correct the abuse if found to exist—and it all ended happily.

I was not a participant in the discussion—simply a medium for exchange of conversation—*and* a few ideas.

While I said nothing I could only think that in my recollection no government but Germany had violated an Embassy. Germany did that of Poland in 1940—on the pretext Poland no longer existed. Even Moscow has respected all the Embassies at the capital. Italy always has with the possible exception of Palazzo Venezia, which once was the Embassy of Venice; later, when Venice was Austrian it became the Embassy of Austria, and in 1915 when Venice was back in Italian jurisdiction and Italy at war with Austria, Italy took it over. We have never violated an Embassy. During 1917–18 the German and the Austrian Embassies continued undisturbed. Ours did in those countries. So Biddle's argument seems to be out of line with my experience and out of tune with my understanding of propriety—even in an all-out war. But I suppose many a precedent will be bowled over during this struggle.

Biddle is an odd genius. He is aggressive, able and courageous—but his philosophies seem to me to get wide of the mark sometimes. On the liberal side he is too liberal and on the conservative side too conservative. They just do not seem to run true. He opposes my attempts to be very careful about the admission of aliens and shows a tender heart to the aliens on the Pacific Coast till public opinion forced the President to turn their case over to the Army. Now, when the property, protected by custom through the ages, belonging to alien governments is concerned he wants to confiscate it in defiance of international law which he said this afternoon was subordinate to United States law. He is hard to follow. . . .

March 30, 1942

Negotiations for the diplomatic exchange still continue. Each country provides some difficulty. Avra Warren[23] is in South America. Yesterday Lima— today to Quito—trying to straighten out troubles. England makes it harder by insisting on providing only conditional or partial safe conducts. Welles talking again to Halifax on the general British policy.

Cripps announces his panacea for Indian support in the war and eventual independence. . . . [24]

April 7, 1942

Four months today since Pearl Harbor—and the situation has deteriorated every minute since. Today the Japs are at the gates of India. The province of Bengal is in a panic. Fifth columnists are rife, the native Bengali is friendly to the Japs—hostile to and resentful of the English. Cripps' proposals are like last season's roses. Delhi is struck with indecision and consternation. The undreamed has happened—or is happening with the rapidity of a holocaust. India is about to fall. The uncomprehending philosophy of England is meeting its reward. Blind, self-centered and tenacious of the phantoms of the past, she refuses to be convinced of vulnerability of England everywhere, but in England. She hangs on to commercial privileges as she always has—even refusing to permit us—now—to use telegraph and telephone facilities unless the agreement includes a warranty that the privilege exist for the duration of the war only. What good will the new cable be from Bombay west—after the

[23] Now ambassador to the Dominican Republic, 1942–1944.

[24] Churchill sent Cripps to India bearing an offer which, it was hoped, would satisfy Gandhi's demand for independence. The offer stated that "immediately upon the cessation of hostilities" Britain would establish an assembly "charged with the task of framing a new constitution for India."

war? How useful will the air beam to New Delhi be, after the war? What value will be placed—for England—on commerce with India, Malaysia and Burma —or with South America—or any other place—after the war unless the war is won completely and unless they let us use their facilities to that end?

"Too Little—and Too Late"—could be written as the title to the chapter of British activity since 1935—starting with the fleet in the Mediterranean to bluff Mussolini—without ammunition. It is short sighted policy. They have fought well, wherever they were, but they were Too Little and Too Late. And India is the same.

Germany is getting ready for the spring drive eastward—but it is not the same German army. They have several uncounted Divisions, discouragement, low morale, lack of confidence. But still a strong army.

Production increases here—but here also the signs all point one way—a changed country, with a new schedule of economic, financial, social and political conditions. The World of Yesterday died. The interment is complete but most people seem to be ignorant of the funeral. We will continue unconquered—but that which will then exist will be of an entirely different character than that which was.

It is a wonderful time to be alive—to be a part of a world in convulsion— to see it writhe and wriggle in convulsion. But it is disheartening too. I have been so discouraged I have not blotted these pages for many days. The present can be seen. The trend is understood. But the future still remains undisclosed—as it always will. It may witness the triumph of a new philosophy— the power of mass mental power superior to that of physical force. Force against an unresisting object loses its spectacle, if not its power. The mass— world-wide—has been inferior to organized power applying force. Will the spectacle of Japanese power applying force now end in a paradox—the inferiority of all force to mass non-resistance? Or, will the new application but reaffirm the concept of our deceased world and soon see it rise to experience an obedience to force applied through a new technique?

At present it is a confusing but absorbing experience.

April 9, 1942

The Bataan defense is broken—outnumbered 15 to 1.[25] The Japs sank two British cruisers in the Bay of Bengal. Still no good news—but it is a little early for the big machine to get under way.

In the meantime what I do seems not even remotely related to action and bullets. Talks with Norman Davis about the Red Cross function and activity abroad; with Joe Davies about Relief activities and their control at home, with Tracy Strong[26] about Y.M.C.A.—at home and abroad—and its relation-

---

[25] Bataan fell to the Japanese on April 9, after resisting a siege of more than three months.
[26] General secretary of the Y.M.C.A., 1937–1953.

ship to Red Cross; correspondence about legislation concerning the procedure of proving citizenship with the Swiss, about a vessel to carry grain to Europe for Switzerland—and the answer no—not now; with Jerry Land about a decent settlement with the Danes whose ships we expropriated; and arrangements in detail of Exchange of Diplomatic and unofficial personnel. It all has to be done—yesterday at the Senate with Barkley—Labor policy and legislative hearings on the forty or forty-eight hour week—and last night on the phone to Montevideo—but no *action* and apparent results.

April 10, 1942
Bill Donovan—"Wild Bill"—is head of the C.I.O.—Coordinator of Information. He has been a thorn in the side of a number of the regular agencies of the Government for some time—including the side of the Department of State—and more particularly recently in Welles'. He is into everybody's business—knows no bounds of jurisdiction—tries to fill the shoes of each agency charged with responsibility for a war activity. He has had almost unlimited money and has a regular army at work and agents all over the world. He does many things under the *nom de guerre* of "Information" but among others he broadcasts news and "propaganda." Often his broadcasts follow a policy widely divergent from the official foreign policy and from time to time make trouble for us abroad. Thanks to my foresight and the President's approval we have a very thorough coverage, by way of monitoring, of all broadcasts from abroad—conducted by the F.C.C. But we have no monitoring of broadcasts emanating in the United States and directed abroad so nobody knows what Donovan and other broadcasting agencies are sending out. . . . One thing seems possible—and that is a licensing of all who appear before the microphone—after they have been thoroughly "looked over," so that only loyal persons have an opportunity to make their voices heard.

April 12, 1942
Sir Ronald Campbell of the British Embassy came in yesterday following a talk Halifax had with Welles in which they were referred to me. They want to exercise a veto over persons we are exchanging with the Germans for our people—in case the British do not like the individual. I explained the situation and let him infer they would have difficulty in preventing us from carrying out our commitments. I immediately cabled London to ask for safe conduct for the *Drottningholm* out of New York for Lisbon April 28th. As the Germans require two weeks that will give them a short time to talk about it—till the 14th. And I am proposing to Welles tomorrow a press announcement of our plans.
Sir Ronald also left a memorandum saying they proposed to make their safe conduct for the evacuation from Japan conditional upon the simultaneous

departure of Americans with that of the English. I told him I would talk to him again on that—and I am getting up steam. I can't tell him just what I think—or am not supposed to tell him—but it might do him a lot of good to hear it. There are enough troubles and complications in this exchange without the British making more. . . .

April 14, 1942

Laval comes back to power in Vichy.[27] Germany is to be in the driver's seat. The fleet is in the balance—our position in North Africa is challenged and our whole policy vis-à-vis Vichy will undergo a sudden change. This has been in the realm of possibility for some time but it developed very suddenly. I am glad I declined the invitation to dine with Henry-Haye for tomorrow as well as for the next night. He was peculiarly persistent in his invitations and for a while it looked as if I might be considered too firm in my refusals but now it is fortunate I was firm for had I accepted I would now drop out. I could not dine with him. It would not have been a pleasure at any time.

Germany held the *Drottningholm* from sailing, for unknown reasons, and London postponed its safe-conduct for the vessel from New York until the Embassy here has cleared the lists of individuals we propose to send home!

April 15, 1942

Subcommittee on Security—under the general committee on post war problems—met in my office today for first meeting under Norman Davis' chairmanship.

Long argument with the Dutch about a Dutch vessel idle in Seattle and under libel. I told them to settle the libel and get the ship to work or we would requisition it. They claim title in Crown—and I say all the more reason to put it to work. Maritime Commission and Justice want to begin proceedings *now*.

Held all French vessels in our harbors till further orders and ordered guards put back on them if any had been removed. . . .

April 20, 1942

Hull back from his long rest—away about two months. He looks rested and well and seems bright and earnest again. I had a good talk with him. He said he had had a long nervous strain—six or eight months—up to Pearl Harbor, had been apprehensive all that time, conscious of his responsibilities, worried day and night, continuously on a strain. The Japanese problem and the Vichy policy had been a two-fold load and though he had always felt

---

[27] In 1940 Pierre Laval had become foreign minister and successor-designate to Marshal Pétain in the Vichy French government. In December 1940, Pétain dismissed him on the suspicion that he was planning a coup d'état. Laval, an advocate of collaboration with Germany, was reinstated by Pétain in April 1942 at Hitler's insistence.

neither of them could be kept at arm's length nor that each could continue indefinitely it was the wise policy to keep them as long as possible. At the end —he was worn out, exhausted. But he had had a good rest and was now full of fight. However he was conscious that the chief responsibility was now on other shoulders. The war had come. It was now military and naval responsibility. He had postponed the event and tried to prevent it but all the while he was conscious of the ultimate futility. However it had been postponed as long as possible and that much time given for preparation and increased production.

[George] Brandt arrived—by air—to be my assistant. He is a realist about German strength for the spring drive and a pessimist as to Italy doing anything but lying down at German feet. . . .

Tokyo, Kobe, etc. are bombed—what damage is not known but we have maintained a perfect silence and there is much mystery about it. We have hit them for the first time.[28]

April 22, 1942

The Republican National Committee yesterday adopted a resolution which disavowed "Isolation" as a party policy. Nothing has gratified me more in years. Shades of Henry Cabot Lodge, of Knox, and Penrose, Pepper and the army of destruction of 1920! They must have turned in their graves. From 1918 to 1942 is a long time but the change is complete—on paper. It will probably rise again in some other form—in some other name—for there are exponents of the philosophy in both parties—Clark for one, Nye and La Follette for others. And this resolution is only an expression of a National Committee. It is entitled to due weight but it is not as binding a commitment of the party as would be an expression of the National Convention. Nevertheless it is a strong indication of the trend of policy—a promise of future commitment—and is most gratifying to me. Had the Republican wrecking crew cooperated with us in 1919 and 1920 the League of Nations might have had the virile strength through our membership to exercise a real influence in the world. There might not have developed this devastating war. I have never wavered in my support of the Wilson policies. I have always been proud of the efforts I made. I have always believed in the righteousness of my stand in those days, now long gone by. And now I am gratified indeed to see the opposition subscribe to the thesis—and welcome them without bitterness— with the single exception that I could never forgive Jim Reed for his perfidy.[29]

[28] On April 18, 1942, carrier-based U.S. Army B-25 bombers led by Major General James H. Doolittle raided Tokyo.

[29] Henry Cabot Lodge, Philander C. Knox, Boies Penrose, and James Reed, were Senators who opposed the League of Nations and who voted against the Treaty of Versailles. George Wharton Pepper, although opposed to the Treaty, did not enter the Senate until 1922.

Pearl Harbor killed isolation—and the political activity taken in its name. It also started another war. But this war is not like the last one—in Washington. The organization for it was different then. The spirit of friendly cooperation and mutual confidence was different then. There was little backbiting, jurisdictional jealousy, personal antagonism. True, there were some differences due to clashing personalities. The Lansings hated the Burlesons, for instance. The Clarks hated the Wilsons—even unto the second generations. There were a few more. I, too, had difficulties with Phillips—the only personal difficulty I remember having had during that whole period—except of course the political difficulties and differences which arose over our foreign policy and which were exemplified by the Republican opposition to the League.[30] But the Republicans were not the Administration. We were. And our family was very happy with a few unimportant and insignificant exceptions—which did not in any way interfere with the operations of government. Political differences did make trouble and out of them did grow the "Lansing incident" which resulted in his resignation being asked for. But we all worked together without bitterness being felt or shown.

Now it is different. I am conscious that some of my colleagues in the Government feel bitterly about me. I know that some of them dislike me intensely. There is some interference with my work—some opposition to my activities—and there has been from time to time some conspiracy against me —some effort to discredit me.

It is difficult to be conscious of these things and not to feel resentment. I fear I am not good enough to be without some resentment. Perhaps I show it —though if I do I am not conscious of that. Whether I do or not I have not tried in any way to retaliate nor have I permitted any personal inclination to enter into my official relationships. I have done my job as best I could and have carried out the President's policies in which I entirely believe—to the best of my ability.

But it is different from the last time—when I was on the most friendly terms with them all—except the Republican opposition in the Congress.

Washington then was gay and confident. Now it is sober. Then it had many aspects of social as well as intellectual leadership. Now it is intellectual without the social setting. Then the whole war effort was treated differently. The leaders of all the world's Governments came to see Mr. Wilson—Balfour,

---

[30] Reference here is to the personal antagonisms between the families of Robert Lansing, Secretary of State, 1915–1920, and Albert Burleson, Postmaster General, 1913–1921. The Clark family referred to is that of Champ Clark, Democrat, U.S. Representative from Missouri, 1893–1895, 1897–1921, and Speaker of the House, 1911–1919. Clark was Wilson's principal rival for the Democratic presidential nomination in 1912. William Phillips, Long's successor in Italy, served as Assistant Secretary of State, 1917–1920, and was Long's immediate superior in the State Department during the Wilson administration.

Viviani and Joffre, Marconi, Ishii—and so many others.[31] They worked—hard—but we all had time to dine out and meet in an atmosphere which was not sombre and which contributed to make the work easier. Then there were State dinners—some of them spectacles—and formality—and congregation of the leaders of all the branches and divisions of the Government—and a camaraderie and a trustfulness—and a cooperation which made the hard work easier—and possibly better.

April 26, 1942

The war has already taken its toll of comforts and conveniences. Labor is at a premium. There are *no* farm hands to be had. I changed the gardener for a farmer—from lawn and flowers to fields and vegetables. I have two Finns—sailors—at least for the moment. The relations of Finland with the Allies are such that our Navy will not allow Finns on any ship. They are not permitted in war industries—and most industry is now in the war effort. So the Finns have difficulty in being placed for work. So I have two who have never before seen a farm. The farmer has trouble getting them to work because he can't talk Finnish—and that is all they know. They are willing but can't understand. Anyhow, vegetables are in the offing. Asparagus is to begin tomorrow—others in due time. Tires are another problem. Gasoline is to be rationed—perhaps 50 gallons a month—which would mean I could not drive to my office every day. Twenty miles each way and a few trips to Laurel runs a minimum of 50 miles a day—using only one car. Six days makes 300 miles a week—1300 miles a month. At 13 miles to the gallon that needs 100 gallons for the month. Then there is the lawnmower and the spray for the fruit, other trees and boxwood—all provided tires hold out and provided further lubricating oil is to be had. Crawford, his wife and Laura the cook are here—but there are three instead of the six or seven of yesteryears—and no more assistant butlers, housemen, kitchen helpers, footmen, etc. They are all in the army or in industry. So we can hardly have guests—two at a time—no one to attend to them. So that purely from the domestic end there are many difficulties.

Transportation curtailment is a severe handicap. It is only just becoming apparent. There are many other difficulties—for instance, priorities which are now preventing purchase of parts for the water supply pump—and prevent

---

[31] Arthur James Balfour, British Foreign Secretary, 1916–1919; René Viviani, French Premier and Minister of Foreign Affairs, 1914–1915; General Joseph Jacques Joffre, Commander-in-Chief of the French Armies, and later of the Allied armies, in France during World War I; Guglielmo Marconi, Italian inventor and Nobel prize winner in physics, 1909, held minor Italian foreign office positions during World War I; Viscount Kikujiro Ishii, Japanese Minister of Foreign Affairs, 1915–1916. As a special envoy to the United States in 1917, he signed the Lansing-Ishii Agreement which limited Japanese immigration to the United States.

purchase of a piece of brass pipe to repair the artesian well of which the iron pipe was corroded so it takes in sand and has ruined the water supply. But it is all part of the general situation—part of the trouble to be cured—part of the reason we are at war—and part of the necessity to win.

We have suffered serious losses in ships. Sinkings have been very heavy— 1,500,000 tons recently.

Yesterday I had a lengthy talk with the Secretary again—subjects I hesitate to put on paper. I can never be sure—entirely sure—other eyes do not see these pages. Some topics are not meant for other eyes. He talked of his solitary conversation with the President—the general suggestions he had made, not in criticism of anything which has been done but pointing out several objectives and indicating how they might be done. He said he had also talked to Welles of that conversation and wanted me to know but would not talk to anyone else. We discussed England, our special representatives there, general policy, leadership, Russia, her western front, her eastern front, her reticence; Turkey, her present and future condition; France—Laval, the withdrawal of our Embassy, the changed and changing relationship; Canada's breach of relations and the difficulty that made for us to continue relations with Vichy. Even though England had begged us to establish, foster and continue our recent policy to Vichy—yet England encourages Canada to act at variance with that policy and is responsible for the embarrassment resulting to us. Relations with Vichy cannot last long. Then Europe will be more difficult and Africa will be more complicated.

April 28, 1942

Russia is pushing England to recognize the Baltic States as Russian—for post war settlement but for commitment now. Russia is using but not mentioning the possibility of a separate arrangement with Germany if that is not agreed to. England needs Russia in the war. She is doing all the real fighting in Europe for the Allies. England hesitates and is tempted. Poland learns of it and protests—that it is immoral from the point of view of the Atlantic Charter and contrary to the spirit and objective of America. Russia is also making a great ado about the trial in Turkey of the Russians charged with complicity in or responsibility for the attempted murder of Von Papen. The fragile good relations between Russia and Turkey are threatened. Russia seems to be provoking an incident. Turkey is a neutral, has had Allied leanings (of doubtful sincerity—but still leanings). A breach between the two would make Turkey lean toward Germany. . . .

If England should refuse to recognize Russia's title to the Baltic States Russia might even the score by letting Germany into the oil fields of Mosul— even Bahrein—1) getting even with England; 2) saving her Caucasus fields for her own use; and 3) paving the easy road to a peace with Germany.

Both Russia and Germany are ready to call their particular war quits. Each is tired—and sore—and hungry. Each has sustained enormous loss in men and material and each is in a state out of which a separate peace could easily be developed. So England might easily be out-foxed. But we would all lose a lot because Germany could then devote her attention to the Mediterranean and Suez and more easily make a juncture with the advancing Japs who now have practically completed their capture of Burma and who are looking west.

This has been building up for some time. The existence of conditions which make for a desire for peace have been inherent in the situation for several months—exhaustion, hunger, discouragement, fear! They have all been on both sides.

When I talked with Standley[32] just before he started for Russia I sketched to him the situation as I saw it and suggested he be on the lookout for symptoms of a developing separate peace between Germany and Russia. He was not inclined to take me seriously. Discerning that I tried to impress him with the thought and at least partly succeeded but I had the impression he could not discount what he termed the rugged national expression of antagonism to Germany. I told him it would come not as an expression of national feeling but as a result of agreement between two men—Hitler and Stalin—and that the reaction would be welcomed by the people of both countries once their struggle was over.

April 30, 1942

This morning I tried to talk with Hull about Russia and the possible significances of the demands on England and the attitude toward Turkey. I just got started and was interrupted by statements that Russian demands vis-à-vis the Baltic States were inconsistent with the Atlantic Charter and an attempt to obtain post war settlements during the war—to both of which I agreed. But I could not get very far—had not time to develop my thoughts when he got word the President wanted to see him right away. So I saw I would have to postpone. . . .

Lunched with Baruch. . . . About the price level fixing Bernie is pretty well satisfied. He has contended for a ceiling over wages as well as over prices of materials because each is a determining factor in cost of the product. He has contended for that for more than a year. Now he sees—and largely through his own influence—the plan take fairly definite shape—and is gratified but not satisfied that it will grow on its own food from now on. He thinks it will need adjustment, readjustment and continuing attention. I agree with him—and have from the start.

About the new tax program with a limit on income of $25,000—he is

[32] Admiral William H. Standley, ambassador to the Soviet Union, 1942–1944.

approving—though it will not bother him personally.[33] He has several million in cash on which he will live at whatever rate he wants—spending out of principal. He has several more in Government bonds. He told me two and five respectively—and various other smaller investments. He has all he wants —has a comparatively small income and is living on cash principal. So from his objective point of view he approves. I have always taken the position that my Government in need could have anything I owned—including me. That is my feeling in this. It will make a vast difference to my family—and I am sorry for them. They have never known privation—of any kind. It is awfully hard to learn privation suddenly after a life of complete luxury. $25,000 is a lot of money—but when you have much more than that you get committed to overhead—several motors, numbers of servants upon whom you depend, several houses which need money for taxes and repairs, payrolls, charitable contributions, all manner of things which become automatic and the elimination of which is impossible in entirety—and so with a much reduced income you find it preallocated and overcharged. The first to get lopped off is extra service.

Bernie and I agreed the world we had known was gone—but that hardly anyone realized it. We do—and have recollections of full lives but cannot divine the future. I cannot create a mental picture of what it will be like— except only it is to be vastly different. He thinks that a State, like Mexico for example—or Canada—could, with its resources and a determination, by selecting its citizens, create a paradise in the future—but I reminded him that while it could be done it could be done only by a highly centralized government which would be a dictatorship of the most developed kind—and that is just what we are fighting against today.

So I guess the future world will "just grow," like Topsy, and to compare it with the dream world of the last sixty years you will have to come back in about a hundred years from now.

May 6, 1942

Another meeting of Defense Sub-Committee of the General Post-War Studies Committee. The minutes are not to show discussion or arguments— only conclusions. Therefore—they probably will be *short*. There are no conclusions yet—only general outlines of possible future conclusions. The General and the Admiral are of mind that only an unconditional surrender will assure the future against German and Japanese aggressions. We had the

[33] Reference here is to the anti-inflationary Price Control Act of 1942 which authorized the Office of Price Administration to fix price ceilings on a wide variety of commodities. It froze salaries of more than $5,000 a year, except where increases were justified by promotions to harder tasks. It directed that "so far as practicable" salaries be limited to $25,000 a year after payment of taxes.

Pershing memos of the last Armistice period—for study and discussion. I agree their objective is best—if obtainable.[34] Then comes the set-up of a political organization—not identical with the League. I threw in the thought of a Court with jurisdiction over political, legal, economic, social and other questions with a "sheriff," with power to act, which would mean that all those nations subscribing would pool sufficient of their forces, as many as necessary, to enforce compliance with the decisions. . . .

May 7, 1942

The *Drottningholm* left this evening from Jersey City carrying the Axis diplomats and other officials from the United States and many of the countries to the south of us. Argentina and Chile have not sent theirs home. Brazil, Uruguay and Paraguay had their own deportation from Rio, except that Paraguay fell down and did not complete the job. All the others were assembled here and are on the way home. Ours are moving from Axis countries by train to Lisbon and will be exchanged under the supervision of Portugal.

I stayed at my desk till 10:30 last night—amongst other things to see Lyon[35] whom I had called back from New York and to whom I entrusted, with the approval of Hull, a confidential oral communication to be made aboard the vessel. He travels on it as the representative of the Department.

This morning the trains conveying to the dock from Cincinatti, Ashville and White Sulphur—six trains arriving an hour apart—seemed to be moving on schedule and under the protection of Frank Haig's [*sic*][36] police, the orderliness of it all being reported as perfect and it all being set up, I thought I might get a change of atmosphere. So I took the noon train and went to Pimlico, where two of my horses were running. On a sloppy track Tilting, making her first start, ran disappointingly, but Equipet won the Carroll Handicap from a band of very good fillies and mares. I was presented with a nice piece of silver plate as a trophy.

May 8, 1942

Had lunch at Russian Embassy and dinner at Norwegian Legation—the latter requested me to wear "blue serge" because the Prime Minister had no evening clothes having just arrived by air and travelling very light. The Crown Prince and Princess were there—and stayed till 1:20 a.m.—so I returned at 2:00 a.m. exhausted.

---

[34] Reference here is to General John Pershing's reports of the proceedings of the Allied Armistice Conference (October 25, 1918) called to formulate surrender terms for Germany. Pershing maintained that "there should be no tendency toward leniency."

[35] Frederick Lyon, assistant, Department of State, 1942–1944.

[36] Frank Hague, mayor of Jersey City, New Jersey, 1917–1947.

May 9, 1942

Hull called me this morning. He is still annoyed at the inroads made on his jurisdiction by the Board of Economic Warfare. In spite of the definition of duty and jurisdiction the President made, the B.E.W. goes on the same. Hull attended a meeting of the Board. After he left Perkins[37] rose and made remarks which were reported to Hull to be an expression of intention to carry on as the authority in charge of foreign relations. Hull is provoked and somewhat mystified. He can't understand how Perkins could continue unless he had been authorized and doubts that he and his group would defy the President's orders. The probable fact is that the delineation between purchasing for war needs and negotiating in conformity with policy has not been nicely drawn and each is partly in the other's territory. In England, the Ministry of Economic Warfare has occupied much of the bailiwick of the Foreign Office —but they have used the personnel of the Foreign Office. Here B.E.W. plans a personnel of its own. The President has a definite understanding of the province of the State Department—an appreciation of Hull's character and help —and a friendly feeling for Welles—but he has a prejudice for the "career" service. He dislikes much of the personnel. So he may not be averse to let Perkins try his hand. The operation will be interesting—but not necessarily successful. These wars within wars! They may ruin us yet. . . .

May 13, 1942

Registration for gasoline today. Because of enemy sinking of our tankers on our own long coastline there is a regional gas shortage. The difficulty of transporting it from producing fields in the Mid- and Southwest causes shortage in the East and Northwest. So we go on ration. I get an unlimited ration for one—temporarily for two—cars; a minimum ration for the other two. The other activities on the farm—mower, sprayer—both motor driven—and the auxilliary power plant in case the electric power line is interrupted, which is also motor driven—are as yet unprovided for in ration cards.

Talked over possibilities of racing being stopped because of gas shortage— at White House with Steve Early. The whole breeding industry depends on racing. It still continues in England, Germany, Italy. The industry here is *very* large—valuable farms and buildings, valuable mares and stallions— thousands of younger stock—millions of bushels of oats and tons of hay grown on commercial basis on other farms, publications—etc.—etc. All are integrated and depend on racing. So we who are interested or commercially occupied in breeding or in racing are hopeful no single thing like a gas short-

[37] Milo Perkins, executive director, Board of Economic Warfare, 1941–1945. This special board was established in 1941 "for the purpose of developing and coordinating policies, plans, and programs designed to strengthen the international economic relations of the United States in the interest of national defense."

age will stop it. Steve and I feel alike but see no action to take at present.

The Germans report heavy action in the Black Sea area and Crimea and claim a considerable victory. It may be the opening of the heralded Spring Offensive—and may not. The mud may still prevent the start further north. Perhaps other causes. I have been suspicious that there may be in prospect an understanding between the two war-weary nations. Cessation of activities would be *very* bad from our point of view. We have been informed Hitler and Stalin have been in contact through intermediaries about peace—but the talks were inconclusive. I finally presented my views to Hull—ten days or more ago.

The little Indian Delegate General[38] came in again this afternoon—to talk communications. He is a very attractive person and a very keen little man. But through his talk I discerned antagonism to England and a certain complacency about developments in India. The Cripps Mission he characterized a "failure"; there was a little irony in his description of England's failure to defend India, and he said that while the situation had not deteriorated particularly it had not improved. He seemed not to expect improvement and seemed to look to us to help India—not with armies, but with things other than military—like transmitters which would be useful to his government rather than to England. I should call him a satisfied defeatist.

May 18, 1942

I have had my 61st birthday.

The Axis diplomats arrived safely at Lisbon—and so have ours. Ours sail for home Friday or Saturday next. The press stories coming out of Lisbon make good reading and all seems to be favorable from the point of view of the Department's work in the premises—and give a good insight of Germany and Italy as of the present. It will be interesting to talk to them on arrival.

Russia seems to be doing well around Karkov [*sic*]—but it is too early yet to judge whether there is *real* fighting going on. The German gains at Kerch[39] and Russian claims at Karkov have not precipitated any general action. The spring battle is not raging—yet.

Gasoline rationing is the principal thought at home. Everybody is glad to give up gas or tires or cars if it will help lick Germany and Japan but not one wants the other fellow to get one drop of gas to use for frivolity or for other than efforts which will help the war effort. Consequently the public is ready to take it out magnificently on the first violator. There is a great dwindling of cars on the streets and roads—particularly the roads in the country.

[38] Sir Gira Shankar Bajpai.

[39] Kharkov, a major industrial center, was the capital of the Ukraine from 1919 until 1934 when it was superseded by Kiev; Kerch is a Crimean seaport on the Black Sea and an industrial center.

May 20, 1942

... Went before the Foreign Relations Committee—all morning—Vichy, Martinique, Mozambique, North Africa, the French fleet—gave them as much background as I could without all details of the Martinique situation and still current negotiations.

We had an important meeting of the Security Committee this afternoon— and have arrived at the point where some definite progress has been made on general conditions and terms for armistice or surrender.

June 1, 1942

The American officials out of Europe arrived on the *Drottningholm* at New York. So one phase of the exchange is completed. Some persons are trying to make it appear we are sending home agents of Germany whose exchange would be against the interest of the United States. On that theory Fahy,[40] the Solicitor General, wrote me a letter in which he proposed to stop the exchange! I called a meeting for 3:00 p.m. He and a young assistant, two F.B.I. representatives, two Army, 3 Navy (including Admiral [*sic*] Wilkinson, Chief of O.N.I.)[41] and 3 of my assistants—and talked 1 1/4 hours—in the aggregate a long day's work of busy men supposedly engaged with important affairs— and to discover Fahy's assistant got his suspicions and started his chief on a chase on the basis of an old list of passengers outbound from which names had been struck which had been objected to by F.B.I., O.N.I., M.I.D. and the British. After a lot of discussion on principles to which we all agreed beforehand it developed the young man had a discarded list. Justice seems to have the idea they have to supervise all my activities!

Molotov has been a secret guest at the White House for some days—a fact not to be mentioned. The Russians are meeting a stiff German drive in the south. Our advices from Teheran indicate there may not be much of a British force in the southern Caucasus to stop them. It may be another too little and too late, if the Russians can't hold them—and then Iraq will go along with Iran.

June 3, 1942

Our telegrams indicate that England's bombing of the Ruhr cities is playing havoc with morale as well as causing great industrial destruction. It has come most opportunely to give Germany something like a second front to think of and to encourage Russia to keep at the fight. The most important thing is to keep Russia fighting.

We are reported to have been raided and bombed in Alaska today at Dutch Harbor but no details are known. The Japs seem to pick on places

[40] Charles Fahy, U.S. Solicitor General, 1941–1945.
[41] Captain Theodore Wilkinson of the Office of Naval Intelligence.

named "Harbor" over here—Pearl Harbor and Dutch Harbor. The Japs used 40 planes, the British 1500 at Cologne, 1100 at Essen and back at Essen again with 500 and another raid reported in progress again this evening.

The Chinese ask us to threaten Japan with retaliation for the use of poison gas—solemnly stating its use. Several months ago there were reports of bacteriological warfare. I have been studying and mulling over the general subject for some time. Today, after his recent talk with Soong,[42] Welles directed the preparation of a memorandum for the President to do as the Chinese suggested. Instead of coming to or through me it went directly back to him—and then I was told and tried to get my recorded thought to catch up with the other memo. I do not agree that we should act quickly. It is a matter for high military policy decision. We are opposed to the practice of such warfare. There are no conventions or treaties prohibiting it. We refused to ratify the only convention ever proposed. It never came into effect. So there are no restrictions—except conscience and humanitarian instinct. These last we have aplenty. But to threaten Japan with reprisal might stimulate her to earlier activity and would frighten and disturb all civilian peoples everywhere. True, it might deter Japan, but she has not yet been known to be deterred by considerations of decent conduct. So I hope my memorandum—two of them —caught up with the file before it reached the President.

The *Drottningholm* sailed eastward again this evening with 1500 enemy aliens aboard. On searching one Nicolaus microfilms of an escape-hatch plans of our submarines stolen from Portsmouth Navy Yard were discovered in the toe of one shoe—and schedules of call signals for radio use with Mexico. He did not sail. He will be interned here for the duration. He is one of Mexico's contingent and we will have to do some explaining to Mexico. . . .

The House passed the war resolution for Hungary, Rumania and Bulgaria today, by unanimous votes. The Senate will get them tomorrow. Sol Bloom's Rabbi had a daughter to whom a visa has been granted. She reached Canada. Being born in Rumania she has not been technically an alien enemy. But as soon as the war proclamation is issued she will automatically become one— probably tomorrow. So I directed she be hurried across the border tonight— and Sol is grateful.

June 5, 1942

Today the President issued the statement about the Japs using poison gas against China and threatening reprisals. I thought it should be handled differently. There is great danger of provocation this way—and the certainty of arousing fear everywhere.

Japan attacked Midway and a battle rages there—but no definite news. . . .

[42] T. V. Soong, Chinese foreign minister.

The exchange with Japan is nearly on the rocks. They have asked guarantees about 700 individuals being included. I cannot guarantee—today. So I am postponing. The intelligence agencies are objecting to various of those the Japs insist on. I am trying to patch up a list which may be satisfactory—but which I doubt. The whole thing is teetering and has caused (on top of everything else) a lot of time and worry today. Tonight I am exhausted.

June 7, 1942

Six months after Pearl Harbor—and we have now claimed a smashing victory at Midway and in its ocean stretches.[43] There is another engagement going on near Dutch Harbor with very little news of it released.

I am still having a very difficult time with the exchange negotiations with Japan.

I am still able to motor in and out to and from my work but the gasoline and rubber situation combine to make the future problematic in that respect. There is a great deal of public dissatisfaction and criticism on account of the gas restriction.

June 9, 1942

Japs postponed safe conduct for repatriation vessel from here to sail the 16th—a delay of a week—and notified the sailing of their vessel from Japan as the 17th. They also demanded certain named individuals. I demanded the whole China list before letting this vessel sail and guaranteed them Ichiro [*sic*] Matsudaira[44] for four named persons of ours, three of them convicted of espionage. Nomura demanded again to stay till the second voyage or until he got orders from his Government. I replied—through the Spanish Ambassador—he was no longer under orders from his Government but from this Government and notified him he would be "escorted" to the vessel. They will all be placed aboard—except certain ones held in reserve—and anchored in the stream until they sail. Cárdenas[45] very busy and excited. He phoned Madrid for instructions. To make our position more difficult the intelligence services object to 51 names booked to sail. A meeting called for tomorrow will try to iron that out. Justice calls this a "repatriation" and do not seem to understand that in an "exchange" you have to give up something to get what you want. . . .

[43] The Battle of Midway (June 3–6, 1942) was one of the decisive Allied victories of World War II. Fought mostly with aircraft, the battle resulted in the destruction of three Japanese aircraft carriers, a loss which crippled the Japanese navy.

[44] Koto Matsudaira, former second secretary at the Japanese embassy in Washington and a member of one of Japan's most distinguished families.

[45] Don Juan F. de Cárdenas, Spanish ambassador to the U.S.

June 11, 1942

Yesterday I took Leland Morris and George Wadsworth[46] to appear before the Senate Foreign Relations Committee. They gave interesting pictures of their impressions of Germany and Italy.

The Jap exchange still on the tight-rope. The Japs have postponed their grant of safe conduct—I am waiting for the list of our people out of China—they are demanding certain named individuals. Cleared with the intelligence agencies the persons whom they objected to and obtained admission from all but Justice that the exchange was a State Department function and our responsibility.

The Secretary is intensely interested in a speech he plans to deliver—considers it most important. The object will be to reexpress our foreign policy in terms of war activity and restate certain aims and objectives. I take it too that it will serve as notice to certain other agencies—particularly the Board of Economic Warfare—that Hull is directing foreign policy—and also to let it be known that certain recent speeches (by Wallace for one) do not exactly conform to Hull's ideas of present and post-war aims. Anyhow, he is much interested and has a group of us, Acheson, Dunn, Pasvolsky, Hackworth, Savage and me. We are reading a draft—changing it—reading a redraft—will be changing it and working into another draft. Each paragraph, each sentence, each word—examined in its relation to the whole picture. . . .

Morris has the understanding Hitler is using the fear of Communism and the fear of a violent hatred by England as reasons to bind the people closer to Germany's victory—to make them fight harder—to stick together for fear they will be individual sufferers. I want to use this speech—which will have wide publicity—to drive a wedge between Hitler and the people of Germany —to point to him, his advisors, his chief lieutenants, as those guilty of taking first Germany to want, fear, disaster and suffering—then the occupied countries—then the world.

Concerning Hitler's personal responsibility—Hull left the meeting for 15 or 20 minutes to sign the Russian agreement with Litvinov.[47] Returning he said he had talked with Litvinov about that phase and the latter had replied he considered Hitler not only personally responsible and directly responsible but to have actually assumed responsibility and publicly announced it.

I loaded all the official Japs and many others on the *Gripsholm*, and the vessel will pull out from the dock and anchor till the time to load the rest and sail.

Equipet was to have run in the Oaks at Delaware Park today. But she stepped on a safety pin yesterday afternoon, punctured her frog badly and had

[46] Leland Morris, former American consul general, Berlin, 1940–1941; George Wadsworth, former counselor of American embassy, Rome, 1941.

[47] Reference here is to the master lend-lease agreement between the United States and the Soviet Union.

to be withdrawn. She was a fit horse and we thought she should win. Instead —lame. She is a bad luck mare.

June 13, 1942

Japs notified us through Swiss they would withhold 160 persons from exchange vessel—This because of Nomura's telegram he sent through Spanish complaining we were withholding 160, which we were not. The only list we recognize is list Spanish have furnished us. Some names on it refused repatriation. Some could not be found. Extra names on other lists furnished by Spanish were added. Of course that did not agree with any list Nomura might have himself compiled. In consequence of it all I talked plainly at length to Spanish Ambassador and advised Swiss Minister—got Spanish Secretary and Brandt to sit down and work on lists and try to bring exact order out of some confusion. Nomura has no place in these negotiations but the Spaniard keeps sending messages for him as if he had authoritative voice. It will probably delay departure still further. We still have no list of persons from China and our vessel will not sail till we get it. Japanese refuse release three persons from jail in Japan and I threaten removal of Matsudaira from vessel. It is all very compliqué and involves a lot of detail.

Held a conference yesterday of the Secretary's advisors to solidify Department understanding of the function of the Secretary of State in relation to exchange—as challenged by Justice. We all agreed. This morning I presented to Hull—in epitome—the question involved and he entirely approved.

The story now first published of the battle of the Coral Sea is most interesting as it throws in bold relief the role of the airplane. The ships engaged were never within range of enemy ships. All destruction was done by airplane with either bomb or torpedo. There as well as at Midway we inflicted *very* heavy damage on Japan—seriously impairing her naval strength. It may mean the end of a naval era in warfare and it may change the status in the Pacific.

Some of our planes made a forced landing in Turkey—and *that* may complicate the political situation there, for it will certainly give Germany a good chance to scold Turkey, even to put more pressure on her.

June 17, 1942

Our people sailed (we assume) from Tokyo after last minute telephone conversation Washington to Bern and Bern to Tokyo. But negotiations still continue here over the telephone between me and the Spanish Ambassador who is aboard the vessel in New York. He comes ashore to telephone and goes back to talk. I told him we wanted the boat to sail and that if there was further delay it would be the responsibility of the Spanish Ambassador as the representative of Japan.

Went with Admiral Leahy to the Senate Foreign Relations Committee this a.m. Afterwards Connally made his usual press interview in spite of the "executive session" secrecy of the meeting.

June 20, 1942

Fights with Germany and Japan. We were advised our people were *still* in Japan and had not sailed as agreed. I got the Spanish Ambassador and talked plainly. He wanted to talk to his foreign office. I expedited the connection and passed him through the Censor. Incidentally—arranged for a transcript of his conversation. It checked with what he said he would say. Arranged with the Navy to take the *Gripsholm* into hand from the high seas and to a port to hold pending developments—if necessary—with the idea of returning them to the United States and to internment camps in due course. Telegraphed strong protest and demands to Tokyo—and am now awaiting results.

Then—tonight—Germany advised the Portuguese they had communicated to the Swiss representative on the *Drottningholm* specifications for a course he should follow. I answered that was inadequate. We wanted no private information for a Swiss representative but public information for communication to the naval and air forces of various belligerents and a performance of Germany's obligation made under the agreement.

Had a talk with Hull this a.m. Hull is quite provoked with Welles because of the speeches he has been making recently about future peace conditions. He said that they were made without consultation with him, without submission of the policy or substance to him, though they had been submitted to [Archibald] McLeish [*sic*] who didn't know anything about whether they were right or not and was not in a position to judge as to whether it was proper to make them. He said he was going to call Welles in this morning and tell him that there were other people in the Department who could make speeches. There seems to be a growing friction between the two.

June 21, 1942

Last midnight the Department got me out of bed to the telephone. Germany offered to let *Drottningholm* sail on directions given in confidence to Swiss representative aboard. In a hot wire in return I said any private information to a neutral individual was unacceptable and entirely inadequate; any such information must be communicated to Governments and be used for the guidance of military, naval and air forces of various belligerents to insure the safe passage of the vessel. Then I called attention to the safe conduct under the protection of which their people had travelled eastward—and to their attempt to renegue on their agreement.

Late this afternoon the answer came. They back down and reaffirm their former assurance. That may be significant because if the mine field (and that is what I think it is) is passable by this vessel it is not so thick that others cannot pass. One vessel was sunk by mine yesterday off Virginia.

June 22, 1942

... For weeks I have been working on a memo for the Secretary to send to the President on a communications policy. The President received the resolution of the War Communications Board to unify control of all international cable and radio-telegraph and sent it to Hull for an expression of thought. He turned it over to me. It is a big, deep and broad subject with a complicated history. I have been in and out of it for 25 years. I tried to boil it down to a short analysis which the President would read. It has the approval of all the people in the Department to whom I have showed it. Now it is ready to go through Welles to Hull.

Churchill is with the President—about to return to England. The British lost from 8000 to 25,000 prisoners in Libya, lost 1009 tanks. Rommel put an anti-tank gun on wheels but not in a tank and just smashed the British. They have had six months to prepare—and now are licked. It is serious now. There are no real fortifications between Rommel and Cairo or Suez—and a broken army. It may easily mean the loss of Egypt—unless *we* can stop it.

The Egyptian Minister came in to see me—much worried—very downcast; asked us to help—afraid Egypt is gone—fears his Government will show its anti-British inclination—and no army to help itself. So they want *us* to help. I told Hull and he is very nervous. He wants the army to tell us what can be done—if anything.

In addition—Laval came out for Germany; Gandhi wrote Chiang Kai-Shek[48] he was against England and irrevocably committed to a Free India; and the damn Japanese advanced along the fogbound islands of the Aleutians toward Alaska and shelled the coast of Oregon.

It is not what I would call a happy day.

June 23, 1942

No word yet to confirm sailing of exchange vessels from Japan. Bern cables they cannot confirm. Our vessel proceeds on her way to Rio—the Navy still thinks it the thing to do and so do we. We get our hands on 403 more Japs there which may count in the scales if we need them. I am preparing for emergency measures if necessary.

I called the Egyptian Minister to keep contact with him and to say only our military authorities are examining what steps might be taken—also to caution him that any communication to his Government might not be magnified into

[48] In January 1942, Chiang Kai-Shek, head of the Nationalist Chinese government, was appointed Supreme Commander of all Allied air and land forces in the Chinese war theater.

a specific hope of definite help from us. He is in a better mood today—but far from happy.

Carlo Sforza came in. Said he assembled a few articles for reprint for use against Fascism and included my Detroit speech which he kindly complimented very highly.

Sevastopol still holds—but that is the only encouraging news of the day. The sinkings off our coast and in the Caribbean assume rather alarming proportions—about 300 ships gone to the bottom.

June 24, 1942

Bad news indeed from Egypt. The Navy advises confidentially Alexandria is to be evacuated and the situation is critical. The remnant of the British Navy will probably try to get through the Canal—then the Canal will be gone —along with "East of Suez"—the near East and North and West Africa. Turkey can hardly withstand the temptation and Iraq and Iran will gladly be relieved of their English occupations. The Negus will again be in exile. India is gone.

> The house of cards is tumbling fast.
> Germany will get her oil.
> Japan has her oil.
> We have our oil.
> From now on it may be an oil war.
> What of the future?

Hitler will have to spend some time mopping up in Africa and Southwest Asia. We will have no bases from which to strike at him there. In three or four months he can be ready to think of other fields.

He can join Japan and we will have to fight the world.

He can seek to join us and destroy Japan.

He will prefer the latter.

There will be a very large element in this country to support the theory that our own best national interest lies in destroying Japan. Certain racial elements and all Communists and extreme left radicals will be so intense in their opposition to Hitler they will choose to fight the world. The large middle ground which is bitterly opposed to Hitlerism and violently anti-Japanese will be the controlling factor and will have a hard time arriving slowly at a national decision.

We may be heading into real trouble at home. . . .

The Vatican desired to help in Prisoner of War work. The field is practically occupied by the Red Cross. The Vatican was able to get lists of prisoners in Germany and wanted Russia to furnish lists in exchange. Russia refused. The Nuncio at Ankara approached Steinhart [*sic*] and referred to us. We were approached by Cicognani[49] here—parried—and said "an opportunity would soon be presented to discuss" it here—meaning Molotov's visit. I presented a memo for Hull to get the President to use in conversation with Molotov. He and the President did, but Molotov pushed it away brusquely—would have nothing to do with it. So today I prepared a note to Cicognani which Welles signed saying nothing further could be done. Tomorrow I will advise Steinhart.

Also the Vatican has been transmitting messages to and from prisoners and persons here and has run afoul of the Censor for communicating with the enemy. So I am to call in Monseignor Ready[50] and take that up and ask Cicognani to cease that. Too bad—but! . . .

June 25, 1942

Busy planning evacuation of unofficial Americans out of Cairo and from Egypt and laying plans for possible evacuation of whole Near East, Palestine, Iraq, Iran, Syria. Talked to Jerry Land about boats—freighters—any boats to get them south to West or South Africa—if. The officials received instructions yesterday through Kirk. If he has to go I want him to go to Saudi Arabia where he is also accredited and to have a plane go and stay with him so he can get out. Only about 400 in Egypt but in other countries there are some thousands who may have a legitimate claim to American citizenship and protection.

This morning I told the Secretary how I felt about the effect of the deteriorating situation in the Near East. He is far from cheerful about it and agrees that the time has come—at least he hopes it has—when command and directorship is to be in our hands. But he feels he has been and is being excluded from any confidential councils on the subject. He has not been asked to sit in or to give advice—or furnished with information. There is a definite and growing feeling in Washington that the British are absolutely incapable of exercising command or using equipment.

June 26, 1942

Lunched in Ed Halsey's office with him and Senators Truman, Guffey, Wheeler and with Chavez, Ellender[51] and several others [*sic*] part-time attend-

[49] Angelo Guiseppe Roncalli, the Nuncio at Ankara (and, later, Pope John XXIII); Laurence A. Steinhardt, now ambassador to Turkey, 1942–1944; Archbishop Amleto Giovanni Cicognani, Apostolic delegate to the United States.

[50] The Right Rev. Mgs. Michael J. Ready, general secretary of the National Catholic Welfare Conference, and member of the President's Advisory Committee on Political Refugees.

[51] Harry S. Truman, Democrat, U.S. Senator from Missouri, 1935–1945; Joseph F. Guffey, Democrat, U.S. Senator from Pennsylvania, 1935–1947; Dennis Chavez, Democrat, U.S. Senator from New Mexico, 1935–1962; Allen Ellender, Democrat, U.S. Senator from Louisiana since 1937.

ants. They are exercised about Egypt and the Near East and all critical in varying degrees of the British—charging them with incompetence. Ellender says he is receiving an astonishing response to his speech criticizing England. They all want a United States Supreme Command—an over-all command— the others to be under United States orders.

Received confirmation our people sailed from Yokohama.

June 28, 1942

. . . Hull talked alone with me. He is irritated and nervous—almost agitated. Said he could no longer trust Welles—he was laying plans for himself, was making speeches without approval and with an illusory consent "weasled," as he called it, out of the White House. He had come to a decision to talk himself with the principal Ambassadors and take up himself that burden because he had to know the trend and development of Department activity and could not be sure of it as it had been going. He is resentful at Wallace and at Rockefeller,[52] thinks they are trying to preempt the Department's function—and is suspicious of them and mad. It is an odd humor for him to be in. He is nervously tired and lacks something of his fire and perspicacity—though he never was decisive. Tenacious to an idea—yes—but very, very awfully slow at decision.

July 6, 1942

The break-through in Russia looks bad. The Don Basin and the Northern Caucasus are in the scales—with oil.[53]

Lunched with Joseph Davies.[54] Not that I admire his judgment or would be guided by it—but he expects Russia to lose. He had just been with Litvinov—though he did not indicate Litvinov agreed with him. Joe is a pessimist on the war—thinks the Russians licked and the English the same. I am looking for a miracle in both places—and need the miracle. The prospect is certainly sombre tonight. . . .

In the meantime I am pushing to eliminate Axis communications from South America—Buenos Aires and Santiago. I held a conference this afternoon to advance that end. . . .

July 9, 1942

. . . Navy wants a monitoring station in Eastern Siberia to monitor Japan's radio—also a transmitting station. Russia at peace with Japan will of course

[52] Nelson A. Rockefeller, coordinator of Inter-American Affairs, 1940–1944.

[53] Reference here is to the German breakthrough in the area of Stalingrad (now Volgograd). The decisive battle for control of this oil-rich area began in September 1942 and lasted until February 1943. The Russian victory signaled a mighty westward drive and the Russians generally remained on the offensive for the remainder of the war.

[54] Davies, now chairman of the War Relief Control Board, 1942–1946, had served as ambassador to the Soviet Union, 1936–1938.

not do it. They had the Naval Attaché in Kuibyshev[55] ask for it. So now the Russians ask us for a radio transmitting station in New York! And we of course cannot do that—and must tell Navy they cannot ask for theirs.

July 19, 1942

Hot Springs, Virginia. Have been here a week—two week-ends—in the hope of a rest and a fresh point of view. I had the rest and feel refreshed—but the fresh point of view is elusive. I see the picture the same as when I left— and start back without a new vision.

July 22, 1942

Still discussion about safe conducts for enemy diplomats moving to and from posts. Our policy has been to deny them except when returning home. It came up yesterday again over Hertelendy, the Hungarian moving [from] Budapest to Argentina, and a Rumanian wife to Argentina. I thought we should refuse. This morning in the Secretary's conference (which he now holds instead of Welles) my decision was agreed to. This afternoon Boström[56] came in about them—he representing Hungarian and Rumanian interests. I told him "no." He had inferred differently from a conversation with Dunn and had cabled a probable approval and is somewhat embarrassed. . . .

July 25, 1942

Hull's speech—and it was well thought out and drafted—was finally completed and the President O.K.'d it. Night before last he delivered it over *all* the radio networks in this country—long and short wave. He asked me to stand by in case his voice gave out so I could take over—and I did sit by him in his office with more microphones than I had seen since the President delivered his address announcing the full emergency. But his voice lasted and I did not have to help out—which was much better. . . .

July 30, 1942

Stanley Reed, here for special Supreme Court session, has been staying with me.

Hired a new farm manager and let the present incumbent go after civil war threatened because the chauffeur held out gasoline from the farmer and the farmer retaliated by holding out milk from the chauffeur.

August 4, 1942

. . . Russia is in dire distress. India is on the eve of a convulsion. The Japs are advancing eastward along the Aleutian chain and are within 300 miles of

---

[55] Between 1941 and 1943 the Soviet government operated from the east central Russian city of Kuibyshev.

[56] W. Boström, Swedish minister to the United States.

Dutch Harbor. In either Russia or Alaska we can lose this war—and I feel so futile—so helpless to help.

Maisky—the Soviet Ambassador in London—made a reasoned logical statement to a group of M.P.'s—A second front *now* or it will be too late, with all the reasons. He wants a large expedition in Europe. And how is it possible? Under our mechanized system it takes 10 tons of shipping to keep *one* man transported and supplied. An army of 1,000,000 means 10,000,000 tons of shipping, on that route alone! Where are the ships? And *one* million men makes a small army these days—and our ships to unload on an hostile shore where there are land-based air forces!

Destructive raids on all shore installations and absolute command of the air would be needed to prepare the landing; and an enormous concentration of naval forces to convoy the fleet. The air forces *could* operate out of England till they got some place of their own on the continent—and it could not be allowed to fail! It must succeed if it is attempted.

If it succeeded it would move the 2nd front from our Atlantic beaches to western Europe. Tonight the 2nd front is about 50 miles east of Laurel. More than 400 ships have been torpedoed off the Atlantic coast.

Gandhi threatens a sit-down.[57] England threatens to arrest Gandhi. In the balance is "India for Japan." The crisis may be day after tomorrow. And with India lost—and Suez—and the Caucasus—an expedition in Europe would find a hard fight against a German army withdrawn from the receding Russian front.

So, tonight I feel sombre and unsatisfied with success in petty details which do not make any difference anyhow—as far as India, and Russia, and Egypt and Alaska are concerned.

August 5, 1942

... The news from Russia continues bad. Reports from Stockholm and other capitals hint of Russian suspicions of England, of bad morale among Russian troops, war-weariness, discouragement, etc. They are not heartening. They think England has failed to assist them and has kept at home an army which might have attracted enough German troops to face them to relieve the pressure on Russia.— The whole Russian picture looks bad—from our point of view—very bad—and yet can anyone fail to understand how the Russians feel about it?

My own peculiar thoughts lead to the continuing suspicion Russia will compromise with Germany—will make a trade, and yield in the Ukraine and

---

[57] On July 14, Gandhi warned the British to accept his "final" demand for immediate Indian independence or he would be unable to prevent widespread rioting by the masses. Gandhi's repeated threats finally caused the British to arrest him and other leaders of his All-India Congress on August 9.

Caucasus for a firm hand in Finland, Northern Norway—and perhaps Sweden. But of course no one agrees with me. That usually happens—even though I am sometimes right—or proven to be right *ex post facto*.

August 8, 1942

No labor to be had. The vegetable gardens lost in weeds—cows and chickens getting just necessary attention. It is all so discouraging.

India on the verge of civil disobedience. Gandhi made his address to his Congress yesterday. Hull talked with me this morning about a proposal to help save the situation. His recent speech is partly applicable to that situation —only those deserve independence who are willing to fight for it; those who want self-government must prepare themselves for that responsibility. In connection with those thoughts—India is unable to oppose Japan by force as the people are untrained and unarmed; so the only way to help herself toward independence is to permit those who are trained and armed to use her soil as a base and to help them to aid China and to conquer Japan with the understanding that upon the success of that undertaking India will share in the common victory by being able to attain independence. . . .

Meanwhile, several American divisions await orders at Karachi, and sections of the British fleet patrol the Bay of Bengal to oppose any naval activity by Japan—and another section of the world slowly assumes a more prominent role in the total state of war which is the struggle between domination by force on one side and regularized independence on the other.

August 26, 1942

Gripsholm landed in N.Y. this morning with her load of diplomats and others from the Far East—glad to get home. Joe Grew phoned me from N.Y. and will come in tomorrow. . . .

August 2 7, 1942

Joe Grew came in this afternoon—looking well. He wants to write some of his impressions and experiences for publication—convinced it is the best contribution he can make to the war effort and needed to arouse the people to a full realization of Japanese peril.

The Japs refuse to allow International Red Cross ship to carry supplies to our prisoners of war and internees into Japanese controlled waters. . . . I had the Red Cross people in and assisted in several cables—one for them to send through Red Cross channels and one for us through Swiss channel. Each needed editing and pointing up. A vain effort to get supplies to our people. It will be principally "for the record" as the Japs will not do it.

September 11, 1942

. . . I was called by Hull—just after his return from a Cabinet meeting. I had talked to him earlier—during the late morning—but we had not finished. He is very much disturbed by a personal scandal—a nasty rumor now in circulation. It is not new to him but it now has apparently gained considerable currency. I shall not repeat it. I heard of it some months ago and dismissed it as malicious, impossible and incredible. But he takes it very seriously, has made some inquiries looking to substantiation or disproof and is very much inclined to believe the story. He has no documentary proof but he has apparently had reports from sources he considers trustworthy, accurate and informed.[58]

I told him I could not believe the report—that I had too much confidence in the man, but that if it was to be bandied about in public it might be alluded to in print—or even published like the nasty charge about Senator Walsh, and if that should happen it would do irreparable harm to the State Department and to its present officers including himself and would also shake the whole Administration. He is uncertain as to his course—whether to report it all and wash his hands of responsibility or to let it take its natural course. He asked my advice. I had little to offer—beyond my own expression of incredulity—except that the person in question be confronted with the charge and given an opportunity to disprove it. That was momentary—impulsive— an honest way to deal with an able man and a nasty situation.

This all came about through a subject introduced at our conference on Wednesday morning when he brought up the subject of "leaks" of information from the Dept.—or attributed to the Dept. and the cause of the President making a decision to keep certain information from the Department—so it could not leak. Hull felt that keenly as a rebuke. He spoke of it pointedly and asked me to consider that situation. It just happened that at lunch that day I sat next to Arthur Krock. He told me he had an informer who gave him in advance news of an astonishing character, obtained by the informer from a "high official"—unnamed, and unknown to Krock, but information which could only come from someone in the intimate confidence of the Department or of the White House—or both. Churchill's visit to the U.S.—two weeks in advance—Early's departure from London two weeks before its announcement—and several other incidents *very* closely kept and others of greater importance. Krock then mentioned this nasty rumor and said his informant had told him that Hull had made certain remarks which he repeated verbatim about the person in question and concerning these rumors. I was astonished— and immediately realized that the informant could be the source of the leaks Hull had mentioned. Thinking that Hull could identify the few persons he had talked to in such an intimate way and that by a process of elimination

[58] See below, pp. 322–325 ff.

he might identify the actual leak to the informer, I went to him and told the Krock story—but not mentioning the scandal or the person concerned. I did tell him I thought he should see Krock and get from him if possible a first hand account of the whole picture of the possible leak. He agreed to do that and intends to do it soon. During our conversation *he* made some critical remarks of a personal kind to elucidate some of the difficulties he labored under officially and then hinted at this scandal in such a way I knew he knew of it. So today it came out nakedly into the open but never specifically named—and all because Krock was the recipient of leaky news of an entirely different variety. When he brought that subject up and Krock had already used that same unpleasant subject to emphasize that he had a direct line to Hull's own confidential conversation, I thought it well to tie the two together and to impress upon Hull the advisability of his having a personal talk with Krock to explore the source of the leak.

September 12, 1942

... I have accepted a proposal to facilitate the reception here of 1,000 Jewish children from France. Another effort will be made to move 6,000 or 8,000 to this hemisphere. They are derelicts. Their elders are being herded like cattle and ordered deported to Poland or to German work-shops. The appeal for asylum is irresistible to any human instinct and the act of barbarity just as repulsive as the result is appalling. But we can not receive into our own midst *all*—or even a large fraction of the oppressed—and no other country will receive them or even a few thousand, except that the President of Santo Domingo offers to receive and care for 3,500 children. Even Myron Taylor, with whom I discussed it on the telephone just before his departure, was doubtful of the sincerity of the offer of Trujillo. My personal reaction to that is that Trujillo was trying to embarrass [Avra] Warren.

September 26, 1942

A lot of things have gone under the bridge recently—none of the greatest consequence but all part of the picture. It is just impossible to set out each day a memo, though it would be very interesting if I could.

Taylor at the Vatican got talked to by the Pope on the theory we are trying to interfere with the humanitarian work of the Vatican in messages to and from prisoners of war. We are bound by the Geneva Convention of '29 and designated the Red Cross to do that—subject to censorship. The Vatican also does it but not under censorship. I have talked to the [Papal] Delegation here and pointed out how censorship regulations *and* the Trading with the Enemy law are being violated. Apparently the Delegation communicated with the Vatican and the Pope used it to offset some proposal Taylor made to him. That caused a cable in semi-frantic terms and we replied that when he returned we could talk it over here. The unusual thing about the reply was that, in order to reach Taylor before his last interview with the Pope this morning, it had to go in plain English and be sent radio from RCA in N.Y. direct to the Vatican radio station. Consequently—with all the world listening in—the message could say very little. The trouble with the system as it now works is that a designing person *can* use the Vatican facilities to transmit funds and directions to carry out a nefarious purpose—without the Vatican authorities having any knowledge of it. The censor is—and for months has been—pressing for a suspension of these activities. . . .

We have agreed to take 1,000 Jewish children out of France. Their families are to be deported to Poland. We have a request to make it 5,000—backed by Mrs. Roosevelt. We are ready to do it but I suggested the President be consulted on that before we acted and he is not able to be reached today. He is away. The President definitely declined to receive 15,000 of these Poles in the Near East. England has much thinly occupied territory in Africa—near there —but they want *us* to take them here. . . .

September 29, 1942
. . . Rabbi Wise's son and Dr. Goldman [*sic*][59] came in with Acheson. They asked to send food to Jews in Warsaw. I said we would agree to $12,000 a month to go to Portugal to buy food there if Treasury would license the transfer of credit. They were pleased. I told Norman Davis and he said his Red Cross would help over there. Then I went to Hull. . . . We again discussed the political reasons against the humanitarian impulses which had motivated us—and the necessity for us to take into consideration the *political consequences* if we are just to say "no" for military reasons and oppose the humanitarian decisions of large groups of our citizens—etc. He approved what I had done about the Jewish proposal and would send a letter for the President's consideration. . . .

October 1, 1942
. . . The decision [to send food parcels from Portugal was taken] on purely political grounds. The total amount of food involved is infinitesimal. But I did not want that policy along with others to serve as the basis for antagonisms toward us after this war . . . so that is our policy.

October 2, 1942
Talked to the Treasury group about the transfer of credits to conform to the policy on food parcels. Presented to them frankly the political considerations and based it squarely on political reasons. Then went into our Security

[59] Nahum Goldmann, representative in America of the Jewish Agency for Palestine, 1940–1946.

Committee. Finished the tentative draft of German surrender terms. I directed the drafting committee to go over the rough proposals for similar terms for Italy and Japan and get them in shape for discussion. General George Strong and [Norman] Davis[60] are old hands at this and are contributing a lot out of their experience.

October 6, 1942

In spare time the last few days, I have drafted a plan for another League of Nations to be submitted to our Security Committee, which has reached the stage—on paper—where we have arrived at security and want to plan how to keep secured!!

There will have to be some kind of an association of nations. It can be based on the ideas of confidence, pure motive and high principles—as was the first, or it will have to be based on the thought that Force is available to secure compliance. The Covenant still exists and can be reinstated. As a basis for discussion I drafted another—very much in the rough—carrying the prospect of Force. These are suggested modifications in Article X, as regards Mandates and as regards Sanctions—i.e. economic and financial sanctions.

I am committed to the idea of a League—by whatever means—and am not wedded to any form if another will more readily and securely attain the objectives.

October 9, 1942

The maneuvers to stop communication with the Axis from Chile became somewhat of a "bloomer"! The company voted to discontinue code messages to all non-American persons—and this cut off the British Ambassador! He did not use the radio to send code messages but seems to feel he is being denied something in theory; something he could not use. The trouble is that if he protests he and the Germans will be on the same side in that fight. So, we cabled London to ask if they would instruct him to let it go at that—and I asked the Embassy here to talk about it and they sent a young man to whom I explained it all and asked them to tell their Government.

In Buenos Aires too the problem is becoming more difficult because the Argentine Government is issuing decrees and preparing the way for taking control itself, which will not stop communication, much of which is against our interest as it concerns ships and cargoes of our vessels which the Axis uses to get a line of them and sink them. . . .

The Germans have not yet taken Stalingrad. It has been a costly experience

[60] General Strong, now head of Military Intelligence, War Department, had served as military adviser to various disarmament conferences held between 1925 and 1934. Norman Davis, now Chairman of the American Red Cross, was an adviser on reparations and finance at the Versailles Conference.

for them. Now they may just try to demolish it. Stalin himself is emphasizing the absence of a second front in Europe—to serve as a counter attraction—and is placing us—or trying to place us—in the position of having failed in our agreements. At the same time the Germans are paying a lot of attention to the possibility of our establishing a second front in Europe or Africa.

I submitted today to the Committee on Security the alternate suggestion for an association of nations based on the availability of force to secure peace —somewhat different in structure and organization from the League and avoiding the unanimity of decisions feature, without sanctions or mandates and with a revised Article X combined with Article XVII.[61]

October 11, 1942

Called in Swiss Minister about reprisals by Germany and counter-reprisals by England in hand-cuffing prisoners of war—contrary to the [Geneva] Convention of 1929. Expressed deep U.S. interest in maintaining practices provided by Convention and our fear of general deterioration of treatment of prisoners by all parties, which would be deplorable and a step backward. He will advise his Govt.

October 13, 1942

Had a long conference with Noel Hall[62] and his two assistants from the British Embassy to which I invited Norman Davis. I took up the question of all kinds of relief being sent into occupied areas in Europe—announced we too would send parcels to several areas—opposed sending bulk shipments— wished to get in coordinated policy with the British—proposed a re-examination of all phases (except parcels) and an agreement after reconsideration to which both Govts. would adhere. They agreed to recommend to their Govt. and advise us promptly when steps would be taken to implement the agreement.

October 21, 1942

. . . This morning the farm manager-foreman notified me he would leave. He does not get along with Connors at the barn—and I can easily understand as the latter is 76 and peculiar—eccentric—bossy. But it leaves me in bad shape—Connors only attends to horses. There are cows, chickens, vegetables, service to the house, kindling, fire logs, and some plowing and planting— more than two men can do well—but *no* labor to be had. So I am to be left short-handed—and without prospects.

[61] Article X of the Covenant of the League of Nations stated that in case of aggression the "Council shall advise upon the means" by which members can help restore peace. Article XVII provided that nonmember states "shall be invited to accept the obligations of membership in the League" in the event of a dispute with a member or with another nonmember. Appropriate action would be taken if this offer should be refused.

[62] British minister to Washington.

While at the Department, I have plenty of work—and when I get home I have more of it.

October 22, 1942

... This afternoon late talked with Hull. He reverted to Welles' recent speech criticizing Argentina and Chile [for not breaking diplomatic relations with the Axis]—which seems to be producing results in Chile. Anyhow, Hull does not like it. Thinks it a departure from "good neighbor" and a resumption of the "big stick." He is quite loquacious on the subject. He had been to the President and had told him so, and had expanded on the thought, saying that he would have sought to gain the collaboration of Mexico, Brazil and one or two more so that a joint approach could have been made in the name of the Hemisphere and by "good neighbors." He said he went on from there to direct the President's attention to the lack of team play in the Government —largely at the expense of the President because he lost power and dignity abroad because his regular Foreign Service was cheapened in the eyes of other Governments by being by-passed by a series of "Personal Representatives," "Special Ambassadors," etc. who visited capitals, assumed a temporary importance, were received by heads of state, in their special and important capacities, who failed to take our regular Ambassadors into their confidence, etc. etc. He quoted Standley, just back from Russia, as very critical and somewhat emphatic in his statements as to the diminishing importance attaching— under those circumstances—to our regular establishments, their loss of prestige, etc. I associated the situation he described [with] the one existing here, with a White House entourage taking away various activities and overlapping of functions and jurisdiction by various organizations and Departments.

November 3, 1942

There is a big movement on—going forward.[63] Hardly anyone knows— only a very few at the top. Each is tense—worried. No one can talk about it, but it can be only a day or so now till it becomes known. I am anxious and hope for its success. . . .

This is Election Day. I voted early. The Republicans will make some gains. Last night at the Pimlico fall sales I sold some horses at the regular auction. They went very low—as thoroughbreds do now because of the threat to the continuance of racing. One mare, one two-year-old and two yearlings brought only $800! . . .

But through the day and the night my mind is always on the big movement —it is probably the turning point of the war. Other things at the office shrink into minor importance—for they all depend now on this. Opposition speeches and candidates—like Wilkie [*sic*]—seem so far away and so false.

[63] On November 7 U.S. and British forces landed in North Africa. This was the first major Allied amphibious operation in this area.

November 4, 1942

We lost a lot of Congressmen and Senators in the election yesterday. The returns are not yet all tabulated but we know we lost about 41 members of the House, bringing the majority down very close to the vanishing point. Seven seats seem still in doubt. We may have a majority of five or six. In the Senate we lost eight and perhaps Murray[64] in Montana—but will have 54 out of 96.[65]

A special session of the War Communications Board this afternoon. Took over the Boston station WRUL—a very delicate job because of its beams to France and Norway and the absolute necessity of maintaining the [original] identity fo : this particular moment. The relation of that to the big movement [the invasion of North Africa] is obvious but as the movement is not known except to the military members and myself, the taking of the station was delicate. Hull tells me Germany knows now—but may not know all. She may put it on the radio any day now. She has withdrawn troops from the Caucasus and Stalingrad fronts. . . . We are keenly on watch. Our whole policy vis-à-vis France is liable to instant change—French vessels to be taken here and our whole [Vichy] policy discarded.

November 7, 1942

The President announced tonight we had entered French territory and called on the French people to be friendly, assuring them we arrived to help France. . . . As soon as I heard the President, I directed that all French vessels in U.S. ports be taken into protective custody and boarded; that the Embassy be placed under police guard "for their protection";—that all telegrams from [Vichy] be accepted but held; that the French and German radio be carefully monitored and I be advised immediately of any unusual development. . . .

The American movement is the culmination of a second front plan. It was carefully planned and kept a secret. Germany on the radio has commented upon the British naval force at Gibraltar but with no reference to our force en route. And so the war is extended again.

In talking with Hull yesterday about North Africa, he got on the lesson in the recent elections. He thinks, and so do I, that there has developed a psychological reaction against the radicals in the Government and their policies. I expressed it as—the President started out with an enormous majority composed of many kinds, each of which he had to recognize. He had, figuratively speaking, 18 horses he was driving. Some on the right and some on the left had to be kept on the tracks. Now he had a smaller team—say 10 horses—and

[64] James Murray, Democrat, U.S. Senator from Montana, 1934–1961.
[65] Congressional, state, and local election returns showed substantial victories for the Republicans, who gained forty-six House seats and nine seats in the Senate. The Democrats, however, retained control of both Houses.

he did not need to pursue the others with recognition as they were getting to be unpopular, possibly politically dangerous. Hull asked me to see the President and talk with him on the political phases of it all. I said when my conclusions were definite, I might ask him to talk with me.

November 8, 1942

We have landed successfully at Oran and Algiers, at Casablanca—and are looking for a landing in Tunis. There was some opposition at first, then acceptance of the situation—later, in Algiers, an armistice reported by the press. Also reported is a naval battle between the French fleet out of Toulon and our Allied forces in the Mediterranean near the coast of Africa.

The Secretary was intent on making some sort of statement to the press to the effect that this was fruition of his "Vichy" policy—rather than a negation of it or a repudiation.[66] Welles, Berle, Atherton, Murray and McDermott and I sat with him for several hours. He is very sensitive to criticism of his policy. Atherton and I agreed there should be no emphasis on Vichy—that this was "regional,"—Mediterranean, Egypt, Africa—the whole area—and that to emphasize Vichy would be a sign of weakness and pique. Welles mentioned that it should not be apologetic. Hull hesitated whether it was the moment to speak. The others said it was—emphatically—and tomorrow would be too late. I kept silent. I could not urge it and I had some reservations. He finally called the President and they agreed to do it. So a lot of historical data for the last two years was rather hurriedly put together—a short statement drawn— and it was decided Hull would just talk but not be quoted—directly.—What the press calls "attributed." Then I left—about 1:30 and came home. Since then the radio announces and quotes the A.P. at Vichy that France has severed diplomatic relations with us.

November 11, 1942

Armistice Day—celebrated in France by Germany denouncing the Armistice and invading heretofore unoccupied France. Germany also takes over Sardinia as Italy invests the Nice area. Our troops push east toward Tunis. All North Africa accepts our occupation. Fighting ceases at all points. The "Vichy" Government is a thing of the past. Our Embassy is closed, our people

[66] Hull had been subjected to savage criticism because he favored diplomatic contacts with the Fascist Vichy government. But the work of American diplomatic officials in France had proved to be indispensable in preparing for the North African invasion. Admiral William Leahy, ambassador to Vichy, had exercised strong influence to counteract German propaganda, to keep the French fleet out of German control, and to prevent French colonies from falling under complete Axis control. With the invasion, our true purposes were revealed and relations with Vichy severed. Hitler now seized unoccupied France, and French naval officers scuttled most of their ships at Toulon to keep them from the Nazis. See Robert Murphy, *Diplomat Among Warriors* (New York: Doubleday, 1964), pp. 49 ff.

under detention and to be removed to Paris till they are exchanged. Here the French Embassy staff is confined to their houses and the Consuls to be collected at Hershey, Pa.—pending exchange. We are now to withhold from Swiss the right to represent "Vichy," because there is no longer a "Vichy" Government—and allow them to exercise their informal good offices on behalf of the "French". . . . In Africa our Consuls are to be instructed to continue their contacts with the officials of those territories as formerly. There are various niceties and nuances of policy inherent in all this. It was all under discussion and decided in conference with the Secretary this a.m. . . . These last few days I have not left my desk from 9:15 to 7:30—even for lunch and have been too exhausted to enter any notes, though I much regret it for it has been most interesting. The Secretary calls me frequently and the unfolding of our decisions on policy around the rapid developments has been worthy of recording. . . .

November 18, 1942

. . . Over here we have had another war—consequent upon the success in Africa. That success opened up needy civilian populations behind our lines as we advanced. On the theory they need food and are apt to be an asset (militarily) rather than a liability if they are fed and contented, we are spreading some relief. Other relief was to go. It was to be handled from here and was (naturally) to have political angles and to carry certain political significance. Who was to do it here? That question posed—the war broke out. Wallace, his Milo Perkins, and Biddle, with a few more, wanted the power in their own hands and encouraged Berle to grab it and cooperate with them. Then Frankfurter and his crew acting through Acheson tried to grab it for themselves. Berle and Acheson were prosecuting this private war over jurisdiction. . . . Hull by-passed both and said he wanted Ray Atherton to do the job. Each said they would support Atherton and each promptly withheld cooperation and assistance in the thought Atherton would need to go to their organizations for help and would be taken into camp and used as a cats-paw. Hull got frantic but was inactive. To me it was a disgusting spectacle.

Atherton refused to act—under those circumstances. . . . It came to a near explosion yesterday. Atherton came to see me to pray for somebody to save the situation. I went directly to the White House and laid all the cards on the table before McIntyre.[67] He went in and talked it over with the President—returned—said the President understood—wanted a memorandum. I sat in my office and wrote a memo in the form of a draft letter purporting to go from Roosevelt to Hull—took it back to "Mac."

This morning, in my absence from the Department before the Ways and

[67] Marvin McIntyre, secretary to the President, 1933–1943.

Means Committee, the same draft arrived with a few additions from the President asking Hull if the text suited him. Acheson and Berle were there. They insisted there should be some clarification to that part which concerned the "staff of your own Department." Hull reluctantly yielded under Berle's aggressive and selfish technique and allowed Berle to take the letter to Mc-Intyre and redraft that part. When I returned this was presented to my attention. I telephoned "Mac" what to expect and not to change the text unless it be to make it stronger. He phoned me later—it was O.K. and the President would sign it in final form and send it over tonight or in the morning.—So that will settle that—put the authority in the Secretary of State and back him up with special instructions from the President. I have not appeared in it at all. Only Atherton, McIntyre and the President know I had anything to do with it. . . .

November 22, 1942

In the Department consultation and bickering about relief and reconstruction work in Africa continued. The President seems to have solved it independently by naming Governor Lehman[68] to handle the relief phases. He will probably act under Hull. It is not yet clear whether he will also have the economic and financial—including the fiscal—phases. Lehman will probably have Poletti[69] with him in January. I hope his appointment will have the wholesome effect of squelching the bickering and petty pushing toward selfish ambitions which has characterized the activities of the Secretary's entourage these last weeks. It has been a sad spectacle in these times. Berle, Acheson, Feis, Pasvolsky and their sattelites [*sic*] have been the principal offenders—and I have kept aloof. Nobody yet knows I had anything to do with the grant of authority and with laying the basis for the solution. But even with the fullest grant of authority any Secretary ever had, Hull was loathe to face the facts and exercise his authority by commanding his subordinates to obey and cooperate under his direction.

November 23, 1942

. . . Hull disclosed this a.m. he is not clear on just what authority Lehman would have with him—"We'll work that out." He hinted that Lehman would be eventually—perhaps soon—head of the whole United Nations relief program and that he would be accepted by all other governments. . . .

[68] Herbert Lehman, Democrat, governor of New York, 1933–1942, resigned that office to become director of the Office of Foreign Relief and Rehabilitation Operations. In 1943 he was appointed director general of the United Nations Relief and Rehabilitation Administration (UNRRA).

[69] Charles Poletti, Democrat, lieutenant governor of New York, 1939–1942, succeeded Lehman as governor and served during December 1942.

December 9, 1942

. . . In the Department personal jealousy and private wars for control continue. I stepped again from an observation post into the ring. . . . Lehman's role is Relief and Rehabilitation—of post-war character. The field is undefined. Its implications are vague. Its objectives somewhat hazy. Lehman's appointment was not popular "on the Hill." Dean Acheson and the Frankfurter contingent have appropriated him. Hull had to accept the appointment and his assignment to the Department but he considers Lehman to be administering a Presidential mandate—not a Departmental one—and has allowed events to take their own course. Today I talked with Hull on the subject and advised him to call Lehman in again to get an expression from him as to his plans and to call in his political advisors for Europe, Near East and Far East and present them to Lehman with the advice that he be free to consult them and ask them for help. This would be for the record. Hull knows that Wallace, Milo Perkins, the Frankfurter influence and the radical thought element will very probably seize control. . . . which neither the Congress nor the People will permit.

December 28, 1942

Long talk with Thurston[70] back from three years in Moscow and en route to be Minister to Costa Rica. He is one of my good younger friends in the Service. I questioned him about the possibilities of a Russo-German peace. He does *not* accept the thought—though he recognizes the possibilities. He feels that *if* it served Russia's long-range advantage it could be done—but does not see the advantage and thinks it would be hard for Stalin to sell the idea to his military chiefs and the Politburo—but that it could be done if decided upon. . . . He said they [the American Embassy] did *not* deliver to Russia the information we sent early in '41 that Germany would attack in June '41. It was withheld because our prestige was supposed to be not too high at the moment—but now considered a mistake to have withheld. . . .

Hull is worried again about "post-war" relief and reconstruction—particularly of the very liberal long-range sort and the unexpurgated Wallace variety. We both fear Congressional difficulties when the Lend-Lease appropriations and the renewal are taken up. I suggested he had better have a memo prepared showing just how far he is implicated and to what extent he has opposed everything.

[70] Walter Thurston, formerly American minister counselor in Moscow.

Preparing for Victory

The New Year got under way with fuel oil, gasoline and motor use restricted more than ever. At Montpelier we have no fuel oil for the house—only just enough to keep the service wing partly heated. All driving for pleasure is eliminated. So with a cold house and no use of the car we are comfortable in the hotel apartment—and walking to and from places necessary to reach. The farmer has oil enough to keep his house at fifty degrees but is helped by the kitchen stove. And so the whole East is rationed . . . .[1]

The French exchange of official personnel is having rough weather. We can only get our people out of France by trading official persons for them. Only six of the French (150 or more here) will go back to Vichy. To force them would be to send them to imprisonment—perhaps to death. They want to join Giraud.[2] A French-North African Military Mission is here and they want to join it or go to Africa to help them there.

Realizing that probable development I planned to use members of the German Armistice Commission we captured in Africa—for exchange. The Secretary of War agreed. We had them held in England "on ice." Now comes word they have been "processed"—i.e. put through a regime of the Army to obtain information. After "processing" they *cannot* be returned to the enemy. So there we are—nobody to exchange—except a handful of civilian officials of the consular type.

So I wired to Africa to see if there were any strays there—or in hospitals—who had not been "processed"; and am negotiating for the few captured at Djubuti—though they really are prisoners of England. On the outcome depends the fate of our people in France—whether they are to stay there for the duration—in confinement.

I offered the French to free their people here, allow them to go to French territory, to expedite their departure—if they would free our people and allow them to leave French territory—to Spain, etc. No answer yet but a negative one expected.

[1] Rationing, an old story in the belligerent and occupied European nations, was introduced to the United States during 1942. Control of rationing became a function of the Office of Price Administration.

[2] Admiral Henri Giraud had been captured by the Germans in May 1940. In April 1942, he made a dramatic escape to unoccupied France and from there to French North Africa. With Admiral Darlan's assassination in December 1942, Giraud succeeded him as high commissioner of French North and West Africa.

The de Gaulle leadership is very aggressive and not at all cooperative. De Gaulle himself and England desire him in charge of *all* French affairs—so England can run France after the war with de Gaulle in power there. It wouldn't work out that way—because they could not rely upon de Gaulle.

We make slow progress—if any—in Tunis, but Hitler is augmenting his forces. It looks like a tough battle over a protracted period—until we can get up men and materiel in sufficient quantity.

Congress opened its new session. They are not in a mood to help our general policies. We will have plenty of trouble with opposition to many of our programs. The immediate effect of it is that our Allies see that Roosevelt will not be a free agent; that he will have a critical and probably a recalcitrant Congress after the war. So they are planning to get along without us. The little Allies are huddling closer to England and will be in her pocket at the Peace Conference—amenable to her leadership—and we will have a hard time to keep from playing a lone—and losing—hand.

Wallace's speeches of post-war plans—and [Herbert] Lehman's appointment in charge of Relief and Reconstruction have done a lot to startle the people and to bolster the opposition in Congress.

January 11, 1943

The Germans put S.S. troops around our official Vichy group—presently confined at Lourdes—and announced they were taking them into Germany. We protested—can do little else. I conferred with the Army about the situation and their plans to hold all military members of the German Armistice Commission as prisoners of war but it seems too late to do anything to undo what they have done— So it looks like Tuck[3] and the 132 others would stay in Germany—though I shall try to trade them out with small fry. The French here are apparently to be sacrificed by the Germans—to stay for the duration.

109 billion dollars worth of budget went to the Congress today for the next fiscal year.

In staff conference this a.m. the Secretary approved Dunn as the member for State on War Planning Committee of the Office of Strategic Service—which is to be responsible for action and intelligence in enemy territory—subject to the Chiefs of Staff. All but one favored Dunn and he favored himself. The Secretary said very definitely he wanted his assistants to keep out of personal participation in such activities—out of the details.

January 14, 1943

The de Gaulle affair is developing more trouble and intensity. We have tried to keep politics out of the North African situation but de Gaulle and his crowd insist upon putting politics into it. He wants political leadership—so he

[3] S. Pinkney Tuck, foreign service officer, American counselor at Vichy, 1941–1942.

can control France after the war. England is encouraging him because England wants an authority in control of France post-war which will be amenable
to England's desires. So both have fostered the program in North Africa and
there is developing a schism there. Of course both de Gaulle and England
antagonized the French at Dakar and again at Oran.[4] Naturally there is no
controlling de Gaulle's faction there. But all not favorable to de Gaulle are
labled as "Vichyites"—which is not true. There are some Vichyites there—
some Monarchists—a lot of good Frenchmen who support neither de Gaulle
nor Vichy—and a progressing acrimony.[5]

Hull discussed it with me at some length yesterday. He has had a visit from
a *New York Tribune* man who brought some letters from their London man
(evidently in the British packet) which denounced United States policy, be-
labored Hull's policy and were altogether critical. Hull was asked why he
opposed de Gaulle. His answer—that he had offered him guns, ammunition,
supplies—to fight the Germans—all the help he could give him to fight and
that that was all the "opposition" he had put in his path; that he had been
hoping a long time to see de Gaulle and his men fighting Germany; otherwise
he had done nothing—particularly of an obstructive nature.

There are the beginnings of real criticism of Eisenhower[6] from those quarters—criticism of his military tactics and judgment as well as the political
accusations—but all with their root in politics. They will try to break him if
it can serve their political ends. And we may—partly on that account as well
as on the tactical situation—have serious trouble in Africa. I look on it with
considerable apprehension—and so does Hull. . . .

The Swiss Minister was in yesterday and said he had instructions to deliver
a protest from the Bey of Tunis about our attacking Tunis and calling the city

[4] In the crucial summer of 1940, Churchill was not prepared to take a chance on Pétain's
being able to pursue a policy independent of Nazi control. On July 3, 1940, therefore, he
ordered the sinking of major units of the French fleet at Oran. The Vichy regime promptly
broke diplomatic relations with Great Britain. During September, French and British
forces led by Charles de Gaulle attacked the French West African city of Dakar. After
several days of fighting, the regular French forces caused the De Gaulle expedition to
withdraw.

[5] The Allied assault on French North Africa, November 7, 1942, ended our diplomatic
dealings with the Vichy government. A bitter struggle among French factions now began
to determine who would lead the French forces. Much to the dismay of de Gaulle supporters, the Allies dealt with Admiral Darlan, former vice premier of Vichy. President
Roosevelt explained that France alone would determine her postwar government, and that
accepting Darlan's cooperation was only "temporary expediency." But liberals throughout
the free world denounced this policy, claiming that the distrusted Darlan was being groomed
as a Fascist dictator for postwar France. De Gaulle, they insisted, should be installed and
supported. American authorities decided it best to fight the war first and let the French
choose their government later.

[6] Dwight D. Eisenhower, Commander of the United States Forces in the European
theater, June 1942–January 1944. Eisenhower commanded the Allied invasion of North
Africa. In January 1944, he was named Supreme Commander of the Allied Expeditionary
Force in Western Europe.

an "open" city. I told him I would receive it and after conferring with Hull decided just to file it and ignore the message sent by the local potentate under control of the Germans. The President addressed him a letter at the time of our landing—amongst others addressed—and this is the first response though the others in one way or another have indicated their friendliness.

January 24, 1943

The top-side conference must be about if not already over in Africa.[7] One of the tops "found it impracticable" to attend in person [Stalin]. At least two are there—perhaps Chiang too. Out of it I hope will come some definite agreement which will be lived up to for military objective, plan and command; and another one to leave politics—such as the fuss about Darlan, Giraud, de Gaulle, etc.—out of the picture till a military decision is reached. The report of the conferees will be of great importance. The President should be able to report by the end of the week.

If he can make a report which will silence some of the carping critics of War Department and State policies the country will be better off. A few columnists and some radio broadcasters are ideologically opposed to us. Defeated by the success of our so-called "Vichy" policy they carry their animosity still and criticize us for being willing to fight with anybody who will fight Germany or Japan. They are partisans of Russia—forgave Russia for her 1939 treaty with Hitler, applaud the Russia which fought against the German attack, as we all do—but can't admit that a Frenchman who was overpowered by Germany in 1940 is to be trusted 10 feet if he has finally got in a position where he can and will fight Germany in 1943 and wants to fight with us! They are quite illogical—but their ideological predilections for Communism will not let them accept the help against Germany of the men who opposed Communism in France and who led their country to defeat because of the situation developed in France by the Communists before, under and after Blum.[8] These critics are themselves the spokesmen of an intellectual cabal characterized by these ideological idiosyncrasies. They and the large number of others who are also articulate are carefully placed in key positions—none of which harbors well for a calm future. Unless somebody puts a firm hand to the throttle the engine is going to get out of control some day. Yesterday I talked with Hull on the whole picture. He is very pessimistic of the future unless a strong hand is applied.

[7] At the Casablanca Conference, January 14–24, President Roosevelt and Prime Minister Churchill declared that the war would be fought until "unconditional surrender" had been secured. Agreement in principle was reached for an invasion of continental Europe—the location, though, was to be determined. The heads of government also appointed General Dwight D. Eisenhower Supreme Commander of the North African theater.

[8] Léon Blum, premier of France, 1936–1938.

February 12, 1943

For the last month Norman Davis, who is Chairman of the Subcommittee on Security has been absent because of his health and I have been serving as Chairman. The Subcommittee had been asked by the Political Committee to present its plan for the security measures to be undertaken by the International Organization. After the discussion got under way several weeks ago it occurred to me that an international air force at the disposal of the central organization and to be the force of the international organization had more possibilities for deterring a violation of the peace or a flagrant aggression than any other form of military or naval activity. I wrote a memorandum about it and gave a copy to Professor Shotwell[9] who immediately accepted the idea. We had some difficulty in persuading the other members of the Committee. During the last four sessions there has been a great deal of discussion and drafts and redrafts and continuing drafts have been made of a plan which can be submitted. Finally today there was unanimous agreement to accept the air force as the most expedient and rapid means of deterring if not preventing a flagrant violation.

It is now proposed that pending the time between the cessation of hostilities and the establishment of an international association on a permanent and satisfactory basis that the Big Four—the United States, England, Russia and China—will assume responsibility for maintaining the peace and will act in concert to do so.

After the establishment of an international force on a satisfactory basis it is now agreed that there shall be an air force of reasonable size at the disposal of the council of the International Organization. In case of a violent aggression or threat of imminent aggression—such as an order of mobilization—the council may immediately dispatch the air force. In the meantime by disarmament agreement anti-aircraft guns will have been abolished. The dispatch of an air force to the area of disturbance would carry the immediate threat of bombing cities, transportation lines and industrial plants. In case that threat is ineffectual the armies will be contributed by the members and will proceed to the scene of action. The beauty about the air force is its mobility and the fact that it can travel within the space of four or five days from Central Europe to Central South America, to Central Africa, or to Southeastern Asia or to Eastern Asia. In the meantime the international society will take such steps as may be possible to force a settlement of the dispute by peaceful means, but if that does not show signs of succeeding the forces of the different contingents from the various government members will be called and will proceed by slower stages.

[9] James Shotwell, Columbia University professor emeritus of international relations 1942–1965, and member of the State Department's Post-War Planning Committee, 1942–1944.

Part of the objection to it was the thought that the United States Senate would not accept such a provision. My answer was that the temper of the people of the United States and the temper of the Senate today was that they would go to any reasonable length to agree to measures which would prevent a repetition of the present difficulty and would insure that every step would be taken to make improbable the recurrence of a world war or even of a serious local war which might spread. The insurance which they would have is the fact that the air force could not operate against the United States without the consent of the United States, because the Big Four would be represented on the executive committee of the council and the executive committee could move only by unanimous consent. So that we would not consent to submit the United States to bombardment, though all the smaller countries in the world and the larger countries of Germany, Italy and Japan would be subject to the combined decision of the Big Four.

Without having made any memoranda recently, I have been very much occupied with a lot of different activities. Amongst them I presented the China Treaty for the abrogation of extraterritorial rights and had it accepted unanimously by the Foreign Relations Committee, and the day following it was accepted without dissenting voice by the Senate.[10]

I have been laying plans for presenting the trade agreements program to the Senate and have had several discussions with them and today lunched with O'Mahoney[11] in which the basis was paved for further discussions, and which I have hope will permit him to support the program. His support is almost essential, because he is the ablest member of the opposition in the Senate. . . .

February 16, 1943

Hull is still having his portrait painted. He calls me in from time to time. The face of the portrait is too flat, stoical, expressionless. But I have not ventured to criticize. He sits on a raised elevation—I on a chair to his right at the corner of the canvas, and the soldier-artist paints away. Whether he is discreet or not I do not know but if he is not he gets many a bit of news to peddle around. This morning Hull took up Lehman during his posing hour and then expressed growing fear of the plans and purposes of the "radical boys"—as Hull calls them—[Milo] Perkins, Wallace, the Agricultural givers

---

[10] In October 1942, the United States and Great Britain announced their intention to relinquish extraterritorial rights in China, rights which had prevailed for a century. The three nations now negotiated new and equal treaties shorn of the humiliating features which the Chinese had resented. The treaties were signed on January 11, 1943. On February 1, the Senate Foreign Relations Committee favorably reported the treaty to the Senate. But contrary to Long's entry, actual ratification did not occur until May 20.

[11] Joseph C. O'Mahoney, Democrat, U.S. Senator from Wyoming, 1934–1953, 1955–1961.

and generally the post-war spreaders of peace, plenty and pulchritude. Lehman is more practical and sees a coming conflict within his own dear jurisdiction. Hull evidently let him talk himself into a projected picture of collision and then the Secretary showed him how he would be cut under, criticized, opposed and interfered with—and elucidated the predicament with some of his own experiences with that same coterie. Their most recent trick is to propose a coalition of Wallace, Perkins, Wickard[12] *and* Lehman to sit with Hull (or Welles) and take over foreign policy!

I took up the conversation there and told Hull the best thing for him to do would be to disconnect Lehman from the State Department—to set him up as an independent agency under the President. That way the Governor would have his own bailiwick but Hull would not be held responsible for his acts. Now he is in the State Department and carries on his plans and signs "Hull" to cables. Some of the things Hull would not approve and they go without his knowledge, but he is responsible, for Lehman is under him. If he was an independent agency he would have to submit his cables to us and we could act in the coordinating capacity over policy we perform for the rest of the Government in foreign affairs.

Eisenhower is Commander in Chief of all forces there now—a result of "Casablanca."

I sent a request to Japan to receive medicines for our sick in prisoner and internee camps to treat them for beri-beri, dysentery and other terrible diseases from which they are suffering—to send supplies by airplane to some convenient place. And I am trying to get a Red Cross ship with larger supplies and foods—a new trial—as soon as the Red Cross, Army and Navy can agree on the text of the proposal. It was all agreed to in principle in my office last week but they have not got a text agreed to yet.

Anthony Eden is coming over. I hope that will help the joint effort. I have been and have been remembered as a critic of his policy vis-à-vis Italy in '35—so I probably will not see him here. . . .

Phillips is having an unhappy few days at New Delhi.[13] Gandhi is fasting again in protest; the Indian Government will not release him unconditionally; the natives are pleading Phillips to intervene, their papers attacking him —and Phillips crying for instructions.[14] When pushed to ask Roosevelt to intervene he replied he had cabled the President but had not heard! This is

---

[12] Claude Wickard, Secretary of Agriculture, 1940–1945.

[13] William Phillips was sent to New Delhi as the personal representative of the President. He held the rank of Ambassador.

[14] The main political development in India during 1943 was the continuance of the deadlock between British authorities and the various Indian groups over the form and extent of the next step toward Indian self-government. Gandhi, in an effort to force the British to release him, began a three-week fast on February 10. This hunger strike quickly centered the world's attention upon the frail, seventy-three year-old leader of the independence movement. The British government of India, however, remained firm in its policy.

the first time Phillips has been in contentious territory and under attack—and he doesn't like it.

March 11, 1943

For some time I have made no entries in this irregular and spasmodic record. Events have changed little. Russia still advances except that the Germans have counter-attacked with effect near Kharkov; Rommel still sits on the Tunisian line with the British in Tripoli behind him and an Allied force to the west of him—albeit his position becomes more precarious; another Jap convoy sunk in the southwest Pacific; a tax bill still in gestation in the Congress and liable to be there a long time yet; and opposition to the domestic policies of the Administration under heavier attack in the Congress—except that Lend-Lease is almost unanimously approved.

Many resolutions are appearing in Congress to consider or investigate various phases of foreign relations—indicative of a desire to take over in spite of the Constitution or to embarrass the President. There is now a plan to give Administration support to a plan to have the President associate himself with a Committee for the purpose of keeping Congress informed in more detail. I have done a good deal of that by my appearances before the Senate Foreign Relations Committee—and it has been very helpful.

Two diplomatic incidents have contributed to the further estrangement of the Congress. Hayes[15] in Madrid made an unauthorized speech outlining how much we had done for Spain—by furnishing gasoline and oil etc.—when we are on short rations of them here. Members of the Congress and of the public blew up! Hayes is coming home for consultation and I have been engaged today in getting an answer to the House Committee to a resolution asking for information. Welles signed it tonight.

Then Standley stated in Moscow that the Russian people had not been told we had given them any help!—another unauthorized remark. The same explosions—plus the press! And Standley may come home. Litvinov made a good and timely speech today at the Lend-Lease anniversary luncheon which I attended—but the trouble is deeper seated than to be cured by a few speeches. There has been sown a seed which will grow resentment. . . .

March 13, 1943

The "Free French"—the de Gaulle element—make the trouble here today. They are being used by the anti-State Department clique to make it difficult for us. . . .

March 15, 1943

Income tax returns and payments due today—and many, many people spent their war wages in a higher scale of living and saved nothing with which to

[15] Carlton J. H. Hayes, ambassador to Spain, 1942–1945.

pay. Fortunately mine was paid—in full—but it was not as large as I had expected.

Giraud made a fine speech from North Africa yesterday. It was a completely satisfactory and reassuring expression of his position. The carping critics here have expected us to make statements or do things in Africa which it was not proper for us to do. It is French territory and under French local authorities—with Giraud over them. We are there as comrades fighting Germany—not as conquerors speaking for the French or telling them what to say. Now, it has been said—but I suppose the critics will find plenty more to carp about, for they are playing politics and want to take over authority and put their own radical schemes in practice—their ideologies. . . .

There is on foot a resolution for the Senate, sponsored by prominent members of *both* parties, to adhere to the "Atlantic Charter," approve a Society of Nations and support the Executive in the big aims of the peace settlement. In the present state of political feeling in the Congress—both House and Senate —it would be a very fortunate and most welcome development for it would take partisanship out of our foreign relations. If this develops and is adopted it will permit of a *national* foreign policy and insure America's cooperation in postwar settlements—provide for it in advance—and permit the negotiation and adoption of treaties during the war which would not only lay down the general principles of the peace but set out agreed methods of implementation. In fact it would *promise* one of the most important developments of our time in American politics. Whether, once the resolution was adopted, the Senators would continue that spirit of cooperation and non-partisan advice is another question—but it would be a good start.

March 16, 1943

Secretary had his staff meeting this a.m. The first since several weeks before he went away. He brought up the question of my jurisdiction over Congressional matters and asked them all to clear through me and went so far as to suggest that I should make all appearances before Committees of the Congress. When he turned to me and asked what I thought of his remarks I said I felt it gave a pretty large order—and that as to appearances I felt my colleagues or those others in the Department whose duty it was to cover specific questions were better qualified than I to testify before Committees but it would be in the interest of better results and orderly process if I should be kept in touch with; that possibly I could help and at least would know what was going on and how it should proceed.

After several other discussions of policy and practice—he took up a telegram from the National Maritime Union—a C.I.O. subsidiary—who wanted him to receive a delegation, and asked me to handle it and receive them. This I did this afternoon—a subcommittee of five—who thought and alleged the

Department was Fascist, who criticized our Spanish policy and of course North Africa and "Vichy." I talked with them freely, frankly and fully—for one hour and twenty minutes—covered trade with Spain—both ways—in detail—and why; politics in North Africa—military command—and why; refugees in North Africa and Spanish internees in whom they were most interested—how many and where etc.—what we were doing and had been trying to do—and why. I covered the whole field, asked them to submit dates, places and vessels they alleged were "cheating" by carrying to the enemy from Spain or fueling subs at sea—thanked them for their help, expressed interest and desire to receive specific data and got them in a better humor by the time they left.

They are a hard lot to deal with. They claim the "privilege"—it is not a right—to supersede their *duty* as citizens of a country at war to strike and re-fuse to load a vessel bound for Spain and thereby to assert their authority superior to the Government offices—including Army and Navy—in carrying out policies which are part of war-time strategy. They are more Fascist than any influence I know in the Government when they take that position.

March 17, 1943

David Sarnoff[16] of R.C.A. came in this a.m.—had seen Welles last evening —talked merger of international broadcasting companies. He favors—but thinks all kinds should be included, telephone, cable, radio telegraphy and voice broadcast. I have been working on the same subject—discussed it at length at Board of War Communications last week and led movement last May to make a recommendation to the President which is as yet unapproved. . . . Right now in North Africa Makay Radio has a contract to operate a cir-cuit with P.T.T. at Algiers but P.T.T. does not agree with the rates so no mes-sages are sent! And all our *news* is filtered through London—even from our Army headquarters—but the situation exists everywhere that any foreign Government in its territory can practically dictate terms to our people in establishing a circuit. Unified control here would stop that.

March 21, 1943

Listened to Churchill over the radio. That part of his speech devoted to foreign policy seemed to corroborate the theory of the recent London *Times* editorial—which Eden disavowed over here. The gist of Churchill's story is that Europe is a European problem and should be treated on a regional basis. England and Russia should take charge after the war, organize it into political entities, supervise their actions, keep them out of wars with one another and get a blank check from the United States to support that system.

[16] President of the Radio Corporation of America, 1930–1947, and chairman of the board of directors, 1947–1965.

The rest of the speech related to domestic issues and had a statesmanlike broad vision and long-range view but he will be a magician indeed if he—or anyone—can work out the program which includes operation of the Beveridge plan from cradle to grave—redemption of the national debt on war cause in a limited number of years—reduction of taxes to a point higher than pre-war levels—retention of the private property system and individual initiative—and government control over industry, business, recreation, health, insurance, babies, food, tariffs and empire coordination.

March 23, 1943

A cable circulated in the Department today from Madrid advised Hayes had been told by his Argentine colleague that he and the Portuguese Ambassador were approached by the Rumanian Ambassador in Madrid under instructions from his Government to ask the Argentine and Portuguese Governments to present Rumania's request for a separate peace with the Allied Powers—the United Nations. The cable was received in the Department at 9:30 p.m. the 21st!! Neither the Secretary nor the European Division had received copies and did not know of it till I asked about it. That is poor administration in the Department!

The circumstance reminds me of the Bulgarian appeal to us in 1918. It was the rift in the clouds then—and circumstances followed quickly one on another till Germany collapsed. This is a little different. Germany is practically in occupation of Rumania today and Rumania's object must be to be entirely occupied so as to curry sympathy with us Allies and thereby help herself at the Peace Conference—if any. But this might be useful. At my suggestion it was repeated to Steinhardt in Ankara hoping the news would reach Turkey and might weaken her position so as to wander, if not rush, into our camp. The effect of that on Bulgaria would be softening and if we could get air bases in either territory so as to bomb the Rumanian oil fields, Germany would be bereft of motive power. Steinhardt is able and resourceful and might be able to use it to advantage. Also from Istanbul came word Rumania was withdrawing her armies from the Russian front and was having internal difficulties.

March 24, 1943

Wellington Koo[17] came in for a very pleasant visit and will dine with me shortly. He looks older but we flattered each other by insisting neither had changed much during the 25 year interval. At least we would easily have recognized one another. I did see him once during the "interval"—at Geneva for a fleeting moment in 1933 when I was on my way to Rome.

[17] Chinese ambassador to Great Britain, 1941–1946.

Held the first session as Chairman of the Committee on Political Planning. The four political advisors, the Economic Advisor and Pasvolsky of Research and Postwar are the members—Chapin[18] secretary. I started with the Rumanian peace rumor and the Japanese executions—to see if the former could be used aggressively to our advantage and to estimate the cost or advantage of publicity for our note in the latter. I think the Committee can be used to foreign policy advantage.

March 25, 1943

Talked to Hull today about Churchill's speech and told him what I thought and felt about it—that it was—in its foreign aspects—most discouraging as choosing a balance of power scheme and a regional treatment—both of which were contrary to our concept of our relationship and to our objectives to secure cooperation from all nations; that the record was there and in effect was a confirmation of the London *Times* editorial—made deliberately while Eden is here—and in the future can be pointed to as an "I told you that in 1943." Further that Eden should be asked to interpret, in writing, while here, specific phases of it and to get his interpretation confirmed by the Prime Minister. Otherwise we would be deserted in the postwar period, would have to fight Japan alone, would be isolated better than the dreams of our own isolationists—as to political responsibility, commerce, communications and all.

He does not like some aspects of it but thinks Churchill was speaking for home consumption and is not to be taken too seriously in his remarks— specifically he was laying the basis for shelving the Beveridge Plan.

Accepting that possibility I maintained that the record was now written and if we let it lie as is we cannot complain if a year from now my fears prove justified. I still thought clarification in writing was in order.

He may approach the subject in his talk with Eden tomorrow, but my guess is that it will ride as is. He certainly does not attribute to it the gloomy importance I do.

March 28, 1943

Sunday. Last week was exhausting. It was just one of those periods which produce more work than usual. Yesterday I was tired to begin with and by late afternoon could hardly keep going. I left the Department at six, went to my room, lay down on the bed with all my clothes on and immediately fell into a profound sleep. Awoke from time to time, but I slept till eleven this morning. By tomorrow I hope to be fairly normal again—but my reserves of nervous and physical energies are lacking. There is no chance to build them

[18] Selden Chapin, foreign service officer, State Department assistant, and executive secretary of the Committee on Political Planning, 1942–1944.

up even if my age and the biological aspects of my stomach would permit it under fairly normal conditions.

Roosevelt, Hull, Welles and Eden are sparring around in their continuing conversations. Eden will not yield one iota in their North African political policy, which is practically in opposition to us. Strang[19] who is with Eden is the one directly in charge of those affairs. De Gaulle is their baby. Giraud is not pliable to their future plans and so they are in opposition to him—and to us, because we are looking to him locally to play ball behind our military lines. But there is no change in the British position. . . .

March 30, 1943

Trade Agreements. Yesterday I conferred with Hull's technical people on the legislative program and we agreed. This morning I had a long session with Hull. I proposed—1) an extended time, three years *and* thereafter until ended by act of Congress; 2) additional latitude of action, reduction range to be increased from 50% to 75% (down to 25% of schedules)—those two being additional powers to us. In return we would 3) incorporate mandatory provision for the "escape clause" and 4) submit each agreement to Congress for disapproval in a stated period. . . . But Hull would not agree to submit to Congress for disapproval. Without that, the others fall. The Congress would give additional authority for an extended time *if* it had a voice in it—but not otherwise. So that was a valiant attempt. Now the program reverts to a straight three-year renewal.

March 31, 1943

Hull seemed to change his mind on the Trade Agreements program I proposed to him the other day. Today he wanted me to go with Sayre and talk to Senator George to seek his advice on doing the very thing he had refused to do. So we went up and presented the picture. I laid emphasis on the postwar phase—on spanning the gulf of economic chaos which is sure to exist for a while—on the non-partisan and statesmanlike approach to the subject which present conditions justify.

George has it under consideration and will talk with us again tomorrow noon—after conferring if he has a chance with a few of his colleagues both Democrats and Republicans. After a thorough conversation his thoughts were to the effect a plain renewal for three years could probably not be passed; that coupled with the veto by the Congress probably could—and easily; to extend the three years "until the Congress by Concurrent Resolution may" end the authority might also pass—in view of the end-of-the-war argument *if* coupled with the veto by Congress; that the increased latitude—from 50% to 75% probably would not pass even if coupled with the other features but

[19] William Strang, British Assistant Undersecretary for Foreign Affairs, 1939–1943.

there was a chance it might. He would be in favor of it all—but he could not tell the temper of the Senate—but he would talk again tomorrow.

April 1, 1943

The Secretary in conference with us this a.m. expressed fear of weakening his consistent position by offering "veto" to the Congress on Trade Agreements. After an hour and more he decided—unless George should have widely separate views as result of his conference—to adopt the three-year limit without any other limitations or additions.

George had his conference with his colleagues—six or seven of them. He reported to the same effect—a straight renewal—with no additions but thought it would be easier to get it through the Senate if it were a request limited to one year.

So the decision was for three years flat—and a bill to that effect sent to Doughton[20] to introduce tomorrow.

If I had my views prevail there would have been no fight. Everybody would have been in agreement. Now we will have a stiff fight to get the three-year conditional bill and may get it amended by adding the provision to submit to the Congress—or get licked.

April 3, 1943

Have been in bed for some days with a virus in my lungs, but managed to conduct a lot of activity over the phone. Had a hard time getting a proper person to head the delegation for the Bermuda Conference.[21] Myron Taylor would not let us use his name. Mr. Justice Roberts said the Chief Justice [Harlan Stone] refused to let him off. President Seymour[22] of Yale first accepted—then said his trustees objected—and withdrew. Finally we got Harold Dodds of Princeton. Rabbi Wise and a few of his colleagues object to Sol Bloom—as not being a representative of Jewry. I reacted that he was a representative of America.

Detail arrangements are being carried out and it is planned they leave New York by plane on Friday.

The Jefferson Memorial was dedicated at noon. I was to have sat in the President's stand but could not attend on account of my illness—though I am allowed out this afternoon. I am also a member of the Jefferson Bicentennial Commission—and this is the 200th anniversary of his birth.

[20] Robert L. Doughton, Democrat, U.S. Representative from North Carolina, 1911–1953, and chairman of the House Ways and Means Committee, 1933–1947, 1949–1953.

[21] During April 1943, an Anglo-American conference met in Bermuda to consider "more effective governmental action on behalf of refugees."

[22] Charles Seymour, president of Yale University, 1937–1950.

April 20, 1943

The "Bermuda Conference" on Refugees has been born. It has taken a lot of nursing but is now in existence. One Jewish faction under the leadership of Rabbi Stephen Wise has been so assiduous in pushing their particular cause—in letters and telegrams to the President, the Secretary and Welles—in public meetings to arouse emotions—in full page newspaper advertisements—in resolutions to be presented to the conference—that they are apt to produce a reaction against their interest. Many public men have signed their broadsides and Johnson[23] of Colorado introduced their resolution into the Senate.

One danger in it all is that their activities may lend color to the charges of Hitler that we are fighting this war on account of and at the instigation and direction of our Jewish citizens, for it is only necessary for Nazi propaganda to republish in the press of neutral countries the resolution introduced in the United States Senate and broadsides bearing the names of high Government officials in order to substantiate their charges in the eyes of doubting neutrals. In Turkey the impression grows—and in Spain it is being circulated—and in Palestine's hinterland and in North Africa the Moslem population will be easy believers in such charges. It might easily be a definite detriment to our war effort.

The Post-War Security takes time each week—seemingly too much time on certain subjects. Trade Agreements supervision, Ways and Means Committee presentations and personal talks with George of Georgia on the maneuvers to follow in the Senate Finance Committee. He and McNary, the Republican leader, have been talking about possible amendments and the latter talking with Joe Martin,[24] the Republican House leader—and then George to me. George is weakening a little and would rather not have a fight. Hull feels any compromise by us will react immediately and adversely abroad to our general postwar plans by convincing our allies as well as our opponents we will be isolationist again and assume no responsibility for Europe or the world. And I agree—but I too would like to see a losing fight avoided. It looks pretty slim in the Senate—but we ought to get by in the House. I talk with Hull about it daily and we are trying now to bolster George by getting some favorable publicity in the big papers in his state —like the Atlanta *Constitution*.

April 21, 1943

... During the morning Hull talked at length with me—earnestly and heatedly on politics—the effect on our world situation of the emphasis being laid on a multiplicity of attentions paid to and publicity about postwar plans

[23] Edwin C. Johnson, Democrat, U.S. Senator from Colorado, 1937–1955.
[24] Joseph Martin, Republican, U.S. Representative from Massachusetts since 1925.

and dreams. We have each—for many months—feared the effect on the war psychology of this country. He is very much disturbed and wants me to find some solution in the Senate. He thinks the President pays too much attention to Wallace and to Welles and gives them too much latitude and relies too much on their recommendations—considering their lack of political experience and judgment. . . . And Hull sees the Trade Agreements legislation as an acid test. If the bill is amended or defeated he sees the nations of the world taking that as a sign America will not assume her international burden after this war any more than it did in 1919–20. The U.P. poll of the Senate showed 32 against an "International Police Force"—whatever that might be defined to be—and that is the 1/3 necessary to defeat ratification of any treaty. Hull thinks the President plays "favorites" too much for the good of the country's better interests.

Out of it all comes a job for me to try to straighten out the Senatorial mind so it will realize that the sober philosophy of Hull will eventually guide the President and all the ballyhoo from Wallace and his clique will not be seriously adopted as Government policy—a job I shall undertake with deliberation and after careful thought, if it is practicable at all. . . .

April 22, 1943

Had a long talk with George to give him the answer to the proposal of McNary and Joe Martin. I told him we could not recede from the three-year term or accept any compromise [over extending Reciprocal Trade Bill] *because* just as soon as we did every Foreign Office in the world would say the United States is drawing out of its commitments and refusing to take part in any post-war responsibilities. Just as soon as that opinion—even now current —was given substance by any State Department concession or other indication of policy the other Allied Governments would immediately begin to draw away from us and to set in motion their own substitute plans for their respective post-war activities. England and Russia would count us out and proceed to plan to divide up spheres in Europe amongst themselves. China would be out on a limb by herself. The smaller nations would throw up their hands and shy away from any commitments with or concerning us. And we would be left with a Pacific war all by ourselves. The Trade Agreements are the first but for that reason the most important of the post-war plans partly because they were the only form extant of international instrumentality to bolster commerce in the period after the fighting and until political stability is achieved. He understood and rather expected that answer and said he would tell McNary today the Democratic leadership would stand pat on the three-year provision.

The Bermuda [Refugee Conference] delegates are sending us some difficult questions to answer. I worked late this evening with Dunn, Atherton, Murray and Brandt outlining our reply to the use of North African territory for an internment camp for German, Czech and stateless Jews now in Spain. To put them in Moslem countries raises political questions which immediately assume a paramount military importance—considering that of the population of 18 million behind our long lines 14 million are Mohamedans. The whole Mohamedan world is tending to flare up at the indications that the Allied forces are trying to locate Jewish people under their protection in Moslem territory. Palestine is verging on the dangerous already, rumblings of definite import are evident in Syria, North Africa is showing its resentment and in Iraq and Iran the situation is lending encouragement to the credibility of German propaganda broadcasts. Altogether it is a bad tendency.

May 7, 1943

The Bermuda Conference adjourned and the delegates back. They met with the Secretary yesterday and me—went over their report. We recommended to the President the grant of certain authority to Myron Taylor, the U.S. man on the Intergovernmental Committee, to carry on the work.[25] Some specific steps can be taken—are being—and can be furthered—out of Spain to North Africa—out of Greece, etc. to Cirenaica—some to Palestine—possibly more to Ethiopia and to Madagascar.

The Trade Agreements bill out of Committee and up on floor of House next Monday—vote by Wednesday—and fear limiting amendments.

May 12, 1943

Churchill arrived yesterday, unheralded, and [Eduard] Beneš today with the fanfare indicating the head of a state—no matter how small. The ceremony is almost under my office window—guards at the side entrance to the White House, Marine band, motorcycle escort, saluting with arms, company formations—and the national anthems. So I have it forced into my consciousness.

Also today we lost a round in the Congress. The House—in committee—accepted an amendment to the Trade Agreements Act cutting it down to two years instead of the customary three. Only two Republicans joined us and we lost about 25. The score 196–153.

It is attributable in part to antagonism against the Administration and the rest is Republican desire to reassume authority—to terminate grants of power to the Executive—partly anti-Roosevelt and partly anti-Democrat.

We had a long conference with Hull this morning. He had been approached

[25] The Anglo-American Conference on Refugees had recommended that the Intergovernmental Committee, formed by the Evian [France] Conference of 1938, be enlarged and its mandate extended. This committee had been empowered to "undertake negotiations to improve the present conditions of [refugee] exodus and to replace them with conditions of orderly emigration."

by Rayburn et al. with a proposal to compromise on two years and prevent any other amendments. He had talked to the President—and during the session talked to Jimmy Byrnes to see if the list of recalcitrants (24 of them) I gave to the White House yesterday had been operated on. They had not. Eleven a.m. today was a little late to operate before twelve noon.

Welles, Sayre and I and several of his technical advisors on trade matters— and all but one—advised [Hull] to get licked rather than himself agree to an amendment which would make him responsible for an act which would indicate that the United States was shortening up its commitments so they would not extend into the post-war world. It would be a retrogression, etc. He was inclined himself that way—and that was the decision—to stand pat and get beat if they beat us. And they did. There is a bare chance tomorrow on roll call before final passage to regain the ground in the House—but the chance is slim. The Senate will be hard too.

The vote is *not* on the merits of the bill. It is just a manifestation of political strength and a warning to this and to all other Governments that America will probably slip back into its shell again after this war as it did in the last return to an "isolation" point of view and withhold cooperation in whole-hearted manner after this war.

I see the signs I saw in 1918.

I hope not to see the consequences.

Tunis is over. Those of the enemy who were not killed in battle or destroyed in attempts to escape surrendered. Prisoners are estimated at 150,000. That opens the Mediterranean and paves the way to Europe.[26]

May 13, 1943

Phillips back from India—says the British are obdurate about Gandhi and about self government. He expects to return but told President he was an embarrassment to him under present conditions—would return if desired— but can do no more unless British make some concession to the Indians—and can do no more than he has now done. Also says the British are doing *nothing* in a military way—Wavell only pecking at Burma—no prospect of a real expedition there—and without the recapture of the Burma Road supplies to China cannot proceed. Also that Chanault [*sic*] and Stilwell[27] are at odds and are here now to straighten out their difficulties. One wants infantry, the other air force—and neither accepts the other's view. To my great surprise Bill [Phillips] is highly critical of the English. He was always an Anglophile—of

[26] The capture of Tunis by Allied forces marked the formal end of the North African campaign. About 250,000 Axis troops surrendered after the battle.

[27] Viscount Archibald Wavell, British Viceroy and Governor General in India, 1943– 1947; General Claire Chenault, chief of the U.S. Air Task Force, Far East, 1943–1945; General Joseph Stilwell, U.S. Army Commander, Southeast Asia, 1942–1944.

marked degree. He played all his cards, at home and vis-à-vis the British, to be Ambassador at London. That was his aim in life. To hear him now—after I have watched him so many years—is a strange experience—and as unexpected as it is strange. . . .

The Trade Agreements got out of the House—without further amendment. After a long time this a.m. Hull decided to let the bill go without insisting on a roll-call on the amendment. Rayburn advised against it. Hull wanted it anyhow—but finally decided to let it ride. Now we are in for a Senate fight. . . .

May 14, 1943

Dined with Beneš at the Czech Legation (or Embassy, I forget which—as all distinction between Embassies and Legations has been extinguished by the elevation of practically all Legations to the higher rank). As a successor to Masaryk he is wanting in the scales—a scheming, unprincipled man.[28] The people in Europe have no confidence in him—but he emerges as President of his state—in exile. Beneš is just a sample of what the difficulties will be when we come to settle the central European questions—boundaries, refugee "rulers," jurisdictions, "official" ambitions, factional disputes, racial distinctions and minorities!!

And there is no answer!!

There was a distinguished company—the Vice President and Mrs. Wallace —Justice Roberts and Mrs.—Rayburn, Halifax, Ickes, Knox, Connally, Strong [Strang?]—and 46 all told. We were asked because the Welles could not go—and they had to have a "State Department" representative—what one might call a "personal compliment."

Welles could not go because he went to New York to talk to the President of Bolivia to finish a talk started here. This a.m. when Welles announced to Hull his visit to New York for that purpose Hull said why could the talk not have been held here—Welles said other engagements he had. Hull asked why he might not have been advised, for he might have taken on the talk.

Just another indication of their difficulties.

Had a long talk this a.m. with Rayburn on the proposed legislation on Chinese immigration. I suggested it would be better to ascertain whether it would not be better to discover if the bill could pass the Congress before proceeding with it. It would be bad to have it defeated—considering China's place in the Big Four. The international effect of defeat would be unfortunate.

---

[28] Thomas Masaryk, a philosopher-statesman, served as the first president of Czechoslovakia from 1918 until 1935, when he resigned because of advanced age. Eduard Beneš succeeded him. After the dismemberment of Czechoslovakia by the Munich Pact (1938), Beneš resigned. During World War II, he headed a provisional Czech government in London.

Rayburn agreed but McCormick was not inclined to agree. He is Irish and a partisan—by nature—likes to fight—not to reason. There is a "drive" on to change the immigration laws to admit Chinese. We are willing—but do not want to offend China by an adverse vote in Congress.[29]

May 16, 1943

62 years gone—40 to go.

Day before yesterday had a long talk with Dan Tobin of the Teamsters Union. We lunched and talked for an hour and a half. He thinks F.D.R. has missed a couple of opportunities. First Lewis agreed to "no strike during the war." Dan says the President should not have taken the air but should have let Dan and his fellow members of the Victory Committee, who sat with Lewis and agreed with him, take the air and tell the country just what Lewis was and is.[30] He talked at length the day before to F.D.R. and—according to Dan—and I do not doubt it, for I know the two intimately—he talked straight out. He needed a Secretary of Labor. He should not take these matters himself but should put responsibility on others. Jim Byrnes has fallen in their estimation. At any rate Lewis *has* to be stopped or inflation is immediately the consequence—The Big Four of the Railroads follow Lewis. The latter are not under W.L.B. [War Labor Board] but their own board of statutory origin. They ought *all* be under one board—and the same board. The price of food and clothes *has* to be related to wages and if one is fixed *both* have to be fixed —otherwise strikes and inflation and worse.

May 19, 1943

Had an important conversation this a.m. with General Strong [of Military Intelligence]. I asked him to come to discuss the contents of a telegram from Woods[31] in Zurich about a German process—it seems it is now more than an experiment—to use uranium powder in connection with split atoms in a compound explosive of alleged incredible violence. Woods is reporting on it and following it as closely as he is able. He says the German military are anxiously awaiting its preparation for actual use and that with it they hope to annihilate England, Russia and us.

[29] The new Chinese immigration bill passed the Congress later in the year, and the President signed it into law on December 17. Chinese living in the United States were made eligible for citizenship. Also, one hundred and five Chinese now could enter the United States annually on a quota basis.

[30] On April 8, 1943, President Roosevelt issued his "hold-the-line" order freezing prices, wages, and salaries. This provoked a strike involving 450,000 soft coal miners and 80,000 anthracite miners. On May 1, Roosevelt ordered Secretary of the Interior Harold Ickes to take over all coal mines in the eastern United States. The President placed responsibility for the stoppage upon John L. Lewis, who halted the strike the following day.

[31] Sam Woods, now consul general, Zurich, 1941–1945.

It was Sam Woods who first reported the magnetic bomb—the trailer transport airplane—and the plan of Germany—five months in advance—to attack Russia in 1941. Having wholesome respect for the accuracy of a lot of his information I nevertheless looked at this a little askance. But Strong was immediately and seriously interested in it—had followed the German experiment—and received this with avidity and concern. It seems we have some plans of our own and want to perfect ours first. He rather doubts Germany has the quantity of uranium they are otherwise reported to have but has followed German purchases of uranium ore. His description of the annihilating effectiveness of the explosive is staggering to the mind. It absolutely destroys all life in an area miles in diameter from the spot of explosion.[32]

I am reminded of my conversation with General George Squire[33] in the summer of 1918 when he reported the "Liberty Eagles" which he thought would revolutionize warfare and render antiquate battleships—large and small. But war and battleships still operate though they have hard going in a flock of torpedo-carrying planes. But they are not "Eagles" as then described by Squire.

Strong is a very thorough thinking, serious minded able officer of sound judgment. His reaction to this was sufficient to impress me with the great importance of this semi-development. I sent a message to Harrison, at Strong's request, to impress him and through him Woods, of the high importance and utmost urgency in obtaining additional information about this. Strong began to act on his own account and from my office called a meeting for his office immediately thereafter with his trusted men. He asked his office to call Dr. Vannevar Bush[34] to meet him there directly. I shall watch the development with keen interest—and hope we beat them to it—for that is what it amounts to.

If they keep up this business of deveoping [sic] more and more devastating explosives they will some day just blow this world out from under us. This thing is awful—or will be if actually put to "practical" use in warfare —but this will not be the end. The next may blow off another chunk to become another moon for some other kind of animal to look at—for it must be another kind of animal as this human kind as we know it will have ceased to exist— by its own smart action.

[32] On October 11, 1939, Albert Einstein and other scientists informed President Roosevelt of the possibility of developing an atomic bomb. Under the command of Brigadier General Leslie R. Groves, actual construction began in September 1942. And on December 2, 1942, scientists working at the University of Chicago effected the first self-sustaining nuclear reaction. The first atomic bomb was exploded at Almogordo, New Mexico on July 16, 1945. The entire project was shrouded with the utmost secrecy, but Long's entry certainly indicates a break in enforcement.

[33] Major General in charge of the Army Air Service, 1916–1918.

[34] Leland Harrison, U.S. minister to Switzerland, 1937–1947; Dr. Bush, chairman, Office of Scientific Research and Development, 1940–1947.

The Trade Agreement bill got amended again in the Senate Finance Committee today—but may be recovered on the floor. Churchill spoke to the Congress and corrected on the record his remarks about war in the Far East —a valuable correction.

May 23, 1943

"Comintern"—the Communist International—is dissolved. Stalin so commands.[35] It will aid the Allied cause in that it will take from the Axis one of their main propaganda charges—that Communism by Russia will be spread throughout western Europe in case of an Allied-Russian victory. Internally— in Russia—it marks the confession of the ascendancy of nationalism over internationalism—a pronouncement post mortem of the victory of Stalin over Trotsky.

In our Post-War Planning Committee work, we have been wrestling with the phraseology to put into a proposed four-power agreement for the U.S.-England-Russia-China to sign and in effect to declare they will after the war agree *not* to interfere in the internal affairs of or violate the territorial integrity of other states—without using these words and without making the statement so frank. The hesitancy and caution have largely been attributable to a desire *not* to offend Russia—to find a formula she would sign—and to make it binding and intelligible to all. This Comintern declaration may permit us to be a bit bolder and suggest a wording all can understand. But the Baltic States and Poland still stand hypothetically in the way because of Russia's known attitude toward them.

June 23, 1943

My entries in this record of activity and thought have been omitted for some weeks. Miss Aderton was away on sick leave, and I was very hard pressed and a little under par physically and not able without an unnecessary effort to use pen and ink in the late hours. I have recently returned from the Mayo Clinic, where I went to have a check-up. No organic difficulty was found but my doctors on the basis of the medical record wanted me to take a thirty-day leave and to rest as well as to take certain medicines which they prescribed and build up my blood count and overcome a tendency to an anemic condition.

During these six or eight weeks a great many things have happened, and it has been a most interesting period in our development. In the course of it I

[35] The dissolving of the "Comintern" meant the passing of the Third International, formed because of an appeal from the Russian Communist party in January 1919. The action, apparently taken without prior consultation with the branches scattered over the world, was designed to facilitate cooperation between the Soviet Union and her allies in the war against Germany. The statement accompanying the dissolution order declared that "the forms, methods, and regulations of the Comintern had become obsolete and in some cases, had actually hindered the workers of the world in their battles against Germany."

have assumed several other responsibilities. I have become Chairman of an active committee—the Political Planning Committee, which is devoted to contemporary phases of war activity with the idea of utilizing or developing policies which would be helpful to us in prosecuting the war.

In addition I have become Chairman of the Post-War Telecommunications Committee. We had our first meeting with the Secretary day before yesterday and will start regular sessions on Friday and will work toward two objectives —first, writing terms of the treaty of surrender imposing conditions on the enemy powers of a punitive nature and of a regulatory nature. The intention is to deprive them of their holdings abroad in communicating facilities so as to prevent their making trouble, particularly in this Hemisphere, in the future and divesting them of their ownership in any United States companies and in the "consortium" companies that are operating in South America. In addition to that it is planned to regulate their activities if they are improperly carried on after the war and after the establishment of peace so that they will not be able to intimidate and terrify their neighboring populations over the radio as they did in the days preceding each of their vicious attacks in this war. After that, and on the basis of the telecommunications world as it may exist or may be envisioned, to formulate an American policy for the approval of the President with the thought that all United States telecommunications companies engaged in foreign activity may be brought under a unified control.

I have also agreed to become Chairman of the Post War Shipping Committee and am now in the process of forming it. I have talked with Admiral Land, head of the War Shipping Administration [1942–1945], who will serve with me, and with him and the Secretary, and am gradually proceeding to fill up the membership. I do not look forward to the future activities of this Committee with the same interest as I do the others, and I accepted with considerable reluctance and after considerable delay the Chairmanship.

I have also got on, over my protest, a Migrations Committee, which is related to my other activity in connection with the refugees because it looks to their return to their homes after the war.

Currently active during the recent weeks has been the French political squabble in North Africa. De Gaulle has proven a thorn in the rose. His personal ambitions seem to have been clashing with what we consider the necessary freedom for military control of the situation in North Africa. He has been a very difficult person to handle. Our objectives in North Africa were purely military and our policy has been to abstain from any contact with political activity. Finally, and only in the last few days, it became necessary to take a strong stand based on military security and to state that it was necessary from our point of view that Giraud be sustained in complete control of French military there.

The refugee question has calmed down. The pressure groups have temporarily withdrawn from the assertion of pressure. Information which we have received indicates very plainly that they now see the correctness of the position which we have maintained from the beginning, which is that we will be glad to help such refugees as find their way out of the clutches of Germany but that we cannot deal with the enemy on the account of refugees any more than we can deal with them or negotiate with them on any other account. The recommendations of the Bermuda Conference have not been carried forward, though I have tried incessantly to secure some agreement between the United States and the British Government, cooperating in that respect with Myron Taylor, who was our member of the Intergovernmental Committee which in itself came out of the Evian Conference of 1938.[36] The British have had a little different idea of the program than we have had and they seem to be stressing the point that there must be a refugee camp in North Africa under our control and as a result of our enterprise. We secured the agreement in principle of Giraud acting through Murphy and Eisenhower and obtained their consent, but the Joint Chiefs of Staff have not given their consent. The President has taken the position that it would be dangerous to have a large number of Jews sent into North Africa—because of the predominant Moslem sentiment and the inherent antagonism existing between the two bodies. We have never agreed to the establishment in North Africa of anything but a temporary camp to which might be transported the Jewish persons evacuated out of Spain who were refugees in Spain and to keep them there only until they could be transferred to places where they could be maintained until the end of the war. The British have misunderstood us and have got firmly fixed in their minds that we had agreed to a considerable refugee camp in North Africa which we would build and maintain. It seems hard to correct their impression, and I am unable to ascertain the origin of their understanding. A telegram is about to go out now which reports the result of a conversation Taylor had with Halifax, but the telegram in my opinion is not adequate.

The truth of the whole thing is that there is no authority in this Government that can make commitments to take refugees in groups and that there are no funds out of which the expenses of refugees could be paid for safe keeping in other localities. There is no authority in this Government, unless the President has special funds, and those funds are neither adequate nor available. The immigration laws stand as a bar to admission of persons unless certain requirements are met, and there is no chance on earth to change those laws in favor of refugees at this time.

The question of Chinese exclusion appeal has been up, and I have had any number of conversations with the Speaker, the last one on yesterday, in

[36] See above, pp. 306–309.

which we agreed that there was no possibility of passing legislation which would permit the immigration of Chinese even as a war measure. It might develop in the future but certainly could not be done now. I have talked before with him and with McCormick, the Majority Leader, and on one occasion with them and certain of the Democratic members of the Immigration Committee. There is a consistent demand from certain elements in this country friendly to China and there are certain reasons why the Chinese Government and its Ambassador here are pressing us for a change in the law which would not discriminate against the Chinese whom we consider one of the Big Four. I must say i is a little inconsistent to claim China as one of our principal allies in war and to deny its citizens admission to the United States. Nevertheless the legislative policy and American sentiment as reflected through its representatives in Congress are not prepared to make any change in the immigration laws.

The exchanges with Japan and with Germany have progressed slowly and it looks now as if we would be ready to send an additional boat-load of Japanese for a boat-load of Americans, and it also looks as if we were nearly at the point of getting the American diplomats formerly accredited to Vichy and now held by the Germans in exchange for certain Germans in this country whom we are holding in confinement. The German attitude toward our people is sure to deteriorate as soon as we begin to operate with more intensity from the air over Germany and there are indications, though they are not very clear, that the Germans may be intending to hold Tuck and his associates as hostages. The Germans demanded the military members of the Armistice Commissions captured in North Africa. The War Department considered them as prisoners of war and said they would not be used for exchange purposes. In that impasse I had a talk with Admiral Leahy, now Chief of Staff to the Commander in Chief [1942–1949]. I met him in the White House last week and found him very much interested because the staff now in Germany was his staff when he was Ambassador in Vichy. He secured from the President a letter directed to the Secretary of War directing him to make these persons available for exchange. It made the War Department mad to have us interfere in what they considered their own matter, but they are preparing to make practically all of them available. As a result of it it looks as if we might get Tuck and his associates out of Germany. The Swiss advised me informally yesterday there was a new German note about to be delivered but that they did not know the contents as it had not been decoded. At any rate it is working gradually toward agreement for exchanges both with Germany and Italy on one side and with the Japanese on the other side.

There has developed a lull on the German east front. Our air forces are battering the German industrial installations and doing a great deal of damage. Whether it is attention to that and the interruptions to transportation is not yet apparent, but the fact is that Germany has not proceeded with its plans to renew the campaign against Russia. On the second anniversary of the attack on Russia Stalin issued a lengthy communique the tail end of which is alleged, but I have not yet seen the text of it, to place insistence upon the opening of a second front in Europe as a prerequisite to victory.

Another question of communications which has been delicate has been the efforts of the Vatican to extend its welfare messages to and from many parts of the world. It had to be very carefully handled, and I tried to keep out of the negotiations but I kept control in every respect, though I did not appear in any of them. As a result the Vatican has been denied the use of the radio for those purposes but has been permitted to use the mails. The present Pope[37] is enormously interested in that phase of the activity. When he was the Cardinal Secretary of State he talked to me in Rome about it. He had had during the last war a wide experience in Germany amongst the prisoners of war and had developed a sentimental tendency to extend the facilities for communications between prisoners and their families, which has later been extended to persons who are not prisoners and their friends in other countries. Without any desire to prevent the communication of these persons with each other through the agency of the Vatican and its very widespread organization, there appeared nevertheless security reasons why we could not assent to the use of the radio. It would be only too easy for designing persons to take advantage of the service which the Vatican was offering and to send a message which would be perfectly innocuous on its face but which could carry a great deal of information. Once such a message was placed on the radio and beamed to a receiving station it is open to the world. It is quite different when messages are sent by cable, because they are not open to interception. After careful consideration and much deliberation the matter was finally decided and the Apostolic Delegate here has been notified. Pending the negotiations and the conversations all communications were held. There were some hundreds of messages from Lima directed to Rome and many messages directed from Rome to Lima which had to be returned to the senders.

Another angle of the Vatican difficulty is now manifesting itself in the Far East. It seems that the Japanese have 18,000,000 Catholics amongst the populations they have conquered in China. There is also the very considerable Catholic population in the Philippines. There are many Japanese priests and there are a lot of Japanese Catholics who have become bishops and some archbishops. The Japanese have not allowed us to be represented in most parts of the countries they have conquered so that the Swiss have no access to our people in prison camps in many places and none at all in the Philippines. The question arose as to whether we should do as the English may be doing by asking the Vatican through their agencies to contact British prisoners and

[37] Pius XII, 1939–1958.

internees. However, it is very hard to visualize an American camp being visited for welfare purposes by Japanese bishops or Japanese priests under the direction of a Japanese bishop. In addition to the attitude of our own people and those who would be visited by a Japanese there is the political question which naturally arises as to what all the other native populations out there would think of the Americans if they came under the care of Japanese.

The question has not been decided here, but it raises some very delicate issues and unless some facts arise which are heavily controlling I think we shall have to take our stand on political grounds and abstain in the future as we have in the past from reliance on any other agency than the Red Cross, which is non-sectarian and without nationality.

July 26, 1943

Mussolini is out. The King dismissed him and appointed Badoglio Prime Minister. Details are lacking. A number of rumors appear in the press from Bern and other sources—among them that Mussolini and his cabinet are prisoners "outside of Rome."[38] He talked with Hitler the day Rome was bombed and it appeared at that time there was not much to talk about but how quick and how Italy would get out of the war. Now Badoglio has two battles on his hands—the Allied Armies approaching from Sicily and the populace of Italy, which, freed from the restraints of Fascism will seek the other extreme and give vent to their long suppressed feelings. Chaos will be manifested in localities and rioting will surely break out intermittently. The Italian populace will welcome American soldiers but they may not like the efforts to restore order.

I am at Wianno, Massachusetts, on the third of a four weeks rest—which I badly needed. I telephoned the Department this a.m. to ask if I should return and the Secretary said there was no need now but would call if he wanted me. I also talked to him on Saturday (day before yesterday). So I continue here at least for the present.

The invasion of Sicily [July 10] and the intensive bombing of military objectives all over Italy created this situation which no doubt will find its repercussions in Hungary, Rumania and the other Balkan states and in all the occupied countries. Russia has been pounding the Germans in the east and the way is rapidly being paved for the fall of Hitler and the collapse of the Nazi dictatorship of Europe. As soon as we secure air fields near enough to

[38] In July 1943, the Fascist Grand Council refused further support to Mussolini's war policies—dictated by Hitler—and King Victor Emmanuel III dismissed him, and placed him under arrest on July 25. Pietro Badoglio, former chief of the Italian General Staff, became prime minister. A daring German rescue two months later freed Mussolini, who now became head of the fascist puppet government established in northern Italy by Hitler. In April 1945, with the German collapse, Mussolini was captured and shot.

really bomb Vienna and Berlin and break up Nazi communications the end will be in sight.

Then we can turn our full attention to Japan. I hope with the aid of Russia. With that development the complete end ought not be delayed too long. But it is still a question in my mind whether Russia will help—or let us get weaker after a long, hard war in the Far East. And the delay which preceded our participation in the war will not make it easier for us to justify their continuance to help us—in spite of the enormous aid we contributed before and the very potent force we have brought to bear since we engaged.

The Russian phase and future role is our hard political problem.

August 9, 1943

Returned to the Department today after a month's absence. One disturbing thing was the possible attitude of Russia. This afternoon I had a talk with the Secretary and Welles and it develops that the rumors of Russian negotiations with Germany are not substantiated. Nevertheless they caused a good deal of concern. It develops that Churchill and the President agreed on the terms of surrender or a peace with Italy. Having agreed amongst themselves they made no provision to consult Russia. Six days later the British, without advising us, gave to the Russian Government in Moscow a copy of the terms, stating that they had been decided upon between us. We did not even know then that England had acted in Moscow. It was three or four days later when Hull and Welles discovered that the White House had not advised Stalin or communicated on the subject. Consequently there is a growing feeling on the part of Stalin that Churchill and Roosevelt are trying to decide the questions of the war without his collaboration and without even notice to him of decisions having been taken.

I stated very frankly and crudely that I thought that Russia was the most important element in this military collaboration at the present time. If Russia should pull out of the war it would leave us in a terrible condition in Europe and would make it infinitely more difficult for us to conquer Japan. I have always had the fear that Russia and Germany would get tired of their particular war and that each would want to make peace. That condition no doubt exists today and each of them would be glad if the war could stop on their respective fronts but to add to that inducement the thought on the part of Stalin that he is not being consulted and that he is not considered a party to the rest of the European war creates an even more dangerous situation. Russia has been vehement in her conversations about a second front in Europe and recently has returned to the charge with the thought that the Allied armies on Sicily are not constituting a second front from the point of view of Russia. This resumed conversation about the second front might easily be a prelude to the excuse that we were not carrying out our part of the military undertaking and would serve to hide the pique and resentment Stalin might feel in case he got the idea that he was not being consulted about questions of the utmost importance.

Aside from that I have checked up on all the divisions in my jurisdiction and have gotten the post war communications committee ready to receive the report of the subcommittee which would lay down the terms to be imposed upon the enemy in connection with our communications. I will call a meeting of the big committee for the latter part of the week.

August 10, 1943

I have got a good deal worried about developments abroad and the potentialities of some of them. Russia has got us in the palm of her hand and can squeeze when Stalin is ready. The recent reiteration of the fact that there was no second front in Europe seems to be a camouflage or a possible basis upon which to place the blame on us for having left him in an "impossible" position.

In Germany Hitler has apparently gone into retirement and active command has been taken over by Goering acting in cooperation with the Chiefs of the Army and the Navy. They can easily dispose of Hitler in the same way Mussolini was deposed and set up a military government with which Stalin would not be averse to dealing.[39] As a matter of fact Stalin's recent "Free Germany" program intimates he would be willing to talk with the Army and states he does not want to destroy the Army.

If this should develop in Germany, a military government could make peace with Russia—and both sides are exhausted and each side would welcome the cessation of hostilities—and then turn to us and say, "You were fighting Mussolini and Hitler. We despised them and got rid of them. You said you were fighting ideologies and were against Fascism and Nazism. We have dispensed with them. Now we have made peace with Germany and we are ready to make peace with you." That would leave us in a very bad position. Psychologically it would be very hard to explain. The matter has been considered by the Secretary and by the President. My impression is that the Secretary does not consider it as seriously as I do. Of course it has not developed. One proposal is made to ask Stalin to sign the Four Power Agreement we have been working on for months in the Political Committee and which is ready for signature.[40] My own thought is that a delegation of highest importance be sent to Moscow with the idea that they take Stalin into our

[39] Long is repeating a rumor which swept the United States during the first week of August. The overthrow of Mussolini, the loss of Kharkov in Russia, and the rapid deterioration of German home front morale under the punishing Anglo-American air raids were the basis for such unconfirmed reports. These rumors appeared sporadically throughout 1943 and 1944.

[40] See below, pp. 323, 331, 333.

confidence and confer with him on the future conduct of the war and the questions which will arise in the settlement that will follow and to make every effort to secure his confidence and to hold them in line.

As it stands at present the Germans are making it very difficult for Badoglio to exercise a free hand and possibly are holding Italy in this state in order that they may have time to negotiate with the Russians. We now know that there have been conversations between the Russians and the Germans. How articulate we do not know, but if Russia should cease its military activities against Germany and Germany should withdraw 190 divisions from the Russian front and move them into France or into Germany we would have a terrible time in Western Europe if we ever set a foot on it and it would be almost humiliating to make a peace under those circumstances.

In addition to that the repercussions in the Far East and the developments out of that in the Far Eastern picture would prolong the war out there for years and make it infinitely more difficult for us to really lick Japan.

I am almost convinced this is the turning point of the war. If we can keep Russia active against Germany there is no doubt in my mind about the eventual end. With Russia out there arises the most serious doubt as to whether Germany can be adequately defeated. . . .

There is only one saving part and that is that in case they do make a peace between Russia and Germany Russia will want to make peace with a Germany which is Free Germany, which is in itself a Communist aggregation, well known to be Communist, and one known by the Germans to be Communist and known by them to be such persons as would institute Communism in Germany if Stalin had his way. This thought may frighten Germany away from any possibility of peace that Stalin would offer, but she knows she is licked if she doesn't make peace with Russia, and she fears Communistic control if she should make peace with Russia. That may prolong the war, but I think we ought to do everything in the world we can, including taking Stalin into our confidence as far as possible and as far as circumstances permit in order to insure that Russia keeps on.

August 29, 1943

Welles is gone. He left the Department a week ago today. Roosevelt and Hull were in Quebec [August 11–24].[41] Prior to their departure for Quebec— as related to me by Hull in his return last Wednesday—it had been agreed Welles would leave, but not in this way. The President wanted to utilize his real abilities but in order to do so his personal reputation had to be protected. He was to keep his position and go to Russia on special mission, still as

[41] At Quebec, President Roosevelt, Prime Minister Churchill, and top ranking advisers reaffirmed May 1, 1944, as the target date for the Normandy invasion, which was to be supplemented by landings in southern France. Also, agreement was reached on increased operations in the Far East, particularly in Burma.

Undersecretary but with the function of Ambassador to attempt the delicate and highly important task of obtaining the agreement of Stalin to a Four Power compact which we have been working on for some months and which is now ready and which was to be the subject of conference with England at Quebec. China was also to be consulted and asked to go along. Welles was familiar with it. His "Political" Committee in conjunction with our "Security" Committee had worked it out under his chairmanship. While away on this mission—and it was assumed it would be a lengthy and dignified as well as a most important work—he would gradually proceed into another field of work and eventually would relinquish the Undersecretaryship.

That was the plan.

Welles knew he was being displaced. Those on the inside would know it. He knew the real reason. Those on the inside would also know that. But his reputation would be spared and the danger of public explosion of the unfortunate facts would be obviated. Suddenly—no one knows why—while Acting Secretary—he left the Department. Two days later he was reported to be at Bar Harbor. He had also been absent from the Department without explanation two days during the preceding week. I knew nothing of it except that Welles was absent and Berle was "Acting" and that the press was speculating.

On Wednesday, the 25th, Berle came in to my office and called my attention to the story in the [Washington] *Post* that said he might resign if I were appointed, in line with his conduct when I was mentioned for Counselor. He said he had no such intention in the present circumstances. He then told me Welles had called him in Sunday morning previous and told him he had resigned and was leaving and for Berle to take over Monday morning as "Acting," which was the regular order.

When Hull arrived that afternoon I had a talk with him. He said Berle had told him Welles had said he had resigned and that his resignation had been accepted. Hull also told me another person whom I do not now recall had told him Welles had resigned but that his resignation had *not* been accepted. The President apparently had not told him anything but was proceeding, supposedly, on the theory Welles was to carry on as indicated above.

I told him then—and I returned to it next morning—that whoever was to succeed him it should be decided and announced as soon as possible because 1) the press and public speculation would cause a rapid deterioration of the situation through which the Department would suffer; 2) the radicals (who hated Hull and me) would strive to embarrass him and cause his downfall through the medium of massed propaganda; and 3) that during it all and as days slipped by the true facts would become public property and Wells would be rendered useless as a public servant. Consequently it was the part of wisdom to finish the business quickly, appoint someone and stop the talk.

And that is the way it stands today—still. I know no more. I have not discussed any phase of it with Hull since and did not see him on it Friday nor did I see him at all yesterday except to pass him in the corridor. Today I have not seen him or anyone else and have just come in from the farm to be quiet here alone and make these notes. . . .

There is a lot of talk about Welles' departure being on account of difference in opinion about policy. That is not the case. The trouble was purely and simply that Welles was accused of a highly immoral bit of conduct, that Bullitt became advised of it, and spread the story. There was an investigation. The office of District Attorney had some part in it I am informed. Hull told me repeatedly about the F.B.I. reports—the file on which was sent to the White House and disappeared for the time. The story was whispered around Washington.

Welles first spoke to me about the story. That was in the spring of 1942. He said Bullitt had started it and that it was a malicious lie. I assumed it was. Bullitt is a person without honor, in my eyes. I have known him a long, long time and know him well but I have *never* had any confidence in him. And—he wanted Welles' position. So I accepted Welles' statement at face value. Even without Bullitt's instigation of the story I would still have accepted Welles' statement. Months later, as appears from time to time in the preceding pages of these notes, Hull talked to me. I tried to calm him, get the two men together, hush the story, keep the boat on an even keel.

But, during last winter and spring it was more and more the subject of his conversation. Hull talked to me at great length on many occasions, expressing his anxiety that the public would get the story, that there would be an explosion and not only the reputation of the Department be involved but, worse, the President himself be besmirched because of the conduct of one of his closest intimates and associates. More recently, before I left on vacation in early July, he took the line that Welles was subject to blackmail by foreign Governments who knew the story. He was genuinely worried about it but was also concerned about Welles' direct contacts with Roosevelt, the products of which he was not always advised of. He felt he was working somewhat in the dark and was being short-circuited—and resented it. But the reputation of the Department and the serious political consequences both to the Department and to the White House were the main theme of his concern.

The lurid story had been circulating for months.[42] A number of people outside the Department had asked me about it. I always passed it off in a light vein and stated my belief that the story was false. It persisted. Finally it got to some Republican members of the Senate. None of them spoke to me about it but the fact that they knew it was dangerous.

Without speaking to Hull on that phase of it I went to Welles himself—

[42] Welles, according to this lurid rumor, had engaged in homosexual activities.

told him the fact and said it was obvious that true or untrue the Republicans would use it to hurt the Administration and that they had no regard for him or personal interest in him which would serve to soften the blows they would make. I laid the cards plainly on the table and discussed the political danger in the circumstances. I then said I thought he should take some action to stop the story circulating—do something to counteract the effect of its undenied circulation. He again said it was a pack of lies, that Bullitt was responsible for the circulation. He proceeded to say that there was nothing one could do. To deny the story publicly would be to add to its currency and would detract from his dignity by mentioning or alluding to a filthy scandal. I admitted the difficulties in the situation but warned him that he was in a serious fix and that unless he did something to correct the impression being fastened in the minds of persons high in authority he might as well expect serious consequences.

He did nothing and we never alluded to it again. . . .

The whole business is unfortunate. The Administration has suffered, the White House has suffered, the State Department has been seriously affected and Welles has been put under a dark cloud from which he may not emerge. Our relations with Russia may have been affected and the American Government has been placed in a most unfortunate light in the eyes of other Governments. Hull has been insisting for months that the President make some disposition of it but he was probably suspect as having personal reasons of jealousy of and animosity toward Welles, so his arguments may not have been received with the same seriousness they were intended to carry. Besides, Welles was a boyhood friend of Roosevelt and Roosevelt sticks by his friends. That is one of his distinct characteristics. He has hardly a more definite trait in his entire and many-sided composition than loyalty to his friends. Sometimes it leads him to embarrassment because his friends are not always capable of discharging the responsibilities of his favor. Welles was capable of it. He is a very able man. And Roosevelt probably could not believe the story relayed by Bullitt—probably continued to discount it—undoubtedly was led to further procrastination in the face of an inevitable decision because of his personal friendship. And the consequence was that delay allowed the tongue of gossip to get too big a start and Welles by his sudden action dramatically precipitated a sordid denouement.

But the world will soon march by the little tragedy and it will be smothered in the dust of rapidly succeeding events.

September 3, 1943

Had a meeting scheduled with our people and the British to reconcile our and their drafts for surrender terms for ships to be taken over from the enemy —beginning with Italy. The British were not ready to discuss so they asked the meeting be postponed. The American draft is the product of my Post War Committee on Shipping. Hull took it to Quebec and after approval by our people there it was presented to Eden. We will meet shortly.

Today my Post War Committee on Communications—after six or eight weeks work—finally completed and agreed to the draft of terms to be required of the enemy concerning communications. It was tenaciously pushed through a long three-hour session in spite of rather less than good-natured criticism by Fly.[43] It was urged through for application to Italy because of the rapidly developing prospect of surrender by Badoglio.

Italy's surrender may occur at any moment—but may be postponed. Allied forces landed on the toe of the boot this morning and the Germans are reported in full retreat in that area.

Sam Woods called by phone from Zurich. Hull asked me to take it but it has not yet been completed because of static. Just after I had retired the overseas operator ("Miss Mary") called to say they were checking on it but could not promise early completion. Sam must have something *awfully* important and urgent to use the radio telephone when every word will be intercepted by the enemy and recorded. But he is a smart person and is sure to have some good purpose.

September 4, 1943

Sam Woods' telephone came through very indistinctly. Had a record of it made by the Censor. The disc was better than my ear. As read back to me several hours later after the text had been ferreted out it seemed to be inconsequential and to pertain to his personal affairs and probably intended for one of the administrative officers—not to my bailiwick. Anyhow, I told him I could not understand him and to cable.

Have spent considerable time these last few days, including today, in conference with Hull and Berle, Hackworth, Dr. Hornbeck, Pasvolsky and Savage working over succeeding drafts of an important series of speeches on foreign policy. Attention is now on the draft of the first speech as the general indicator of policy. Therefore it assumes a real importance.

The purpose is to make a general survey of the history of our policy so the present will tie in with the past and point the way to the future. The decision to do it now has its roots in the widespread criticism of our policies. Lippmann's[44] book is wrong in many, many particulars, facts, assumptions and conclusions. A number of memoranda have been received in the Department from persons outside—Charles Warren, Quincy Shaw and several other able, competent and qualified commentators, including one of my own, which

[43] James Fly, chairman of the Board of War Communications, 1940–1944, and chairman of the Federal Communications Commission, 1939–1944.

[44] Walter Lippmann, noted essayist and columnist.

take direct exception to Lippmann's book [*U.S. Foreign Policy: Shield of the Republic*]. Nevertheless its role is widespread—one of the "best sellers"—and apt to mislead the reading public.

The Welles incident has called forth—starting with the radical element and gradually gathering momentum and strength from various other sources—a veritable broadside, some in support of but most in criticism of our policies and the personnel of the Department. The reasons and the motives behind them vary. But Hull himself is criticized, either directly or inferentially, in such papers as the Washington *Post* and the St. Louis *Post Dispatch* in well-reasoned but in the case of the *Post* prejudicial articles—and defended ably by the Baltimore *Sun* and some other important papers. I get it both ways—but the radical press is particularly denunciatory. Berle gets plenty. Dunn gets little praise and many "slings and arrows." Acheson, being the pet of Frankfurter and the hope of the radicals, so far escapes much comment but is headed for plenty too. But it all goes to the competence of the Department to handle its enormous load in those epochal times and circumstances—to the competence of or to the political intent of its policy-making officers.

Hull is supersensitive to criticism. Consequently all this avalanche spurs him on to make—not a defense, but—a calm review and statement. This will be along the historical line of a memo I wrote as a supplement to my memo on Lippmann's book. Others wrote memos and have done more of the drafting than I have but the difference between the first draft and the present working copy elucidates what I mean though I am not trying to assume personal credit for the present copy. . . . So that is why a series of speeches will be made and why the first one will be the basis for those shortly to follow.

September 6, 1943

Worked with the group three hours—10:15 to 1:15—on the speech. This afternoon I spoke to Hull again about the serious damage to the Department and to our influence in foreign fields by letting the present press campaign proceed. The standing of the Department was being seriously affected. The only way to stop it was for the President to put somebody in the Department promptly—quickly. That would give them something else to talk about.

He said he agreed thoroughly but that the President was delaying action because he wanted Welles to do the Russian job. Hull told him Welles was now disqualified for that job. The President however was still of the opinion it could be worked out. He agreed with everything I said but stated he had done all he could. He suggested I communicate my thoughts to the President—and I declined. I told him I had sent a message to Frank Walker[45] just along the line of my earlier conversation with him—but had done nothing else. He

[45] Now U.S. Postmaster General, 1940–1945, and chairman of the Democratic National Committee, 1943–1944.

agreed with it all but thought he could not do more immediately. During the talk I said that a lot of this was levelled against him and if it went on and on he would suffer. He said he realized that—but—just nothing to do.

September 7, 1943

This evening I was talking to Hull about some other matters and he brought up the Welles succession, said he had been talking to the President and he had mentioned to Hull several names. The names were not repeated. He went on to say "it looked like the President still wanted to run the State Department" and that he "didn't know what other advice the President was getting from some people around him." The inference was rather clear that my name and others had been discussed, that no decision had been made and that the President was going to choose whom he wanted whether Hull quite agreed or not —and that Hull was not going to make any issue of it. That is the first and only time he has mentioned it to me. I said nothing except that if he got someone who was not in sympathy with him he would have another lot of trouble on his hands—to which he agreed.

Some others came in—Pasvolsky and Gray[46]—and after sitting and discussing other topics a few minutes I rose and started to the door. He called me back and said in the presence of the others—"Breck, I want you to know I told the President you had always been in accord with me and that you and I were going to shape foreign policies in here."

What the purpose of that remark was I was at a loss to understand and do not still see. He is such a canny person and it was so deliberately done in the presence of others that he must have had some purpose. It was either to alibi himself for any thought or suggestion he had not gone to all proper lengths to advocate my appointment—or with the honest intent to let the Department know he placed just reliance on me—or—what?

It was just mysterious.

September 8, 1943

Italy surrenders. Eisenhower accepts from Badoglio. American forces land on the continent all around Naples and both above and below it. The Italian fleet is included in the terms but it is not clear yet that the war ships will be delivered. It will take some days to unscramble the news so one can see just what has happened but it looks now as if we would take over up to the Pisa-Florence line, and perhaps up to the Genoa-Venice line, and the Germans try to hold north of that. But we get air fields closer and closer to Berlin and can now fly from them to bomb Berlin and go on to England to reload and return. It is much closer than North Africa—where the armies were six weeks ago.

Worked three or four hours more on the speech—redrafting.

[46] Cecil Gray, foreign service officer, assistant to Secretary Hull, 1939–1944.

September 9, 1943

Finished the speech draft about noon. Hull took it over to the President and had him read it to get his approval. He called Roosevelt's attention and asked him to read carefully the remarks which over-rule the Wallace theories of "a bottle of milk a day" for every child in the world—as our donation to uplifting the backward peoples. The President read it—so Hull advised us this afternoon and gave it his definite endorsement. He called us in about 3:30 and related his interview with the President and reported the President as saying in substance, "it is not worth taking too much exception to them (the Wallace group). Let them talk if they want to. They will not last very long."

This confirms again my impression the President is a little fed up with some of his radical friends and with their unsubstantial ravings and plannings. He is turning away from them—slowly. The last previous confirmation was at the East-Wing of the White House the other day when I talked with Jim Byrnes. . . . When finishing the conversation, he said "We are getting some of these radical boys out of the way and more will go—but it is better to do it gradually." To all of this I expressed my agreement.

September 13, 1943

Late yesterday afternoon Hull phoned me and asked me to sit by and be prepared to take over the microphone if his voice gave out—so I met him at the broadcast studio and stood by. His delivery is never good—usually poor —and last night it was at best poor. His voice—very bad at first—improved somewhat and he got through with it. But he makes an impression of "old age" on the public. There is no evidence of virility or "punch" in his voice and there is fertile suspicion of "old age" which is propagated by the impression his delivery makes.

This morning I drafted a short Departmental Order—"Supervision of the Visa Division is hereby transferred from A-L to U." A-L is my office symbol —U that of the Undersecretary. I took it to the Secretary, told him I had decided I had won all the battles and the war in the immigration fight, that it was in smooth, systematic order, that all the vilification and abuse that had been heaped on me by the radicals was on account of my fair administration of the issues involved and while I would not quit in a fight I felt that having won I would take this instant to be relieved of that work. I had asked no favors. I had received no open support from any quarter. I had been the target of character assassins. I did not admit people promiscuously without proper examination and safeguard. I had executed in a humane spirit the laws I was sworn to uphold. I wanted to be free of that job after three and a half years of handling the most complex and worst job in the Government. I had won my fights. Now I wanted to give someone else a chance at it.

Hull signed the order and it has been promulgated. So I am free.

Welles at Bar Harbor is carrying on the war against Hull from there. He sails every afternoon with Pulitzer of the St. Louis *Post Dispatch*—talks anti-Hull and anti-policy to him. That was the cause back of the article by Marquis Childs.[47] Also there came to see me today Charles Ross. He is a Washington representative of the *Post Dispatch*. He had a telegram from Pulitzer at Bar Harbor saying he had information a basic reason for not recognizing the French Committee as a *government* was because we would have to give them the French funds blocked here. He asked me if it was true. I said it seemed to put recognition on a very sordid scale—that the Committee got many millions in gold with Martinique—that they had all the revenues from the colonial governments of France, their balance on that account running to a hundred million dollars here—that they did not need the money blocked here—that that had had nothing to do with it and—that the policy was that of the President himself. . . .[48] Now it appears Walter Lippmann has been at Bar Harbor—is just back—and lunched with Welles at least once and spent one whole morning with him. Also, Wallace phoned him and sent two men to see him. They travelled by plane—one had a long talk with him and the other sat out—and they left by plane.

The point is all these men, Pulitzer, Welles, Wallace, Lippmann, are bitter critics of our foreign policy and of Hull and that those who talk with Welles print or speak in distortion of our policies and in criticism of Hull.

September 26, 1943

Last night the radio announced Stettinius had been selected for Under Secretary. I did not hear it. Miss Aderton called me and told me. Shortly thereafter Hull called me by phone, said he had tried to talk with me during the day but was tied up till after I left—the President had picked Stettinius all the names had been knocked down—he had urged the President to appoint me but the President wanted to make his own decision—did not know Stettinius but casually but thought him a man of honorable intent. I replied I had had no personal ambition in the complicated scheme of things and thought Stettinius better than all the others mentioned. Hull said he was going to the Russian–English Conference, would be away a few days at Hot Springs. Then here preparing to go to London—probably. There would be other organizational moves in the Department but they would have to wait till his return.

[47] Joseph Pulitzer, publisher of the *St. Louis Post-Dispatch*, 1912–1955; Marquis Childs, correspondent for the *St. Louis Post-Dispatch* since 1926.

[48] President Roosevelt and Secretary Hull adopted the view that the United States should do nothing that would impose a government upon the French people. Therefore, the French National Committee in London headed by General Charles de Gaulle was not recognized as the legitimate French government by the United States until two months after the fall of Paris (October 23, 1944). Hull was then convinced "that the great majority of the French people, at least for the period of the emergency, freely accepted the leadership of General de Gaulle and the administration that he had set up on French soil."

He wanted to talk to me briefly before the Conference on that subject but at length on his return. He said Crowley[49] was to head up all the economic activities in foreign fields and become "Economic Advisor" of the Department and in charge of all those subjects under him—thought it would work well. He was to leave for a rest this morning.

Stettinius is an able fellow—energetic—capable—has done a good job on Lend-Lease. What he knows of foreign affairs I do not know. As far as I know him I like him. I knew his father in the last war when he was Assistant Secretary of the Treasury and member of the Morgan firm.

My own thoughts about my future in the Department are that I must be rid of the executive details connected with supervision of the very active divisions I have under me. That has to be arranged soon. I have been filling two positions and doing the work of the Counselor and that of an Assistant Secretary. I have served my apprenticeship—did that in the last war—came into this office reluctantly but in a spirit of service and glad to serve but still looking toward a field of work which will not carry with it the minutiae of executive supervision and direction.

November 3, 1943

For a number of weeks I have omitted to make any notes. Much seems to have happened. Mr. Stettinius was appointed and took over just before the Secretary left for Moscow[50] and has been Acting Secretary. Hull took with him twelve or thirteen members of the Department staff and safely arrived in Moscow. The results of the deliberations there are the Four Power Declaration in regard to the continuation of the war and cooperation after the war through the stages which will follow and until there will be set up an international organization which each of the Powers pledges support. The Declaration has closed the door to Germany and Japan to obtain a separate peace or to separate the Allies. It is a most important political as well as military Declaration and has been received with perfect agreement in this country. The Declaration was released in the midst of the Senate debate on some kind of a resolution which would indicate that the United States would support the Allies, running along a similar line. After ten days of debate during which period the Moscow agreement was published, no definite stand developed on the part of the Senate. I brought this to the attention of the Acting Secretary. Up to this point, we had considered it a Senate matter. However, now the action of the Senate might serve to divide the executive from the legislative

[49] Leo T. Crowley, foreign economic administrator, 1943–1945.

[50] The Moscow Conference of Foreign Ministers (October 19–30) was attended by Hull, Anthony Eden, and V. M. Molotov, together with United States, British, and Soviet military officials. The closing declaration recognized "the necessity of establishing . . . a general international organization" for the "maintenance of international peace and security."

branch and would be of assistance to Germany. He suggested that I talk to Connally. I said I would be glad to talk with him if my conversation had White House approval. Either the President should take cognizance of the situation and act himself or someone should go to the Senate to present the situation.

After conferring with the White House it was decided that I should go. I immediately telephoned Connally, and he said that he would talk with me. So I went to the Senate but was not immediately received. During the interval Hatch, Burton, Hill and Austin came through and I talked with them a few minutes and then talked to Connally alone.[51] I presented to him the serious thought that the matter had now developed to a point where it transcended in importance a purely Senatorial matter and became in substance a matter of international political consequence and that the Senate was in a position where it should take some stand on the Moscow Resolution. Otherwise, its position would be misunderstood. I emphasized that I was not there to talk to him casually and that my visit was an indication that the Department of State and the executive branch of the Government considered the situation of utmost importance from the point of view of international politics and Allied cooperation. Connally expressed himself as being in entire accord with these thoughts. . . .

November 7, 1943

I am very happy and pleased about the action of the Senate [in passing the Connally Resolution]. 85 to 5 is practically unanimous. Two recalcitrant Democrats, two Republicans and Shipstead.[52] LaFollette would have voted "no" if he had been able to be present. Of the two Democrats Reynolds[52] is doomed to defeat in the coming primary and is believed by his colleagues to have deliberately taken the position to give public excuse for his coming and admitted repudiation. The other, Wheeler, is just naturally antagonistic and by design was carrying out a policy of opposition to Roosevelt—a policy he has pursued for years. Bennett Clark voted with us and confirmed the shift from his 1918–20 position—taken then because of his father.

As a whole the action is most gratifying. It takes partisanship out of the question and puts both major parties in line on the great question of foreign

[51] In March 1943, Senators Carl Hatch (Democrat, New Mexico), Harold Burton (Republican, Ohio), Lister Hill (Democrat, Alabama), and Warren Austin (Republican, Vermont) began a bi-partisan movement to commit the U.S. Senate to participation in an international organization. On September 21, the House adopted the Fulbright Resolution favoring "the creation of appropriate international machinery with power adequate to establish and to maintain a just and lasting peace." On November 5, a similar resolution introduced by Senator Connally passed in the Senate.

[52] Henrik Shipstead, Farmer-Laborite (Republican after 1940), U.S. Senator from Minnesota, 1923–1947; Robert Reynolds, Democrat, U.S. Senator from North Carolina, 1932–1945.

policy which has caused so much trouble in this country and in the world since the days of Wilson. Personally, I am happy that I have kept the faith these many years—now to find myself vindicated—and gratified that I had a considerable part in the maneuver. . . . Now we are back on the main track—after being side-tracked and nearly wrecked in 1920.

November 18, 1943

Hull delivered his address to the Joint Meeting of Congress today. I went up—sat on the Floor—and was interested to see him get quite an ovation and deliver his remarks forcibly. He returned about a week ago. We all went to the airport to meet him and Roosevelt went too. He spent a few days in retirement—tired out. Since then we have been working on his speech. We worked with him steadily two and a half days and parts of the Saturday and Monday preceding. But we turned out an excellent document which was not finished till ten this a.m.—and delivered at 12:30!

He is very well satisfied with his trip and the things he accomplished. The Four Power Pact was possible as a Four Power Agreement only two days before the end because Stalin would not till then agree to admit China as signatory. But Hull wore him down and Molotov finally consented. Eden did not help to that end.

The terms of the pact itself had been worked out in the Department in our Committees—Welles' Political and our Security Committees—so called. The provisions as we drafted them through weeks of consideration were adopted practically verbatim.[53]

Designed as a Four Power Agreement it took all of Hull's persistence and patience to get Russia to extend signature to China. Hull liked Stalin. Formed a real admiration for him. They sat next to one another at dinner and he made friends with him. He appealed to his self-consciousness and told him he did not appreciate the power for good he could exercise in the world through his enormous influence—Hull did not get the impression Stalin realized what a power he might exercise if he exerted his influence for the stabilization of the world in the postwar era.

Eden made a poor impression and Hull reports that Stalin sort of waved him aside—paid little attention to his proposals or recommendations. This was so to the extent Hull thought it wise to write Eden an effulgent letter about his work at Moscow—fearing he would react unfavorably toward the United States after his return home.

[53] In addition to recognizing the need for an international organization, the Moscow Conference of Foreign Ministers established a European Advisory Commission to formulate a postwar policy for Germany. The United States and Great Britain assured Russia that preparations for a second European front were under way, and the Soviets made an unconditional promise to enter the war against Japan after Germany's defeat.

Some of those with Hull—Hackworth, for instance, obtained a very poor impression of Eden and said that even members of his own delegation allowed their unflattering opinions to be known to members of our delegation. They gave the impression they felt Eden was trying to use the Conference to further his personal political ambitions at home to become Prime Minister. It was that atmosphere which warned Hull he should try to placate a disappointed Eden so he would not turn against the United States to cover his failure in Russia.

Eden sat between two astute poker-players—and got outplayed.

The address to the Congress was a distinct success but it was a lot of hard work preparing it. Hackworth with a bad tooth—Dunn tired out—Pasvolsky, McDermott, Savage and I—with Stettinius from time to time and Berle part of the time—wrestled with Hull till it was dragged through five drafts and each word of each draft weighed, passed, transposed or substituted or eliminated. One who has not been through one of those searching, prolonged sessions cannot realize what microscopic examination is given to every phrase in the lights of grammar, inflexes, syntax, history, politics, psychology and structural position—all the nuances of meaning and all the implications of use—alone or in relation to its context. Such a session is truly an ordeal—but an interesting experience. The result is a short, compact, logical, correct statement of a political situation—and hard to deny or refute.

1944

January 1, 1944

The new year—another new year—is here. We are in a better situation in the war—both in Europe and in the Far East—as a result of operations during its course but there is probably much trouble ahead and heavy fighting in front of us.

Here I have been enmeshed in the executive activities of prisoners of war, POWs as they are written, of Americans in camps abroad, in exchange of personnel with the enemies, in telecommunications, shipping, visas, refugees, Congressional legislation of many kinds and the Jewish problems. I made a statement to the Foreign Affairs Committee of the House which was subsequently printed and in the course of a long four-hour inquisition made several statements which were not accurate—for I spoke without notes, from a memory of four years, without preparation and on one day's notice. It is remarkable I did not make more inaccurate statements. But the radical press, always prone to attack me, and the Jewish press have turned their barrage against me and made life somewhat uncomfortable. I said "We have taken into this country approximately 580,000 refugees" (in ten years) and I should have said "We have authorized visas to come to this country." The figures are 568,000 authorized of which 545,000 issued. On that basis I have been pilloried as an enemy of the Jew and as trying to discredit them. Anyhow I have written to [Sol] Bloom to straighten it out. The Jewish agitation depends on attacking some individual. Otherwise they would have no publicity. So for the time being I am the bull's eye. . . .[54]

The Palestine question is one of those pressing for some solution. I have made known my thoughts and the Jewish organizations—with a lot of Christian names signed to petitions, are pressing for the creation of a State—a Jewish State—a political Jewish entity. Juridically speaking we are not in the picture—have no responsibility—and I want us to assume no political responsibility but to induce England to take some reasonable action in the premises—to pass the question over till after the war so that the nations of the world in the next League of Nations can decide the question—in their full responsibility—in justice to both sides, on humanitarian grounds and in keeping with the deep religious sentiments involved. And that is a big order.[55]

The British have responsibility for the Arab and we have the question of the Jewish demands. They are really irreconcilable—but will have to be worked out. But I do not want us to get the political responsibility saddled on us. We were not parties to the original and still continuing agreement, had no responsibility for issuing the mandate—and have none now. But we have an interest in the peace of the world, in the humanitarian questions involved, and in the satisfaction of the religious sentiments implicit in any settlement. And on those grounds we should approach England. . . .

Sam Woods and I got in one good lick in Germany the other night when the bombers flattened out one industry. But that cannot be written now. There is involved a German "prisoner of war," a message through O.S.S. and a bomber activity—of which more can be written in safety some time later. It is a fascinating story.

January 11, 1944

Unable yet to relinquish jurisdiction over the refugee problem—or over my other executive activities—I carry on—as today. Rabbi Willes [?] and a

[54] Long's misleading and secret testimony on November 26, 1943, however, had convinced the House Foreign Affairs Committee to oppose two bills providing for the creation of a commission "to effectuate the rescue of the Jewish people of Europe." Long testified that the majority of the 580,000 refugees admitted had been Jews and said that the proposed legislation would "constitute a criticism of what the State Department had done quietly to this end." On December 12, the day after Long's statement had been made public, Representative Emanuel Celler (Democrat, New York) assailed the Assistant Secretary as being the "least sympathetic to refugees in all the State Department." The 580,000 persons whom Long had described as Nazi refugees were, according to Celler, regular quota immigrants, and the majority of these were non-Jews.

[55] Throughout 1942 and 1943, Zionist organizations in the United States and Great Britain continued to agitate for a Jewish national state in Palestine at the end of the war. Although the war had diminished political tensions between the Jews and Arabs, the Palestinian problem remained acute.

colleague came to talk about Jews in Poland escaping into Hungary and the possibilities of our sending a message to an agent in Switzerland to encourage the practice—and I said we could. . . . The Jewish organizations are all divided and in controversies of their own. The world Jewish Congress is one, the American Jewish Committee is quite another and opposed, the Jewish Joint Distribution Committee is another and a fine lot of citizens engaged purely in charity and relief—not in politics, as the others are—the Emergency Committee to Rescue the Jews Under Hitler—another which is anathema to all the above named—etc. There is no adhesion nor any sympathetic collaboration—rather rivalry, jealousy and antagonism. Some are pro-Zion, some not, but no Jew can wholly oppose the idea of a Jewish Home in Palestine because it becomes almost a part of Judaism. But there is a difference between a "Jewish Homeland in Palestine" and a "Jewish National State of Palestine." The World Jewish Congress contends for the latter and is provoked because the "Emergency Committee" has stolen its thunder. The others are for a "Homeland"—or oblivious to the struggle going on amongst their confreres. But it will be only a few days now before I relinquish jurisdiction in connection with refugees and let somebody else have the fun. And it has been a heavy responsibility—domestic as well as foreign, because there are 5 million Jews in the country, of whom 4 million are concentrated in and around New York City. And we have *no* Arab or Moslem population but we do have increasingly important commercial interests—principally oil—in the Moslem countries. In addition our ally England has hardly any Jewish citizenship but a very large political interest in the Near East. So our policy increasingly is based in part—a large part—on a domestic situation, while England's is based entirely on a foreign affairs base—and the two are hard to reconcile. . . .

January 24, 1944

The President has appointed a Refugee Board consisting of the Secretaries of State, War, and Treasury—they to appoint a Director to save the refugees in German control. And it is good news for me. This "Director," when chosen, will take over—this insures me staying out. What they can do that I have not done I cannot imagine. However, they can try. I will advise them, if they want—but the Director should do the work. I hope they succeed but there are already rumblings from abroad. Canada advises us orally they will consider withdrawal from the I.G.C. [International Governmental Committee on Refugees] in case this pyramids. We have not heard from England but I expect they will not look with favor on it. However, I think it a good move—for local political reasons—for there are 4 million Jews in New York and its environs who feel themselves related to the refugees and because of the persecutions of the Jews, and who have been demanding special attention and treatment. This will encourage them to think the persecuted may be saved and possibly satisfy them—politically—but in my opinion the Board will not save any persecuted people I could not save under my recent and long suffering administration. . . . The first meeting of the Board will be in Hull's office Wednesday. He has asked me for a memo as to what to propose to it. I told him he ought to name Stettinius as his alternate on the Board and syphon through him. I will get him a memo. . . .

January 25, 1944

Hull has been slightly under the weather for two days and confined to his room. I went out this afternoon and had an hour with him. First we discussed the Refugee Board and a memo on the subject I had prepared at his request dealing with the 1st meeting tomorrow. He agrees that the Director should be outside the Dept. as an independent agency and that the Dept. should help whenever possible—but no longer be responsible. So we are in entire accord—and Stettinius to be his alternate.

Then I took up the "International Political Organization" subject, stated we should get the draft in finished form, get agreement to it here, be ready and proceed thereafter as quickly as possible to submit it to our principal Allies, seek their agreement as promptly as possible and then lay it before the Senate for ratification. This is an election year. It should be laid before the Senate in time for it to act on it before election—for the "Connally Resolution" was only an expression of the individual Senators. It was not only not binding on them but had no official status. However, it was a promise of support—but would not bind the members of the next Senate. Therefore we should put it before them in the sense of the Moscow Declaration and have them face the alternative of passing the resolution of ratification or suffer the decision of the people at the polls. If it was promptly done the whole matter would be taken out of politics—as between the parties—and then it could be opened for signatures by the other nations of the world in the confidence the U.S. would be a member . . . We discussed this and Hull is of the same mind— and that it be done as promptly as practical. We agree about the political elements concerned—and all. He said he had intended to speed the President's approval of the draft and to have a small gathering in his own office to get it going—and that he would proceed to this in a few days.

February 29, 1944

Resolutions were introduced in each House to open up Palestine to immigration so they could develop a Jewish *commonwealth*—a political state. Hearings were to proceed—just when our negotiations with King Ibn Saud[56] for the great Arabian oil deposit and the grant of concessions to

[56] King of Saudi Arabia, 1932–1953.
Reference here is to a plan by which the Petroleum Reserves Corporation, owned and operated by the United States and administered by the Department of the Interior, would

American companies was maturing. Also a pipe-line across Arabia was under consideration. That would all be jeopardized by injecting the Palestine issue —and serious considerations of a military character effecting our supply lines in North Africa and our losses in the Near East be raised. The oil supply is one of the largest ones known and use of it will save our dwindling supply— so necessary if we are ever to fight another war. After talking with Hull at length it was decided that the Senate leaders should know about the oil. I went in secret to a meeting with Connally, George, Barkley, Vandenberg and LaFollette. For an hour I presented the picture and answered questions. They were somewhat stunned and astounded. A letter to Hull had preceded my visit and I insisted one go also to the Secretary of War—and it did—and he answered the resolution should not be passed—or even discussed—because of military necessity. . . . The Arab states began to protest, Iraq, Egypt, Syria. We sent cables to quiet them—and so it stands. But as a consequence I now have the whole politics of the region and the whole of the oil question crossing my desk—and a Congressional investigation of the whole oil business is getting under way. . . .

March 3, 1944

The post-war studies move very slowly into recommendations and conclusions. Part of the delay is due to the failing of Pasvolsky to let anyone peek at the work. Hull told him a month ago to give me all the papers on the "Political Organization" (League of Nations)—and I asked him a week later to do as the Secretary directed. Each time he said he would—but so far I have not had one bit of paper. And that is the way he does all the post-war work of any importance. I shall not speak with him again but when Hull returns I shall see if the whole system can not be shaken up and some results produced.

March 11, 1944

On February 23rd Mr. Stettinius discussed a possible international organization with the President. During the conversation the cables to the Prime Minister and Stalin were discussed and Mr. Stettinius notified the Secretary that the President is now thinking in terms of having the framework of the United Nations organization established so that a meeting could take place in June. [Roosevelt] feels that by using the organization for war purposes, starting with the economic problems outlined in the cables, that Congressional action would not be necessary.

---

have constructed pipelines from the oil-producing fields in Kuwait, Iraq, and Saudi Arabia to the Mediterranean ports of Alexandria and Haifa—building refineries in these cities. Controversies between British officials, American private oil companies, and Washington authorities caused the project to die before the end of June.

I told the Secretary when he returned that the proposal to have all the United Nations take part in drafting the framework of an international political society and to use that organization for war purposes without submitting it to the Congress is a very dangerous procedure and I did not think it could succeed. Mr. Hull agreed, and agreed further that it was necessary in the very near future to discuss the general principles involved with members of the Senate from both parties and about the same time to discuss the matter with England, Russia and China on exactly the same lines and to see if we could not get agreement amongst these four governments and then get informal agreement of the Senate and then submit to the Senate the agreement as signed by the four governments. The agreement could then be open later for signature of the United Nations and the details of it could be worked out later. Hull wanted a number of persons of national prominence associated at the same time. He mentioned John Davis, Jim Cox, Homer Cummings, Chief Justice Stone and former Chief Justice Hughes.[57]

March 15, 1944

... Spent most of the day at the Capitol—Connally, Bloom, Truman, Kilgore,[58] O'Mahoney—and several others on oil, Palestine, and Arabia.

The study for the new "League of Nations" was received from the drafters. Including its security features, it is the product of two years' work. It is pretty good—but a little unbalanced as to powers between the Council and Assembly. I have been over it with care and with some doubts but feel it can be placed in adjustment.

March 19, 1944

We took up the International Society document in the Policy Committee—for a preliminary general discussion. I urged immediate and continuing study. ... There are several defects in the document as submitted—too much power in "Council"—not enough in "Assembly"—no "Administrative Offices" to carry on in recess or adjournment. There is also too much definition of power and authority which ought to be in general terms. ... Most of this was discussed in detail in our Security Committee last July—and it should have been put together six months ago—not just now.

March 21, 1944

Yesterday March entered the lion stage—rain, hail, sleet and ice. This morning the sun shone beautifully and every bush and tree glistened in its

[57] James Cox, Democratic presidential nominee in 1920; Harlan Stone, Associate Justice of the U.S. Supreme Court, 1925–1941, and Chief Justice, 1941–1946; Charles Evans Hughes, Associate Justice of the U.S. Supreme Court, 1910–1916, and Chief Justice, 1930–1941.

[58] Harley Kilgore, Democrat, U.S. Senator from West Virginia, 1941–1956.

light. Spring is here. And yesterday with the "International Organization," the Post War Committee made slow progress. At the present rate of discussion, we will continue till after the war. Something must be done to speed it up, and make something concrete and specific to be signed—something in written terms one can approve, amend or disapprove. Today Indian immigration, "stockpile" bill, Mexican Water Treaty, Palestine, Arabian oil, the Secretary's presentation of statement to the Senate Foreign Relations Committee, criticism of the Department due to lack of particulars in its public relations, the "International Organization," and the "unconditional surrender" phrase as our war objective against Germany— I object to the last because it solidifies the German people through fear. It helps the enemy. I think Russia's formula better and I argued for a restatement of our purpose so as to take the advantage to the enemy out of our program. Am told the President insists on the phrase. . . .

April 23, 1944

Last week we had up again the directions to the Army for occupation of Japan and the questions proposed by the Army. Again the Far Eastern division [of the State Department] relies on Japanese psychology and wants to retain the Emperor and treat him and his successors with glories. I argued for rough treatment—to root out the system which permitted a predatory policy—even if it means deposition for the "Son of Heaven" and his potential successors in office—all of them. They argue for an "institution" and the advisability of retaining it—but I see a three-faced body—the Army, the political establishment (filled by the Army) and the ecclesiastical system with the Emperor at the top (which welds the others together and inspires them). . . . All of which should go. They think my position extreme. I think theirs is soft—compromising—ineffectual. Anyhow, some of the papers are to be re-written and we will look at them again.[59]

April 26, 1944

Another long argument in Post War Committee on Japan and the directions to the Army for occupation which somehow degenerated into an argu-

---

[59] The Cairo Declaration of December 1, 1943, committed the United States, Great Britain, and China to strip Japan of her conquests. In the Potsdam Declaration of July 26, 1945, the same powers, with the Soviet Union adhering later, demanded unconditional surrender and announced their intention to occupy Japan until certain broad objectives were achieved. After Japan's surrender in September 1945, the nation remained under Allied military occupation and subject to the orders of a Supreme Commander for the Allied Powers (SCAP) until April 28, 1952. The planning of postwar Japanese policy had begun in 1942; the State Department and other divisions working on this problem were deeply divided over the issue of a "hard" or "soft" peace. The sharpest disagreement concerned treatment of the emperor—the result was that the emperor renounced his divine powers and supreme sovereignty, but remained in charge of ceremonial functions.

ment by the proponents of the paper in support of the Emperor and of the
institution of Emperor. Joe Grew joined them and read a proposed statement arguing for the dynasty as the best agency to rule Japan—divested (or
suspended from the use of) some of its prerogatives during but restored to
full authority after the occupation. I again said I was not interested in the
Emperor or his successors or in the dynasty. I was however very deeply
interested in making Japan incapable of disturbing the peace of the Pacific or
of the United States in the future. But I did not see how that objective could
be obtained with the centralized authority and power concentrated in the
Emperor and his immediate entourage. I was for the destruction of the system
which made aggression possible. . . . I want the *system* broken up and de-
centralized and the army and navy disarmed and the basis laid so that when
we withdraw it will not be easy to put the pieces together so that a theocratic
personage commanding fealty and obedience from all shall not weld together the political structure and the military forces to be used for predatory
purposes in the name of and under authority of religion. The argument was
adjourned till tomorrow.

May 1, 1944

The International Organization to Secure the Peace is the thing just now
receiving the top side attention. The principal point to be solved is the use of
force—by what authority, how and when. That looks like the bone of contention with the Special Senate Committee.[60] Hull meets them for the second
conference tomorrow. The first time he gave them our papers and they took
them away to study. That was our third (or fourth) draft. Since then we have
another draft. Tomorrow we expect [to discuss] the vital question of the use
of force. We have discussed it a lot amongst ourselves—all phases of it. . . .
We fear the Senators will take the Congressional attitude that the use of
force is making war—and that the Constitution declares the Congress shall
declare war. It does. But it does not limit it to the Congress. It also provides
the President shall use the armed forces to suppress insurrections and to repel
invasion. Both of those are acts of war, one civil—one against a foreign foe.

These Senators are *politicians*. Vandenberg claims he will be guided by his
conscience and non-partisan judgment—but he hates Roosevelt so he is not
normal on any proposal which would give him any power nor to admit he
had a power.

---

[60] On March 22, Secretary Hull expressed his desire to work closely with the Senate
Foreign Relations Committee in establishing an international organization. He suggested
that key members meet with him without fanfare of publicity so that the issue could be
explored informally. Senator Connally agreed and appointed four Republicans—Senators
LaFollette, Austin, Wallace White (Maine, 1931–1949), and Arthur Vandenberg (Michigan,
1928–1951); and four Democrats—Senators Guy Gillette (Iowa, 1936–1945, 1949–1955),
Barkley, George, and himself. The first meeting with Hull occurred on April 25.

LaFollette is congenitally opposed. His father was one of the willful members in the earlier tragedy but he sees some of the changes time has wrought.

Austin is on our side.

On our side George is with us—Connally is jealous of the prerogatives of the Senate and Gillette is inconsistent and unpredictable. A Democrat from Iowa usually would be. . . .

May 3, 1944

The conference with the Senators went quite satisfactorily yesterday, according to Hull . . . However, they did not get into the questionable field of executive authority. Twice Hull broached the subject but each time they shied away. Vandenberg and LaFollette gave some inclination of a possible ground (or excuse) for future opposition. It was—What kind of a peace are we going to have? A good one, or a bad one? If it is bad, the International Organization would be bad. Hull said the Treaty would be partly their responsibility. He might have added—the worse the peace the more the need for the International Organization.

Joe Grew has taken over the Jap occupation and peace terms work. He and I have had several talks and he now agrees with me on the basic principles involved and a re-draft of the whole thing is under way on a basis which will meet my objections.

May 8, 1944

Had two days away from town—at the farm. The flowers and fields, the birds and the horses—all are part of May. Pimlico on Saturday. I lost on the Derby but won on the Dixie—and had my fun at no expense and enjoyed the change of scene. Sunday I worked a few hours but relaxed and slept eleven hours one night and ten the next.

Today is another day. We have had another session on the International Organization. Hull is sure the Republican Senators in his Committee are going to stick for Congressional approval of any move to dispatch troops to any place abroad to enforce decisions of the Council of the organization. If they do take that position, it will prevent any other government from joining the Organization. They will not put this reliance in nor will they be party to a compact in which they all agree to *perform* their part and then at the crucial moment be uncertain as to what we will do and *wait* till Congress debates the issue—and maybe decide NOT to go along. We have been trying to work out a formula—a protocol—which would set out the respective functions of the Congress and the President but I have no use for such a procedure. . . . Hull is inclined to agree with me but Acheson, Hackworth and Pasvolsky are still discussing drafts of agreements between the President and the Congress.

... And so the battle goes. Tomorrow Hull meets the Senators for his third talk. Stettinius—just back—reported to the Policy Committee this a.m. and had agreed to talk to the British here the 3rd week in May—on this subject. I wanted to ask "How about the Russians?" but did not. We should talk to them at the same time.

May 11, 1944

The Senators postponed their conversation till tomorrow. In the meantime, we have had, through Myron Taylor, the benefit of advices from the "Three Wise Men"—great lawyers all. . . . They would not care to have their names used in connection with such work, nor to be quoted—nor even to have it known or recorded that they had been consulted [about the constitutionality of allowing the President to use troops in enforcing decisions of the International Organization's Council]. I suppose an opinion from such an exalted source is worth considering seriously even under the conditions imposed. Taylor seems to be somewhat puffed up about his role and acts as a curtain shield for the great actors. Their names begin with H.—D.—and M.—but it would possibly incriminate them to further identify them.[61]

However, their opinions—for there are three—all agree as to the constitutionality of the program. Amongst them they make three reservations which are sound—and acceptable. The principal one is that there be no illustrious person selected "President" of the whole show—that the Council select one of its own members to preside over that [body]. The argument is there would be politics or competition for the honor and perhaps Stalin or Churchill might be put forth—etc. It is a sound argument—and is accepted. The other two were sound and were accepted. Otherwise, it had their undivided and joint blessing—but entirely "off the record." In their oral opinions at the only meeting with Hull which was in Taylor's apartment—they advised postponement till after election!! That is *not* sound and will not be adopted—under existing circumstances. We cannot keep the thing secret. The American people will respect secrecy while we are talking to other governments—for a reasonable length of time but not indefinitely. So we can't follow that course.

May 12, 1944

The Senators came this morning and practically gave the green light. We had expected to be debated and questioned [about] the right of the President to use force, if necessary, without the consent of the Congress. In spite of the fact he has always had and used that power, we were fearful the prerogative of the Congress to declare war would be interpreted by them as demanding

[61] Reference here is to former Chief Justice Charles Evans Hughes and to Supreme Court Justices William Douglas and Frank Murphy.

the President secure the authority of the Congress before complying with the call of the Council to furnish our share of an international expedition. But that was not raised. Instead, they reverted to the only objection—that raised by LaFollette and Vandenberg—that it was necessary to know what kind of peace—good or bad—would be accomplished before they would consecrate the international organization—and force—to uphold it. Hull's answer is the same—and they did not refute it. . . .

May 19, 1944

. . . Another objection [raised by Hughes, Douglas, and Murphy] was that the statute for the World Court be in a separate instrument. This is also the British position. Its advocates believe it would be more satisfactory to have a separate statute for the Court and that if the Court is treated separately from the political organization it may out-last the other and not be dependent upon it. After considerable discussion of the matter we decided to adopt that suggestion.

During the period the Secretary had been carrying on his conversations with the eight Senators constituting the special committee, we had also been approaching the time when it would be necessary to deliver copies of these documents to the British, Russians and Chinese. But, the British and Russian situation is imminent. Consequently time becomes of the essence. Under these circumstances Connally notified Hull that he would be able to report to him on Wednesday last, which was the 17th. However, the text that [the Senate Committee] agreed upon was unsatisfactory. It had a number of reservations and plainly indicated that [the Senators] were withholding commitment to the principles involved. That evening having had the paper read to him over the telephone by Connally and Hull having a cold so that he could not carry on a conversation, he asked me to get in touch with Connally. I tried that night but Connally was physically indisposed himself. Consequently yesterday morning I met Connally, read the draft and discussed the very great importance of the situation in which the Senate committee was an elemental part of the picture. I presented to him very plainly these different topics. First, the great responsibility which lay upon his shoulders and the members of his committee in this situation. Second, that if the committee made reservations Hull would have his hands tied because other governments would immediately point to the fact that the committee had not accepted Hull's program. Third, that the paper that they were willing to sign did not express approval of the principles involved in the particular documents which had been submitted to them. Fourth, that the documents which had been submitted to them and which must be the basis of the proposals made to the other governments had been approved by them orally and that their assent to the use of the idea involved was essential to further progress along this road. After a long conversation Connally asked me to take the document he had written and to redraft it.

Connally is having serious difficulty because Barkley and Austin (each of them a strong supporter) are out of the city and because LaFollette is very hesitant; Vandenberg desirous of conserving his record so that he can take advantage of some political maneuver if advantageous for him to do so; and Gillette for some strange reason has different ideas—just what they are is difficult to understand. Anyhow, Connally let me read the original record in which these men had made their own comment on his original draft. I returned with my redraft and Connally and I sat there and drafted and redrafted and exercised all the ingenuity each of us had to weave our way around the idea of commitment and yet giving substantial support to the Committee's document. After four or five different drafts we finally arrived at a formula which appeared as the #6 in my file. I read that over the telephone to Hull who was back in bed and he made two suggestions in it, one of which would favor them and one of which would favor us.

So this morning I cleared those with Connally and he accepted the phraseology which has evolved out of this process. I begged him to get Barkley back here or to talk to him over the telephone and obtain his strong support and also urged that he reach Austin in Vermont and secure his complete support. . . . He is trying to get his committee together at 2:30 this afternoon and has asked me to stand by so that if there is serious disagreement he will ask me to meet with them. I have cleared that with Hull, who is still in bed, and he has authorized me to speak for him.

If we can only keep this out of politics and get Democrats and Republicans to accept the document as it now exists we will have accomplished our purpose which is to authorize Hull to go to the other nations with the apparent support of the leaders of the Senate of the United States. . . . What these men really want is to hold off to see whether the peace is good or bad. They say if it is a good peace they will be glad to enforce it. If it is a bad peace they do not want to be obligated. But their holding out prevents us from operating along the lines to secure a good peace. The consequence of it is that this very movement is the crux of the whole program. If we can obtain their assent to the program stated in the draft numbered 6, or even if some words in it are changed but the idea retained, we will have succeeded.

. . . After waiting an hour and a half and no word from Connally I phoned his office at five o'clock and was advised the meeting had adjourned fifteen minutes previous and dispersed and he had gone to another committee! He was expected back in half an hour and they would tell him I would appreciate a call. At six Connally phoned and said they had not been able to agree. They objected to the word "document." I replied to find a synonym like "plan"—"proposal"—anything definite. He thought he could use some suitable phraseology that would pass. They [the Committee] also objected to publication of their letter [of agreement] before the "document" was published because no one would know what they had approved. To which I replied we could hold their letter till the "document" was published but we would have to have some statement from Connally they had agreed the plan was sound enough for us to proceed with conversations. George and Austin were absent today. He expects them present Monday at 10:30 and *hopes* for agreement—but is not enthusiastic of unanimity.

May 22, 1944

. . . The desire of the Senators not to commit themselves [to an international organization] is inherent in Senatorship as such. All of these men are political figures. They all want to be free to act in their own interest and in the interest of their respective constituencies. They do not want to have their course in the future bound in any respect by anything they may have agreed to which was not finished business. And as a matter of fact in the last analysis what we are submitting to them is a statement of principles and not a definitive document such as to be laid eventually before the Senate. The document has not been reduced to actual draft terms—as far as I know. But only a definitive document signed and agreed to could be submitted officially to the Senate in the form of a treaty or agreement or to the Congress for legislative purposes. So that we are not on very sound ground when we try to get that we call a "green light" from Senators on a statement of general principles. We must expect that they will react just as they are reacting—that is, they are shying away like a horse from a snake.

Hull thinks that because Connally dislikes him personally there may be additional obstacles. I told him that I was not intimately acquainted with his own personal relationship with Connally but that in all my dealings with Connally I had had from him only the impression of confidence and respect as regards Hull.

Of course Vandenberg hates Roosevelt. The word "hate" is used advisedly. He thinks Roosevelt stands for everything bad and for nothing good. His sentiment is rancorous. But he is the only one of the group that has that antipathy to Roosevelt and suspicion of every move he makes. Austin is the most reasonable. White, while Assistant Republican Leader, is interested and apparently willing to go quite a distance. LaFollette is bound by the tradition of his family and the opposition of his father to the League of Nations and has a psychological reaction from the treatment his father received from the public in the last war. Gillette is wobbly. I can never tell what he thinks or what he will think about any particular proposition. There seems to be no rule by which to prejudge his actions. George is surprisingly a little off the reservation to the extent that he wants to see what kind of a peace we have to enforce. Barkley is entirely in line and Connally is trying to weave their different political and personal characters into some kind of a pattern which would be satisfactory to us, but I really do not think he is very enthusiastic about his job in this particular and I have a feeling that he would probably prefer not to be committed to anything himself, though he is perfectly willing to go along and try to commit the others. . . .

May 23, 1944

Not one word from Connally today. Have talked to Hull several times—still in bed. He wanted me to get in touch with Connally this morning. I told him I thought it was the wrong thing to do, that I had better wait and give Connally more time. He agreed.

Somewhat later we talked again and he then thought that it was just as well to wait because the Republican members might have felt under some political obligation to consult their own theoretical leadership—that is the Republican Chairman Spangler and Governor Dewey or Governor Bricker[62] or possibly Willkie. To do that would take time. The time elapsed would hardly have been sufficient for them to do so. Consequently it was probably better to let the matter slide for the moment. With all this I was in entire accord. And so that has been today. Nothing has happened.

About 5:30 the Secretary advised me that Connally's office had called his office and had asked for an engagement for Connally as the representative of the committee to see him. He was having his doctor in tonight to see if he can get out tomorrow or the next day and if able to get down to his office he will see Connally day after tomorrow morning. He had no information other than that and we speculate that Connally is to convey to him what will be the final answer of the committee and do it orally so there will be no record.

May 25, 1944

The Secretary telephoned me this morning that he had had his talk with Connally. It lasted two hours. As a result of it Connally learned a good deal about the point of view of the Secretary and about the serious responsibility confronting his committee. Connally has taken the whole thing rather cavalierly and the Secretary made up his mind to make him take it very seriously. Apparently it had that result because Connally returned to his committee and said that he would immediately present it again and would try to get another statement which would refer to the Moscow Declaration and to the Connally Resolution each by name and which would state that the Department of State had taken long steps to implement the spirit of those resolutions and that on

[62] Harrison Spangler, chairman of the Republican National Committee, 1942–1944; Thomas E. Dewey, now governor of New York (1943–1955), will be the 1944 Republican presidential nominee; John Bricker, governor of Ohio (1939–1945), will be the 1944 vice-presidential nominee.

that basis the committee was of the opinion that conversations should proceed with the other governments.

May 27, 1944

Yesterday afternoon the committee of Senators had their last meeting alone and some of them telephoned to Hull to say that the committee would like to meet with him on the 29th, which will be Monday, in the morning. I went to a small reception for Harold Dodds of Princeton and there met Warren Austin. Austin said that the committee could not agree on any formula but would be willing to make an oral statement to Hull. He was somewhat belligerent and rather critical of Vandenberg and LaFollette but said there was nothing that could be done to get them to the point of subscribing a statement to which the others would be willing to agree. He thought it possible to wage a fight and to place the matter before the people of the country in such a way that those men would be seriously criticized.

This morning we have had a very long conversation—Acheson, Norman Davis, Hackworth, Pasvolsky and myself. The whole history of the thing was reviewed. An article just appeared in the *Saturday Evening Post* of May 20 written by Forrest Davis. It is the second of two articles. The first appeared a week ago. They concern the conference at Teheran and purport to give the President's views and a statement of his mental activities there.[63] This article has hurt the situation because it has come on top of several other articles in the press which indicate to these recalcitrant Senators that the President does not take the Department of State into his confidence and that agreements made with the Department of State are not binding upon him and which cause these Senators to back farther away from any commitment. They feel that it would be useless for them to make any agreement about a matter and then to have some other authority not bound by it take a different course. Vandenberg is particularly ferocious in his attitude toward Roosevelt and these recent articles, if they do not fortify him, will serve as additional pretexts upon which he can hang his recalcitrant position. White is perfectly willing to go along but will not sign any statement unless it is unanimously agreed upon. So that leaves three of the eight Senators outside of the agreement if it is to be signed. Three is more than one-third of the eight. These men represent the various shades of political opinion of the Senate and it only takes one-third of the Senate to block a treaty. The world might figure it on that basis, and if it did so any signed agreement would do more harm than it could possibly do good.

[63] At the Teheran [Iran] Conference, November 28—December 1, 1943, Roosevelt, Churchill, and Stalin agreed on the scope and timing of military operations against Germany, including plans for the Allied invasion of France. Stalin reaffirmed his pledge to commit Soviet forces against Japan after the defeat of Germany. The three leaders also stressed the need for a United Nations.

At least that was the argument I made this morning. I related the history of the whole movement from the work of the Security Committee three years ago and coming up through the Mackinaw-Fulbright Resolutions, the Moscow Agreement and the Connally Resolution; then the presentation of the documents which were statements of principle but which were specific in that they had physical form and political substance though the language was not in such shape that it could be signed as a document to be agreed to by the parties concerned. Nevertheless it was a specific document. The country knew that it had been on the basis of this document the Secretary had had his conversations with the Senators; then had come the conferences with the Senators and Monday was to be the last. We were now at the fork of the roads. We had come up this road which I have just indicated. We now had to go either to the left or to the right. One way led to disagreement—open and vitriolic and extensive and which might find its way into the political arena.

The other road accepts what we have got and takes the best we can get and makes the best use of it. I stated that I had only two objectives in life. One was to win this war and the other was to see set up an international organization to secure the peace if possible. I had no other ambitions, sentiments, or objectives in either public or private life and that anything that I could do in either capacity to further those ends I was going to do. I thought most of the American people felt the same way. Consequently I passed on that sentiment and in relation to that history I recommended that he meet with the Senators Monday and make one last effort to get their agreement in writing but that if that were not possible that he thank them for the time spent in their collaboration and that he then make a very carefully prepared statement which would be short and which would be to the effect that he had had a number of discussions with the Senators who represented every shade of political opinion in the United States Senate. In consideration of the agreement at Moscow and in the spirit of the Connally Resolution, he had made a proposal of general principles to serve as the basis for preliminary conversations with other governments for the implementation of an international security organization. Now that the conversations with the Senators were concluded he had been sufficiently encouraged to proceed to converse with the other governments and that he was so proceeding. . . .

After two hours of conversation the Secretary left—I am quite sure with the thought that he would follow the course that I had outlined—and he went across the street to talk with the President and to lay the whole matter before him and to ask what he would care to have done in the circumstances. With him he took the Davis articles I have mentioned above and he took a copy of a letter Vandenberg had written him some time ago, shortly after their conversations began, and in which Vandenberg laid the basis for the position he has since followed.

May 28, 1944

Yesterday Hull saw the President and had a very full and frank conversation with him. It covered all phases of the present situation including the recent publicity. I called Hull in the evening on the telephone and he said the President had appreciated the significance of the situation and had volunteered to call in each of the eight Senators and have a personal talk with them and assure them that the statements made in the public press were incorrect and that the President was entirely sincere in his efforts to work this thing out to the best advantage. The plan was that he would begin with Vandenberg and have his first talk with him. I was asked what I thought of it. I said I thought it was dangerous; that Vandenberg's position was animated partly by personal animus to Roosevelt and partly by political considerations. He undoubtedly wanted to proceed with some kind of international organization and in my mind was sincere in that but his attitude toward the President was such that I thought no statement to him by the President would change that attitude. It was of too long standing and too deep. I also discussed with him an article appearing in the *Saturday Evening Post* by Demory Best which apparently had been written from the information contained in the Forrest Davis story and the information had been obtained by access to the advance sheets of the Davis story and it looked as if not only Vandenberg might have had knowledge in advance of both stories but that Dewey's foreign advisor [John Foster] Dulles had also been party to it. At least from my knowledge of Vandenberg's reactions and from conversations with him I gained that definite impression.

I called him [Hull] about noon today and had another considerable conversation. He said that he had thought over night about the conversations on the part of the President with these individuals and had come to the conclusion, largely based on his own political judgment and reinforced by my reactions, they should not be held and had telephoned the President this morning and had told him he thought it better not to do it that way. The President agreed and cancelled the program. The President also agreed that Hull in his conversations tomorrow with the members of the committee should say to them what the President would have said and invite them individually to go to the President if they so desired and he would give to them individually the same assurances which Mr. Hull would give them but that they would have the opportunity to get it direct from the President if they so desired.

May 29, 1944

This morning the Senators returned for the last of their conferences. It ended as expected—nothing in writing. Only Vandenberg and LaFollette held out. White was willing to sign. Lacking unanimity there was nothing in writing.

This afternoon we of the Department—the same group—met with Hull and agreed upon a statement which he issued and which was in line with the suggestion I made last week. Hull added a last phrase about "non-partisan" treatment of the subject by the Department of State. Pasvolsky objected to the phraseology of the "non-partisan" phrase. He said it was awkwardly expressed. Hull replied that if it was awkward enough to attract attention it was all right with him. He hoped it would stick out like a sore thumb so that everybody would look at it and understand the emphasis he was putting on it. Consequently if he could make it a little more awkward and still carry the sense he would be glad to do it.

The point of all this is that there had been a considerable difficulty in preparing the statement. Hull wanted to insert into it something to cut the ground from under the objecting Senators and had inserted in the statement a sentence to the effect that everybody wanted a good peace and was striving for it and every official had a responsibility in connection with it and that nobody wanted to preserve a peace that was not worth preserving. I objected to that because it was argumentative. This was a statement and not an argument. Acheson tried to get around it by some other phraseology. Finally the whole sentence was stricken out and any allusion to the subject was eliminated. But then Hull put onto the end of it the phrase about non-partisan treatment of the subject by the Department of State and that was intended to serve as the background for any criticism of the statement that emanate from the two recalcitrant Senators.

Recalcitrant is hardly the proper word. LaFollette is just constitutionally opposed. His heredity and his whole attitude seem to deny the thought that he can support [the international organization]. I rather look for him to end up against it. On the other hand I rather expect Vandenberg to support it. But they are recalcitrant in that they will not agree with their colleagues and with us in giving any kind of assurance that they are satisfied even for the time being with the developments up to their present stage.

Hull phoned Halifax and the Soviet Ambassador to come in tomorrow at eleven to discuss a meeting of the three governments to exchange plans and views—and they accepted.

June 6, 1944

The invasion of France began this morning. Beachheads on a wide front have been established in Normandy. The whole world is excited by it—the radios are all busy with the story and the event has overshadowed everything else.

I talked with Pershing in 1917 the night before he went to France—and last night I talked with Marshall. I think he is due in England. He was still here at noon. Last night the Russian Ambassador decorated him with

Russia's highest award—at the Russian Embassy—and I got home late at 9:30 for dinner after the ceremony and vodka. Marshall is a very able, solid, forceful, decisive person. I think I have higher regard for him than for any of his predecessors I have known—and they include Scott, March[64] and McArthur [sic].

We passed the recommendations on France through the Post War Committee this morning, after debate on only two items. One was remanded for redraft and I was in the minority seeking amendment of the other.

Hull is away for ten days rest. Stettinius handed me a file in disagreement between the European and Near Eastern Divisions and asked me to get a recommendation by morning. It involves a British proposal to Russia—and we were not consulted till Russia asked if we agreed—to assign Rumania to Russia and Greece to Britain for their respective independent control over "affairs" in those two countries. Churchill cabled F.D.R. and I am proposing an answer in the negative.

June 7, 1944

We are pursuing disorganized Germans north of Rome—and may expect heavy fighting again near or before the Arno—and resistance has stiffened today in France with a more active enemy air force. But the combination of the two events must have a strong psychological influence in Germany. We have been busy helping by preventing necessary supplies reaching Germany. Wolfram from Spain—nearly stopped; wolfram from Portugal—stopped; chrome from Turkey—stopped; ball bearings from Sweden—slowed up and still in dispute. Mikolajczyk of Poland is here.[65] Conversations do not indicate a yielding frame of mind. I have not seen him yet but the report of his talks with Stettinius and the European Division are not encouraging.

June 9, 1944

I have dined twice on two successive evenings with the Prime Minister of Poland but there has been no political conversation between us on the delicate subject. Tonight Frankfurter sat between me and him. Frankfurter was in a most talkative mood with Vandenberg on the other side of the Prime Minister. However nothing of political consequence developed except the expression of bitter opposition to Germany in all of its forms and practices.

[64] Hugh L. Scott, U.S. Army chief of staff, 1914–1917; Peyton C. March, U.S. Army chief of staff, 1918–1921.

[65] Stanislaw Mikolajczyk, prime minister of the Polish government-in-exile.

Reference here is to the complicated Polish situation. The U.S. and Great Britain backed the Polish government in London and urged its leaders to settle territorial differences with the Soviet Union. The Soviets supported the Communist-dominated Polish Committee of National Liberation (the Lublin government), which declared itself the rightful Polish authority on December 31, 1944.

It is bad weather and hard going in France. It goes much better in Italy and we have even passed Civitavecchia on the way north. Madame Lipovatz, the niece of the Queen of Italy, came in worried about her mother and I got off a cable to Kirk,[66] and I did the same thing a day or so before to get food and medicine to Ascanio Colonna who was reported as quite ill at a hotel in Rome and lacking food and medicine.

June 10, 1944

We finished up Yugoslavia in the Post War Committee but the questions of the British-Russian agreements as to Greece and Rumania were still unfinished. However I approved a final draft during the morning and early this afternoon it was dispatched. It expresses the point of view that I have maintained from the start but which I had considerable difficulty in having approved.

The question of an additional agreement with England over surplus military supplies and their disposition freely by Great Britain in the form of goods similar to Lend Lease was not disposed of. I have come to what I think is a proper solution of it and have the agreement at least of a large sector of the Department's opinion in using exactly the same phraseology to England that we are proposing to use to Russia. I have reason to believe that that will prevail but it will not be finished until Monday. It involved the furnishing of 10,000 guns by the British to Ibn Saud and there was also the question of Russian tanks being furnished to Iran while we are furnishing tanks to Russia. To my mind the question is fundamental though there is a good deal of sympathy on the part of certain persons in the Department for a modification of views in that respect.

June 13, 1944

The President yesterday had a last talk with Mikolajczyk (euphonistically it would be spelled Mikolochik—and I wish the Poles indulged in that form of alphabetical ostentation) and told him that the Poles should not take an irrevocable or intransigent position vis-à-vis Russia; that they should expect fair treatment and a just settlement from Russia; but should not take their stand on a geographical parallel in East Prussia; but should be ready to adjust themselves to the possibility of legitimate claims on the part of others; and should be ready to be compensated for variations in the east by the accession of East Prussia; and should consider an indefinite line between their eastern claim and the Curzon Line. So the Poles ought to know now that they ought to be reasonable. But by temperament they are not a reasonable race—so it may not result in any change.

[66] In addition to his responsibilities as ambassador to Egypt, Alexander Kirk served as the U.S. ambassador to the Advisory Council for Italy, 1944.

This Polish question is a great problem for us here. Detroit, Chicago, Buffalo, etc. contain great settlements which are especially articulate in an election year. I have talked to some of their "leaders" who are reasonable and see the problem from the United States point of view but apparently they are not actual "leaders" for their Buffalo convention [of the Polish-American Congress, May 28–30] popped off in a nationalistic (Polish) direction instead of the American tone indicated by their "statement of principles." The appeal to former allegiance apparently had a deciding effect on the delegates for they ended up their resolutions on a foreign theme. I did the best I could with them and found the "leaders" understanding and sympathetic. The whole problem —not only a just settlement in Europe but a solution (or a position) satisfactory to the Poles here seems difficult—and they *may* hold the balance of power in votes in Illinois, Ohio and New York—and Pennsylvania—though it is improbable they will control in the last two.

Another bad one is de Gaulle. He is cutting up again—insists on "Provisional *Government* of France." The President has asked him here to talk and no doubt he will come—and be a hero in our press as he is now in England where he was invited for invasion day. But when he got there he refused to cooperate and ordered to refrain from invasion all the liaison forces who had been trained in England and at their and our expense for a year—500 of them. Next day he consented that 20 go—but I believe only *one* actually went and he has kept the others in England. And he is fussing because we are expending invasion francs in France instead of some currency he would agree to spend and *authorize*!

The radical press here is enthusiastic for him and hypercritical of us. As usual, they espouse some foreign cause to champion rather than advocate the *American* point of view or propose some practice in our own interest. And the circle of their ranks is spreading. It is already an embarrassing question— and may, probably will, become very troublesome. But if you accept the theory which seems to me fundamental that we want the people of France to choose their own government—how are we to justify choosing one for them?

De Gaulle had a conference with Churchill and Eden. Churchill took the President's line but Eden waded in and condemned that policy, said it was United States policy, England not responsible for it, and the Foreign Office not only did not agree with the Prime Minister but wanted to recognize— in the presence of de Gaulle—all of which makes it so much "easier" for us to hold the line. We are "obdurate," "out of harmony," "selfish," "unimaginative," "impractical" and "wrong."

We finished Formosa this morning in Post War Committee and Austria too. We had a deadline of June 15 to finish all—but can't do it. We have extended it one week, are working every day and expect to be all through by the end of next week. And it is heavy going—with every political problem and most of the economic problems in the world paraded across your desk in rapid succession.

June 14, 1944

Hull talked over plans for the conversations with the other Governments about the Security Organization. Halifax will represent Eden and Cadogan[67] will come over. Soong apparently wants to come for China. We have not heard from the Russians and decided to send a cable to Harriman to let them know the progress with the others with the thought they should let us know. Gromyko[68] has just left for Moscow—three or four days ago—and they might be waiting to talk to him. We hope they will send a top-side man.

As to procedure here—Hull will talk to them as to the fundamentals and seek agreement on them in principle. That may take a week. Then the principles agreed upon are to go to "technicians" for incorporation in a draft. That may take two weeks. Then the drafts will go back to the top level for discussion and agreement. If all goes well that may take a week—four weeks in all. Perhaps it can be done in three.

The conversations will all be in Washington. Eden prefers it here in spite of the heat so he can be kept constantly in touch—and there would be a delay in transmission and in speed if the conversations were out of town as originally considered possible. We of course prefer Washington—in spite of the heat probable in August, perhaps late July.

June 15, 1944

Bright and early this morning we were taken into conference on the general subject of Security Organization. I missed (we all did) the Post War Committee. Isaiah Bowman,[69] Pasvolsky, Dunn, Hackworth, Hull and myself. The subject matter had been up yesterday. It was—a public statement giving some description of the International Organization proposed by the United States. The people want details. They want to know what the general idea is. There have been recently attacks of critical nature based on ignorance or misunderstanding. Culbertson, the bridge professional recently turned super-statesman, did it on the radio.[70] Columnists have fulminated. Editorialists have criticized. So it was talked out yesterday. A radio speech was suggested. I opposed that. It is too close to the Republican Convention to do that and keep politics out of it. A press interview, suggested. I doubted that —for the same reason but less cogent. So this morning it came up—quick—

---

[67] Alexander Cadogan, British Undersecretary for Foreign Affairs, 1938–1946.

[68] Andrei Gromyko, Soviet ambassador to the United States, 1943–1946.

[69] President of Johns Hopkins University, 1935–1950, and vice-chairman of the State Department's Post-War Advisory Council, 1943–1944.

[70] Ely Culbertson, international contract bridge expert, proposed that every nation in the postwar international organization be considered equal in all decisions and on all councils.

had to be done—*now*. We met at 9:30 and talked. Hull dictated a paper. Hurriedly written up. Then at 10:00 Bowman, Hackworth, Pasvolsky and I were detailed to redraft and enlarge. Have it finished *before* eleven o'clock— and we did.

Then Hull took Pasvolsky and Bowman over to the President and annexed Norman Davis and the President was asked to approve and issue it. It was drawn as a statement for him to issue and he approved and issued.

The reason for this technique does not appear on the face of it—or in connection with it. The reason was that Hull is now attacked by those who say *he* is not running foreign policy—the President is; *he* does not know what the President says nor the commitments he makes—so any argument Hull makes lacks authority—even knowledge. He is not in the inner confidence of the President—and that is a telling factor. Vandenberg uses it. The Forrest Davis articles put fuel on the flames. The impression was growing. So this was conceived to tie the President in to the whole works and commit him to Hull's program—which, in the last analysis, of course, is the President's program— for we are all under him and *his* administration will get the credit for all of it or any of it which succeeds.

And so it was done.

I have suggested to Hull that I be authorized to talk to Warren Austin— perhaps others of that group—and try to get the Republican Resolutions Committee to go along the road very far in our direction—with the concurrent agreement we will not attack them politically if they do. They will probably want to stand on the "Mackinac" line.[71] But a lot has happened since Mackinac. It would be better to bring their stand up to date and include some of the features of the plan. And that would take the *whole thing* right out of politics. More—it would put the *next* Senate on record for us because the men to sit in the next Senate will be elected on the two platforms about to be drafted. And my personal relations with *all* those men are such I can talk straight politics *and* statecraft.

But he is too cautious for that. I will broach the subject once more—but without his and the President's authority I will do nothing more than I have done which is that I talked lightly on the subject and played with the thought in talking with Vandenberg and Austin at the Polish Embassy last week. They were each interested—but the subject was not pursued.

June 17, 1944

Yesterday afternoon I made an engagement with Senator Warren Austin to see him this morning. Then I saw Hull, told him I was to see Austin and

[71] The postwar advisory council of the Republican party met at Mackinac Island, Michigan, during September 1943, and pledged "responsible participation" in an "organization of sovereign nations" to prevent future military aggression and attain peace "with organized justice in a free world."

renewed the suggestion I had made that I present the possibilities of a Republican platform which would coincide in principle with ours—keep the Security Organization out of politics—and commit both parties and *all* candidates for office on either ticket to the principles—incidentally fixing the moral obligation to support an organization based on those principles upon every member of the next House and in one-third of the next Senate. I proposed as the mechanics that I talk with Austin and I offer to be his contact here while he is in Chicago—not to embarrass him by a call from me but to be available to discuss any matter which might trouble him and to try to straighten out any obstacle or to engage to obtain any pledge of cooperation to further the desired end. Hull agreed (and he is also seeing Will Hays—but Will is *not* a delegate. He got beat by the powers who choose—so he will not be in Chicago).

This morning at 10:30 I met Austin in his office. We got into the subject of the International Organization. He stated again his keen interest, traced the questionable recent history of the Republican party, castigated its 1940 platform, then the dawning of a better day with the 1942 Republican National Committee resolution, the Mackinac Statement—his own considerable activity in that body and service on the drafting sub-committee of which Vandenberg was chairman—his conferences with the Secretary, as member of the select Senate Committee and his sincere ambition to take it all out of politics and to put it on a national basis as a national need.

Then he said he could not work effectively on the Resolutions Committee —of which he is a member—or on the floor of the Convention in case there was a fight on the floor—unless he was free to talk of some of the subjects and matters which composed our program and which had been discussed in secret by Hull with his Committee. He felt his hands were tied and his utility to the cause was thereby circumscribed and limited. I agreed with him and undertook to get him freed from some of it—as much as was possible from the point of view of our needed courtesy and consideration for the proprieties of our contacts with the other governments. —And he agreed to the liaison with me by telephone, day or night, while he was in Chicago—if it would be helpful—but to originate with *him*, not at all to come from me. After nearly and hour I went back to the Department and saw Hull—laid before him the whole conversation—advised that we free him as far as diplomatic practice and necessity would permit. After twenty minutes or more of conversation Hull agreed—and I suggested and he agreed neither of us would mention the agreement or the conversations to *anybody else*.

By 12:30 I was back in Austin's office, freed him from his obligations of secrecy, agreed he might talk more freely but limited his freedom by 1) no quotation of Hull; 2) no direct reference to a particular feature of the plan as being a part of the plan, but, to talk, if in his discretion it would be wise for him to do so in furtherance of a resolution to conform to our program and to describe the whole organization if necessary to accomplish that objective but to do it as of his own knowledge and understanding resulting from his conferences with Hull and with quotations and direct references to Hull's Easter speech, my New York speech, the President's statement of yesterday and any other public utterance actually made by Hull or Roosevelt. He agreed. I then explained why we could not turn him loose entirely—because the program had *not* been delivered to the other governments and could not be (in our interest) until the expected meeting at which there would be an exchange of plans. Prior to that we all had to be bound by secrecy. He understood and agreed and said he saw the whole thing in a better light and was ready for the fray.

I impressed upon him the necessity of bringing any resolution up to date *since* Mackinac—that a lot of water and some implementation of principle had passed over the dam since then. If they were to be in step with us they had to do more than reaffirm Mackinac. Since then had been Moscow, Connally and Fulbright[72] and the conversations with Senators and a unanimous agreement Hull should talk to other governments—and the evolution of a definite program he well knew.

After that I met Jimmie Reynolds[73]—who is leaving tomorrow for Chicago. I met him by appointment at the Metropolitan Club and put the same proposal to him—individually, separately and secretly. He has as many contacts with the real leaders as any man in his party and is *still* an effective mechanic in practical political affairs. Jim agreed to my program and will do all he can to work a resolution which will be in harmony with the International Organization I outlined to him—in secret, not for quotation, for his guidance and basic knowledge only. So now we will wait and see whether a rose grows in the garden—or a pumpkin. If it should be a rose it will be my first success in a *Republican* convention.

June 20, 1944

The British Minister of Munitions made a most inept and to us embarrassing speech in London today. He interpolated a statement to the effect that Japan had been justified in attacking us because we had provoked the attack by giving aid and comfort to her enemies—or words which had that effect. Then somebody tried to explain it away and made it worse. It became prime business for us. Facing a situation in France that statement would give a fine line of propaganda for Germany in Europe and would substantiate Japan's story to her own people. It was bad enough for enemy propaganda but at home here it is almost as bad because there is the Wheeler-Nye and other

[72] See above, pp. 323, n. 51; 356, n. 71.
[73] James Reynolds, former secretary of the Republican National Committee, 1912–1920.

charges that Roosevelt deliberately led us into this war by secret and un-authorized dealings with Churchill.[74] It is a current brand of conversation. And the Republican Convention is about to meet in the course of which our opposition is looking for some substantiation of just such talk.

After Halifax had been talked to but not heard from after five or six hours and after talking to Winant—who hadn't heard it—we decided to issue a statement of denial and reaffirmation of our historic position. We—the same group—worked with Hull, he cleared it with the President in our presence by phone, and the statement was issued saying the orator was "entirely in error as to the facts" and failed to "state the true attitude of the United States" dur-ing the earlier stages of aggression as well as the later stages—and specifying again Japan's aggressions beginning in 1931. And it was issued. This lasted till eight o'clock.

Senators Ball, Burton, Hatch and Hill—the "H_2B_2" group as someone facetiously called them—are coming in to see Hull Thursday on Post War Security Organization.[75] We discussed that before the declaration and we were all in accord at the end that Hull use his discretion during the talk to determine whether he should hand them copies like the other Senators got. The decision—to do so if it seemed they would expect it and accept the secrecy injunction. Otherwise not.

June 21, 1944

The longest day in the year, and the shortest seems only a few weeks ago. At such rapid pace do we race through "age."

This morning I had to leave the Post War Committee early to go before the Senate Foreign Relations Committee. After failing to get their approval (and being unwise to press it) for an Iranian boy to enter West Point we went into secret session and on request I took up successively Finland (they were all sympathetic to Finland and thought us harsh),[76] de Gaulle and Latin America—with particular reference to Argentina—the one black sheep. Then I stayed to lunch with ten or twelve of them and did some legislative and some political work with individual members.

[74] Reference here is to a speech delivered by Oliver Lyttelton, British Minister of Production (not of Munitions). Lyttelton claimed that his views were misrepresented by reporters. The previous day, June 19, Senators Wheeler and Nye had asked for a Senatorial inquiry to determine whether Churchill had received Roosevelt's assurances of U.S. aid before 1940.

[75] During 1943, Senators Joseph Ball (Republican, Minnesota, 1940–1942, 1943–1949), Burton, Hatch, and Hill had sponsored the so-called B_2H_2 resolution calling for United States participation in a postwar international organization. Senator Connally, chairman of the Foreign Relations Committee, shunted aside their resolution in favor of his own. The Connally Resolution, which included the B_2H_2 principles, passed the Senate on November 5, 1943.

[76] On June 30, the United States broke diplomatic relations with Finland. Secretary Hull charged that the Finnish government had become "a puppet of Nazi Germany."

Having come to decision to recognize Bolivia (the 23rd), we are taking up Argentina to bring that situation to a head. Armour is being "recalled for consultation" and a bill of particulars of Argentina's misdeeds is being prepared for circulation to the other republics. Hull this evening asked me to pull it together and it is started and will be ready for presentation tomorrow. The columnists—Welles and others—are critical of us in respect to Argentina in particular and Latin America in general—and we are somewhat vulnerable but have had to proceed cautiously.[77]

June 22, 1944

In the Post War Committee we had the revised paper on "Trusteeships" for backward territories and mandated areas and I was successful in having held open for United States ownership, if that should prove desirable, the Japanese mandated islands in the Pacific and any other islands taken from Japan.[78] So after twenty-five years I made a little progress.

We got final clearance for the statement about Bolivia's recognition. That is the end of that. We got policy on Argentina—settled—a long telegram setting out a bill of particulars against Argentina. There was division in the ranks of the South American advisors but the Secretary handed it to me for settlement last evening and in two sessions today we had it all set out and ready for Hull's approval—which he gave in the third session which was with him. So that is that for the moment.

June 26, 1944

Talked to George Creel[79] today before he left for the Republican Convention and asked him to try to guide the important reporters and radio commentators in their presentation of the Republican foreign relations plank. I presented the thought that if the plank proposed by the Austin subcommittee was adopted by the whole committee and by the Convention it might be the biggest story any of them ever wrote; that if they could bring it into close harmony with the international organization outlined by Roosevelt recently and by Hull and myself the effect would be that foreign relations as such were on a non-partisan basis and that the approach to the establishment of an international organization would be an American policy—not a party

[77] Argentina's pro-Fascist leanings, and her support of a Fascist *coup* in tin-rich Bolivia, caused Washington much consternation during the war years. It was not until March 27, 1945, that Argentina unenthusiastically declared war on Japan and Germany, but genuine democratic elements were still stifled in the militaristic nation.

[78] Under the Treaty of Versailles (1919), Japan administered the former German possessions in the Pacific. The mandate comprised some 1400 islands, islets, and reefs, three main groups of which were the Marianas, Marshalls, and Carolines. Following the Japanese defeat, the islands passed under Allied control. On November 6, 1946, at the request of the United States, the islands were placed under United Nations trusteeship with the United States as administering authority.

[79] Journalist, and former chairman of the Committee on Public Information, 1917–1918.

program. That would be most important. It *might* change the course of future history. The commentators could guide public thoughts and impress that upon the public mind right at the most important moment. The psychological impression would be very strong and might be lasting. They could hardly do a better service to their country. . . . So between George Creel, Will Hays, Warren Austin and Jimmy Reynolds I have covered as best I can the Republican platform committee, the Republican organization as such and the translators to the public of the events of the convention.

I understand from fairly well informed source that Dewey, if nominated, will ask facilities for travel to England, France, Italy, Russia and China. The reason would be that he could answer the charge he did not know anything about foreign affairs. He could presumably learn it all in a few weeks—and how to win the war too! Like "One World" Willkie he would be "One Trip" Dewey. I told Steve Early—thinking the President might be interested.

June 26, 1944

We have been examining in the Post War Committee the question of Germany's post war treatment, and there are of course the preliminary stages of occupation which are practically military provisions. Then comes an intermediate provision and finally there comes the ultimate disposition.

Everyone is agreed upon occupation by the three Powers as representatives of the United Nations. The Department has been thinking along the lines of a united Germany with the exception that East Prussia and Silesia be divested and added to Poland and that certain rectifications be made along the western region of the Rhine. In my own mind I have had difficulty in coming to a conclusion as to the best course to pursue and I am still in a bit of a quandary. However, as it now develops it seems that my objections to the Department's program—which objections I have not been able to convince myself of as to their correctness—have also found place in the minds of the big three, Roosevelt, Churchill and Stalin. My information now is that each of the three is for partition of Germany. Roosevelt wants it in three parts; Churchill in five; and Stalin in seven. They mean to break up Germany as a going concern, having already in mind the probability that East Prussia and Silesia will go to Poland. What would remain would be divided up into a number of parts.

One of the questions I have been cogitating for a long time and since the matter first came up in the Security Committee was whether partition would help to break up German unity or whether it would not create an underlying sympathetic relationship between the various parts which would be more serious in the end and which would linger on in much the same manner that it has in Poland for the last 120 years and as it did in Bohemia. The Germans have had it ingrained in them for the last thousand years that wherever they may be all over the world they are Germans at heart. We have found it so in this country in two wars with Germany. We have found it so in every country in South America which has a German population even though it be a small minority. It has been found particularly so in Brazil, which imported from Russia at one time what they thought were going to be Russians but they turned out to be Germans who had 200 years previously moved into Russia and who still considered themselves Germans and who continued to act as Germans when they were settled in southern Brazil. That being the history of the animal, it is hard to see how a theoretical boundary line would separate them in sympathy or deprive them of the desire to be reunited. It is further hard to see that such reaction against the known psychological characteristics of the German people would deprive them of a common impulse or a common ambition to be reunited and to reassert themselves in what in the future will seem to be a "former grandeur."

In studying the papers the Committee has had I have attempted to guide the policy to be a destruction of the bureaucratic system of Germany, including not only the military, naval and commercial bureaucracies and the industrial bureaucracy but even the educational and religious organization of the country which heads up into the central state and is directed by the central state, all the teachers being appointed and paid by the central government irrespective of the desires of the local community and the pastors and preachers in Germany being more or less controlled by the central government by virtue of the taxes imposed throughout Germany of which each congregation is the beneficiary.

However, any responsibility of decision will apparently be taken off my shoulders if the report is correct that the three great men have made up their minds to do something quite different than the Department was proposing. While I am not sure that the carrying out of that decision will change a situation which we know to have existed since the days that Caesar wrote his Gallic Wars [sic], it will be just as satisfactory to my own sense of responsibility as it would be if Germany was to be left as a single state. My one belief is that the bureaucratic system must be destroyed. It is hard to see how it could really be destroyed if the single state is to be continued because there would always be a gravitation back to what is the present norm in Germany and has been the norm since the practice was started by Frederick the Great. It is reasonable to suppose that if Germany were broken up into a number of states the bureaucratic system could not be larger than the confines of the state and, in that respect, what I consider to be the *sine qua non* in a settlement of the German problem will automatically have been brought about. Perhaps that is the only proper solution and I am inclined to think that I agree with it much more fully than I do with the idea of leaving Germany as a single state even divested of East Prussia and Silesia.

June 28, 1944

The Republican platform on foreign relations is a disappointment. It is so far from being specific or concrete or definite and so remote from ours that I don't see how we can keep the difference from becoming the subject of political discussion—consequently, we cannot keep it out of politics as I had hoped. On such a platform Dewey was nominated. His speech of acceptance tonight was about as commonplace as that of any little two-by-four orator I ever heard. He said absolutely nothing. Idealism was absent, constructive thought was silent, platitudes were abundant and even criticism poorly done.

June 29, 1944

Hull was upset this morning by Dewey's speech. He seemed to take personal umbrage at the use of the words "old," "tired," "quarrelsome"—used to criticize the Administration. I thought the whole speech should be turned aside—overlooked. He felt differently—wanted to wade right in and say something about it. Several short statements were dictated. I did not like any of them—pointed out we had tried hard to get our foreign relations on a non-partisan basis and it did not make sense to be thrown off base by one speech which unless we magnified it out of all proportion to its merits would be forgotten in a week. I urged that he pass it all over but if he had to say anything to say: "I am glad that the Republican platform relating to foreign relations and the speeches in the convention which touched on that subject avoided partisan treatment of those important matters. Our effort has been to keep out of partisan politics foreign relations in general and post-war methods of international cooperation in particular. I hope we can continue on that level."

Strange to relate Berle was the only one who approved. Then Hull dictated another. I said I did not like it at all. He asked why. I said it sounded like he was tooting his own horn. He replied if he did not the opposition would not. He retorted his record spoke for itself. But he was unconvinced and unmoved. He was plainly exaggerating first the importance of the remarks of Dewey and second the applicability to him of the offensive comment. He is sensitive to criticism these days. But he was also losing sight of the main line which is that, while the platform and speeches do not closely approximate our position, the fact is they do not take issue with us in principle and partisan attack in principle is absent. Anyhow, he went to talk with the President and when he came back met the press. The President must have agreed with me for he passed it all over when he was asked by the press the only one question put to him on that subject.

The question of nomination for Vice President has been much under discussion. Wallace is generally and almost universally disliked. The President has stood for him in spite of all the criticism. Texas is one example of the trouble it can get him in on that account. Now I understand the President is weakening. Barkley, Rayburn, etc. are not approved but Henry Kaiser[80]— the boat builder magician—is reported as acceptable as a compromise. It sounds like a red herring—but it may be true. Barkley is to be Keynoter again—according to my information.

July 13, 1944

Roosevelt announced yesterday he would accept the Democratic nomination and if elected would serve. My information from Early previously had been to that effect—and further that he wanted to be elected to finish the war —which is quite natural, proper, and, from my point of view, very desirable. But there has been great and widespread opposition to Wallace as Vice President again. He was a good Secretary of Agriculture but has been a distinct failure as Vice President. He has attached to himself radicals, has espoused wild theories, has been inconsistent and has been very provocative.

Roosevelt's announcement stirred up the Vice Presidential situation as that remains the only thing in doubt. Barkley, Rayburn, Byrnes and Truman (of Missouri) are being advocated by various elements. Different reasons are advanced against each. They have been the subject of discussion by the President with his political advisors—who are few. He has raised objections to each, is reported (quite directly) to prefer Wallace but to realize the opposition and its meritorious grounding and to be disposed to let the Convention decide. The latest report is that he feels that if he were a delegate he would vote for Wallace but would accept the Convention's choice.

According to Early, he feels different this time than last—four years ago. Then he did *not* desire the nomination—was actually drafted—and under those circumstances felt justified in insisting upon the choice of his running-mate. He chose Wallace because he had entire confidence that Wallace would in case of succession, carry out F.D.R.'s policies because he actually and entirely accepted and espoused all of F.D.R.'s policies and their concepts. This time it is different. Now he would like to be nominated and reelected. In these circumstances he does not feel he can or should insist on his running-mate.

I had half-way planned to leave tomorrow for Chicago—early—but I am holding back. Sunday in Chicago offers no allurements. The Convention does not open till Wednesday. I have no duties there—would not want to get in the limelight or to butt into Convention business. The Platform Committee meets Monday. The text of the Resolutions has not been submitted to us. It is reported to be a White House document and only 500 words in length. The danger with extreme brevity is that you cannot lay your predicates and

[80] Henry Kaiser, an industrialist whose several corporations made exceptional contributions to the war effort, producing ships, planes, and military vehicles in vast numbers.

may by omission lay yourself open to severe attack. What it says about foreign affairs we have not the slightest intimation.

Not quite so with the Keynote Speech. It was written by or for Kerr[81] and was to be referred to Hull who asked it be sent directly to me. I waited two days for it to arrive, then reported to him it had not come. Later we were advised the copy had been taken to Chicago—and it was suggested I should ask Kerr for it in Chicago—but I replied I was not trying to seek out the speech but only to be of help if they cared to submit it. . . .

In the meantime I will watch the Vice Presidential battle from afar—though the swell of a Convention fight still fascinates me and attracts me like a magnet. I had such an early education in City Conventions, then in State Conventions beginning in 1910 and then National Conventions in 1912, '16, '24, '28, '32 and '40—and all those campaigns and others in "off-years"—that I have difficulty in resisting the appeal to excitement and to take another hand in the game. But I have no longer a political base. Since 1924 I have been "a man without a country." I left Missouri—and have eschewed politics in Maryland. In 1928 I went as a delegate from the District of Columbia, lonely fate for a war horse—and was drafted in '32 to be floor manager for Roosevelt in Chicago but was not then a delegate—though I was a very effective agent on the floor. My first role in that capacity was for McAdoo at Madison Square in 1924.

Hull has talked twice to the President—once about foreign affairs and the other—about what principally I do not know—but he got into the Wallace business and told the President the election of Wallace would place him (Hull) "in an impossible position." He told me that this evening—said he did not know whether the President appreciated the implications and added that he "could not support" Wallace. He said Wallace was "intellectually dishonest" and that he literally could not support him under present circumstances.

Hull started to reinforce that by talking to General Watson on the phone and asking him to remind the President of his statement. He actually got Watson on the phone while I sat with him. The President was just about to leave—on his long trip—but he only talked to him about not having seen the platform or Kerr's speech, though he had helped Jackson with his—and in a way disavowed any responsibility for foreign affairs in the platform by taking the position it was now too late to take it up. It was from him I learned of the 500 words' length—which seemed to relieve his mind somewhat because he figured they could not say much about foreign affairs if all they had was 500 words for it all. But he hung up without mentioning Wallace again.

I am getting just a little discouraged at the way things are breaking. The mutual confidence which once existed seems either to be vanishing or to have gone. Hull relies on me, confides at great length to me. I try to respect that

[81] Robert S. Kerr, Democrat, governor of Oklahoma, 1943–1947.

confidence. But my loyalty is not to him. My loyalty is to Roosevelt—just as it once was to Wilson. I once had Roosevelt's confidence. That seems to have been withdrawn. Passing me over for appointment on two different occasions—once under unfortunate circumstances—has been a definite announcement of less than full confidence to say the least. Yet I have stuck to a duty as a soldier. I did not want my present position. I accepted it reluctantly. I have discharged its responsibilities fully. And I have stuck to a war job. On the first of those occasions I felt terribly hurt—possibly should have resigned then. And other vacancies I have seen filled by promotions from below—like Forrestal and Bard[82] just recently—which emphasize the treatment in my own case. But I have not wavered in my loyalty to the President. I have supported him completely—but I have not even seen him except at a formal occasion and at a distance for more than two years. I have not been invited to the White House on a formal occasion or to talk with him for more than three years. I have not been asked to meet any single one of the heads and chiefs of Government who have been here during three years. Churchill, Madame Chiang,[83] de Gaulle—nor any other. Eden wandered into my office once with Halifax—but I was not taken into any conference with them or with any of the others. But I have done my duty to my government—thoroughly—and was thrown to the wolves and took the brunt of the worst attack made against *any* officer of this Government and which raged in the press and on the radio for a full year—ending only last winter—and without help of any kind from *any* quarter—when my attackers included other persons in responsible positions in other departments in the Government, as well as slanderers and Jack-a-napes on the floor of the Congress. All this—and a continuing loyalty to a Chief in whom I still believe—and through it all I have done my duty and fought my own battles in my own way.

But I begin to see animosity in other places. And I begin to feel a discouragement. But I don't want to quit in time of war. Neither do I want to have any mistake as to where my loyalty rests. When I am on the team I play ball as the Captain says. When I don't do that I get off the team. And I have no reason of loyalty to get off the team—but, if my services are desired till the war is won—I will continue a war job—until that time—though I shall soon give another opportunity—as I did after election in 1940—to my Chief to make his own decision in that respect.

July 15, 1944

The draft of the plank on foreign relations for the platform has been submitted to us and we have examined and approved it. Connally has been

---

[82] James Forrestal, Under Secretary of the Navy, 1940–1944, promoted to Secretary in 1944; Ralph Bard, Assistant Secretary of the Navy, promoted to Under Secretary in 1944.
[83] Madame Meiling Soong Chiang, wife of Chiang Kai-Shek, and adviser to him.

designated to go to Chicago primarily to handle the H_2's [Senators Hatch and Hill] of the B_2H_2 group. They will want to go farther than the platform but the platform goes to the very limit of public expression by the President, the Secretary and incidentally myself. The phraseology is very similar to the Connally Resolution, which in itself was repetitive of the Moscow Declaration. The B_2H_2 group want to go farther but the Government is not ready to take another position until it has talked to the other Great Powers. So I am proceeding to Chicago tomorrow and have already established contact with Connally and arranged for our collaboration there. I will have copies of such papers as the Department has furnished Connally and I will be available by telephone with the Department.

As regards the Vice Presidential question I have talked this morning with Stanley. It seems that Byrnes is still a possibility but Rayburn is eliminated and Truman has withdrawn. That leaves only Byrnes and Barkley. In order to organize the forces against Wallace it has been decided to have a meeting in Chicago and I have offered my quarters. Homer Cummings, Stanley, Max Gardner[84] and one or two others from other sections will be a nucleus.

We are momentarily awaiting final word from Russia as to her final agreement to enter into conversations with us in August. It would be very helpful if this could be announced before the Convention meets. As soon as the word comes it will be relayed to me for Connally's use.

July 25, 1944—Rochester, Minnesota

Am at the Mayo Clinic undergoing a "check up" as I have done every year or so since my serious operation in 1936. This time I am having them investigate a sinus ailment which has bothered me considerably for seven months. They may tell me it is super-induced by excessive smoking—but it may be only the Washington smoke and dampness which causes it.

I came here after the Chicago Democratic Convention—where I was an interested spectator and a "behind the scenes" contact on the foreign relations parts of the platform. Being undecided as to whether I should go while the final studies for the Four Power conversations were proceeding but naturally drawn to conventions of my party it was finally decided I should be there to help the Resolutions Committee members if they wanted. So I went —arriving two days before the convention opened and for three days sat in my room practically *all* the time to be available from either end—Hull on one and the Committee members on the other—and it was worth while. I brought along a draft Connally had proposed and which we had amended in some respects. I talked with Connally several times—one evening at length. We dined in my apartment and talked rather late. John McCormack was Chairman of the big Committee and of the subcommittee. I talked with him—and

[84] Oliver Max Gardner, Democrat, former governor of North Carolina, 1929–1933.

checked with Hull—and talked again with him, on the foreign relations plank and again on the foreign trade references. Josephus Daniels asked me to talk with him—and I went to his rooms and talked it out. Senator Green[85] wanted help and I talked with him. After four days of consideration, argument and compromises the Committee was finally ready and reported the text we prepared practically as amended and approved by us. . . .

Roosevelt's nomination could have been done by acclamation but the roll had to be called. He subsequently addressed the Convention by radio and made what I think was the best speech he has ever made. There was a fight—short and somewhat acrimonious—over the Vice Presidential nomination which went to Truman on the second ballot. Wallace was an active candidate for renomination and there was much opposition to him from important elements of the party in every section of the country. I did not want to see him renominated and when I felt I was free of Presidential restraint I did what I could for Truman. When I arrived in Chicago it looked as though Barkley would win it. The next day it looked like Byrnes. I would have been glad to see either one chosen. Roosevelt turned thumbs down on Byrnes—which Jimmy took very hard. The reasons underlying the rejection seemed to lie on grounds of religion, negro opposition because of South Carolina, the existence of important enemies properly antagonized in prosecution of the war's business—and each quite potent—but also I felt that Byrnes was so close and intimate a member of the President's official family Roosevelt believed it would be better to have someone else. So he was eliminated—and Barkley reappeared as the probable choice to be submerged the next day by the rising tide of Truman.

As a matter of fact the Convention did not want Wallace. There was danger of his nomination unless opposition to it could be organized. Organization meant concentration—as far as possible—on one man. Wallace had delegates instructed for him—but many of them personally desired another—were opposed to Wallace. Even members of his own Iowa delegation were bitterly opposed to him—had talked to me of their opposition and intention to vote for someone else.

The C.I.O. made the mistake—political mistake—of coming into a Democratic Party Convention and using coercive methods and gangster tactics to impose him on the Convention. They packed the galleries and the aisles. One night it constituted a serious hazard to the physical safety of the enormous crowd in that hall. The aisles were so packed no one could move—and as soon as business and parliamentary procedure permitted the Convention adjourned. The speeches made by some of these people in support of Wallace were in bad taste and turned away from him many an individual delegate who

[85] Josephus Daniels, journalist, and former ambassador to Mexico, 1933–1941; Theodore Green, Democrat, U.S. Senator from Rhode Island, 1937–1960.

was inclined to be for him. I estimated from conversations I had there that he lost 40 to 50 delegates for that reason alone—which reason only confirmed the expressed fears of many others who were definitely opposed to Wallace.

I had a box almost opposite the Speakers stand—right on the aisle—and was easily accessible to anyone. Besides I had been furnished with a special badge which permitted me to move anywhere. Many, many of them stopped as they passed by or came up to talk with me. Among them I remember [Bennett Champ] Clark, Howard Cook (Missouri); Governor O'Connor [*sic*], Tydings, Brooke Lee (Maryland); Connally (Texas); Farley, Eisner, Flynn (New York); Guldoni (St. Louis); Lucas (Illinois); Herring (Iowa);[86] O'Mahoney (Wyoming); Chavez (New Mexico); Biffle (Arkansas and Sergeant at Arms)—and a lot of others from more than half the states—including some lowly but active members of the organization who had been with me in past fights, who were in touch with the current developments and from whom I could receive this or that or send them to do this or that—loyal personally and good organization Democrats. So I could keep in touch with what was going on under the surface and could be of some assistance in the platform and in nominating someone other than Wallace.

I was glad to help Truman—a fellow Missourian—in spite of the opposition his crowd afforded me in my entire political activity in Missouri. He is a product of machine politics but he is entirely honest, has his feet on the ground, is bright and capable and where he himself does not know he will rely on good sound advice from those he trusts—and he trusts practical minded, intelligent men. We have been friends for years and he has frequently told me how sorry he was of the vicious treatment his gang bestowed upon me years ago.

Some moments during the Convention moved me very much. The platform about foreign relations and references by the different speakers to the struggle of the Wilson era several times brought an urge to cry. A quarter of a century ago I made a hard fight for the League of Nations. I believed in its principles, in its ideals, in its purposes. I gave all I had in that fight. I emerged, after seven years, a political derelict. I knew I was right. I saw America abstain—and weaken the League. I saw a separate treaty of peace with Germany. I saw first England and then France use the machinery of the League as a political instrument for their own national advantage, which they could not have done with us present. I saw the League suffer, decline and collapse.

[86] Howard Cook, Jefferson City, Missouri lawyer active in state politics; Herbert O'Conor, Democrat, governor of Maryland, 1939–1947; Millard Tydings, Democrat, U.S. Senator from Maryland, 1927–1951; Col. Edward B. Lee, active in Maryland Democratic politics, and son of Blair Lee, U.S. Senator from Maryland, 1913–1917; Mark Eisner, lawyer, former chairman of the Board of Higher Education of the City of New York, 1926–1938; Louis J. Guldoni, St. Louis automobile dealer active in Missouri Democratic politics; Scott Lucas, Democrat, U.S. Senator from Illinois, 1939–1953; Clyde Herring, Democrat, U.S. Senator from Iowa, 1937–1943.

For years I have been working to rebuild a world almost destroyed by the violence of a war which still rages but which should never have been allowed to start. And now I see my party espouse the cause I fought for and believed in and see the opposing party generally endorse the idea. And it is but natural I feel happy, gratified. Perhaps I will soon feel compensated for myself, confident of peace for my grandchildren.

August 18, 1944

For the last two weeks we have been engaged in rather an intensive study of the American proposals which will be laid on the table at the conferences on the International Security Organization which will begin next week. These have been only a continuation of the studies that we have been engaged in over a period which now runs back two and a half years and which started in the Security Subcommittee of the general study group. We had evolved what was a pretty good understanding of American policy which was expressed in terms of a document Mr. Hull used as the basis of conversations with the special committee of the Senate. After discussion with those Senators a continuing study produced certain changes in that document, though they were largely changes of a minor nature. On the basis of those changes a new draft was submitted to the three other Governments, England, Russia and China, simply with the idea of informing them of the line along which our thoughts were proceeding. It was not considered that this document should be considered at all binding or in the nature of a firm proposal. While we have had very little comment from China, we understand from Russia that they are in general sympathetic to the proposal in that document and from England we hear that they are in general accord, though there are a few points of difference. It is also probably correct to say that there are a few points of difference with the Russians. However after we delivered that document to them we continued to study and have made several minor changes in it, all of which appear in a redraft which was circulated the first part of the current week to the members of the American delegation and those associated with us who composed this study group. That document has undergone intensive study during the current week. It has been read section by section and either passed or slightly amended.

In the meantime the British have submitted to us their thought and the Russians have now submitted a paper which embodies their ideas. It has just indicated these ideas are in sympathy with ours except for a few conflicts. Primarily the differences are, first, as regards Russia that they would like to confine the organization to purely security functions at first with very little addition in the way of economic, cultural and other activities, though they have now accepted the idea of a world court as a part of the organization to which they originally objected. On the other hand, they had some idea originally about a police force of the air but they seem now to have accepted the thought of armed forces supplied by nations to be selected by a separate agreement. Consequently they seem more or less in line.

The British have had several different ideas. In the first place they feel that a member of the Executive Council who is a party to a dispute should not be allowed to vote in matters before the Council affecting the interests of that state. This is probably the most difficult situation which we will have to face. Mr. Hull and the President will eventually have to decide whether the United States can modify its position. Our position heretofore has been that on security matters alone the Big Four would have to stand together and that any one of them would have a veto over the application of force directed against it or on behalf of the Council directed against any other state. In our discussion with the Senate it developed that the idea of preserving a veto by the United States in matters affecting its own security and the security of the world in general were necessary in order to obtain the approval of the Senate. It has been considered necessary in view of the political situation in the United States to retain that position. At a meeting on yesterday it was decided to recommend a modification of the United States position in that respect. I am not of the belief that the Secretary or the President will feel justified in approving that proposal without consultation with members of the Senate; and I clearly doubt that the members of the Senate with whom we have been in consultation will accede to it. So I see no alternative but to persuade the British to accept our draft. . . .

Further, the British have a thought that the program is a little too much inclined to develop into a "super state." They fear an assumption on the part of the Council or the delegation to the Council of too much power. They feel that whereas the Council should have authority to investigate differences and propose settlements that there should not be in the Council the power and authority to enforce decisions unless they actually result in warfare or threaten to end in warfare. I am not averse to this except that it is difficult to see how controversies could ever be terminated under that procedure. The only way they could be terminated would be for one of the parties to begin the use of force, thereby calling in power the security arrangements of the Council, or have the Council of its own accord to find that the situation in that particular area and because of the international actions of one of the parties constituted a menace to the peace or a threat to the peace. Even considering my doubts in the matter I am inclined to accept the proposal even though it does detract and possibly because it does detract from the power of the Council and the eventual charge that the exercise of the deleted power would cause the organization to be a super-state. This modification will no doubt appear in the revised document which we will submit at the opening of the conference and lay on the table as the American proposal. Whether the other revised section concerning the voting will be in the document is one which I will have to discuss before the decision is made to include it because I am not now prepared to go along with it. But as it stands there are no irreconcilable differences. . . .

We have been holding these last preparatory meetings at Dumbarton Oaks, the former home of Bob Bliss, and will proceed there on Monday morning to open the conference—provided the Russians arrive on time.

In the meantime the war is progressing most favorably on every front. We are closer and closer to the mainland of Japan. We have landed on the French Riviera and have moved well in. The forces have broken out from Normandy and are almost if not quite at Paris. The Russian armies are still battling and far westward and are at the borderland of East Prussia and at the gates of Warsaw. The synchronization, supply and deployment of troops has been carried out with complete success. The air, marine and land forces have cooperated and have been integrated. The President has just returned from Honolulu and the Aleutians and everything is progressing smoothly. Some of the President's advisors wanted him to take hold of the [Dumbarton Oaks] conference[87] and to address a message of welcome but when he talked to Hull it was decided that Mr. Hull's statement would be so phrased as to include the message of the President and that he might take some occasion after the arrival of all the delegations to make some expression of his own to them.

Governor Dewey's effort to inject himself into the picture of the International Conference and within the orb of the movement to establish an organization for peace and security has resulted in his hooking himself completely to our program. . . . His communication to the Secretary about the appointment of Dulles [as an observer at Dumbarton Oaks] has committed him and through him his element in the Republican Party to our whole program. It probably assures the approval of the Senate and will expedite the whole thing because it will tend to eliminate a lot of delaying tactics on the part of opponents to the program. So that it may turn out to be the most beneficent situation that could have been developed. However, that was not Mr. Dewey's intention.

August 21, 1944

The Dumbarton Oaks Conference opened this morning with formalities— Hull, Gromyko and Cadogan read statements. They were all harmonious and it seemed to get off to a good start. The rest of the time was for photographs

[87] The Dumbarton Oaks Conference (August 21–October 7) was attended by representatives of the United States, Great Britain, the Soviet Union, and China. (The Soviet Union and China did not attend meetings together because the Soviets were still at peace with Japan.) The conference discussed the charter draft for a permanent postwar international organization designed to maintain peace and security. The proposals of the conference, known as the Dumbarton Oaks plan, served as the basis for the Charter of the United Nations.

—inside during the readings of statements—outside in the garden and again inside as if simulating the work of the Conference. The real conversations will begin tomorrow. We are prepared—all but on one point and that concerns the right of any state member of the Council to sit in judgment on and to vote on questions affecting that state. It consequently involves the right of veto which would pertain to any of the Big Four if unanimity of the Big Four was to be required as part of any decision. It also affects the power of the Council—whether it shall or shall not have the authority to *enforce* its decision by arms. . . .

August 23, 1944

Events are following fast—one after another. Paris has fallen to us—Rumania has surrendered to Russia and joined the United Nations to fight against the Germans. Our armies have crossed the Seine and now threaten two great German armies with destruction. The landing on the Riviera has spread out and penetrated far inland.

I went to the White House today—not specially invited but as a member of the Dumbarton Oaks conference. It was the first time I had seen the President face to face for three and a half years—if I remember correctly. I hesitated a bit about going—because I was not sure he really wanted me and might not realize I was a member of the American delegation. I went over with Hull. He, Stettinius, Gromyko and Halifax went in first. Then the Russians and English. So it happened I led the American Delegation into the room. I was stunned to see him. He must have lost fifty to sixty pounds and aged *years* since I saw him close up. It was a shock to me to realize he had spent so much in physical resource.

I think he had the same or a similar feeling about me. I am sure he was incredulous when he looked at me as I approached him at the head of the line. Whether it was my whitening hairs, my deeply lined face and my 122 pounds —or—whether he had missed a cog and had not wanted me there—I could not guess. His face at first was inscrutable. Then I smiled—he smiled—we shook hands—and he said—"Mr. Long"—nothing else. As far as my recollection goes it is the only time in my memory he has called me anything but "Breck." It might have been facetious—and it might have been earnest. I could not tell.

Then he addressed a most informal but most felicitous running comment for ten minutes—and we left.

In thinking it all over I cannot make up my mind about his attitude. Perhaps I should—and should act on my decision. If I incur his displeasure or lack his confidence I ought to remove myself. But I cannot—in view of the antecedents—bring myself to that thought. And if I am to err during the war —I err on the side of subordinating my personal pride to the exigencies of duty to my country. The question has vexed me for years—and I am no nearer a solution tonight because I cannot evaluate my observations of his reactions on looking me in the eye.

But what difference does it make? I have given my all in the war effort. My work has been exactly and effectively done for five long years. The war is being won—rapidly now. The end is in sight. The effort for a security organization has had the benefit of all I could contribute toward it. For two and a half years already I have been one of those responsible for it and now one of the American group to formulate the plan with our great allies. I have spared no effort. I have given all I have had of mental, nervous and physical effort. I have grown old like Roosevelt—in the same service. He has always had my resignation because I serve at his pleasure. If he had wanted my resignation it was his for the asking—and I offered it in 1940.

In the light of it all the experience today was enigmatic—the querulous expression, the moment of incredulity, the kindly smile, the "Mr. Long"— without being able to label it as formal or facetious—and my own saddening reaction at his appearance—But I am still sure I have followed the right course and that my deletion from White House lists is not attributable to him personally.

August 24, 1944

This morning we had an American delegation meeting and tried to define a specific position on several different points. One concerned the power of the Council in case a decision had been rendered against a state. Thereafter what were the powers of the Council. First—obviously—is to try some other method of settlement—some new device or some method untried in that particular dispute. But suppose the state against which decision has been rendered is recalcitrant, refuses to accept even after additional procedures have been attempted. Suppose further that state prepares to use force or actually does use force. What then are the residuary powers of the Council? It can use force to suppress either the preparation to use or the actual use of force. But having used that force, what power does the Council still have? Can it then force compliance with the decision? Or, having suppressed the use of force, does it withdraw and leave the whole thing hanging in air? Some argued "no." Some argued "maybe." Neither of which was conclusive or, to me, satisfactory. So I suggested that if, in those circumstances, the Council became seized of jurisdiction and used its force under its authority that it followed *automatically* that the Council could continue to use the same force to *settle* the dispute by enforcing compliance. But I was summarily contradicted —by Pasvolsky and Ben Cohen[88]—and I think also by several others. Never-

[88] Benjamin V. Cohen, now general counsel to the office of War Mobilization and Reconversion, 1943–1945.

theless, I contend no other answer is reasonable. Firstly, the state becomes an outlaw when the Council decides to use force against it. That in my mind is axiomatic. That state is automatically suspended from membership—or should be—so it can enjoy none of the privileges, rights, or immunities of membership. Secondly, a state of war exists—*de facto*—between all other members and that state. Thirdly, when the force of that state is overcome it will be in the same situation that Germany or Japan will be when we finally lick them. As an enemy state a surrender and a treaty will be entered into by the Council and that state, and in that instrument will set out the terms of peace and future conduct which will in fact be the imposition of the conditions of the original decision—or some variation of it. At least, it will be a definite and final disposition of the matter and settlement of the dispute.

But I was stated to be wrong in my conclusion.

Anyhow, that and several other questions had to be decided. Stettinius insisted on following the time schedule—in spite of the inconclusion—and taking it up with the President. So there was a meeting to be had with him at 12:30 (cars leave at 12:15 sharp). Stettinius, Dunn, Hackworth and Pasvolsky were to consult the President. . . .

The Dewey-Dulles thing came up. At 4:45 Dulles was due for his second talk [with Hull]—having conferred with Dewey. Hull and I went over a paper for Dulles to agree to. For the better part of an hour we examined language to commit Dewey to a *non*-partisan course in relation to the World Organization —and succeeded in getting one on paper in terms satisfactory to us. Dulles (for Dewey) takes the position on a *bi*-partisan treatment. We did not want that. *Non-* is simple and all-inclusive. *Bi-* puts it *into* politics by bringing both political parties into the argument. They want to put it *into* politics. We want to keep it *out*. The choice of words is important.

I left just as Dulles was arriving. After an hour Hull asked me to meet him in his ante-room. He brought out an enlarged statement. Our language was there but Dulles wanted some of his language there. So Hull was thinking over Dulles' suggestions. We sat there and examined it critically. He had induced Dulles to add the words "so as to keep it *non*-partisan" after the word "bi-partisan," which Dulles had insisted on. Hull's addition killed the Dulles implication and Dulles was ready to agree. Hull suggested I call the President while he returned to Dulles so he would not leave him alone too long. I thought he ought to call the President himself—so he did—told the President I was with him and agreed on the text. The President agreed it was O.K. Hull returned to his big office and I left. Shortly Dulles left and I returned only to learn Dulles had signed his name in his own right and not as representative of Dewey—so it would be a personal arrangement between Hull and Dulles. Hull refused to accept that signature and Dulles said he would have to call Dewey for authority and return at eleven a.m. tomorrow.

So as it stands they are hooked if he signs and they are sunk if they don't—for all we would have to do would be to publish the text and say they refused to sign after agreeing to do so.

August 25, 1944

Dulles talked with Dewey and the latter failed to accept certain phraseology in the draft. So Dulles came back to the Secretary late that a.m. and proposed a substitute paragraph which was in part unacceptable. With that paragraph revised to omit the objectionable language and with the use of "non-partisan" ("bi-partisan" has been eliminated), the Secretary was satisfied. He sent for me again and we studied it carefully in his ante-room. I agreed as I thought he was well protected and left in control of the situation. So we agreed to accept and Dulles was to call Dewey by phone from here and get authority to sign. I did not see Dulles. I left at that stage. Soon the paper was issued to the press in that form. . . .

If Dewey lives up to it all—including "non-partisan" discussion—the fight is practically won as far as Senate approval is concerned. If he does not live up to this agreement then the whole program is in jeopardy because his action may prevent Senate approval—and without that approval and *our* cooperation *this* time there will be *no* World Organization and we might as well get ready for World War III and the end. This is our last chance—and this agreement may so bind the political opposition it cannot defeat us or this issue.

There was another agreement—a separate oral one; that they would not disclose the contents of the document we gave Dulles. That document is the one we laid on the table at Dumbarton as the American plan. They cannot publish it, or disclose it for quotation or comment, or discuss its proposals in any way until the document is released by us. We do not intend to do that until we arrive at agreement at Dumbarton, until our respective governments have agreed and until it has been submitted to "other peace-loving states."

August 30, 1944

Koo brought his delegation to the Department and was received by Hull and some of us. It was quite informal and for fifteen minutes the discussion touched only the philosophy of a world movement for peace. As Koo went out he stopped by me a moment, renewed his friendly expressions and said he wanted to have a visit with me in the next few days.

The matters at Dumbarton seem to be getting settled. There are only a comparatively few divergencies—only two or three of moment—and even drafting of specific provisions is in advanced form. So it looks as if we could finish by the middle or latter part of next week and start with the Chinese the following week. Koo today said he had no disposition to quibble about any details; that the most important thing was to agree to *something*; that practically any provision we should want would be approached by them in the belief that any United States serious proposal would be fair and without selfish intent. So it looks as if anything we agree to with the United Kingdom, and the U.S.S.R. will be accepted by China. And that makes the work as a whole look good—as far as the international aspects go.

But—

I had an engagement tonight with Walter George, Senator of Georgia. He is probably the ablest man in the Senate. His judgment, reason, poise and experience, together with his character and acumen, have combined to create a reputation for solidarity and ability which he richly deserves. He has the confidence of the Senate as no other member has. We have been just a little concerned lest he do not view the international organization under consideration in exactly the same light we do—and it was my aim to sound him out tonight on the question of the use of force. We were fearful he would not accept our position—completely. The object was to ascertain that but *if* he agreed to ascertain whether he felt deeply enough to be our advocate on the floor of the Senate. I approached him cautiously—and was eventually surprised to find him entirely in accord and willing to assume an active part in a possible (probable) debate on the Senate floor—but—before I had opened the subject he told me he had had a disappointing experience today in that same connection.

I go into detail because it is *so* important.

Wallace White, of Maine, had called on him today much disturbed. White had been called on by Vandenberg and LaFollette. For two hours they had confronted him and hedged him around with questions to demand an answer to the question whether he would "vote for force, the force to be decided by the vote of United States representatives on the Council"—with all the ancillary statements and positions of the old "isolationist" technique. White answered that he thought they had all agreed to use force if necessary; that he was convinced it was necessary to have the right to use force in the last analysis. They were not satisfied. They wanted to know whether he as Republican leader in the Senate would stand with them or would not. They were pointed, definite, positive. They wanted a "yes" answer. They approached the point from different angles. They used all the old isolationist arguments. They insisted on a categoric answer. They did not get their categoric answer. They got the argument they had all agreed to the ultimate use of force— But they were not satisfied. Neither was White satisfied. He was much troubled. He saw—but he did not openly say to George, though he arranged the plain inference—that there was a deep political move to defeat the whole movement for a peace and security organization. He had to talk. So he sought out George—and talked and asked for advice. That in itself was an oddity in American politics. For the Republican leader to seek advice on a political matter from a Democratic colleague was in itself most unusual, if not unique, but a compliment to the stature and character of both men.

George received permission to speak to me or to Hull and seek advice and to lay the basis for serious warning of real political trouble ahead. So instead of me talking to George, George talked to me. He was troubled. He saw the implication in it all. He realized the political danger signal's meaning. He bound me to absolute secrecy—except as to Hull.

I listened to it all—not entirely unprepared. . . . I asked George to talk to White and tell him we would get word to him later; that I would talk to Hull —and to no one else—and would let him know our reactions. It was during the course of this I asked George if he would be spokesman for "force"—and that long argument of mine served as a predicate for the question—and he said he would. I also asked him if he agreed that no nation should sit in the decision of a case in which it itself was directly involved. He said he was definitely of opinion no state should have a controlling voice in such case— even the United States. I explained that even if we should be involved, should not sit, should have decision against us, should violate our pledge and proceed to use force contrary to the decision—even all that—nobody could *force* us. If that happened it would be the end of the organization—but no one could force us.

This all presages a nasty partisan Republican attack—during the Dumbarton meeting—against the movement to secure peace and prevent war. What is more unfortunate—Vandenberg can muster probably fifteen, perhaps eighteen, Republican votes to follow him and add to them at least five Democratic votes—probably more—Wheeler, McCarran, Reynolds, Walsh (Massachusetts)[89] and there will develop others. The attack would be very disturbing to other governments—but it cannot be allowed to prevail.

September 8, 1944
    . . . At Dumbarton much of the text of the final document is agreed to. Some few points have been placed before the Big Three. The President lent his hand this morning in a talk with Gromyko and wired Stalin on one of the stumbling blocks—disqualification from voting of a state when involved in a dispute before the Council. We definitely oppose a state's sitting in judgment of itself. England now agrees. Russia holds out. And because she holds firm on that she refuses to yield and accept the economic section. But if one breaks the other will follow. The principle of unanimity is involved and the Russians think that is essential for real security. So do we as among the Big Four but the principle of unbiased decision is more important and must prevail.

In the last analysis it makes no difference because *if* we were a party to a

[89] Patrick McCarran, Democrat, U.S. Senator from Nevada, 1933–1954; David Walsh, Democrat, U.S. Senator from Massachusetts, 1926–1947.

dispute and could not vote and Russia and England tried to enforce a decision we did not agree with and could not accept or abide by—they could *not* enforce it—but the partnership would end—the organization would dissolve. But as that is an improbable development the question impinges on the academic.

I have been at Dumbarton practically all day every day this week—as last week—and we hope either to finish the Russian conversations by Monday or to suspend them so as to proceed with the Chinese and finish it all by the end of next week—the 16th—and then to the United Nations for study and to the press.

The Senate orated one day—and will again—but it is due to adjourn next week till election. Dewey is going to speak about the subject and may get it muddled—but the prospect is still good for general acceptance even though the opposition will be strong in the Senate.

One thing at Dumbarton we agreed to accept but I did not like *at all* was the provision for "*periodic* meetings of the Council at which should be present" *important members of the government of members*. The British insisted on "Cabinet rank" visitors but eventually yielded to the point of "important members of" or some such phrase. I fought it steadily. It makes a "super Council" when they meet, subordinates the regular delegate, detracts from his importance, prestige and effectiveness. It will create a three ring circus with a Super Council (for important matters), a Council (for ordinary affairs) and an Assembly (for other matters). They yielded to the point of leaving the Council to "function continuously" and the delegate "reside" at the seat but I do not like the prospect for I am sure England, France, Russia (if advisable) and all the near-by powers will send their Prime Ministers to outshine the others on occasions most important to them—or their Foreign Ministers in important matters—and pass on to the *ordinary* meetings of the Council *ordinary* matters. . . . But British acceptance of other things depended on our acceptance of some device to establish that bad practice and I finally said I would not object to the form as adopted—but did not like it.

September 13, 1944

This afternoon at Dumbarton we ran head-on into collision with the Russians. The Russians view this whole movement as a security measure. Consequently they insist upon the application of the doctrine of unanimity when it comes to decisions of the Big Four in the Council. We had that position for a long time. Recently we have adopted the other position, that a party to a dispute should not sit in his own case even though he was a permanent member of the Council or any other member of the Council. The latter involves the principle of fair play and the ordinary rules by which we decide problems under our own political system. On the other hand, the other is a general adherence to the doctrine that this is an organization to preserve the peace and that the peace can only be preserved by the Big Four standing together because it is the Big Four which has the power and which can apply it.

The American group was called together in special session to draft proposals which would save both positions. We were unable to agree to any one but did adopt a report which would go to Stettinius, the Secretary and the President, Stettinius being the negotiator, the Secretary and the President being the ultimate authorities. This report contained four different plans proposed by individuals or groups. I proposed one reading as follows: "Each member of the S. [Security] Council would have one vote; would make decisions by simple majority of those voting provided the members having permanent seats be part of the majority. Each member may abstain from voting and the majority will be counted without the participation of that member. In case a state member of the Council shall be party to a dispute before the Council the Council shall refer the entire matter to the General Assembly which shall reach decision by three-quarters vote of all members (including all parties to the dispute) which decision shall be final." That was considered to be a rough draft.

The conference has now run into the fourth week and we are not in agreement on a very vital part of the whole thing. . . . There are two principles involved and they clash head-on. It gets down to the point of whether a state furnishing the power and force necessary to preserve the peace is to be excluded from voting in a matter in which its own vital interests may be concerned or whether the ideology which excludes a person or a state from sitting in judgment in his own case are directly in conflict.

It is argued on one side that the small states would not accept the decision. It is argued on the other side that unless the four states stick together in all matters there is no hope of success. The introduction of the use of force concentrated in the hands of four nations places into the general understanding the one element which was lacking from the League of Nations. There the League required unanimity and lacked force or the power to apply it. If we can solve this one problem the Dumbarton Conference will be a success. To my mind it is unthinkable that it should not be solved but tonight it is in a very precarious condition.

September 19, 1944

Last week at Dumbarton it began to look as if we were moving into a deadlock with Russia on the question of voting in the Council. Wednesday, the 13th, the question loomed up as to what we should do in case of this development. I took very little part in the conversation except to interrupt a talk of Ben Cohen at a point where he indicated that it might be a good idea to suspend the conference and to leave open the question of voting. . . . I called attention to the fact that it would be dangerous to the cause to engage in a [national] debate which would become vitriolic at times and would lend itself to every caprice of political ingenuity to stir up opposition. It would make it extremely difficult in the future to secure the required two-thirds majority in the Senate because members would themselves be engaged in these conversations with the chances that they would spread upon party lines. Once that happened we would be in a very serious situation. . . . It was eventually decided that nothing could be done until we had some further word from the Russians and that they had to have time to hear from Moscow about a proposal which had been made to the three Governments in the form of a compromise on the veto provision.

So the meetings were adjourned until Monday morning. That was yesterday. Stettinius announced that he had been in serious conversation with Gromyko and that Gromyko had told him it was his opinion that the Russian Government would not agree to the voting provision and would insist upon an agreement here and would refrain from joining in another conference of the United Nations unless the question was settled here. It developed that that was his personal opinion of his Government's position but not a final official expression. Stettinius very properly asked him to obtain a final official expression of that point. This he agreed to do and had telegraphed. . . .

September 20, 1944

The crisis was precipitated by a statement by Stettinius that the Russian Ambassador had told him that he would not agree to waive the right of veto and would insist on unanimity even in case Russia was party to a dispute with another state. Further, that was an expression of the personal view of the Ambassador. He would telegraph for an official answer but he had reason to believe his understanding would be the position of his Government. Further, that Russia would not agree that we start conversations with the Chinese before the final termination of the conversations with Russia. The Russian Ambassador further stated that Russia would not agree to invite the other states to a United Nations conference unless that question was settled first.

The American delegation was confronted with the alternative of suspension of conversations with the Russians at Dumbarton Oaks and proceeding with the conversations with the Chinese or continuing conversations with Russia so that at Dumbarton Oaks there might be agreement with Russia.

All agreed as to the desirability of agreement.

All agreed as to the necessity of avoiding a break here.

There was division [in the State Department] position of the United States. . . . Today we worked on a statement to the President. He did not return this morning but will tomorrow morning.[90] We finished it at 11 p.m.—having worked all day. Most of the time—until dinner—was taken in finishing negotiations with Russia. There are five outstanding points remaining yet to be agreed upon. They will be submitted "on high." They are Amendment, Voting, Human Rights and Freedoms, and two others.

September 26, 1944

Yesterday and today the Secretary talked to me under suppressed nervous excitement and a great emotional strain. He is all upset about the Morgenthau activity in connection with the German post war plan. It seems that Morgenthau went to the President with a plan and the President took him to Quebec to talk with Churchill.[91]

Previous to that we had been in negotiations with the British to open up British trade areas and to break down the Empire preference program in favor of our trade agreements and were making the continuance of Lease Lend after the war a part of those negotiations. This had nothing to do with the German peace arrangement. Suddenly, the Morgenthau program for Germany was submitted to the President. It involved both the Secretary of War and the Secretary of State because the Secretary of War was responsible for the interim period and the Secretary of State for the long-range program in Germany or at least in making plans with other Governments for the treatment of Germany in post-war phases. The President put Harry Hopkins in as mediator and there were several meetings, both Stimson and Hull from their respective points of view differing from Morgenthau.

Now it appears that out of Quebec came several understandings. One is that under the Morgenthau proposal to take over the Ruhr and the Rheinland [sic] and segregate it from Germany—which was not part of our plan to control the manufacturing facilities and natural assets of Germany so that they could be used only on a controlled basis—this segregated area is given to England. England would get the Ruhr and all of the Rheinland. Just in what capacity or for how long and to what degree the assets of the area would be given to England is not yet clear in my mind except that it would in its drastic extreme destroy all the manufacturing facilities and turn the country into an agricultural area with the probable exception that the mines and other sources of natural wealth would be under the control of England for an indefinite period, perhaps in perpetuity.

[90] President Roosevelt met with Prime Minister Churchill (September 11–16) in Quebec to consider strategic plans for final victory over Germany and Japan. The main subjects discussed were the demarcation of the zones of occupation following the defeat of Germany, and the postwar treatment of that nation.

[91] Secretary of the Treasury Henry Morgenthau, Jr. proposed reducing Germany to an agrarian economy. This plan was tentatively approved at the Quebec Conference, but President Roosevelt rejected it three weeks later.

Second, it appears that they agreed to pay England six and a half billion dollars under Lend Lease in the first year after the war without any conditions or strings attached. And the effect of this is to throw into the discard the trade agreements program because the bargaining power to get England to consent to our trade agreements program was the prospect of Lend Lease.

So if the present plan matures Morgenthau will emerge as the Lease Lend agent in charge of those activities which have heretofore been run through the Department of State as the arbiter of all policy in regard to it and he will also appear as the member of the commission to do the settlement with Germany.

Naturally this is very disconcerting to Mr. Hull. He is in the worst humor I have ever seen him. He is worried sick and has not slept for two or three nights and finds it impossible to get this off his mind. He feels that it is a repudiation and that it has placed him in a position which he may not for very long be able to maintain. He has not said that in so many words but that is the exact state of his mental operations during these last two days at least. He feels that a rift between him and the President has become real and that his position under these circumstances may not long be tenable.

This is Tuesday, the 26th of September. No word has yet come from Russia as to whether or not the text of the so-called final document to emanate from Dumbarton is agreeable to her. We are waiting day by day and the conversations are in a state of suspension pending final word so that we can either hold the plenary session and adjourn the Russian phases of the conversations—and then begin the Chinese—or indulge in some more conversation and try to reach some kind of an understanding. In the meantime the movement in the press which has a good deal to do with molding public opinion, indicates that the British position and the American position are identical on the voting features, with Russia in a position of holding out. The consequence of that is that the public is getting an impression that Russia is the obstacle to agreement—which is not exactly the case because England is also a hold-out from the strict Russian point of view—but is liable to give Russia the impression that we are trying to force her hand and thereby complicate the whole problem.

In the meantime there is nothing to do but wait.

September 27, 1944

This morning we had another session of the American delegation. It developed that Gromyko had received his final instructions. They accepted the amendment provision for inclusion in the article and several other small matters but did not answer the question of voting. That remains as the only important question open. They did, however, accept the mention of human rights and freedoms in what seems an appropriate place.

We all agreed to accept the text as thus modified as the final text. It had been telegraphed to London and Moscow and each of them has now agreed to that text. It will be published on October 9 after we have finished with the Chinese. We will have a plenary session tomorrow to formally accept the text and to end the Russian conference. The next day we will begin with the Chinese. The question of voting will be taken up on the level of the President, Prime Minister and Marshal [Stalin] and between them they will come to some agreement but it is going to be difficult for Stalin to agree to exclude Russia from participation and from voting when Russia is a party in interest. . . .[92]

Somehow this will be worked out on a higher level and it will have to be worked out before there is an international conference if Russia is to be at the conference and if Russia maintains to her present position that she will not attend a conference unless it is settled in advance. If she should do so she would find herself faced with all the other nations of the world and would be in a very difficult and practically untenable position from the point of view of world public opinion. Of course all the little states would be on the other side but they would be on the other side because it appealed to their own vital interests—just the same reason it appeals to Russia.

Sometimes in the arguments the question has been asked what the little states could expect out of an organization where unanimity was required and one of the Big Four could vote in its own behalf. My answer has consistently been that the little states would find protection, and complete protection, for the simple reason that force could not be used against them unless the United States should concur in the application of force even though one of the Big Four should be the party in interest against them for the United States would not vote "yes" on the question to apply force unjustly to a small state—and no force could be exercised unless it was decided by the unanimous vote of the Big Four.

So it is now arranged that the conference will adjourn tomorrow and the object of my impassioned contention last week has been achieved. Had we acted precipitately and closed the meeting last Wednesday the blame would have been upon us and Russia might, and most probably would, have been seriously offended. As it is today the world has got the opinion that Russia is holding out and the onus is laid at her doorstep—if there is any onus to be

[92] At the Yalta Conference (February 4–11, 1945), Roosevelt, Churchill, and Stalin announced that they had worked out a formula for voting procedure in the Security Council. At the United Nations Conference on International Organization held in San Francisco (April 26–June 26, 1945), the Russians interpreted the Yalta voting formula to mean that a nation could use the veto to forbid the Security Council from even discussing questions which might require force in their settlement. A deadlock developed, with the United States threatening not to participate in the organization unless the Russians yielded. Finally, Stalin agreed that the veto should not be used to prevent discussion. Following this announcement of June 7, a draft charter was worked out and signed on June 26.

laid. And we now have an opportunity to work out on the highest level the one question which has proven insurmountable in this particular conference and the meeting of the United Nations conference to consider this question has not been set so that there is no deadline. In consequence this question may drag on for a long time which is regrettable but unavoidable under present circumstances.

During this whole period the Chinese delegation has been waiting. It has got to the point of embarrassment both for us and for them. Koo has been here more than three weeks and has not been able to have any conversations because the Russians took the flat position that they could not consider that we were talking to the Chinese while the Russian conversations were pending. This got very embarrassing for Koo. He was unable to telegraph his Government anything for the simple reason he was unable to have a conversation with anybody on the subject which he came to Washington to discuss. His Government probably could not understand the lack of information from him. He and I have been warm friends since the last war so one afternoon he came to see me. It was nearly two weeks ago. I could not refuse to talk with him on the general subject of international cooperation and various angles of it and I did so but I was careful to have him understand that I was not discussing any particular paper or any plan or any particular proposal which was pending at Dumbarton Oaks. We were together for an hour and discussed a number of subjects and then I telegraphed to Chungking the fact that I had had the conversation with him but that I had refrained from discussing matters pending at the conference.

Friday that will all be changed and we will start regular conversations with him and probably will finish up sometime during the latter part of next week. . . .

September 29, 1944

The Russian conversations were ended in a plenary session yesterday and the final text initialed by the chiefs of the three delegations. There is agreement on everything but the voting provision except that there are a few general things which may need some addition and revision such as who shall be the initial members and details of that character.

Today we met with the Chinese delegation. Mr. Hull, Kung the Vice President of the Council in China, and Wellington Koo representing the Chinese, Halifax and Cadogan at the head of the British delegation. Koo made a very felicitous address characteristic of his understanding and use of the English language. Mr. Hull and Cadogan, each of them, made very appropriate speeches. The conversations will be resumed on Monday after the Chinese have had an opportunity to examine the documents with care.

The rift in the Cabinet over the treatment of Germany has been settled.

The settlement followed an outbreak in the press that was almost unanimous condemning the Morgenthau plan. The publicity of the plan did us a good deal of injury in that it helped Goebbels stiffen up the German people. As a consequence of the rift the President has now thrown over the Morgenthau proposal and put the thing back on the main line with military affairs under the control of the War Department and economic affairs under the Foreign Economic Administration with policy decisions in the Department of State.

That does not cure, however, the difficulties attending the decision at Quebec to give England six and one half billion Lend Lease in the first year after the war and to put that under Morgenthau. The wreckage that might occur to the trade agreements policy and to the establishment of a world trade after the war by breaking down trade barriers is still more than a potential danger. This probably will have to be straightened out too.

October 1, 1944

Yesterday about four p.m. there came to me for action a decision of W.P.B., [the War Production Board] Ration Board and White House to ration coffee—to announce it yesterday evening and to put it into effect immediately. I did not like the pre-election effect of rationing coffee again and went into action. I got Hull's authority, then talked to Jim Byrnes at the White House, had Caffery and Wright[93] (of American Republics Division) with me and finally secured twenty-four hours postponement—till four p.m. today. We talked to Rio and concentrated on getting firm agreements to effect shipments of coffee up to one million bags a month for four months— and by noon today had the assurance. Then that was presented to the authorities here—they accepted—and the ration is cancelled—thanks to my strenuous efforts.

Hull had a fever today. I stayed home in the country—did the coffee job over the phone. When I wanted to get his final approval of the arrangement I called him at home but Mrs. Hull said he was in bed under doctor's care and had a fever about 100°. He had an engagement with the President this afternoon but it looked at one o'clock as if he could not keep it. It was to have been a very important talk. He told me yesterday what he was going to say— but he enjoined me to absolute secrecy and said I was the only person he would talk to about it.[94] He is *not* a well man. He has had a very heavy responsibility—very heavy—and certain attitudes have made it more difficult for him to perform his duties and discharge his responsibilities—as he sees it.

---

[93] Jefferson Caffery, ambassador to Brazil, 1937–1944, now assigned to State Department, Division of American Republics; James H. Wright, foreign service officer, assistant to the director of the American Republics Division, 1944.

[94] Hull told Long that he intended to submit his resignation.

October 4, 1944

. . . We have arrived at the stage which now practically secures the adoption by the Chinese of the text as presently written. This means that the conference has been a success in so far as it has gone. It lacks a spark plug because there is no provision for voting. That will be presented to the higher authorities and I hope that they can agree along the lines of my formula, which is to disqualify a party in interest in all stages of a dispute up to the time it comes to voting on the use of force but in that particular instance to require a unanimity on the part of the Big Four. If that is not provided it will simply invite a disintegration of the Big Four and it will place one of the Big Four—or more—in the potential position of declaring war on the other member because it will invite the way for three members who are not parties to the dispute to be of a majority in a decision to use force which would be aimed at the fourth member—and that would be another world war because one of the Great Powers cannot fight another of the Great Powers without involving a war. And that is directly opposed to the purpose and objectives of the organization.

October 18, 1944

Hull has not been to the Department since he had that serious talk with the President. This is the third week of his absence—

When he talked with me [October 1st entry] the day before he talked with the President he told me he was practically through. He was going to see the President and tell him that while he would not resign before election that he would leave immediately after that. He would *not* make any speeches. His doctor had advised him that his throat was in very bad shape—that there might be some serious trouble with it—that his general health as a result of it was impaired and he was *not* in physical condition to carry the burdens and undergo the strain and that he was through. He said that he was not telling anybody else and asked me to keep it a profound secret—not to tell a soul. The conversation then ranged around the past intrigues against him—Wallace's activities, Welles' White House connections and activities—the manner in which Hull had been embarrassed—policy decided without his knowledge from time to time—Morgenthau being taken to Quebec the last time and the ill-starred decision to give England six and a half billion Lend-Lease without *quid pro quo* which would ruin the Trade Agreement arrangement with England—probably jeopardize the whole program—because England would be now enabled to set up her "Empire Preference" program against us and knock the basis out from under the Trade Agreements—etc., etc.

It was a sombre conversation. The ghosts of Moley, George Peek—each of his former enemies—were dragged across the stage. His pet policy was shorn of its raiment and allowed to collapse limply to the floor. He was tired of intrigue. He was tired of being by-passed. He was tired of being relied upon in public and ignored in private. He was tired of fighting battles which were not appreciated. He was tired of making speeches and holding press interviews—tired of talking and tired of service. But he would not take any public step before election. However he thought the President should know—and he was going to tell him. Of course I am not surprised. All the elements have been there and little by little the accumulation has piled up resentment—something of smoldering anger—and the end of a long career is near at hand—ending not in satisfaction, as it should, but in bitterness.

Hull is still mad. He sent me word by his secretary Gray to get reinstated in the President's speech a deleted sentence which mentioned honorably the work of the State Department. I communicated it through the secretary of Rosenman[95]—as close as one can get to him—and sent a memo—but I do not know the effect of my intervention. Gray said he "had fire in his eye" when he said he wanted it reinstated. That is just another manifestation of the fire which has been smoldering inside and which was fanned into flame by the Morgenthau incident. But the same fire consumes his energy and keeps him weak and has contributed to his undoing.

It will not be long till there is a successor to Hull to be named. If it is to be only till January 20 it probably would be Stettinius. But if it is for a long tenure it might be either Henry Wallace, Don Nelson or Frank Walker—with Bill Phillips in the background because of his relationship to Mrs. Roosevelt and his "safeness"—even including his Indian Affairs letter. I would discount Wallace except for F.D.'s personal attachment to him. He certainly is not my choice. Walker is safe—sound—and personally very friendly with F.D.R.—intimate. Nelson is currently in favor and able but not versed in politics. Then there is Winant if we want a radical and pro-British policy. But I can't imagine a "fresh young man" to be chosen.

October 24, 1944

The political campaign proceeds with some fury. For a long time there was a lethargy but in these last ten days the tempo has increased and it looks as if it would be as hectic as usual from now till two weeks from today—when it will be over.

Dewey does fairly well with his material. He marshals it well and delivers it well. Except for his attack on Roosevelt he is platitudinous in the extreme. As for policies—he has adopted practically all the so-called "New Deal"—even including Social Security legislation, which he would further extend—and today has adopted the A.A.A. His song is he could do it better and tonight made a good political speech trying to show how he would do it better by

[95] Samuel I. Rosenman, special counsel to the President, 1943–1945.

cooperation with the Congress in the Dumbarton plans. While he could not possibly change the spots of his leopard skin obstructionist party members in the Congress he can make a show for it in the campaign.

October 26, 1944

We have won a great naval victory at the Philippines. The *Princeton* was sunk but the enemy lost a lot of battleships, carriers, destroyers, etc. and was routed—probably—incapable of forming a serious menace in the Pacific from now on. It may have been one of the great naval victories of history—for major forces were involved.

Hull's statement was issued—supporting F.D.R. for reelection. Savage drafted it—Hackworth and I redrafted it yesterday and day before, Hull through Stettinius approved it and I, by request, sent it to F.D.R. for approval —which he did.

Frank Walker talked with me today. He says the President wants Stettinius to make a speech or a statement at least. Stettinius had decided he would not —I told Frank I could not direct my superiors in office. He insisted I talk to Stettinius and I agreed to do so. Frank says he is talking with authority of the President and that I am the designee for such matters in the Department—so —he expects and the President expects me to arrange it for Stettinius to do something.

When I tried to talk to Stettinius it was laid over till tomorrow—It is always difficult for me to talk with him except over the phone—and when that happens there is a record made—surreptitiously—on his end. So I do *not* talk with him on the phone—unless he calls me and then I am guarded. If it was announced there was to be a record I would not object—but his office and several other offices (Biddle's for one) always make either a stenographic record or a recording of conversations—unknown, supposedly, to the other party.

Perhaps tomorrow I can talk—in person.

November 8, 1944

We have won the election for the fourth consecutive time—the Presidency for another four years, increased our majority in the Senate and established a comfortable majority in the House.[96] Now we can go ahead with the war and exercise our authority, which assumes the form of a mandate, to arrange a peace organization and take steps to stabilize our economy at home.

---

[96] On November 7, Roosevelt was elected to an unprecedented fourth term. The Democrats won 243 of the 435 House seats, and they increased their Senate membership to 57 of the total 96 seats.

November 10, 1944

This evening I went to see Mrs. Hull. My primary purpose was to ask her to tell the Secretary that I was intending to submit my resignation tomorrow. I thought he should know it. I added that I would not be surprised if it were accepted. I also wanted to ask about his own health. She said that he was much better but far from being strong. She did not know when he would return to the hotel from the hospital but it would be ten days or two weeks. After that it would be an additional period of rest. She said that she did not know that he would return as Secretary and he had asked her to tell me that he had not changed his mind since he talked to me and had no change to make in his statement made to me. Mrs. Hull added that she did not know what he had said to me—and I did not enlighten her.

She said that the President had been there recently to talk with him and they had not talked politics nor official matters but had just had a general personal conversation with jokes and good-natured conversation. However, during the course of it the President had said that he wanted him to preside over the coming peace conference.

I told Mrs. Hull that I thought he ought to do it. I was sure he could muster up the strength to do that. There were others he might have around him who would do some of the arduous things in connection with the presiding officer and his name would add so much to the peace of mind of the conference. Besides it would be a fitting and proper climax in case he was unable to resume the rather arduous duties of the Secretaryship. And in addition it would postpone the break. She said she would tell him what I thought.

I also told her that Arthur Krock had told me he was going to send in his resignation as manager of the *New York Times* office here for he thought that his paper should have as its representative in Washington a person who was *persona grata* at the White House and that he himself had antagonized the White House. While he had told me that in confidence I was sure that he would expect me to send word to Mr. Hull and she said she would deliver the word.

November 27, 1944

Palm Beach, Florida. The President today announced Hull's resignation and the appointment of Stettinius[97] to succeed him.

November 28, 1944

Following quickly on yesterday's events my resignation was practically accepted today by the offer of the Embassy at Mexico—which I declined. Harry Hopkins called me by phone, said the President just before he left for Warm Springs asked him to ask me if I would accept it. I replied the altitude

[97] Edward Stettinius served as Secretary of State from December 1, 1944, to July 3, 1945.

would prevent it—and the language would make it difficult besides. He suggested I write to the President direct—which I did this evening—thanking him for the offer and stating my office was ready to be vacated—but would await the signal from him.

November 29, 1944

Late tonight received long telegram purporting to be from the President proposing Cuba instead of Mexico. Mi non piaci. Hesitate to decline but cannot see way clear to accept.

December 2, 1944—Miami, Florida

Stettinius phoned at night. Asked if reference in my telegram to letter of 28th was a "routine" resignation. I answered "No"—I had sent a real resignation just after election—on November 10 or 11—it was an honest-to-goodness resignation. He said he had not seen it or heard of it and added "we" did not know about that. So I suggested he ask my office for a copy of it—and went on to say he hoped I would be available for service later, to which I replied that rest and some rehabilitation was my first requirement, that I was very tired. After that—I did not want a "job"—or just an office—but if there was a real work to be done and it was important to have done and if the President wanted me to do it of course I would be available to him. He then mentioned the Dumbarton program and said he hoped I could help with it. I said of course—under the same conditions—and I refrained my saying that my interest and activity in connection with it began in 1916, had continued since and in office or out of office would continue to be expressed.

December 4, 1944

So, I am out of office—and a free man again—free to rest a little, readjust my life and plan for the future at the age of 63 1/2. My record in the Department speaks for itself. I am satisfied and happy. . . . I do not consider myself a scholar—rather a man of action—perhaps somewhat slowed up by age. And Stettinius is certainly no scholar, and is definitely a man of action—but his methods, background and lack of experience grated on me. There is no alternative in such cases but separation. . . .

And we have arrived at the end of *that* chapter.

Postscript

After his retirement from the State Department, Long never held another government position. On July 28, 1945, he sat in the Senate gallery and heard the close of the debate and the roll-call on the resolution consenting to ratification of the United Nations Charter—"It was very gratifying to me to witness the formal acceptance of the principle of international collaboration to maintain the peace, after so many years of advocacy. This has been the motivating thought of my political life for about thirty years. . . . The faith of Woodrow Wilson has been vindicated. Civilization has a better chance to survive—but the will to make it work will be a continuing necessity."

Long died on September 26, 1958.

Acknowledgements

In the preparation of this manuscript I have incurred many agreeable debts of gratitude. My colleague Professor James Watts made numerous suggestions and generously shared with me his knowledge of the Long papers. The courteous staff of the Manuscript Division, Library of Congress, were of immeasurable assistance. Mrs. Shirley Lerman of Arverne, New York, skillfully typed this manuscript and aided me in deciphering Long's difficult handwriting, which in places was almost illegible. Invaluable secretarial help came from patient and understanding Mrs. Grace Cacioppo of Brooklyn, New York. A generous grant from the City College Faculty Research Fund facilitated the preparation of this book.

F. L. I.

Index